The Homeless Mentally Ill

Task Force on the Homeless Mentally Ill

H. Richard Lamb, M.D. *(Chairperson)*
Frank R. Lipton, M.D.
Charles A. Kaufmann, M.D.
A. Anthony Arce, M.D.
Rodger Farr, M.D.
Leona L. Bachrach, Ph.D.
Ellen Baxter
Roger Peele, M.D.
Mokarram Jafri, M.D.

The Homeless Mentally Ill

A Task Force Report of the
American Psychiatric Association

Edited by H. Richard Lamb, M.D.

Published by the
American Psychiatric Association
1400 K Street, N.W.
Washington, D.C. 20005

NOTE: The contributors have worked to ensure that all information in this book concerning drug doses, schedules, and routes
of administration is accurate at the time of publication and consistent with standards set by the U.S. Food and Drug Administration and the general medical community. As medical research and
practice advance, however, therapeutic standards may change.
For this reason and because human and mechanical errors sometimes occur, we recommend that readers follow the advice of a
physician directly involved in their care or the care of a member
of their family.

The findings, opinions, and conclusions of the report do not
necessarily represent the views of the officers, trustees, or all
members of the Association. Each report, however, does represent the thoughtful judgment and findings of the task force of
experts who composed it. These reports are considered a substantive contribution to the ongoing analysis and evaluation of problems, programs, issues, and practices in a given area of concern.

Library of Congress Cataloging in Publication Data
Main entry under title:

The Homeless mentally ill.

  Includes bibliographies and index.
  1. Mental health services—United States.
2. Mentally ill—Care and treatment—United States.
3. Homelessness—United States. I. Lamb, H. Richard,
1929–   . II. American Psychiatric Association. [DNLM:
1. Transients and Migrants—psychology. 2. Mental Health
Services. 3. Mental Disorders. WM 31 A512h]
RA790.6.H66   1984   362.2'0973   84-16916
ISBN 0-89042-200-1

Contents

Contributors

David A. Adler, M.D.
Associate Professor
Department of Psychiatry
Tufts University School of Medicine
Associate Chief
Division of Adult Psychiatry
New England Medical Center
Boston, Massachusetts

A. Anthony Arce, M.D.
Executive Director
John F. Kennedy Community Mental Health–Mental
    Retardation Center
Professor and Deputy Chairman
Department of Mental Health Sciences
Hahnemann University
Philadelphia, Pennsylvania

Bernard Arons, M.D.
Director, Dixon Implementation Office
St. Elizabeths Hospital
Associate Clinical Professor of Psychiatry
George Washington University
Washington, D.C.

Leona L. Bachrach, Ph.D.
Research Professor of Psychiatry
Maryland Psychiatric Research Center
University of Maryland School of Medicine
Catonsville, Maryland
Senior Consultant in Deinstitutionalization
    and Community Support System Planning
Maryland Mental Hygiene Administration

Ellen L. Bassuk, M.D.
Associate Professor of Psychiatry
Harvard Medical School
Boston, Massachusetts

Ellen Baxter
Research Associate
Community Service Society
New York, New York

Philip W. Brickner, M.D.
Director, Department of Community Medicine
St. Vincent's Hospital and Medical Center of New York
New York, New York

Linda Chafetz, R.N., D.N.S.
Associate Professor
Department of Mental Health and Community Nursing
School of Nursing
University of California, San Francisco

Barbara Conanan, R.N.
Director, SRO/Homeless Program
Department of Community Medicine
St. Vincent's Hospital and Medical Center of New York
New York, New York

Robert E. Drake, M.D., Ph.D.
Instructor, Department of Psychiatry
Harvard Medical School
Boston, Massachusetts
Co-director, Ambulatory Community Services
Cambridge-Somerville Mental Health Center
Cambridge, Massachusetts

Alexander Elvy, M.S.W.
Social Worker and Community Organizer
Department of Community Medicine
St. Vincent's Hospital and Medical Center of New York
New York, New York

Elizabeth Farrell, M.S., M.S.W.
Director, Work and Leisure Activities
Takoma Park, Maryland

Thomas Filardo, M.D.
Assistant Professor in Family Practice
University of Illinois College of Medicine at Urbana/Champaign

Stephen M. Goldfinger, M.D.
Assistant Clincial Professor of Psychiatry
University of California, San Francisco
Director, Outpatient Services
San Francisco General Hospital

Richard Green, M.D.
Associate Attending Physician in Dermatology
New York University Medical Center
New York, New York

Bruce Gross, Ph.D., J.D.
Acting Director, Institute of Psychiatry, Law,
    and Behavioral Science
University of Southern California School of Medicine
Los Angeles, California

Agnes B. Hatfield, Ph.D.
Associate Professor of Education
Department of Human Development
University of Maryland College of Education
College Park, Maryland
Past-President, National Alliance for the Mentally Ill

Kim Hopper
Research Associate
Community Service Society
New York, New York

Michael Iseman, M.D.
Associate Professor of Medicine
Division of Pulmonary Sciences
University of Colorado School of Medicine
Denver, Colorado

Mokarram Jafri, M.D.
Commissioner, Broome County Mental Health Services
Binghamton, New York

Charles A. Kaufmann, M.D.
Senior Staff Fellow
Adult Psychiatry Branch
Intramural Research Program
National Institute of Mental Health

St. Elizabeths Hospital
Washington, D.C.

H. Richard Lamb, M.D.
Professor of Psychiatry
University of Southern California School of Medicine
Los Angeles, California

Alison S. Lauriat, M.A.
Independent Consultant on Issues of Public Policy and
    Homelessness
Boston, Massachusetts

Irene Shifren Levine, Ph.D.
Coordinator, Program for the Homeless Mentally Ill
National Institute of Mental Health
Rockville, Maryland

Frank R. Lipton, M.D.
Director, Emergency Services
Bellevue Psychiatric Hospital
Assistant Clinical Professor of Psychiatry
New York University School of Medicine
New York, New York

Roger Peele, M.D.
Chair, Department of Psychiatry
St. Elizabeths Hospital
Clinical Professor of Psychiatry
George Washington University
Washington, D.C.

Albert Sabatini, M.D.
Medical Director
Bellevue Psychiatric Hospital
Associate Professor of Clinical Psychiatry
New York University School of Medicine
New York, New York

Shirley Starr, M.A.
Chairman, Mental Disability Committee
President's Committee on Employment of the Handicapped
Past-President, National Alliance for the Mentally Ill

John A. Talbott, M.D.
Professor of Psychiatry
Cornell University Medical College
Associate Medical Director
Payne Whitney Psychiatric Clinic
New York Hospital
New York, New York
President, American Psychiatric Association, 1984–85

Michael J. Vergare, M.D.
Associate Chairman
Department of Psychiatry
Albert Einstein Medical Center, Northern Division
Associate Professor of Psychiatry
Temple University School of Medicine
Philadelphia, Pennsylvania

Foreword

Deinstitutionalization, begun with so little preparation or planning 30 years ago, has had a profound impact on the delivery of mental health services in America today. Despite the fact that we now refer to it as a movement or development, it was only in retrospect that we gave it a name. Indeed, the forces that propelled it, such as the community mental health philosophy, social and pharmacological therapeutics, legal and legislative pressures, and economic incentives, were largely recognized as causal only after the fact.

The concept of moving comprehensive treatment and care of most of the chronically mentally ill from institutional to community auspices was basically a good one—and for many patients has resulted in their successful return to family, neighborhood, and purposeful activity. But, as with so many other movements embraced enthusiastically by zealous Americans, its implementation was flawed, and many persons were terribly adversely affected. Again in retrospect, it is clear that for them, nursing homes, welfare hotels, and prisons were in no way adequate replacements for state hospitals. In addition, there were those too sick, too impaired, or too socially unskilled to survive in alternative settings, and many of these persons spilled over into our streets.

Homelessness in America is not a new phenomenon. Colonial documents reveal the existence of wanderers; indeed, almshouses, workhouses, and poorhouses were established partly to serve those without adequate housing. More recently, especially during the

Great Depression of the 1930s, hoboes and vagabonds were commonplace in urban and rural areas. In addition, for years certain individuals living on the margins of society, such as skid-row alcoholics, have been without permanent housing. But most recently, and without precedent, we have witnessed the dramatic growth of one homeless subgroup—the homeless mentally ill.

Although the media have documented the problems of this group, until relatively recently we psychiatrists made no professional acknowledgment of their existence. Partly this was due to our failure to know how to address the problem and our reliance on "traditional" techniques and services; partly to the victims' own suspiciousness of authority and mental health professionals and their inability or unwillingness to form interpersonal relationships, as well as their mental disability; and partly to the reluctance of nonmedical caregivers to work with this population.

In any case, while we have all been appalled by the seemingly large number of the homeless mentally ill, we have lacked the knowledge of who they are, how ill and disabled they are, what their needs are (in terms of generic services, shelter, and psychiatric treatment), and what sort of plan can ameliorate their plight.

This volume, for the first time, begins to provide answers to these questions. It assembles the results of our first attempts to study the population of homeless mentally ill; begins to document their complex unmet needs; and proposes solutions, both short-term and long-term, that must be incorporated into a comprehensive public policy if we are to adequately address the current problem. The contributors to this monograph include the leading experts in the field, many of whose individual efforts were pioneering ones. To some extent the book continues the commitment of the American Psychiatric Association to the pursuit of better care and treatment of the chronically mentally ill, begun in its original book on the subject entitled *The Chronic Mental Patient: Problems, Solutions, and Recommendations for a Public Policy* (Talbott 1978). That book was followed by two additional works initiated by APA's Committee on the Chronically Mentally Ill: *The Chronic Mentally Ill: Treatment, Programs, Systems* (Talbott 1981) and *The Chronic Mentally Ill: Five Years Later* (Talbott in press).

This report will be of great value to government officials, planners, and mental health practitioners concerned with the homeless mentally ill, as well as to all those involved in the problems of homelessness and deinstitutionalization. The data and the concepts will challenge not only researchers but those whose duty it is to translate these findings into public policy.

Deinstitutionalization was not a universal disaster—for many it was humane and successful. But any program that injures a significant number even though helping others must provide a safety net for those for whom it is not successful. As a concerned society, we can do no less. This book provides a foundation upon which society can begin to remedy those defects in implementing the policy of deinstitutionalization that have hurt some Americans so severely. It will not be an easy task, but it is an essential one.

John A. Talbott, M.D.
President
American Psychiatric Association

References

Talbott JA (ed). Washington, American Psychiatric Association, 1978
Talbott JA (ed). New York, Human Sciences Press, 1981
Talbott JA (ed). New York, Grune & Stratton (in press)

Preface

There was a sense of urgency when the American Psychiatric Association's Task Force on the Homeless Mentally Ill was formed. The problem was so serious, the plight of the homeless mentally ill so desperate, that we were asked to have our report and recommendations completed and ready for publication within a year. Our charge was to gather all the research, data, and knowledge available, to prepare a substantive volume that contained an up-to-date summary of what is known about the problems of the homeless mentally ill, and to formulate recommendations for dealing with these problems.

The authors who contributed to this volume are all persons with considerable knowledge and experience in the area of service delivery to the chronically mentally ill, including those who are homeless. After considerable discussion with all the participants, chapters were assigned based on individual areas of expertise and interest. It was decided that the entire Task Force would comment on drafts of each chapter and give input and suggestions. But the authors of each chapter were to have the final say about what the final drafts of their chapters contained. And, in fact, that is how we did it.

When it came to the recommendations, however, we wanted to reach a consensus to the extent possible with such a diverse group. This proved easier than any of us had imagined. We found that we all agreed that simply providing shelter was a symptomatic approach, and that we must address the underlying problems of the chronically mentally ill in the community. Homelessness among the mentally ill was not seen as the result of deinstitutionalization per se, but rather of the way deinstitutionalization has been implemented. It seemed clear to all of us that what is needed is a vast expansion of community housing and services and a revamping of the mental health delivery system to meet the needs of the chronically mentally ill. And so it went. There was even agreement on the need to change the laws in order to facilitate involuntary treatment, though here there were somewhat differing views about how and to what extent it should be done.

A grant was obtained from the Alcohol, Drug Abuse, and Mental Health Administration (ADAMHA) to enable the Task Force to visit programs providing services to the homeless mentally ill around the country. From November 1983 to February 1984, we visited a variety of programs in Boston, New York City, Washington, D.C., Los Angeles, and San Francisco. Many were highly innovative and of excellent quality. A few illustrated the poor quality of services for the homeless mentally ill. All pointed up the vast unmet needs of this population.

The experience of seeing the patients themselves was a grim reminder that the chronically mentally ill have been cast adrift under conditions that most persons think can no longer exist in this country. Sometimes their situation was the result of inhumane treatment, but more often it seemed to be simply neglect. If these tragic scenes have any positive aspect, it is that they take place out in the community for all to see, and may arouse our society to take some definitive action for dealing with the problems of the chronically mentally ill. But given society's history of neglect of the mentally ill, this result is far from certain.

This book deals primarily with the homeless mentally ill 18 years of age or older. Because of our time limitations and the lack of definitive information, we were unable to investigate possible relationships between the homeless mentally ill and homeless youth. Clearly this is one of many areas of the exceedingly complex phenomenon of the homeless mentally ill where more research is needed.

Many persons in addition to the authors of this volume made important contributions to the work of the Task Force. I would like to single out for special commendation Claudia (Corky) Hart of the American Psychiatric Association, who coordinated the Task Force's efforts and whose exceptional competence helped make this work possible, and Betty Cochran, who helped to give the text its final shape and whose dedication to editorial excellence added much to the quality of this book.

H. Richard Lamb, M.D.
Los Angeles, California

Chapter 1

Summary and Recommendations

John A. Talbott, M.D.
H. Richard Lamb, M.D.

A large number of difficult and often seemingly overwhelming social issues, most of which elude easy solutions, confront us today. Principal among them is the widespread, serious, and increasing phenomenon of homelessness in America, many of whose victims are seriously and/or chronically mentally ill. To address this problem, the American Psychiatric Association appointed a Task Force on the Homeless Mentally Ill in 1983, realizing that while all citizens have a responsibility for the welfare of the homeless, psychiatrists have an additional responsibility for the mentally ill among them.

The recommendations in this report reflect that general obligation as citizens to address the problems of this heterogeneous population as well as our specific obligation as psychiatrists to help the large number of homeless mentally ill. Recommendations for additional action on the part of the American Psychiatric Association and American psychiatrists will be contained in a joint position paper formulated by the Association's Task Force on the Homeless Mentally Ill, its Committee on the Chronically Mentally Ill, and its Council on Psychiatric Services.

Dr. Talbott is professor of psychiatry at Cornell University Medical College and associate medical director of the Payne Whitney Psychiatric Clinic of the New York Hospital in New York City; he is president of the American Psychiatric Association for 1984-85. Dr. Lamb is professor of psychiatry at the University of Southern California School of Medicine in Los Angeles and chairperson of the American Psychiatric Association's Task Force on the Homeless Mentally Ill.

To provide a basis for the recommendations below, we will begin by summarizing the major points of this study of the homeless mentally ill in America. Both here and in the recommendations, the reader is referred to individual chapters for more detailed information. It should be noted, however, that most of the points are discussed in more than one chapter.

Summary

Homelessness is not a new phenomenon. Large urban centers have always attracted vagabonds, derelicts, and hoboes, but until recently these unfortunate individuals tended to cluster in certain areas, often called skid rows. Today, however, we are experiencing a new phenomenon—one of unprecedented magnitude and complexity— and hardly a section of the country, urban or rural, has escaped the ubiquitous presence of ragged, ill, and hallucinating human beings, wandering through our city streets, huddled in alleyways, or sleeping over vents.

This rapidly growing problem of homelessness has emerged as a major societal tragedy and has recently commanded increasing attention from all segments of society, including the government, the media, and the public at large. The individuals affected are now regarded as an eyesore at best and the victims of a moral scandal at worst.

It now is apparent that a substantial portion of the homeless are chronically and severely mentally ill men and women who in years past would have been long-term residents of state hospitals. They now have no place to live because of efforts to depopulate public hospitals coupled with the unavailability of suitable housing and supervised living arrangements in "the community," inadequate continuing medical-psychiatric care and other supportive services, and poorly thought-out changes in the laws governing involuntary treatment.

Homelessness has historically reflected the interaction between the most vulnerable of our population and the scarcity or plenty of our resources. Those members of society least able to care for themselves have always been at greatest risk for loss of residence and affiliation—for example, the never-institutionalized alcoholic, the unemployed, and the migrant and the refugee. Today their ranks are swelled by the addition of thousands of people suffering from severe and chronic mental disorders, including major psychotic disorders, alcoholism, drug abuse, and severe personality disorders, who have been discharged or diverted from institutions.

The causes of homelessness are many and complex, and the homeless comprise different populations with different needs. Some of the homeless are undomiciled because they have lost their jobs, others because of the gentrification of urban areas without a concomitant replacement of inexpensive housing. Still others suffer from substance abuse or severe and chronic mental disorder and disability. Thus each person's needs can be identified only by knowing which subset of the homeless population he or she belongs to.

The concept of deinstitutionalization per se was not bad. The idea that many, if not most, of the severely and chronically mentally ill suffering from serious illnesses such as schizophrenia and manic-depression could be cared for as well in community programs as in institutions, if not better, was in itself not a bad idea. It was clinically sound and economically feasible.

However, the way deinstitutionalization was originally carried out, through the poorly planned discharge of thousands of mentally ill residents of state hospitals into inadequately prepared or programmatically deficient communities, was another thing altogether. In addition, as a result of the states' admission diversion policies, increasing numbers of "new" chronically mentally ill individuals have never been institutionalized, and have further expanded the homeless mentally ill population.

Vital resources for both groups have been lacking. They include adequate and integrated community programs for these individuals; an adequate number and range of community residential settings, with varying degrees of supervision and structure; a system of follow-up, monitoring, and responsibility for ensuring that services are provided to those unable to obtain them; and easy access to short-term and long-term inpatient care when indicated. The consequences of these gaps in essential resources have been disastrous (see chapters 2 and 3).

An emphasis on homelessness per se deflects attention from the basic, underlying problem of the lack of a comprehensive support system for the severely and chronically mentally ill. As was noted above, it was not the concept of deinstitutionalization, but its implementation, that was flawed. All services available to patients while they resided in state facilities, including the function of asylum, were not available when they returned to community settings (see chapter 3). In addition, in hospitals such services are provided under one roof, and no such umbrella existed in the community.

While temporary housing such as shelters may be an important stopgap measure for many of the homeless mentally ill, increasing the number of shelters merely postpones the day of reckoning when we will have to try to provide all the services needed as well as a system to glue them together. Such a support system can be familial or institutional (that is, provided by mental health programs), or a combination of both, but society must ensure that the system exists and is adequate.

Society's ambivalence about wanting the mentally ill kept out of sight, while at the same time opposing involuntary incarceration, must be better resolved. When deinstitutionalization occurred, society reacted vehemently to the presence on our cities' streets of the most seriously and chronically ill patients. Yet society has increasingly rejected the idea of involuntarily committing such patients to state hospitals for long periods of time. Currently few states have commitment laws that give family members or those responsible for treatment easy access to prompt treatment for persons whose mental illness has worsened or whose condition has deteriorated severely. Society cannot continue to have it both ways.

These major points of the Task Force report lead to three general statements that relate to proposed solutions to the problems of the homeless mentally ill.

First, there is no single, simple solution to the problems of homelessness. Because of the different subpopulations of the homeless, the different causes of and reasons for homelessness, and the different needs of the various subgroups, no one solution will meet all the needs of the homeless. Moreover, while temporary housing, such as shelters, is a necessary step, it is only a short-term solution.

Second, solutions must be targeted to the differing populations. Obviously such diverse groups as the unemployed, those displaced by gentrification, alcoholics and drug abusers, and the severely and chronically mentally ill have very different needs. The solutions for those who are unemployed include job assessment, placement, and retraining; for those displaced by gentrification, an ambitious new program of low-cost housing; for those suffering primarily from substance abuse and alcoholism, outreach services, detoxification facilities, medical treatment, and a host of specialized programs; and for those suffering from severe and chronic mental illnesses, supervised housing, medical and psychiatric care, aggressive case management and follow-up, and a multiplicity of other services.

Lastly, the recommendations that follow will deal only with the mentally ill homeless, the group with which this report deals, not with the homeless in general. To come to grips with the problems of the homeless mentally ill, we must address both short- and long-term issues simultaneously; thus the recommendations suggest both immediate and long-range actions. While other advocates and agencies will address the problems of other groups of homeless Americans, and some of their proposals will apply to the entire population of the homeless, we will confine our recommendations specifically to the homeless mentally ill.

The recommendations that follow are proposed as optimal solutions that all concerned segments of society should work to carry out. Clearly their implementation, however, will depend on society's willingness to reallocate resources to meet this pressing problem.

Recommendations of the Task Force

Major Recommendation

To address the problems of the homeless mentally ill in America, a comprehensive and integrated system of care for this vulnerable population of the mentally ill, with designated responsibility, with accountability, and with adequate fiscal resources, must be established.

Derivative Recommendations

1) *Any attempt to address the problems of the homeless mentally ill must begin with provisions for meeting their basic needs: food, shelter, and clothing.* The chronically mentally ill have a *right*, equal to that of other groups, to these needs being met.

2) *An adequate number and ample range of graded, step-wise, super-*

vised community housing settings must be established. (See chapter 6.)
While many of the homeless may benefit from temporary housing
such as shelters, and some small portion of the severely and chronically mentally ill can graduate to independent living, for the vast
majority neither shelters nor mainstream low-cost housing are
appropriate. Most housing settings that require people to manage
by themselves are beyond the capabilities of the chronically mentally
ill. Instead, there must be settings offering different levels of supervision, both more and less intensive, including quarterway and
halfway houses, lodges and camps, board-and-care homes, satellite
housing, foster or family care, and crisis or temporary hostels.

3) *Adequate, comprehensive, and accessible psychiatric and rehabilitative services must be available, and must be assertively provided
through outreach services when necessary.* (See chapters 5, 8, and 9.)
First, there must be an adequate number of direct psychiatric services, both on the streets and in the shelters when appropriate, that
provide (a) outreach contact with the mentally ill in the community,
(b) psychiatric assessment and evaluation, (c) crisis intervention,
including hospitalization, (d) individualized treatment plans, (e)
psychotropic medication and other somatic therapies, and (f)
psychosocial treatment. Second, there must be an adequate number
of rehabilitative services, providing socialization experiences, training in the skills of everyday living, and social rehabilitation. Third,
both treatment and rehabilitative services must be provided assertively—for instance, by going out to patients' living settings if they
do not or cannot come to a centralized program. And fourth, the
difficulty of working with some of these patients must not be under-
estimated (see chapters 7, 9, and 11).

4) *General medical assessment and care must be available.* (See chapter
11.) Since we know that the chronically mentally ill have three
times the morbidity and mortality of their counterparts of the same
age in the general population, and the homeless even higher rates,
the ready availability of general medical care is essential and critical.

5) *Crisis services must be available and accessible to both the chronically mentally ill homeless and the chronically mentally ill in general.*
Too often, the homeless mentally ill who are in crisis are ignored
because they are presumed, as part of the larger homeless population, to reject all conventional forms of help. Even more inappropriately, they may be put into inpatient hospital units when
rapid, specific interventions such as medication or crisis housing
would be more effective and less costly. Others, in need of acute

hospitalization, are denied it because of restrictive admission criteria or commitment laws. In any case, it will be difficult to provide adequate crisis services to the homeless mentally ill until they are conceptualized and treated separately from the large numbers of other homeless persons.

6) *A system of responsibility for the chronically mentally ill living in the community must be established, with the goal of ensuring that ultimately each patient has one person responsible for his or her care.* Clearly the shift of psychiatric care from institutional to community settings does not in any way eliminate the need to continue the provision of comprehensive services to mentally ill persons. As a result, society must declare a public policy of responsibility for the mentally ill who are unable to meet their own needs; governments must designate programs in each region or locale as core agencies responsible and accountable for the care of the chronically mentally ill living there; and the staff of these agencies must be assigned individual patients for whom they are responsible. The ultimate goal must be to ensure that each chronically mentally ill person in this country has one person—such as a case manager or resource manager—who is responsible for his or her treatment and care.

For the more than 50 percent of the chronically ill population living at home or for those with positive ongoing relationships with their families, programs and respite care must be provided to enhance the family's ability to provide a support system. Where the use of family systems is not feasible, the patient must be linked up with a formal community support system. In any case, the entire burden of deinstitutionalization must not be allowed to fall upon families (see chapter 13).

7) *Basic changes must be made in legal and administrative procedures to ensure continuing community care for the chronically mentally ill.* (See chapter 12.) In the 1960s and 1970s more stringent commitment laws and patients' rights advocacy remedied some egregious abuses in public hospital care, but at the same time these changes neglected patients' right to high-quality comprehensive outpatient care as well as the rights of families and society. New laws and procedures must be developed to ensure provision of psychiatric care in the community—that is, to guarantee a right to treatment in the community.

It must become easier to obtain conservatorship status for outpatients who are so gravely disabled and/or have such impaired judgment that they cannot care for themselves in the community without legally sanctioned supervision. Involuntary commitment laws must be made more humane to permit prompt return to active inpatient treatment for patients when acute exacerbations of their illnesses make their lives in the community chaotic and unbearable. Involuntary treatment laws should be revised to allow the option of outpatient civil commitment; in states that already have provisions for such treatment, that mechanism should be more widely used. Finally, advocacy efforts should be focused on the availability of competent care in the community.

8) *A system of coordination among funding sources and implementation agencies must be established.* (See chapters 2, 5, and 8.) Because the problems of the mentally ill homeless must be addressed by multiple public and private authorities, coordination, so lacking in the deinstitutionalization process, must become a primary goal. The ultimate objective must be a true system of care rather than a loose network of services, and an ease of communication among different types of agencies (for example, psychiatric, social, vocational, and housing) as well as up and down the governmental ladder, from local through federal. One characteristic of a genuine system is the ability to flexibly alter roles, responsibilities, and programs as specific service needs change, and this ultimate end must be striven for.

9) *An adequate number of professionals and paraprofessionals must be trained for community care of the chronically ill.* Among the additional specially trained workers needed, four groups are particularly important for this population: (a) psychiatrists who are skilled in, and interested in, working with the chronically mentally ill[1]; (b) outreach workers who can engage the homeless mentally ill on the streets; (c) case managers, preferably with sufficient training to provide therapeutic interventions themselves; and (d) conservators, to act for patients too disabled to make clinically and economically sound decisions.

10) *General social services must be provided.* Besides the need for specialized social services such as socialization experiences and training

---

[1]Readers desiring specifics of how to interest psychiatrists in treating the chronically mentally ill and how to provide relevant training are referred to "Encouraging Psychiatrists to Work With Chronic Patients: Opportunities and Limitations of Residency Education," by Arthur C. Nielsen, Leonard I. Stein, John A. Talbott, and others in *Hospital and Community Psychiatry*, volume 32, 1981, pages 767-775, and "Treatment and Care of the Chronically Mentally Ill, chapter 7 in *The Chronic Mental Patient: Five Years Later*, edited by John A. Talbott, Grune & Stratton, in press for 1984.

in the skills of everyday living (referred to in Recommendation 3), there is also a pressing need for generic social services. Such services include escort services to agencies and potential residential placements, help with applications to entitlement programs, and assistance in mobilizing the resources of the family.

11) *Ongoing asylum and sanctuary should be available for that small proportion of the chronically mentally ill who do not respond to current methods of treatment and rehabilitation.* (See chapter 3.) Some patients, even with high-quality treatment and rehabilitation efforts, remain dangerous or gravely disabled. For these patients, there is a pressing need for ongoing asylum in long-term settings, whether in hospitals or in facilities such as California's locked skilled nursing facilities that have special programs for the mentally ill.

12) *Research into the causes and treatment of both chronic mental illness and homelessness needs to be expanded.* While our knowledge has greatly advanced in recent years (see chapters 4 and 10), it is still limited. Treatment of chronic mental illness remains largely palliative, and definitive treatment will occur only with an adequate understanding of etiologic processes. In addition, our understanding of differential therapeutics—that is, what treatment works for which patients in what settings—is in its infancy and requires increased resources and attention.

13) *More accurate epidemiological data need to be gathered and analyzed.* Currently the research findings of incidence of mental illness among homeless groups are highly variable, ranging up to 91 percent; these differences depend largely on such methodological issues as where the sample is taken, whether standardized scales or comparable criteria of illness are used, and theoretical biases (see chapters 4 and 14). Better data, using recognized diagnostic criteria, need to be acquired.

14) *Finally, additional monies must be expended for longer-term solutions for the homeless mentally ill.* Although health and mental health costs and funding in this country have recently increased, the homeless mentally ill have not been beneficiaries of this increase. Therefore, adequate new monies must be found to finance the system of care we envision, which incorporates supervised living arrangements, assertive case management, and an array of other services. In addition, financial support from existing entitlement programs such as Supplemental Security Income and Medicaid must be ensured.

In summary, the solutions to the problems of the mentally ill homeless are as manifold as the problems they seek to remedy. However, only with comprehensive short- and long-term solutions will the plight of this most neglected population in America be addressed.

Chapter 2

The Homeless Mentally Ill and Mental Health Services: An Analytical Review of the Literature

Leona L. Bachrach, Ph.D.

Who are the homeless and what services do they need? As individual citizens we may feel deep compassion for the many human beings who lack residences and live on the fringes of our society. Our wish to help them may prompt us to seek ways to reduce their pain and to solve their problems in living. But what should be the limits of our professional concern with homeless individuals?

This question is one that currently concerns psychiatrists and other professionals who work with the mentally ill (APA Report 1983; Jones 1983; Nelson 1983; Psychiatrists to Study 1983; Talbott 1983a). It is an important question, for failure to address it carefully and answer it judiciously may lead to a repetition of the errors associated with past service delivery initiatives. It is now generally understood, for example, that the failure to define the chronically mentally ill with precision, and to focus on their unique service needs, has led to some of the serious problems we are presently encountering in serving them in deinstitutionalized service systems (Group for the Advancement of Psychiatry 1983; Langsley 1980; Zusman and Lamb 1977).

Dr. Bachrach is research professor of psychiatry at the Maryland Psychiatric Research Center of the University of Maryland School of Medicine, Catonsville, Maryland, and senior consultant in deinstitutionalization and community support system planning to the Maryland Mental Hygiene Administration. This review of the literature was supported in part by a contract from the Alcohol, Drug Abuse, and Mental Health Administration, which is distributing a version of this chapter.

Moreover, professional concern with the homeless is being prodded today by numerous media reports that deplore the fate of the undomiciled and lay much of the blame at the door of the psychiatric service system (Gargan 1983; Overend 1983; Rule 1983b; Thimmesch 1983; Torrey 1983). Statements like this are not uncommon:

> The American Psychiatric Association [has] formed a task force . . . to study the homeless and their needs. The studying shouldn't be hard. Church groups, for whom service to the outcast poor is the essence of religion, have opened shelters in all the large cities, and more and more of the small ones. The shelter providers have all the facts and insights the American Psychiatric Association will ever need, beginning with the observation that it shouldn't have taken this long for the doctors to get involved (McCarthy 1983).

Indeed, we have ample reason to anticipate that, unless the mental health professions make an effort to examine the limits of their responsibility to the homeless, the media will assume that task. In the process, they will only oversimplify and confuse the issues surrounding the care of homeless individuals, including the mentally ill among them.

This chapter is based on the assumption that it is important for psychiatry and allied professions to focus their concern with the homeless—that too broad a preoccupation with the entire population of "street people," "bag ladies," "grate gentlemen," and other undomiciled individuals will ultimately blur the boundaries of social and professional responsibility. Accordingly, this discussion addresses the service needs not of homeless people per se, but rather those of seriously mentally ill persons who ordinarily fall within the compass of psychiatry's concern and who also happen to be homeless. These are individuals whose homelessness is either an expression of their complicated psychopathology or else contributes significantly to the course of that pathology.

In limiting the scope of this chapter in this way, I should like to note the concerns of those who speculate that any individual forced to, or choosing to, live on the streets necessarily has sufficient psychopathology to warrant the attention of the psychiatric service system. Although I share this view to some extent, I am mindful of the need to draw boundaries, even if they are arbitrary, for purposes of policy formulation. Thus this chapter deals exclusively with individuals whose pathology and symptomatology are clearly those of the chronically mentally ill.

The definition of chronicity in mental illness has, in fact, undergone considerable change in recent years. Currently the chronically mentally ill individual is generally regarded as a person who has a major mental disorder and "needs psychiatric services indefinitely to attain and preserve the maximum possible independence from a substantially disabling mental illness and its consequences" (Peele and Palmer 1980, 63), irrespective of his or her diagnosis or length of stay in a psychiatric inpatient facility. Severity and persistence of disability and dependency of indefinite duration are thus the distinguishing hallmarks of chronicity in today's essentially noninstitutional system of care (Bachrach 1983c).

From this perspective, certain important questions begin to take form. For example, we may inquire about the extent to which current service delivery modes contribute to the probability that some among the chronically mentally ill will become, and remain, homeless. More specifically, we may focus on the speculation that deinstitutionalization has exacerbated the problems of certain chronically mentally ill individuals and led to their homelessness. In a similar vein, we may ask what steps planners and providers of psychiatric services may take in an effort to reduce homelessness among the chronically mentally ill.

This chapter assesses the findings of two bodies of literature in an effort to shed some light on these and related questions. The first consists of a limited selection of current writings that focus on the homeless mentally ill and contribute to our understanding of their epidemiology, psychopathology, sociology, and special service needs. The second, which has emerged over the past several decades in response to problems associated with deinstitutionalization, deals with specialized service needs of the chronically mentally ill. Considered separately, each of these two bodies of literature gives very partial answers to our questions about how to make the psychiatric service system responsive to the specialized needs of the homeless mentally ill. Viewed together, however, they begin to strengthen our understanding of the extraordinary service needs of this vulnerable and underserved population.

A substantial portion of the literature reviewed here appears in the popular press and in official documents with limited circulation. Reliance on such "fugitive" literature results partly from the fact that concern for the homeless mentally ill achieved earlier prominence in the popular than in the professional literature. The professional focus is actually quite recent.

Beyond this, however, it must be acknowledged that popular sources have often contained insightful and sensitive accounts and analyses of issues surrounding the care of this population, and the professional reader stands to gain from familiarity with those descriptions (Bachrach in press a). Indeed, vignettes from the popular media at times provide a dimension of reality to the problems of the homeless mentally ill that is often absent from professional accounts. A recent newspaper article by Dorothy Gilliam (1984), for example, describes a Veterans Administration surgeon's report of an "epidemic" of limb amputations occasioned by an increased incidence of frostbite among homeless people in Washington, D.C.

Growth of the Homeless Mentally Ill Population

Professional and popular sources appear to agree on three major points concerning the homeless in America today: that their numbers are growing steadily (Hayes 1982; Herman 1982a; U.S. Senate 1983); that their average age is dropping precipitously (Leaf and Cohen 1982; New York State 1982; Reich and Siegel 1978); and that the percentage who are chronically mentally ill, by any definition, is increasing rapidly (Drake 1982; Hayes 1982; Larew 1980; Reich and Siegel 1978; U.S. Department of Health and Human Services 1983; U.S. Senate 1983).

To what may we attribute these trends? Actually, the increasing prominence of the homeless mentally ill in our society results from a confluence of forces. In part, they represent the group of individuals who, two or three decades ago, probably would have been admitted to institutions for indefinite lengths of stay. Today, very much as the result of deinstitutionalization policies and practices, they have become more visible. Some are diverted from institutional care as the result of aggressive "admission diversion" policies (Dionne 1978; Morrissey and McGreevy 1982; Pepper and Ryglewicz 1982a; Sullivan 1979a, 1979b). Others enter institutions but tend to stay for only a short while before they are returned to the community (Bachrach 1978; Goldman et al. 1983).

However, the growth of a homeless mentally ill population is not a simple phenomenon, and it should not be concluded that it is entirely an artifact of deinstitutionalization. Its prominence also results in large part from the nation's changing demography. An accumulation of young adults in our population has been very marked in recent years as successive cohorts of post-World War II baby-boom babies have reached maturity. As the result of the coming of age of 64 million babies born between 1946 and 1961, the absolute number of young persons at risk for developing schizophrenia and other chronic mental disorders has increased dramatically (Bachrach 1982).

The interaction of deinstitutionalization and demography has had profound consequences for the chronically mentally ill. It has provided the younger members of that population with opportunities to emulate their age-peers who are not mentally ill. Like other young adults in the population (U.S. Bureau of the Census 1980), those who are mentally ill tend to be very mobile. They travel extensively and relocate frequently within and between major cities, and also move in and out of small cities and rural communities (Bachrach 1983d; Farr 1982; Macklin 1983; Travelers Aid 1976). Many of them are episodically or permanently homeless.

In fact, there are probably certain "magnet" communities that attract the more mobile of the homeless mentally ill. There is evidence of several migration streams within which the chronically mentally ill move. A typical one covers the northern portions of New England and extends down through the metropolitan areas of New York, Pennsylvania, and Washington, D.C., to the south (Bachrach 1982). Similar migration streams probably exist in the West (Raine 1982; Timnick 1981), and anecdotes abound of the movement of chronically mentally ill individuals into and out of the national parks and between the communities on the highways that connect those parks. Washington County, Vermont, reports an influx of chronically mentally ill young adults who typically arrive with acute treatment, welfare, and support service requirements (R. DeForge, personal communication, 1981). And a community mental health center in the Virgin Islands reports itself often faced with having to choose between caring for young adult in-migrants or financing their passage back to the mainland (M.A. Weston, personal communication, 1982).

Another behavior pattern that young adults with chronic mental illnesses apparently share with many of their age-peers is the recreational use of addictive substances (Pepper et al. 1981). However, alcohol and drugs often exacerbate the symptoms of illness and may seriously alter its clinical course (Pearlson 1981; Treffert 1978). In fact, exposure to alcohol and street drugs is thought to contribute materially to the noted volatility and noncompliance of mobile young adults with chronic mental illnesses (Glass 1982; Schwartz and Goldfinger 1981).

Other cultural trends may also have played a role in the increased visibility of the homeless mentally ill. Prager (1982) suggests that many of those who exist in isolation on the streets today were protected a decade or more ago by the counterculture on whose fringes they lived, a view supported by the research of Harris and Bergman (1983). Today little counterculture survives, and the mentally ill who once benefited from its tolerance and supportive milieu have become more exposed.

To recapitulate, the growing homeless mentally ill population results from a complex of forces. Two major variables—deinstitutionalization and demography—and several attendant or intervening variables, such as exposure to street drugs, geographic mobility, and loss of a "cover," have interacted to produce a numerically significant population of chronically mentally ill individuals with specialized service needs. Those who lack residences are highly visible, a situation that intensifies their problems. Larew (1980) aptly notes that "the public's attitude toward homeless persons tends to be one of intolerance when their visibility increases" so that a common concern is the "removal, relocation, or elimination of these undesirables" (p. 108).

At times, in fact, the effort to remove "undesirables" may take on malicious overtones, as is demonstrated in a suggestion by a Fort Lauderdale, Florida, city commissioner that beach-area garbage cans be sprayed with kerosene in order to discourage homeless individuals from foraging for food (New Migrants 1982; Plan to Spray 1981). His rationale, that "the way to get rid of roaches or other vermin in the house is to get rid of their food supply" (Garbage Consumption 1981), was endorsed by the city's mayor and is a chilling reminder that the limits of society's tolerance are finite.

Recent Studies of the Homeless Mentally Ill

A number of recent works have carved out selected portions of the population of homeless mentally ill individuals and reported on their characteristics and service needs:

• Arce and his colleagues (1983) determined the prevalence of mental illness among 193 homeless men and women brought to a city-run emergency shelter in Philadelphia in December of 1981. A subsample of 179 received psychiatric examinations, and 40 percent of those were found to have major mental disorders. The leading primary diagnoses were schizophrenia, for more than one-third of the cases, and substance abuse, for one-fourth. Secondary diagnoses of substance abuse were made for an additional 18 percent.

• Barrow and Lovell (1983b) studied referral patterns among a sample of 159 enrollees in two New York City outreach programs for the homeless mentally ill during a three-month period in 1983. For the subsample of 96 individuals judged to need mental health services, referral patterns often clustered. For example, individuals who were referred for housing were also more likely to have been referred for mental health services. In addition, younger persons in the sample were more likely to have been given mental health referrals than were older persons, and males were more likely to have received mental health referrals than were females. In all, at least one mental health referral was made for 31 percent of the sample.

• On five consecutive nights in the spring of 1983, Bassuk (1983) studied the psychiatric status of 78 shelter residents in a facility deemed to be representative of shelters in the Boston-Cambridge area. The median age of the population was 34, and males exceeded females by a ratio of four to one. Psychiatric evaluations revealed that 40 percent had major mental disorders. One-fifth of the shelter residents had lived continuously on the streets or in shelters for a minimum of two years.

• Baxter and Hopper's (1981) classic field study, updated a year later by Hopper and his colleagues (1982), assessed mental disability and service needs among the homeless on New York City streets. Yielding insights and information of a primarily qualitative nature, these landmark studies provided vivid descriptions of the homeless population and suggested that as many as half may suffer from serious psychiatric disorders. At the same time, however, these reports pointed out the necessity for controlling for the confounding effects of physical illness in assigning psychiatric diagnoses to the homeless.

• Brown and his colleagues (1983) used both sampling and census techniques to estimate the prevalence of mental disability among homeless individuals in Phoenix during a three-week period in 1983. Interviews conducted on two samples of food-line users (150 and 195 subjects) revealed that about three in ten individuals had at some time been in mental institutions. The most striking findings in this report concerned the wide-ranging transiency of Phoenix' homeless population. Only 5 percent of those whose residential histories were taken were Phoenix natives. More than half had been in Phoenix for six months or less.

• Chmiel and his colleagues (1979) reviewed the records of 35 "long distance patients" (that is, transient in-migrants) presenting at the emergency service of a mental health center in Charlottesville, Virginia, between July and December of 1974. Of this number 26 percent received diagnoses of schizophrenia and 17 percent of affective disorder.

• Depp and Ackiss (1983) determined the psychiatric history and status of 65 residents in a women's shelter in Washington, D.C., in 1983. Forty-eight percent were found to be in need of psychiatric treatment.

• Leaf and Cohen (1982) detailed demographic and diagnostic changes in the population of homeless men in New York City shelters between 1970 and 1980. The investigation found significant changes in age and racial composition of the two cohorts. The 1980 grouping was a younger population and had relatively higher percentages of blacks and Hispanics. There was, in addition, a shift from a population "composed largely of alcoholics to one with significant numbers of former mental patients" (p. 8).

• Lewis (1978) studied 76 "transient mentally disabled" individuals applying for services at the Travelers Aid Society of San Francisco during the winter of 1977-78. Applicants had arrived from all regions of the United States. Fewer than half had come from California. More than 60 percent had recently been under psychiatric care.

• Lipton and his colleagues (1983) examined the psychiatric histories and demographic characteristics of 100 homeless patients presenting consecutively at the emergency psychiatric service at Bellevue Hospital in New York City. Seventy-two percent had diagnoses of schizophrenia, and 6 percent of affective disorder. Two in five patients acknowledged the use of alcohol or drugs, and 97 percent had had prior psychiatric hospitalizations. This study made a number of important observations regarding the unique treatment needs of homeless mentally ill individuals.

• The results of interviews with 107 randomly selected men using New York City shelters during the summer of 1981 were reported by the New York State Office of Mental Health (1982). Fewer than a quarter of those interviewed were determined to be in need of psychiatric services.

• In order to determine the extent of social deficit in a mentally ill vagrant population, Segal and his colleagues (1977) surveyed 295 primarily young adult patrons of a soup line in Berkeley, California, in 1973. The resulting data, supplemented by systematic observations of street life, yielded a seminal theoretical analysis of the place of homeless mentally ill individuals in street culture. The concept of limited "social margin" for these individuals was developed.

• Streltzer (1979) reviewed the charts of all individuals given psychiatric diagnoses at the emergency room of a general hospital in Hawaii during five months in 1976. The incidence of psychiatric emergencies was estimated to be 1,250 per 100,000 persons per year for the local population and 2,250 per 100,000 persons per year for transient newcomers. Two in five transient newcomers received diagnoses of schizophrenia and frequently reflected the "coconuts and bananas syndrome"—that is, they believed the myth, responsible for heavy in-migration to Hawaii, that "life is so easy in Hawaii that one can simply pick food off of trees" (p. 143).

• Tabler (1982) studied the mental health status of 269 individuals in a Baltimore city shelter during six months in 1981-82. Thirty-one percent had psychiatric histories consisting of inpatient or outpatient treatment, psychotherapy, or chemotherapy. This brief report commented on the probability that the prevalence of psychopathology is understated when it is estimated on the basis of psychiatric history per se and called for more accurate and complete mental health needs assessments among the homeless.

• The Travelers Aid Society of New Orleans (1976) surveyed the records of 62 mentally ill homeless individuals utilizing its services in order to establish the prevalence of geographic mobility. Thirty-four individuals were reported to be on the rolls of at least one other Travelers Aid Society facility in the United States.

These selected studies constitute a small sampling of a rapidly growing body of research. Together they provide a wealth of detail about the homeless mentally ill. Yet they establish few generalizable principles to guide us in developing a global picture of this population. Many of these reports, in fact, contain disclaimers and remind readers that they deal with only a small portion of the homeless mentally ill.

A major reason for the limited generalizability of the results is that they are not in any sense based on systematic samples from the universe of homeless mentally ill individuals. Rather, each investigates the parameters of a small and finite portion of that universe. This does not in any sense alter the value of these studies as hypothesis-generating efforts, but it vastly limits the degree to which they may be compared with one another and the extent to which their findings may be said to represent the larger universe.

Problems in Defining and Counting

In fact, there are serious conceptual and methodological impediments to defining and counting the homeless mentally ill population. They include difficulties in defining homelessness per se, problems in establishing the presence of psychopathology, overlap of the homeless mentally ill with other populations, heterogeneity within the population, and geographic variability.

Defining Homelessness

At a conference held recently in New York State, a county director of mental health services remarked, "We don't have any homelessness in our community. If someone sees a person without a home out on the streets, they call Social Services. Social Services come and put the person up in a hotel. So we never have any homeless people here." Yet most service providers who work directly with the homeless would almost certainly contend that homelessness is something more than a mere lack of residence. As Lipton and Sabatini point out in their chapter in this report, the homeless lack not only shelter but also food, clothing, medical services, and social supports. They are multiply disadvantaged individuals.

It is apparent that a major deterrent to defining the homeless mentally ill population lies in our uncertainty about the precise meaning of homelessness. Are all unsheltered individuals homeless? What of migrant farmworkers who "live in squalid little camps sometimes five or six in a single room, in barracks or huts that lack basic sanitary facilities" (Sinclair 1981)? What of the Kickapoo Indian tribe whose members live in reed huts in a park under a bridge across the Rio Grande at Eagle Pass, Texas ("Lost" Indian Tribe 1981)?

Several investigators have sought to define homelessness, but their definitions tend to be more descriptive than operational. Larew

(1980), in an essentially sociological definition, defines homelessness as "a human condition of disaffiliation and detachment . . . from the primary agents of social structure" (p. 107). Bassuk (1983) focuses on the intrapsychic nature of homelessness and describes it as "more than the lack of a home; it is a metaphor for profound disconnection from other people and social institutions." The Alcohol, Drug Abuse, and Mental Health Administration (ADAMHA) offers a multiplex definition of the homeless individual as one who "lacks adequate shelter, resources, and community ties" (Levine 1983).

Even if it were possible to reach consensus on the precise properties of homelessness, it would still be difficult to count homeless people. Thus Ross (1983) reports a San Francisco Police Department count of 245 homeless individuals but remarks that "what the SFPD cannot see, of course, are the homeless who hide from them—at least 2,000 more than are publicly sheltered each evening" (p. 10).

ADAMHA estimates the total number of homeless persons in the United States to be about 2,000,000, with the possibility that as many as half suffer from alcohol, drug abuse, or mental health problems (The Homeless 1983). However, this estimate is, of necessity, very approximate.

Establishing Psychopathology

In testimony before the New York Governor's Task Force on the Homeless, Kennedy (1983) stated: "I recognize and want to emphasize that those individuals who are chronically mentally ill constitute only a percent of those who are homeless and those who are homeless constitute only a percent of those who are chronically mentally ill." These words indicate a second major difficulty in defining and counting the homeless mentally ill: there are obvious difficulties in confirming the presence of psychopathology among individuals who are often shy and frightened, who frequently use alcohol and drugs, and who are likely to have a subculture encompassing different values and normative expressions from those of most mental health workers and researchers (Ball 1982; Barrow and Lovell 1982, 1983a; Segal and Baumohl 1980; Segal et al. 1977).

The fact that homeless individuals are also usually physically debilitated does not help efforts to establish the presence of psychopathology. Baxter and Hopper (1982) are concerned with the validity of diagnoses made on individuals whose basic subsistence needs are unmet and caution that "were the same individuals to receive several nights of sleep, an adequate diet, and warm social contact, some of their symptoms might subside" (p. 402).

It is worth noting parenthetically that homeless individuals themselves do not necessarily share the definitional problems experienced by professionals. Those among the homeless who are not mentally ill tend to shun those who are (Baxter and Hopper 1982). Segal and Baumohl (1980) refer to mentally ill street people as "space cases," who are "judged by other street people to be delusionary, unpredictable, and unreliable—in the lexicon of the street, 'burned out,' 'fried,' or 'spaced'" (p. 358).

Overlap With Other Populations

Problems in defining and counting the homeless mentally ill are further complicated by the overlap of this population with other populations. The characteristics of the homeless mentally ill as a group are not readily distinguishable from those of other chronically mentally ill groups such as "revolving door" patients (Geller 1982), "difficult" patients (Neill 1979; Robbins et al. 1978; H. White 1981), "treatment resistant" patients (Goldfinger et al. 1984), "chronic crisis" patients (Bassuk and Gerson 1980), and, most recently, "young adult chronic" patients (Bachrach 1982; Pepper et al. 1981).

Goldfinger and his colleagues (1984) in fact identify a subgroup of chronic mental patients who fit all of these labels. They are frequent users of emergency and inpatient psychiatric services at San Francisco General Hospital and also of outpatient, residential, and day treatment services. Many of these "acute care recidivists" are also intermittently homeless. In another study of the same population, Chafetz and Goldfinger (1984) establish that 46 percent of a sample of admissions to psychiatric emergency services were or had at some time been without stable housing, and they conclude that domiciled and undomiciled patients come from a common demographic pool.

The homeless mentally ill are also at times difficult to differentiate from populations in jails and correctional facilities (Drake 1982; Stelovich 1979; R. White 1981). Earley (1983), in an article in the *Washington Post*, asserts that jails have become the "social agencies of last resort" for many mentally ill individuals: that "cuts in social reform programs, hard economic times, and the development of psychotropic medicines which have allowed large numbers of disturbed persons to leave mental institutions have contributed to a dramatic increase in persons jailed for non-serious crimes." This finding is reinforced by reports in the professional literature. Lamb and Grant (1982, 1983), for example, write that 36 percent of male and 42 percent of female inmates at Los Angeles County jail facilities who were referred for psychiatric evaluation had been living as transients on the streets, on the beach, or in missions at the time of their arrests.

The homeless mentally ill even overlap to some extent with the population of migrant farmworkers. There are reports that homeless mentally ill individuals are at times shanghaied into migrant labor streams (Baxter and Hopper 1982; Henry 1983; Herman 1979).

Heterogeneity

The homeless mentally ill are also frequently difficult to define and count because of their extreme diversity—a blind-man-and-elephant kind of methodological limitation. Like the chronically mentally ill in general (Goldman et al. 1981), these individuals do not constitute a uniform population either diagnostically, demographically, functionally, or in terms of their residential histories (Arce et al. 1983; Barrow and Lovell 1982; Bassuk 1983; Baxter and Hopper 1982; Down and Out 1982; Lipton et al. 1983; Project HELP 1983; Rousseau 1981).

Arce (1983) and Arce and his colleagues (1983) divide the homeless mentally ill population into two groups. "Street people" usually have diagnoses of schizophrenia, substance abuse, or both; a history of hospitalization in a public mental hospital; and a variety of health problems. They tend to be floridly psychotic. The "episodic homeless" are usually younger than the street people and tend to have diagnoses of personality disorder, affective disorder, or substance abuse. They tend also to use a wide variety of mental health services sporadically and are likely to be regarded as "difficult" patients. (A third category of homeless individuals described by Arce, the "situationally homeless," is identified by situational stress instead of psychopathology. For this population the lack of shelter is generally temporary, and the disaffiliation less pronounced.)

Nor do the homeless mentally ill constitute a uniform group in terms of appearance. Project HELP (1983) in New York City is targeted toward a severely disabled subgroup distinguished by "certain key visual and behavioral characteristics":

> The primary visual indicators include: extremely dirty and di-shevelled appearance; obvious lice infestation; torn, dirty, and/or layered clothing; weather inappropriate clothing (especially heavy coats and woolen hats in mid-summer); and a cache of belongings in bags, boxes, shopping carts, etc. The primary behavioral indi-cators include: walking in traffic, urinating and/or defecating in public, remaining mute and withdrawn" (p. 4).

At the opposite pole are the individuals described in Reich and Siegel's (1978) analysis of recent arrivals to the Bowery in New York City:

> Most of these men are intelligent and have better than the usual education found on the Bowery. They present a fairly intact appearance even when undergoing severe inner disturbance and thus can avoid unwanted hospitalization even when their situation destabilizes and there is a threat of erupting violence" (pp. 195-196).

The parents of John Hinckley (1983) remind us that people often find it difficult to accept the presence of severe mental illness in an individual who "looks and acts so 'sane'" (p. 3).

Geographic Variability

Finally, it is difficult to define and count the homeless mentally ill because they are often hard to locate. Although frequently associated with inner-city residence, they are also, as previously noted, found in small cities and in suburban and rural areas (Bachrach 1983d; Melton 1983; Young 1983). Even within cities there are distinctive concentrations of the homeless mentally ill. Barrow and Lovell (1982) distinguish between Upper West Side "street" people and Central Park "park" people in New York City. The latter are characterized by a substantially heavier concentration of males, a markedly higher prevalence of severe psychopathology, and a lower prevalence of substance abuse.

Not only do the homeless mentally ill differ according to where they are; they also vary in how long they have been there. Some are part of an essentially stationary population that is relatively fixed within defined geographic limits, sometimes as small as a few city blocks (Larew 1980). Others are characterized by extremes of mobility that may cover vast areas. As long as 15 years ago Travelers Aid Society (TAS) units throughout the country were noting an upsurge of clients in "psychological flight" (New Tasks 1969). A number of TAS studies have addressed problems in identifying and serving travelers with severe psychiatric disabilities (Goldberg 1972; Health and Welfare Council 1983; Lewis 1978; Smith 1980; Travelers Aid 1976). One particularly interesting contribution notes a group of severely mentally ill clients identified both in New Orleans and in TAS facilities in other parts of the country. In this population 55 percent were seen in at least one other city, 45 percent in at least three other cities, and 22 percent in at least six other cities (Travelers Aid 1976).

Indeed, migrating homeless mentally ill individuals have been documented in a number of places including Arizona (Brown et al. 1983), California (Farr 1982), Virginia (Chmiel et al. 1979), and Hawaii (Kimura et al. 1975; Streltzer 1979). The common finding in all of these studies is summed up neatly in a single sentence in Streltzer's (1979) report: "Those [transients] who were attempting to escape psychosis continued to be psychotic in Hawaii" (p. 468).

In summary, a number of complex problems inhibit efforts to define and count the homeless mentally ill. In the absence of accurate estimates, disagreements over the size of the population are sometimes bitter and fuel political debate (New York State 1980). Frequent articles in the *New York Times* chronicle an ongoing battle in which city and state officials hold one another responsible for the plight of homeless mentally ill individuals whose precise numbers are a source of disagreement (Barbanel 1983; Blum 1983; Gargan 1983; Sullivan 1983b, 1983c). Such rancor is not in the best interests of the homeless mentally ill, who have somehow become unwitting pawns in a political struggle that they have no hope of influencing.

The Context of Care for the Homeless Mentally Ill

Like other chronically mentally ill individuals, those who are homeless have been profoundly affected by the ideology of and service practices within deinstitutionalized service systems (Jones 1983; Slavinsky and Cousins 1982). The younger members of that population have indeed lived their entire adult lives in an era of deinstitutionalization. Thus it is appropriate, before considering the service needs of the homeless mentally ill, to describe the current status of deinstitutionalization and to point out some of its consequences.

The resident population of the nation's public mental hospitals peaked at about 559,000 in 1955 (Goldman et al. 1983). A quarter of a century later, in 1980, the count stood at approximately 132,000 (Redick and Witkin 1983)—a drop of about three-quarters. This dramatic decline has taken place within the context of deinstitutionalization, a policy stressing the avoidance of traditional institutional settings, and the concurrent development of community-based alternatives, for the care of the chronically mentally ill (Bachrach 1976). The basic assumptions of deinstitutionalization—that community-based care represents a highly therapeutic option for some, if not all, chronic mental patients; that communities have the potential for providing a full and relevant array of services to people who are severely mentally disabled; and that communities may be persuaded to assume responsibility for the care of those individuals—today permeate service planning for all chronically mentally ill persons, including those who have never been institutionalized (Bachrach 1978, 1983b).

There is evidence that deinstitutionalization has had mixed outcomes (Bachrach 1983a). On the positive side, a number of successful community-based alternatives to institutional care have been developed and tested and have shown positive results (Stein and Test 1978; Talbott 1981). They demonstrate that the chronically mentally ill stand to benefit from deinstitutionalized service initiatives when those initiatives are implemented under ideal circumstances. Indeed, the success of programs that "work" is a testimony to the ability of some communities to confront their service delivery problems and to institute aggressive efforts to overcome them.

However, although deinstitutionalization has provided creative and encouraging responses to the service needs of some chronically mentally ill individuals, it has also generated a series of unprecedented service problems. Most communities have had relatively little success in dealing with those problems, and there is evidence that the majority of the chronically mentally ill in the United States today have not been fortunate enough to experience deinstitutionalization under optimal conditions. Problems associated with deinstitutionalization include the need for highly diversified programming, difficulties in achieving both continuity and comprehensiveness of care, the emergence of a population of system "misfits," and service systems' failure to designate the dimensions of their responsibility to the chronically mentally ill.

Need for Diversified Programs

A major problem in deinstitutionalized service systems revolves around the complexity of planning. What was once a relatively uniform population of chronic mental patients living inside public institutions has been splintered into a variety of groups with different treatment histories and different program requirements (Bachrach 1983b; Dorwart 1980; Shore and Shapiro 1979). Some patients have been released from institutions after as many as five or six decades in residence, while others, who are equally ill, have received no inpatient care at all (Bachrach 1978, 1982; Pepper and Ryglewicz 1983). Many of those released have been shunted to minimal kinds of facilities where, by most measures, the quality of their lives has actually deteriorated (Bachrach 1980a). Others have exhibited persistent dependency on institutional care and have developed patterns of repeated readmission and discharge. Still other patients have been deemed "poor risks" for discharge and have remained on the rolls of public mental hospitals despite the idealization of community-based care (Peele 1983).

This extreme diversity in the treatment histories of chronic mental patients, when coupled with their varied symptoms and functional levels, has created a need for highly diversified programs—a circumstance for which our imagination, our creativity, and our pocketbooks have generally, at least on a nationwide basis, not been adequate.

Continuity of Care

A second problem accompanying deinstitutionalization has to do with the complexities of implementing continuity in the care of chronic mental patients (Bachrach 1981; Peterson 1978; Schwartz et al. 1983). Since the service needs of these individuals tend to endure over time, efforts must be made to reduce the possibility that hiatuses in service delivery will occur. This, in turn, requires the design of proactive and carefully detailed program plans, as well as the presence of "continuity agents" (Granet and Talbott 1978) to anticipate and mitigate barriers to care. In contrast to these

requirements, however, deinstitutionalized program initiatives tend
to be designed for the "single-episode user of services" and thus,
in the words of Hansell (1978), to exhibit "a deficiency of interest
in people with lifelong disorders" (p. 105).

Comprehensive Care

Third, there have been serious practical difficulties associated with
the provision of comprehensive services to chronic mental patients.
These individuals require an intricate array of psychiatric, medical,
social, rehabilitative, vocational, and quasi-vocational services. In
the past, when all of these needs could at least potentially be met
within a single physical setting, providing comprehensive care was
relatively easy. In deinstitutionalized service systems, however, where
programmatic offerings are typically divided among many health
and human service agencies in the public and private sectors, the
potential for comprehensiveness is greatly reduced. The programs
in which specific services are offered—if they exist at all—are sometimes reserved for less impaired target populations and are effectively unavailable to the most seriously mentally ill. In other instances,
although the services may be open to them, the chronically mentally
ill may not know where or how to gain access to them—a circumstance not rare among severely disabled individuals. To use a cliché,
community-based psychiatric service systems are often hopelessly
fragmented, and their fragmentation leads to insuperable barriers
to care among the chronically mentally ill.

The failure to provide comprehensive care to the chronically
mentally ill is often an outgrowth of the fact that communities do
not always fully understand the implications of their charge. Even
communities that are genuinely committed to serving this population have at times not anticipated the difficulties inherent in
providing substitutes for the full array of services formerly provided,
for better or worse, within institutional settings. Institutional care,
whatever its past shortcomings may have been, performed a complex
and extensive set of functions in the service of chronic mental patients
(Bachrach 1976). Extending beyond long-term residential, psychiatric, and adjunctive care, these functions included some less readily perceived and acknowledged services, such as assistance to patients
in gaining access to their entitlements, regular physical and mental
health care monitoring, opportunities for social intercourse, and
relief for overburdened families (Thurer 1983).

A basic function fulfilled by institutions that is of particular importance to the homeless mentally ill was—and in many cases continues to be—the provision of safety and security for individuals in need of refuge. Known as asylum, this function is associated with the offer of safe haven to those mentally ill persons who need to escape from the stresses of community living for either short or long periods of time. The function of asylum is conspicuously absent in most community-based systems of care (Bachrach 1984), and this deficiency has greatly limited the effectiveness of deinstitutionalized service systems for many chronically mentally ill individuals.

System "Misfits"

Failure to provide comprehensive and continuous care in the community has been associated with a fourth problem, the presence of many chronically mentally ill individuals who have no niche, either within society or within the system of care. This situation is graphically described by Schwartz and his colleagues (1983):

> In any one setting—hospital, clinic, and so forth—patients are cared for and considered the responsibility of that setting only as long as they are well enough to be contained by it and sick enough to need it. Although some attempts may be made to ensure continuity, transfer to another setting generally involves new counselors, new rules, new treatment approaches, and new goals. One facility usually will not consider itself responsible for a patient after the patient is transferred to another facility (p. 32).

Given these circumstances, it is hardly surprising that a subpopulation described by the New York State Office of Mental Health (1980) as "homeless, mentally ill, and disaffiliated" (p. 1) has emerged in this era of deinstitutionalization. If the professional literature has until now given scant attention to their needs, they have not escaped the notice of the popular media, which often portray them as disruptive and frightening to other citizens.

I am particularly struck by a pair of articles in the *New York Times* discussing the use of public libraries by the homeless mentally ill. One reports on the situation in New York City and quotes an assistant police commissioner as saying, "'We've lost the subways and most of the parks [to this population] and we just can't afford to lose our libraries'" (Basler 1981). The second reports similar situations in other parts of the country—Miami, Los Angeles, Seattle, and Washington, D.C.: "Many city librarians say privately that the 'disturbed patron' has taken the enjoyment out of the job, if not, in some cases, the personal safety as well" (Jaynes 1981). In fact, the California Library Association in 1980 conducted a special workshop for librarians on how to deal with these "disturbed patrons" (Jaynes 1981).

Nonspecific Responsibility

A final major issue, although it is implicit in the problems noted above, warrants separate consideration. It involves a frequent failure of deinstitutionalized service systems to designate with precision the dimensions of their responsibility to the chronically mentally ill. The result is that many efforts ostensibly designed for chronic mental patients actually are directed toward the needs of a population described by Zusman and Lamb (1977) as "healthy but unhappy." There is, in fact, a deepening concern that scarce resources are increasingly being deflected toward patients with less severe disabilities at the expense of those who are most disabled and least able to compete successfully (Langsley 1980).

This situation is, in part, an outgrowth of the stigma that continues to attach to the chronically mentally ill and to those services and individuals who care for them (Baron 1981; Report of Task Panel 1978; Stern and Minkoff 1979). Negative attitudes toward the chronically mentally ill are found among service providers as well as the general public and have been exceedingly difficult to neutralize.

Stigma is, however, not the sole cause. The problem is also often one of insufficient resources for multiple competing populations, a legacy of the expansiveness of early community mental health planning. Many of the pioneer deinstitutionalization efforts adopted a markedly broader view of their mission than did traditional psychiatric service systems, and concerned themselves with clientele and social problems not previously regarded as the domain of traditional systems. This has resulted in the creation of "boundaryless" programs capable of "busting the boundaries" of psychiatric service systems (Dinitz and Beran 1971).

Today it is increasingly acknowledged that the prevalence of chronic mental illness is not synonymous with the existence of social problems: that the populations subsumed under these two headings, though at times overlapping, are not coterminous (Langsley 1980; Stern and Minkoff 1979). But the early failure to assign clear priorities in the distribution of program resources continues to affect the selection of patients to be served in deinstitutionalized service systems today. It is not at all unusual for program administrators or even clinicians in these systems to insist that the most severely disabled belong "someplace else, not here," without a clear understanding that available service opportunities are in fact more sparse than are the proverbial cracks through which these patients are said to fall.

Barriers to Care for the Homeless Mentally Ill

It is against this backdrop of general problems and issues that we must consider the unique needs of the homeless mentally ill. Although certainly not all of these individuals are public mental hospital dischargees, they are, as a group, essentially deinstitutionalized persons, for they must seek treatment and support in service systems that are primarily deinstitutionalized. The homeless mentally ill are thus profoundly affected by the policies, the practices, and the priorities of the deinstitutionalization movement, and it is deinstitutionalization that gives substance to their problems in receiving adequate care.

Because those among the chronically mentally ill who are homeless are particularly vulnerable to the effects of the problems summarized above, they tend to experience today's psychiatric service system as a series of paradoxes defying ready solution (Homeless in America 1984; Minkoff 1982; Stern and Minkoff 1979). They generally encounter severe impediments to care. These barriers fall into several interrelated broad categories: preclusive admission policies, inadequate services, geographically determined responsibility, inappropriate expectations, and social distance.

Preclusive Admission Policies

Specific services for the homeless mentally ill, like those for other chronically mentally ill individuals, are often targeted toward the highest functioning members of that population. The result is that programs may be totally unavailable to those who require services most. A newspaper article describes a suburban community outside

Washington, D.C., for example, as having "a fledgling supervised-apartment program and a group home for the mentally ill, but only for those who have been judged capable of being rehabilitated, not for the so-called hopeless cases" (Sugawara 1983).

That such preclusive admission policies flourish should come as no surprise. Service planners and providers may be expected to do what they know how to do—to treat those who best respond to their efforts—and higher functioning individuals must not be abandoned simply because the "answers" to problems of caring for the most disturbed are so elusive. Exclusory policies are, moreover, reinforced by certain attitude sets of service providers. Not only. does the stigma of working with the most severely ill influence gatekeeping behavior, but service providers tend to measure their effectiveness in terms of "cures" for their patients (Stern and Minkoff 1979). The cure rate among the homeless is not demonstrably high.

Other preclusive admission policies result from a failure by service planners to perceive accurately the program needs of the population they are attempting to serve. There is often a time lag between the identification of service needs and the implementation of programs directed toward those needs. In the case of the chronically mentally ill, that lag is manifested in initiatives designed for earlier generations of institutionalized patients. "Aftercare," assisting long-time residents of institutions to adapt to life in the community, is a fundamental program planning concept today (Meyerson and Herman 1983; Cutler 1983). Yet an aftercare focus denies the essentially noninstitutional cast of today's chronically mentally ill population and overlooks the existence of a rapidly growing portion of that population that has never had hospitalizations of any kind. Many of these individuals are homeless (Bachrach 1982; Segal et al. 1977).

Inadequate Services

Very often specific services that the homeless mentally ill require simply do not exist as part of the psychiatric service system's offerings. One reason for this deficit is that the homeless mentally ill have service needs that are extraordinary in both number and content. In keeping with the complex nature of homelessness—it is more than a simple lack of shelter—Barrow and Lovell (1982) list 70 separate services needed by members of this population, including some not very traditional ones like delousing and showering. Providers may be hard pressed to make placements that will ensure the complete array of needed services.

The absence of adequate services may also result from a failure in concept. Planners often view alternatives for the homeless mentally ill in absolute terms. In the well-chosen words of Baxter and Hopper (in press), it is a "Hobson's choice which depicts options as either mental hospitalization or a life on the streets." Yet many who spend time with the homeless mentally ill are adamant in their belief that there are shades in between these two extremes and that more moderate options are viable (Baxter and Hopper in press; Hombs and Snyder 1982).

Homeless mentally ill persons with substance abuse problems— by all accounts a substantial percentage—apparently have particular difficulty in finding adequate services because they often fail to meet categorical admission criteria for either mental health or substance abuse programs (Barrow and Lovell 1983b).

When appropriate placements cannot be made, there is a tendency to "dump" individuals—to shunt them into places that ignore the specificity of their individual needs. This is evident in the way that shelter facilities are often used for the homeless mentally ill population. Bassuk (1983) aptly points out that shelters usually are not connected with clinical services and thus stand outside the spectrum of linked psychiatric services within a community.

Geographically Determined Responsibility

Historically, one of the major philosophical underpinnings of the community mental health movement involved fixing responsibility for the chronically mentally ill within defined geographic areas (Group for the Advancement of Psychiatry 1983). Although such "catchmenting" is rarely a major topic in today's literature, its original intent, to force providers to assume responsibility for the care of persons within definite boundaries so that none would be overlooked (Panzetta 1971), continues to influence the provision of services. More generally, in order to qualify for care in many facilities, the chronically mentally ill must meet a variety of residency requirements. Obviously such a policy imposes severe barriers to care for those who have no home and no fixed address.

Residence-based requirements for eligibility also often affect the ability of many homeless mentally ill individuals to qualify for social service and medical treatment entitlements (Barrow and Lovell 1983b;

Bassuk 1983; Christmas and Food Lines 1983; Homeless in America 1984). Segal and his colleagues (1977), for example, note that the lack of a permanent address "greatly increases the likelihood that an individual's SSI application will not be processed" (p. 398). Even if the application is processed, the applicant may still experience difficulty in receiving entitlements, because "notification of psychiatric appointments, requests for additional information or release forms, and all other communications from the Social Security Office are routinely conducted by mail" (Segal et al. 1977, 398).

It may be noted parenthetically that, despite the emphasis on geographic responsibility, there are times when the homeless mentally ill are actively extruded from their communities. Wealthy suburbs sometimes refer seriously ill citizens to inner-city agencies (Muscatine 1983). Whether those referrals are actually completed is questionable.

Inappropriate Expectations

The homeless mentally ill are often further impeded in their access to psychiatric and related services by unrealistic expectations on the part of service planners and providers. Some investigators conclude that there is a great need for highly structured treatment settings where these individuals can receive at least a minimum of attention and will not be exposed to the uncertainties and rigors of street life (Lamb and Grant 1982, 1983). However, the needs of the homeless mentally ill who require such structure are in direct conflict with societal norms that encourage freedom for the mentally ill and define that freedom on the basis of individuals' consent to be placed in treatment settings. Often homeless mentally ill people are unwilling or unable to give that consent (Barrow and Lovell 1983b; Bassuk 1983; Drake 1982; Kamen 1982; Quindlen 1982; Sullivan 1983b).

This paradox is illustrated by the poignant example of the late Rebecca Smith, a "bag lady" who, two winters ago, died of hypothermia in her home, a cardboard box on the streets of New York City. Ms. Smith had previously been a patient in a public mental hospital and had steadfastly rejected readmission. At the time of her death city officials were attempting to obtain a court order for her rehospitalization, but Ms. Smith wished to live independently on the streets (Death in a Cardboard Box 1982). It is ironic that "independent living" is a central goal of deinstitutionalization (Bachrach 1980a), one that was being pursued vigorously for chronic mental patients in New York at the very time of Ms. Smith's death (Allen 1982; Herman 1982b).

Situations like Ms. Smith's might be avoided by involuntary commitment procedures, but these are often slow, ponderous, and difficult to implement. In many states, involuntary commitment is generally reserved for persons who are dangerous to themselves or to others, but today dangerousness is being ever more narrowly defined (Rachlin 1983). While the quest for "independence" may be, as in the case of Ms. Smith, ultimately and terminally dangerous to oneself, it is becoming increasingly difficult to invoke the self-destructive effects of undomiciled existence as evidence of dangerousness.

However, not all the homeless mentally ill are in need of structured treatment settings. Barrow and Lovell (1982) see a need for less structure than is generally offered in services for much of this population, and they support the use of drop-in centers operated by a staff specially skilled in working with homeless people. Segal and Baumohl (1980) concur in this view.

The two positions regarding structure noted here, though polarized, are not necessarily contradictory, for the homeless mentally ill are a diverse population, and different individuals in it have different service needs. What both of these viewpoints point up is a frequent failure on the part of service planners and providers to plan a realistic array of service structures for the target population and to assess, on an individualized basis, the appropriate placement of those who utilize their services.

Social Distance

Closely related to the inconsistency between professionals' expectations and many homeless mentally ill persons' capabilities is a paradox created by the fact that, for all practical purposes, they live in different worlds. The homeless mentally ill tend to have a unique cultural identity and a limited universe of discourse with those who attempt to serve them (O'Connor 1983; Segal et al. 1977; Sullivan 1983a). Their respective values differ, and certainly the norms that govern their behavior are often disparate. Baxter and Hopper (1981) provide forceful documentation of the existence of a separate culture among homeless street people, a culture that often

escapes the notice of those who provide them with services.
Larew (1980) explains the social distance paradox:

> An inability [on the part of the homeless individual] to live in a
> traditional lifestyle poses a special problem for the traditional
> service providers and for the community planners that offer serv-
> ices to transients. Traditional services are geared toward either
> religious evangelism or rehabilitation, with an emphasis on gain-
> ing employable skills. These two goals conflict with the transients'
> inability to look beyond the next meal or bed. Workers who
> deliver the services often place the highest value on the client
> who least fulfills the transient criteria. The transient who most
> frequently needs a variety of services is left unattended (p. 109).

Carried to extremes, this kind of cultural bias may result in public
policy that denies basic necessities to the homeless on the assumption that their failure to look after themselves bespeaks a disincli-
nation to "earn" their keep and an eagerness to acquire unneeded,
and undeserved, handouts (Engel and Sargent 1983; Meese 1983).

In summary, those among the chronically mentally ill who are
homeless have a special relationship to deinstitutionalization in that
the benefits of that basically humanistic movement have largely
eluded them. These individuals, usually unable to surmount barriers
to care, have fallen prey to the disaffiliation and detachment that
are the conditions of homelessness. Once homeless, they usually
have not had the resources to escape that status. Although they are
often geographically mobile, they lack the personal and social
resources—the constellation of attributes that Segal and his colleagues
(1977) call "social margin"—to be vertically mobile, to become
something other than what they are.

Planning Principles

What can be done to overcome these barriers? The problems outlined
here may well lead to pessimism, to the notion that there are no
effective solutions to meeting the needs of the homeless mentally
ill. Yet from another perspective, our ability to summarize and
analyze these difficulties indicates that we are beginning to build a
body of knowledge about the service needs of this population.

Thus, even though our services for these individuals are certainly
inadequate, and even though our efforts to reach them are frequently

misdirected, it is possible today to enumerate a series of planning principles that may be applied in designing programs for the homeless mentally ill. These principles parallel those I have described elsewhere (Bachrach in press b) as basic to the planning of humane and relevant services for the chronically mentally ill, whoever and wherever they are. They include formulating precise goals and objectives, assigning priorities in service delivery, reassessing institutional alternatives, arranging an array of comprehensive service interventions, ensuring interagency cooperation, designing individualized programs, utilizing flexible program formats, designing culturally relevant programs, and exercising caution and restraint.

Precise Goals and Objectives

Programs for the chronically mentally ill, including those for the homeless, require competent goal-setting (Bachrach 1974; Bachrach and Lamb 1982; Hagedorn 1977). Goals must be precisely stated, they must be reasonable, and they must be consistent with the resources of the target population.

An excellent report on California's mental health system (Teknekron 1977) illustrates the importance of precision in goal-setting for the chronically mentally ill by isolating several disiderata in service planning. They include letting patients reside in the community, minimizing hospitalization, maximizing independence, and curing or eliminating mental illness. The relative implications of goals such as these for the homeless mentally ill are readily apparent. If the first two goals, living in the community and minimizing hospitalization, are to be pursued, an individual's mere presence in the community, even on the streets, provides evidence of a successful outcome. But if the last two, maximizing independence and eliminating mental illness, are to be pursued—if, in fact, they are even realistic—the program planning process becomes infinitely more complicated.

Once goals have been enunciated, they must be translated into precise objectives or implementation strategies. Objectives are operational statements that specify the means for pursuing selected goals. They must demonstrate relevance to those goals, they must be practicable, and they must be measurable (Bachrach 1974).

Priority-Setting

Closely related to the need for defining goals and stating program
objectives is a second planning principle, the assignment of unam-
biguous priority to the homeless mentally ill in systems of care that
seek to serve them. Because these individuals generally do not advocate effectively on their own behalf, they do not fare well when
they must compete for scarce resources with others who are less
severely impaired and often more attractive to staff. Because the
homeless are unlikely to act aggressively to avail themselves of
services, any program purporting to serve them must back up that
intention by removing barriers to care—whether those barriers are
physical, economic, regulatory, social, or psychological.

This planning principle does not imply that every psychiatric
service facility must direct its efforts toward the needs of the homeless mentally ill at the expense of other patients. It does mean that,
when the homeless have been targeted as the recipients of services,
special efforts must be undertaken to assure that they are not somehow pushed aside. An article in the *Philadelphia Inquirer* clearly
illustrates this principle in a story about a city-run shelter for the
homeless that had been pre-empted by a group of angry individuals
who were "able to work but unable to find jobs" (Kaufman 1983).
The director of the shelter was quoted as saying that the facility
was "being used by a different group of people than it was intended
for."

Reassessment of Institutional Alternatives

A clear statement of goals and objectives also invites reassessment
of the possible role that institutions may play in the spectrum of
services for the homeless mentally ill, a third planning principle.
In recent years, the exclusive superiority of community-based care
has increasingly come into question (Peele et al. 1977; Spiro 1982;
Treffert 1977; Zaleski et al. 1979), and the polarized views that
characterized the early years of deinstitutionalization have moder-
ated. This change in thinking accompanies the understanding that
institutionalism may occur in community-based facilities as well as
in public mental hospitals unless individual patients' needs are carefully assessed and met. It acknowledges that where care is given is
less important than what happens within a program, and that well-
designed institution-based programs may also be capable of sensi-

tivity (Massachusetts Association for Mental Health 1981; McGuire 1982).

The professional literature is even beginning to feature contributions that view institutional care as something other than systems failure (Group for the Advancement of Psychiatry 1982), a real departure from the early years of deinstitutionalization. Increasingly there are suggestions that chronic mental patients, like patients with other chronic illnesses, may even benefit from periods of hospitalization, either short- or long-term, and that there are sometimes therapeutic advantages in patients' removal from the community (Strange 1981).

Comprehensive Services

This chapter has repeatedly noted the diversity of the homeless mentally ill and their extensive needs. A fourth planning principle is that service systems that target these individuals for care must consist of networks of interrelated programs that meet the needs of a very heterogeneous and multiply disadvantaged population. In practical terms this means that the service system must not settle for just one modality or approach, because there are too many different kinds of people who must be served. If we have learned one major lesson from the experience of deinstitutionalization, it is that there is no single right way, or place, to treat the chronically mentally ill.

Viewed structurally, service systems for the homeless mentally ill should contain screening and referral services, crisis stabilization services, a network of residential alternatives, a comprehensive array of treatment settings, a network of treatment services, transportation services, and information and evaluation services (Bachrach 1983c). Since these components are described at some length in other chapters of this report, I shall not elaborate upon them. However, it is critical that each of these service categories be considered as a separate entity in the planning process. A tendency to think of them interchangeably has, in fact, often been detrimental to the welfare of chronically mentally ill individuals—particularly the frequent confusion of residential and treatment settings. Although some sites provide both residential and treatment services, as in the case of the psychiatric hospital, recognition that the two functions are distinct must guide the planning process.

Confusing residential and treatment settings has had particularly

powerful consequences for the homeless mentally ill. It is not unusual
for planners to think of the residential needs of these individuals
but to ignore their various treatment needs, including their frequent
need for medical care (Arce et al. 1983; Baxter and Hopper 1982;
Rule 1983a) and psychiatric care (Bassuk 1983). Because the homeless mentally ill are multiply handicapped, housing is not enough.

Comprehensive care, a concept much in vogue in service planning, has unique connotations for the homeless mentally ill, who
generally have nothing and need everything. Thus the cornerstone
of planning for this population must be provision of services that
meet their basic survival needs. Until these have been met, clinical
and rehabilitative efforts will have little positive effect (Baxter and
Hopper 1982). SOME (So Others Might Eat), a unique soup kitchen
in Washington, D.C., credits much of its success in reaching the
homeless mentally ill to its provision of on-site medical, dental, and
psychiatric services (SOME, undated).

Interagency Cooperation

Precise delineation of goals and objectives, assignment of service
priorities, and designation of an array of service interventions are
all dependent upon cooperative enterprise. The multiplicity of
agencies and authorities typically involved in providing services to
the homeless mentally ill thus leads to a fifth principle, the need
for cooperation, communication, and linkages among the agencies
and personnel involved in their care. Cooperation among agencies
is essential for integrating service delivery, for avoiding duplication,
for controlling or reducing service delivery costs, and for attacking
turf-related opposition to specific program initiatives (Hagedorn
1977).

In some communities it has been possible to unify services for
the chronically mentally ill on the administrative level, so that all
the agencies offering treatment and support come under a single
planning and coordinating authority (Talbott 1983b). Pepper and
Ryglewicz (1982b) summarize as the major benefit of unified service
systems "the shift from an inherently competitive model of service
provision, plagued by inconsistent policies of diverse agencies, to
an integrated system that, while it may not achieve continuously
smooth operation, at least cherishes integration and consistency of
goals" (p. 764). Indeed, where such administrative arrangements
are possible, the unified service approach appears to hold great

potential for enhancing the quality of care delivered to the chronically mentally ill, including those among them who are homeless.

Even in a unified system of care, however, the importance of participating agencies' maintaining their unique identities must be stressed (Pepper and Ryglewicz 1982b). It is essential that efforts to establish interagency cooperation on behalf of the homeless mentally ill not be confused with a quest for regulated coordination and blurring of agencies' identities. There are genuine categorical differences in the needs of the homeless mentally ill, and the possibility that separate and highly focused programs may at times be more responsive to those differences should not be overlooked (Austin 1983; Hidden Resource 1981).

Individualized Programming

A sixth planning principle involves the necessity for individually designed treatment regimens (Anthony et al. 1983; Bachrach 1980b; Cotton 1983; Lamb 1982). Individualized programming is an essential part of treatment for the chronically mentally ill in general, whether the intervention is chemotherapy, psychotherapy, psychosocial rehabilitation, or some combination of these or other treatment modalities. For the homeless in that population, individualized programming is particularly critical, because of their fearfulness, resistance, and general inaccessibility.

The simplest kind of individualized programming involves placing a patient in a program that is compatible with his or her current level of functioning. Even greater sensitivity is introduced when the patient's potential is anticipated, and he or she is placed in a program that provides resources for skill development. With such an individualized skill training or rehabilitation approach, placement is based on the individual's potential for future development, and capabilities, not disabilities, are stressed.

There are, however, many chronically mentally ill individuals, particularly among the homeless, who cannot respond to skill training. It is essential that their care also be assured in service planning and that they not be abandoned for patients who show greater "promise." The critical point in planning services for the homeless mentally ill is that treatments be individually and realistically prescribed.

Flexible Format

Closely related to the principle of individualized treatment is a seventh principle: that program formats for the homeless mentally ill be flexible enough to be responsive to their ever-changing needs. Flexibility relieves the service recipient of pressures always to exhibit "progress," to move "forward" along a continuum (Abbott 1978; Bachrach 1981). It acknowledges that, as with other chronically ill individuals, it is generally inappropriate to think in terms of linear progress. A flexible format in programs for the homeless mentally ill permits the flow in services to correspond to changes in their circumstances, whether they progress or decompensate.

Flexible program formats not only respond to the changing needs of individual homeless persons; they also make it easier to modify the service system in accord with changes in aggregate service demand. It may be anticipated that the homeless mentally ill population will become even more heterogeneous in years to come. It will almost certainly be necessary to provide for an ever-growing population of noninstitutionalized individuals, increasing percentages of whom have never been hospitalized. The service needs of that population will change as its members age.

Cultural Relevance

An eighth principle, that of cultural relevance, is critical in the design of programs for chronic mental patients (Bachrach 1980b). It is not enough for services to be oriented toward individual patients; they must also be tailored to conform to the local realities of the communities in which they are offered. Abbott (1978) points out that any successful program for chronic mental patients reflects the "character of the community in which the patients are being served" (p. 35).

Cultural specificity is certainly required for programs for the homeless mentally ill. Many services that might be appropriate for "space cases" in Berkeley, California (Segal and Baumohl 1980), will have limited value for the "episodic homeless" in Philadelphia (Arce et al. 1983). However, responsiveness to the local culture is only one aspect of cultural relevance for this special population; even within their communities, these individuals are not in the cultural mainstream, and their subcultural norms must be heeded (Minkoff 1982).

The extremes of social distance that separate the homeless mentally ill from the mainstream of society and from those who attempt to care for them lead Barrow and Lovell (1982) to assert that initial psychiatric assessments in the population are often necessarily "based on fairly obvious and extreme symptoms," while "more subtle" disabilities are routinely overlooked (p. 4). Inculcating planners and service providers with a sensitivity to these cultural differences must be a first step in overcoming irrelevance in program initiatives.

Caution and Restraint

A final planning principle, one that is implicit in all the others discussed, involves the need to guard against being seduced by the "quick fix," an understandable tendency when the wish to help is strong. Service planning for the homeless mentally ill is far too complex a process to be amenable to quick-and-easy solutions, and new initiatives should be adopted cautiously. This is not always easy to do. In these times of scarce resources there is often a great deal of pressure to produce programmatic solutions that will quickly eliminate the serious disjunctions between our intentions and results.

Case management is one of many service initiatives that may be used to illustrate the principle of exercising caution and restraint. Case management is, of course, a perfectly valid concept that includes such essential activities as arranging appointments and referrals, arranging and monitoring actual service delivery, coordinating personnel from multiple agencies, and providing active patient advocacy (Buckingham and Lupu 1982). It is specifically directed toward assuring implementation of an individualized treatment plan and facilitating continuity of care. The function of case management is thus implicit in and central to all the planning principles discussed here.

In recent years the introduction of case managers has been promoted in an effort to combat fragmentation in service delivery to the chronically mentally ill (Intagliata 1982; Johnson and Rubin 1983; Schwartz et al. 1982). There is, however, a fundamental difference between the function of case management and the role of the case manager that is often overlooked. Introducing a separate bureaucratic stratum of case managers will not by itself assure the provision of case management, and it may even foster a false sense of security. By interchanging the presence of a bureaucratically defined case manager with the responsible execution of the complex function of case management, the planning process may easily fall victim to the error of confusing the container with the thing contained—all too common a tendency in services for the chronically mentally ill.

The principle of caution and restraint encourages planners and service providers to look beyond slogans, catchwords, and stereotyped service interventions to confront the complexities inherent in planning for the homeless mentally ill. There are few shortcuts to good care for this population.

Summary and Conclusions

Recent demographic changes in the nation have interacted with the effects of deinstitutionalization to produce a numerically significant population of chronically mentally ill individuals with highly specialized service needs. The growth of a homeless mentally ill subpopulation throws the problems associated with deinstitutionalization into bold relief. Even more than the domiciled chronically mentally ill, those who are homeless are impeded from access to care by the absence of a comprehensive array of basic services, by the difficulties associated with implementing continuity in their care, and by uncertainty regarding their status as rightful recipients of services. They are usually trapped in living situations that give them little hope. Thus planning for this population requires the formulation of complex public policy decisions and implementation strategies (Marcos and Gill 1983).

Our knowledge of how to overcome problems inherent in serving the homeless mentally ill is imperfect. There is still much to learn. The director of policy studies of the Health and Welfare Council of Central Maryland has stated in a public television interview that the homeless mentally ill "didn't get sick in a day, and they won't get well in a day" (No Place 1983). Yet it is possible today to enunciate some fundamental planning principles to assist us in designing sensitive and relevant services for the homeless mentally ill. These principles are neither new nor startling. They are, in fact, very much the same principles that we must employ in planning for domiciled chronically mentally ill individuals.

However, the application of these principles to the needs of the homeless mentally ill must be based on an understanding of the unique interaction of chronicity and homelessness. Adapting these principles to the special concerns of the homeless mentally ill represents an initial step in the challenge of systematizing care for this vulnerable population.

References

Abbott B: Tailoring the service system to the community. Hosp Community Psychiatry 29:35-36, 1978

Allen A: Who killed Rebecca Smith? Foundation News 24:13-16, 1982

Anthony WA, Cohen MR, Cohen BF: Philosophy, treatment process, and principles of the psychiatric rehabilitation approach. New Directions for Mental Health Services, no 17:67-69, 1983

APA Report, Sept 16, 1983, p 1

Arce AA: Statement Before the Committee on Appropriations, in US Senate Special Hearing on Street People. Washington, US Government Printing Office, 1983

Arce AA, Tadlock M, Vergare MJ, et al: A psychiatric profile of street people admitted to an emergency shelter. Hosp Community Psychiatry 34:812-817, 1983

Austin C: Churches see charity's limits. New York Times, July 31, 1983, p 20E

Bachrach LL: Developing objectives in community mental health planning. Am J Public Health 64:1162-1163, 1974

Bachrach LL: Deinstitutionalization: An Analytical Review and Sociological Perspective. Rockville, Md, National Institute of Mental Health, 1976

Bachrach LL: A conceptual approach to deinstitutionalization. Hosp Community Psychiatry 29:573-578, 1978

Bachrach LL: Is the least restrictive environment always the best? sociological and semantic implications. Hosp Community Psychiatry 31:97-103, 1980a

Bachrach LL: Overview: model programs for chronic mental patients. Am J Psychiatry 137:1023-1031, 1980b

Bachrach LL: Continuity of care for chronic mental patients: a conceptual analysis. Am J Psychiatry 138:1449-1456, 1981

Bachrach LL: Young adult chronic patients: an analytical review of the literature. Hosp Community Psychiatry 33:189-197, 1982

Bachrach LL: Evaluating the consequences of deinstitutionalization. Hosp Community Psychiatry 34:105, 1983a

Bachrach LL: An overview of deinstitutionalization. New Directions for Mental Health Services, no 17:5-14, 1983b

Bachrach LL: Planning services for chronically mentally ill patients. Bull Menninger Clin 47:163-188, 1983c

Bachrach LL: Psychiatric services in rural areas: a sociological overview. Hosp Community Psychiatry 34:215-226, 1983d

Bachrach LL: Asylum and chronically ill psychiatric patients. Am J Psychiatry 141:975-978, 1984

Bachrach LL: Deinstitutionalization and women: assessing the consequences of public policy. Am Psychol (in press a)

Bachrach LL: Principles of planning for chronic psychiatric patients: a
synthesis, in The Chronic Mental Patient: Five Years Later. Edited by
Talbott JA. New York, Grune & Stratton (in press b)

Bachrach LL, Lamb HR: Conceptual issues in the evaluation of the dein-
stitutionalization movement, in Innovative Approaches to Mental Health
Evaluation. Edited by Stahler GJ, Tash WR. New York, Academic
Press, 1982

Ball FLJ: San Francisco's Homeless Consumers of Psychiatric Services:
Demographic Characteristics and Expressed Needs. San Francisco
Community Mental Health Services, May 1982

Barbanel J: Cuomo promises to restore cuts in funds for mental health
clinics. New York Times, Dec 9, 1983, p B1

Baron RC: Changing public attitudes about the mentally ill in the community. Hosp Community Psychiatry 32:173-178, 1981

Barrow S, Lovell AM: Evaluation of Project Reach Out, 1981-82. New
York, New York State Psychiatric Institute, June 30, 1982

Barrow S, Lovell AM: CSS Preliminary Report. New York, New York
State Psychiatric Institute, Apr 15, 1983a

Barrow S, Lovell AM: Evaluation of the Referral of Outreach Clients to
Mental Health Services, Private Proprietary Homes for Adults, CSS
Eligibility, and the Acute Day Hospitals. New York, New York State
Psychiatric Institute, June 30, 1983b

Basler B: Addicts and vandals troubling city libraries. New York Times,
July 11, 1981, pp 1, 16

Bassuk EL: Addressing the needs of the homeless. Boston Globe Magazine, Nov 6, 1983, pp 12, 60ff

Bassuk E, Gerson S: Chronic crisis patients: a discrete clinical group. Am
J Psychiatry 137:1513-1517, 1980

Baxter E, Hopper K: Private Lives/Public Spaces: Homeless Adults on
the Streets of New York City. New York, Community Service Society,
1981

Baxter E, Hopper K: The new mendicancy: homeless in New York City.
Am J Orthopsychiatry 52:393-408, 1982

Baxter E, Hopper K: Troubled on the streets: the mentally disabled homeless poor, in The Chronic Mental Patient: Five Years Later. Edited by
Talbott JA. New York, Grune & Stratton (in press)

Blum H: Creedmoor homeless plan disputed. New York Times, Dec 6,
1983, p B4

Brown C, MacFarlane S, Paredes R, et al: the Homeless of Phoenix: Who
Are They? And What Should Be Done? Phoenix South Community
Mental Health Center, 1983

Buckingham RW, Lupu D: A comparative study of hospice services in
the United States. Am J Public Health 72:455-463, 1982

Chafetz L, Goldfinger SM: Residential instability in a psychiatric emergency setting. Psychiatr Q 56:20-34, 1984

Chmiel AJ, Akhtar S, Morris J: The long-distance psychiatric patient in the emergency room. Int J Soc Psychiatry 25:38-46, 1979

Christmas and food lines. Washington Post, Dec 25, 1983, p B6

Cotton PG: Psychiatric care of the deinstitutionalized patient. New Directions for Mental Health Service, no 17:55-56, 1983

Cutler DL (ed): Effective Aftercare for the 1980s. New Directions for Mental Health Service, no 19, 1983

Death in a cardboard box. Psychiatric News, Apr 2, 1982, p 40

Depp FC, Ackiss V: Assessing needs among sheltered homeless women. Presented at the Conference on Homelessness: A Time for New Directions, Washington, July 19, 1983

Dinitz S, Beran N: Community mental health as a boundaryless and boundary-busting system. J Health Soc Behav 12:99-108, 1971

Dionne EJ: Mental patient cutbacks planned. New York Times, Dec 8, 1978, p B3

Dorwart RA: Deinstitutionalization: who is left behind? Hosp Community Psychiatry 31:336-338, 1980

Down and out in America. Newsweek, Mar 15, 1982, pp 28-29

Drake DC: The Forsaken. Philadelphia Inquirer series, July 18-24, 1982

Earley P: Jails are becoming "dumping grounds," federal government advisory panel told. Washington Post, June 17, 1983, p A12

Engel M, Sargent ED: Meese's hunger remarks stir more outrage among groups. Washington Post, Dec 11, 1983, pp A1, A10

Farr RK: Skid Row Project. Los Angeles County Department of Mental Health, Jan 18, 1982

Garbage consumption by humans irks resort. New York Times, Oct 22, 1981, p 18

Gargan EA: Ducking for cover over the homeless. New York Times, Nov 27, 1983, p E7

Geller MP: The "revolving door": a trap or a life style? Hosp Community Psychiatry 33:388-389, 1982

Gilliam D: Amputees. Washington Post, Mar 12, 1984, p B1

Glass J: Summary of Proceedings: The Young Adult Chronic Patient, an ADM Working Conference, Oct 21-22, 1982. Rockville, Md, Alcohol, Drug Abuse, and Mental Health Administration

Goldberg M: The runaway Americans. Mental Hygiene 56:13-21, 1972

Goldfinger SM, Hopkin JT, Surber RW: Treatment resisters or system resisters? toward a better service system for acute care recidivists. New Directions for Mental Health Services, no 21:17-27, 1984

Goldman HH, Gattozzi AA, Taube CA: Defining and counting the chronically mentally ill. Hosp Community Psychiatry 32:21-27, 1981

Goldman HH, Adams NH, Taube CA: Deinstitutionalization: the data demythologized. Hosp Community Psychiatry 34:129-134, 1983

Granet RB, Talbott JA: The continuity agent: creating a new role to bridge the gaps in the mental health system. Hosp Community Psychiatry 29:132-133, 1978

Group for the Advancement of Psychiatry: The Positive Aspects of Long Term Hospitalization in the Public Sector for Chronic Psychiatric Patients. New York, Mental Health Materials Center, 1982

Group for the Advancement of Psychiatry: Community Psychiatry: A Reappraisal. New York, Mental Health Materials Center, 1983

Hagedorn H: A Manual on State Mental Health Planning. Rockville, Md, National Institute of Mental Health, 1977

Hansell N: Services for schizophrenics: a lifelong approach to treatment. Hosp Community Psychiatry 29:105-109, 1978

Harris M, Bergman HC: Youth of the '60s. Hosp Community Psychiatry 34:1164, 1983

Hayes RM: Reforming current city policies. CBC Quarterly 2:1-4, 1982

Health and Welfare Council of Central Maryland: A Report to the Greater Baltimore Shelter Network on Homelessness in Central Maryland. Baltimore, June 1983

Henry N: The long, hot wait for pickin' work. Washington Post, Oct 9, 1983, pp A1, A16

Herman R: Some freed mental patients make it, some do not. New York Times, Nov 19, 1979, pp B1, B4

Herman R: City's homeless: story of Bobby Cruz. New York Times, Jan 16, 1982, pp 27, 31 (1982a)

Herman R: One of city's homeless goes home—in death. New York Times, Jan 31, 1982, p 34 (1982b)

Hidden resource for the homeless. New York Times, Dec 22, 1981, p A18

Hinckley J, Hinckley JA: Illness is the culprit! Reader's Digest, Mar 1983, pp 2-6

Hombs ME, Snyder M: Homeless in America: A Forced March to Nowhere. Washington, Community for Creative Nonviolence, 1982

The homeless. ADAMHA News. June 24, 1983, pp 1,6

Homeless in America. Newsweek, Jan 2, 1984, pp 20-29

Hopper K, Baxter E, Cox S, et al: One Year Later: The Homeless Poor in New York City, 1982. New York, Community Service Society, 1982

Intagliata J: Improving the quality of community care for the chronically mentally disabled: the role of case management. Schizophr Bull 8:655-674, 1982

Jaynes G: Urban librarians seek ways to deal with "disturbed patrons." New York Times, Nov 24, 1981, p A16

Johnson PJ, Rubin A: Case management in mental health: a social work domain? Social Work 28:49-55, 1983

Jones RE: Street people and psychiatry: an introduction. Hosp Community Psychiatry 34:807-811, 1983

Kamen A: The right to refuse treatment. Washington Post, May 20, 1982, pp B1, B4

Kaufman M: Stormy times for city shelter. Philadelphia Inquirer, Nov 22, 1983, pp 1B, 2B

Kennedy C: Testimony Before Governor's Task Force on the Homeless, New York City, Apr 21, 1983

Kimura SP, Mikolashek PL, Kirk SA: Madness in paradise: psychiatric crises among newcomers in Honolulu. Hawaii Med J 34:275-278, 1975

Lamb HR: Treating the Long-Term Mentally Ill: Beyond Deinstitution-alization. San Francisco, Jossey-Bass, 1982

Lamb HR, Grant RW: The mentally ill in an urban county jail. Arch Gen Psychiatry 39:17-22, 1982

Lamb HR, Grant RW: Mentally ill women in a county jail. Arch Gen Psychiatry 40:363-368, 1983

Langsley DG: The community mental health center: does it treat patients? Hosp Community Psychiatry 31:815-819, 1980

Larew BI: Strange strangers: serving transients. Social Casework 63:107-113, 1980

Leaf A, Cohen M: Providing Services for the Homeless: The New York City Program. City of New York Human Resources Administration, Dec 1982

Levine IS: Homelessness: its implications for mental health policy and practice. Presented at the annual meeting of the American Psychological Association, Anaheim, Calif, Aug 30, 1983

Lewis N: Community Intake Services for the Transient Mentally Disabled (TMD). Travelers Aid Society of San Francisco, 1978

Lipton FR, Sabatini A, Katz SE: Down and out in the city: the homeless mentally ill. Hosp Community Psychiatry 34:818-821, 1983

"Lost" Indian tribe seeks recognition and a home. New York Times, Dec 26, 1981, p 12

Macklin B: Mentally unfit: no place to stay. Tulsa World, Aug 11, 1983, p E1

Marcos LR, Gil RM: Muddling through mental health policies. Am J Psychiatry 140:853-856, 1983

Massachusetts Association for Mental Health: Statement on the Fiscal Year 1982 Budget for the Massachusetts Department of Mental Health. Boston, May 28, 1981

McCarthy C: A doctor's house call on the homeless. Washington Post, Nov 5, 1983, p A17

McGuire PA: Young, idealistic psychiatrists win acclaim for state hospitals. Baltimore Sun, Dec 19, 1982, pp A1, A14

Meese: "The food is free and . . . that's easier than paying for it." Washington Post, Dec 10, 1983, p A8

Melton RH: Shelter gives lift to down and out. Washington Post, Dec 23, 1983, pp C1, C7

Meyerson AT, Herman GS: What's new in aftercare? a review of recent literature. Hosp Community Psychiatry 34:333-342, 1983

Minkoff K: Deinstitutionalization: problems and prospects: clinical implications for "new" chronic patients. Presented at the Institute on Hospital and Community Psychiatry, Louisville, Oct 1982

Morrissey JP, McGreevy MM: The fates of applicants denied admission to state mental hospitals: some unexamined consequences of deinstitutionalization in the USA. Presented at the meeting of the International Sociological Association, Mexico City, Aug 1982

Muscatine A: Suburbs send homeless to DC shelters. Washington Post, Feb 19, 1983, pp A1, A31

Neill JR: The difficult patient: identification and response. J Clinical Psychiatry 40:209-212, 1979

Nelson B: Nation's psychiatrists give "high priority" to the homeless. New York Times, May 10, 1983, pp C1, C2

The new migrants. Washington Post, Dec 26, 1982, p D6

New tasks faced by Travelers Aid. New York Times, May 4, 1969, p 53

New York State Office of Mental Health and Department of Social Services: New York State's Versus New York City's Record in Mental Health and Social Services. Albany, Dec 29, 1980

New York State Office of Mental Health: Who Are the Homeless? a Study of Randomly Selected Men Who Use the New York City Shelters. Albany, May 1982

No Place Like Home. Aired on the State Line Series, Maryland Public Television, Channel 22, Annapolis, Dec 25, 1983

O'Connor J: Sheltering the homeless in the nation's capital. Hosp Community Psychiatry 34:863-879, 1983

Overend W: What can be done about Laura Juarez? Los Angeles Times, Oct 9, 1983, Part 7, pp 1, 16-18

Panzetta A: Community Mental Health: Myth and Reality. Philadelphia, Lea & Febiger, 1971

Pearlson GD: Psychiatric and medical syndromes associated with phencyclidine (PCP) abuse. Johns Hopkins Med J 148:25-33, 1981

Peele R: We need insane asylums; ask Joe, 68 years at St E's. Washington Post, Oct 30, 1983, pp C1, C3

Peele R, Luisada PV, Lucas MJ, et al: Asylums revisited. Am J Psychiatry 134:1077-1081, 1977

Peele R, Palmer RR: Patient rights and patient chronicity. Journal of Psychiatry and Law: 59-71, Spring 1980

Pepper B, Kirshner MC, Ryglewicz H: The young adult chronic patient: overview of a population. Hosp Community Psychiatry 32:463-469, 1981

Pepper B, Ryglewicz H: Testimony for the neglected: the mentally ill in the post-deinstitutionalized age. Am J Orthopsychiatry 52:388-392, 1982a

Pepper B, Ryglewicz H: Unified services: concept and practice. Hosp Community Psychiatry 33:762-765, 1982b

Pepper B, Ryglewicz H: The young adult chronic patient: an uninstitutionalized generation. Presented at the Fourth Annual Conference on the Young Adult Chronic Patient, Los Angeles, Oct 21, 1983

Peterson I: Former mental patients a source of pity and anger on Long Island. New York Times, Jan 1, 1978, p 22

Plan to spray garbage has mixed response. Philadelphia Inquirer, Nov 8, 1981, p 15A

Prager D: Hippies still survive where it all started. Washington Post, Apr 5, 1982, p A2

Project HELP Summary, October 30, 1982–August 31, 1983. New York State Community Support Services, Gouverneur Hospital, New York City, 1983

Psychiatrists to study street people. Washington Post, Sept 1, 1983, p A7

Quindlen A: About New York. New York Times, Dec 15, 1982, p B3

Rachlin S: The influence of law on deinstitutionalization. New Directions for Mental Health Services, no 17:41-54, 1983

Raine G: Energy states turning cold to transients. New York Times, Feb 2, 1982, pp A2, A12

Redick RW, Witkin MJ: State and County Mental Hospitals, United States, 1979-80 and 1980-81. Mental Health Statistical Note No 165. Rockville, Md, National Institute of Mental Health, Aug 1983

Reich R, Siegel L: The emergence of the Bowery as a psychiatric dumping ground. Psychiatr Q 50:191-201, 1978

Report of the Task Panel on Deinstitutionalization, Rehabilitation, and Long-Term Care, in President's Commission on Mental Health: Report to the President, vol 2. Washington, US Government Printing Office, 1978

Robbins E, Stern M, Robbins L, et al: Unwelcome patients: where can they find asylum? Hosp Community Psychiatry 29:44-46, 1978

Ross J: The homeless are still with us. San Francisco Bay Guardian, Dec 7, 1983, pp 9-13

Rousseau AM: Shopping Bag Ladies. New York, Pilgrim Press, 1981

Rule S: Outlook for homeless ill called grim. New York Times, Oct 29, 1983, p 31 (1983a)

Rule S: New York plans 2,000 new beds for its homeless. New York Times, Nov 24, 1983, pp A1, B9 (1983b)

Schwartz SR, Goldfinger SM: The new chronic patient: clinical characteristics of an emerging subgroup. Hosp Community Psychiatry 32:470-474, 1981

Schwartz SR, Goldfinger SM, Ratener M, et al: The young adult chronic patient and the care system: fragmentation prototypes. New Directions for Mental Health Services, no 19:23-35, 1983

Schwartz SR, Goldman HH, Churgin S: Case management for the chronic mentally ill: models and dimensions. Hosp Community Psychiatry 33:1006-1009, 1982

Segal SP, Baumohl J: Engaging the disengaged: proposals on madness and vagrancy. Social Work 25:358-365, 1980

Segal SP, Baumohl J, Johnson E: Falling through the cracks: mental disorder and social margin in a young vagrant population. Social Problems 24:387-400, 1977

Shore MF, Shapiro R: The effect of deinstitutionalization on the state hospital. Hosp Community Psychiatry 30:605-608, 1979

Sinclair W: Needed workers are caught in the stream. Washington Post, Aug 23, 1981, pp A1, A18

Slavinsky A, Cousins A: Homeless women. Nursing Outlook 30:358-362, 1982

Smith HA: Psycho-social development of flight chronic clients. New Orleans, Travelers Aid Society, 1980

SOME: Hospitality in the Shadow of the Nation's Capitol. Washington, undated

Spiro HR: Reforming the state hospital in a unified care system. Hosp Community Psychiatry 33:722-728, 1982

Stein LI, Test MA (eds): Alternatives to Mental Hospital Treatment. New York, Plenum, 1978

Stelovich S: From the hospital to the prison: a step forward in deinstitutionalization? Hosp Community Psychiatry 30:618-620, 1979

Stern R, Minkoff K: Paradoxes in programming for chronic patients in a community clinic. Hosp Community Psychiatry 30:613-617, 1979

Strange RE: The rise, fall, and rebirth of hospital psychiatry. Advance 31:16-18, Winter 1981

Streltzer J: Psychiatric emergencies in travelers to Hawaii. Compr Psychiatry 20:463-468, 1979

Sugawara S: Mentally ill often are left on their own in Fairfax. Washington Post, Nov 20, 1983, pp B1, B2

Sullivan R: Hospital forced to oust patients with psychoses. New York Times, Nov 8, 1979, p B3 (1979a)

Sullivan R: Hospitals will gain by cutting bed use. New York Times, Dec 31, 1979, p A1 (1979b)

Sullivan R: Officials say that homeless often refuse aid from city. New York Times, Oct 22, 1983 (1983a)

Sullivan R: New York to give funds to operate 15 mental clinics. New York Times, Nov 23, 1983 (1983b)

Sullivan R: The homeless: officials differ on the causes. New York Times, Nov 24, 1983 (1983c)

Tabler DL: Preliminary Report: Emergency Adult-at-Risk Shelter: A BCDSS Demonstration Project. Baltimore Department of Social Services, Sept 20, 1982

Talbott JA (ed): The Chronic Mentally Ill: Treatment, Programs, Systems. New York, Human Sciences Press, 1981

Talbott JA: The shame of the cities. Hosp Community Psychiatry 34:773, 1983a

Talbott JA (ed): Unified Mental Health Systems: Utopia Unrealized. New Directions for Mental Health Services, no 18:107-111, 1983b

Teknekron, Inc: Improving California's Mental Health System: A Framework for Public Contributions. Berkeley, Calif, 1977

Thimmesch N: Free to suffer. Washington Post, May 3, 1983, p A13

Thurer SL: Deinstitutionalization and women: where the buck stops. Hosp Community Psychiatry 34:1162-1163, 1983

Timnick L: The new drifters: society's costly and dangerous burden. Los Angeles Times, July 20, 1981, p 13

Torrey EF: The real twilight zone. Washington Post, Aug 26, 1983

Travelers Aid Society of Greater New Orleans: Summary of Study of Wandering Mentally Ill, 1976

Treffert DA: Sane asylum: an alternative to the mental hospital. Curr Psychiatr Ther 17:309-314, 1977

Treffert DA: Marijuana use in schizophrenia: a clear hazard. Am J Psychiatry 135:1213-1215, 1978

US Bureau of the Census: Geographical Mobility: March 1975 to March

1979. Washington, US Government Printing Office, 1980

US Department of Health and Human Services and US Department of Housing and Urban Development: Report on Federal Efforts to Respond to the Shelter and Basic Living Needs of Chronically Mentally Ill Individuals. Washington, Department of Health and Human Services, Feb 1983

US Senate, Committee on Appropriations: Special Hearing on Street People. Washington, US Government Printing Office, 1983

White HS: Managing the difficult patient in the community residence. New Directions for Mental Health Services, no 11:5-17, 1981

White RD: Mentally ill, retarded suffer in crowded jails. Washington Post, Nov 19, 1981, pp Md1, Md7

Young BJ: Testimony, in Homelessness in America: Hearing Before the Subcommittee on Housing and Community Development, US House of Representatives Committee on Banking, Finance, and Urban Affairs, Dec 15, 1982. Washington, US Government Printing Office, 1983

Zaleski J, Gale MS, Winget C: Extended hospital care as treatment of choice. Hosp Community Psychiatry 30:399-401, 1979

Zusman J, Lamb HR: In defense of community mental health. Am J Psychiatry 134:887-890, 1977

Chapter 3

Deinstitutionalization and the Homeless Mentally Ill

H. Richard Lamb, M.D.

Is deinstitutionalization the cause of homelessness? Some would say yes and send the chronically mentally ill back to the hospitals. A main thesis of this chapter, however, is that problems such as homelessness are not the result of deinstitutionalization per se but rather of the way deinstitutionalization has been implemented. It is the purpose of this chapter to describe these problems of implementation and the related problem of the lack of clear understanding of the needs of the chronically mentally ill in the community. The discussion then turns to some additional unintended results of these problems, such as the criminalization of the mentally ill that usually accompanies homelessness. The chapter concludes with some ways of resolving these problems.

To see and experience the appalling conditions under which the homeless mentally ill exist has a profound impact upon us; our natural reaction is to want to rectify the horrors of what we see with a quick, bold stroke. But for the chronically mentally ill, homelessness is a complex problem with multiple causative factors; in our analysis of this problem we need to guard against settling for simplistic explanations and solutions.

Dr. Lamb is professor of psychiatry at the University of Southern California School of Medicine in Los Angeles. This chapter also appears in *Hospital and Community Psychiatry*, volume 35, September 1984, in a special section on the homeless mentally ill.

For instance, homelessness is closely linked with deinstitution-alization in the sense that three decades ago most of the chronically mentally ill had a home—the state hospital. Without deinstitution-alization it is unlikely there would be large numbers of homeless mentally ill. Thus in countries such as Israel, where deinstitution-alization has barely begun, homelessness of the chronically mentally ill is not a significant problem. But that does not mean we can simply explain homelessness as a result of deinstitutionalization; we have to look at what conditions these mentally ill persons must face in the community, what needed resources are lacking, and the nature of mental illness itself.

With the mass exodus into the community that deinstitutional-ization brought, we are faced with the need to understand the reactions and tolerance of the chronically mentally ill to the stresses of the community. And we must determine what has become of them without the state hospitals, and why. There is now evidence that nationwide very substantial numbers of the severely mentally ill are homeless at any given time (Arce et al. 1983; Baxter and Hopper in press; Lipton et al. 1983). Some are homeless contin-uously and some intermittently (see chapter 5). We need to under-stand what characteristics of society and the mentally ill themselves have interacted to produce such an unforeseen and grave problem as homelessness. Without that understanding, we will not be able to conceptualize and then implement what needs to be done to resolve the problems of homelessness.

With the advantage of hindsight, we can see that the era of deinstitutionalization was ushered in with much naivete and many simplistic notions about what would become of the chronically and severely mentally ill. The importance of psychoactive medication and a stable source of financial support was perceived, but the importance of developing such fundamental resources as supportive living arrangements was often not clearly seen, or at least not imple-mented. "Community treatment" was much discussed, but there was no clear idea as to what it should consist of, and the resistance of community mental health centers to providing services to the chronically mentally ill was not anticipated. Nor was it foreseen how reluctant many states would be to allocate funds for commu-nity-based services.

It had been observed that persons who spend long periods in hospitals develop what has come to be known as institutionalism—a syndrome characterized by lack of initiative, apathy, withdrawal,

submissiveness to authority, and excessive dependence on the institution (Wing and Brown 1970). It had also been observed, however,
that this syndrome may not be entirely the outcome of living in
dehumanizing institutions; at least in part, it may be characteristic
of the schizophrenic process itself (Johnstone et al. 1981). Many
patients who are liable to institutionalism and vulnerable to external
stimulation may develop dependence on any other way of life outside
hospitals that provides minimal social stimulation and allows them
to be socially inactive (Brown et al. 1966). These aspects of institutionalism were often not recognized or were overlooked in the
early enthusiasm about deinstitutionalization.

In the midst of very valid concerns about the shortcomings and
antitherapeutic aspects of state hospitals, it was not appreciated
that the state hospitals fulfilled some very crucial functions for the
chronically and severely mentally ill. The term "asylum" was in
many ways an appropriate one, for these imperfect institutions did
provide asylum and sanctuary from the pressures of the world with
which, in varying degrees, most of these patients were unable to
cope (Lamb and Peele in press). Further, these institutions provided
such services as medical care, patient monitoring, respite for the
patient's family, and a social network for the patient as well as food
and shelter and needed support and structure (Bachrach 1984).

Fernandez (1983), working in Dublin, recognizes these needs
that used to be met, though not well, by state hospitals. He warns
about the tendency to "equate the concept of homelessness exclusively with the lack of a permanent roof over one's head. This
deflects attention from what is believed to be the essential deficit
of homelessness, namely, the absence of a stable base of caring or
supportive individuals whose concern and support help buffer the
homeless against the vicissitudes of life. In this context, it is felt
that the absence of such a base, or the inability to establish or to
approximate such a base, is the essential deficit of patients with
'no-fixed-abode'" (p. 7).

In the state hospitals what treatment and services that did exist
were in one place and under one administration. In the community
the situation is very different. Services and treatment are under
various administrative jurisdictions and in various locations. Even
the mentally healthy have difficulty dealing with a number of
bureaucracies, both governmental and private, and getting their
needs met. Further, patients can easily get lost in the community
as compared to a hospital, where they may have been neglected but

at least their whereabouts were known. It is these problems that have led to the recognition of the importance of case management. It is probable that many of the homeless mentally ill would not be on the streets if they were on the caseload of a professional or paraprofessional trained to deal with the problems of the chronically mentally ill, monitor them (with considerable persistence when necessary), and facilitate their receiving services.

In my experience (Lamb 1981) and that of others (Baxter and Hopper 1982), the survival of long-term patients, let alone their rehabilitation, begins with an appropriately supportive and structured living arrangement. Other treatment and rehabilitation are of little avail until patients feel secure and are stabilized in their living situation. Deinstitutionalization means granting asylum in the community to a large marginal population, many of whom can cope to only a limited extent with the ordinary demands of life, have strong dependency needs, and are unable to live independently.

Moreover, that some patients might need to reside in a long-term, locked, intensively supervised community facility was a foreign thought to most who advocated return to the community in the early years of emptying the state hospitals. "Patients who need a secure environment can remain in the state hospital" was the rationale. But in those early years most people seemed to think that such patients were few, and that community treatment and modern psychoactive medications would take care of most problems. More people are now recognizing that a number of severely disabled patients present major problems in management, and can survive and have their basic needs met outside of state hospitals only if they have a sufficiently structured community facility or other mechanism that provides support and controls (Lamb 1980b). Some of the homeless appear to be in this group. A function of the old state hospitals often given too little weight is that of providing structure. Without this structure, many of the chronically mentally ill feel lost and cast adrift in the community—however much they may deny it.

There is currently much emphasis on providing emergency shelter to the homeless, and certainly this must be done. But it is important to put the "shelter approach" into perspective; it is a necessary stopgap, symptomatic measure, but does not address the basic causes of homelessness. Too much emphasis on shelters can only delay our coming to grips with the underlying problems that result in homelessness. We must keep these problems in mind even as we sharpen our techniques for working with mentally ill persons who are already homeless.

Most mental health professionals are disinclined to treat "street people" or "transients" (Larew 1980). Moreover, in the case of many of the homeless, we are working with persons whose lack of trust and desire for autonomy cause them to not give us their real names, to refuse our services, and to move along because of their fear of closeness, of losing their autonomy, or of acquiring a mentally ill identity. Providing food and shelter with no strings attached, especially in a facility that has a close involvement with mental health professionals, a clear conception of the needs of the mentally ill, and the ready availability of other services, can be an opening wedge that ultimately will give us the opportunity to treat a few of this population.

At the same time we have learned that we must beware of simple solutions and recognize that this shelter approach is not a definitive solution to the basic problems of the homeless mentally ill. It does not substitute for the array of measures that will be effective in both significantly reducing and preventing homelessness: a full range of residential placements, aggressive case management, changes in the legal system that will facilitate involuntary treatment (see chapter 12), a stable source of income for each patient, and access to acute hospitalization and other vitally needed community services.

Still another problem with the shelter approach is that many of the homeless mentally ill will accept shelter but nothing more, and they eventually return to a wretched and dangerous life on the streets. A case example will illustrate.

A 28-year-old man was brought to a California state hospital with a diagnosis of acute paranoid schizophrenia. He had been living under a freeway overpass for the past six weeks. There was no prior record of his hospitalization in the state. After a month in the hospital he had gone into partial remission and was transferred to a community residential program. There he was assigned to a skilled, low-key, sensitive clinician. Over a period of several weeks he gradually improved and returned to what was probably his normal state of being guarded and suspicious but not overtly psychotic.

Though he isolated himself much of the time, he appeared quite comfortable with the program and with the staff and indicated that he would, if allowed, stay indefinitely. He denied possessing a birth certificate, baptismal certificate, driver's license, or any other proof of identity. He steadfastly refused to give the whereabouts of his family or reveal his place of birth or anything else about his identity, even though he realized such information was necessary to qualify him for any type of financial or housing assistance. Clearly his autonomy was precious to him. And in an unguarded moment he said, "I couldn't bear to have my family know what a failure I have been." At the end of three months, the maximum length of stay allowed by the community program's contract, he had to be discharged to a mission.

What was not foreseen in the midst of the early optimism about returning the mentally ill to the community and restoring and rehabilitating them so they could take their places in the mainstream of society was what was actually to befall them. Certainly it was not anticipated that criminalization and homelessness would be the lot for many. But first let us briefly look at how deinstitutionalization came about.

A Brief History of Deinstitutionalization

For more than half of this century, the state hospitals fulfilled the function for society of keeping the mentally ill out of sight and thus out of mind. Moreover, the controls and structure provided by the state hospitals, as well as the granting of almost total asylum, may have been necessary for many of the long-term mentally ill before the advent of modern psychoactive medications. Unfortunately, the ways in which state hospitals achieved this structure and asylum led to everyday abuses that have left scars on the mental health professions as well as on the patients.

The stage was set for deinstitutionalization by the periodic public outcries about these deplorable conditions, documented by journalists such as Albert Deutsch (1948); mental health professionals and their organizational leaders also expressed growing concern. These concerns led ultimately to the formation of the Joint Commission on Mental Illness and Health in 1955 and its recommendations for community alternatives to state hospitals, published in 1961 as a widely read book, *Action for Mental Health*.

When the new psychoactive medications appeared (Brill and Patton 1957; Kris 1971), along with a new philosophy of social treatment (Greenblatt 1977), the great majority of the chronic psychotic population was left in a state hospital environment that was now clearly unnecessary and even inappropriate for them, though, as noted above, it met many needs. Still other factors came into play. First was a conviction that mental patients receive better and more humanitarian treatment in the community than in state hospitals far removed from home. This belief was a philosophical keystone in the origins of the community mental health movement. Another powerful motivating force was concern about the civil rights of psychiatric patients; the system then employed of commitment and institutionalization in many ways deprived them of their civil rights. Not the least of the motivating factors was financial. State governments wished to shift some of the fiscal burden for these patients to federal and local government—that is, to federal Supplemental Security Income (SSI) and Medicaid and local law enforcement agencies and emergency health and mental health services (Borus 1981; Goldman et al. 1983).

The process of deinstitutionalization was considerably accelerated by two significant federal developments in 1963. First, categorical Aid to the Disabled (ATD) became available to the mentally ill, which made them eligible for the first time for federal financial support in the community. Second, the community mental health centers legislation was passed.

With ATD, psychiatric patients and mental health professionals acting on their behalf now had access to federal grants-in-aid, in some states supplemented by state funds, which enabled patients to support themselves or be supported either at home or in such facilities as board-and-care homes or old hotels at comparatively little cost to the state. Although the amount of money available to patients under ATD was not a princely sum, it was sufficient to maintain a low standard of living in the community. Thus the states, even those that provided generous ATD supplements, found it cost far less to maintain patients in the community than in the hospital. (ATD is now called Supplemental Security Income and is administered by the Social Security Administration.)

The second significant federal development of 1963 was the passage of the Mental Retardation Facilities and Community Mental Health Centers Construction Act, amended in 1965 to provide grants for the initial costs of staffing the newly constructed centers. This legislation was a strong incentive to the development of community programs with the potential to treat people whose main recourse previously had been the state hospital. It is important to note, however, that although rehabilitative services and precare and after-care services were among the services eligible for funding, an agency did not have to offer them in order to qualify for funding as a comprehensive community mental health center.

Also contributing to deinstitutionalization were sweeping changes in the commitment laws of the various states. In California, for instance, the Lanterman-Petris-Short Act of 1968 provided further impetus for the movement of patients out of hospitals. Behind this legislation was a concern for the civil rights of the psychiatric patient, much of it from civil rights groups and individuals outside the mental health professions. The act made the involuntary commitment of psychiatric patients a much more complex process, and it became difficult to hold psychiatric patients indefinitely against their will in mental hospitals. Thus the initial stage of what had formerly been the career of the long-term hospitalized patient— namely, an involuntary, indefinite commitment—became a thing of the past (Lamb et al. 1981).

Some clearly recognized that while many abuses needed to be corrected, this legislation went too far in the other direction and no longer safeguarded the welfare of the patients. (For instance, Richard Levy, M.D., of San Mateo, California, argued this point long and vigorously.) But these were voices in the wilderness. We have still not found a way to help some mental health lawyers and patients' rights advocates see that they have contributed heavily to the problem of homelessness—that patients' rights to freedom are not synonymous with releasing them to the streets where they cannot take care of themselves, are too disorganized or fearful to avail themselves of what help is available, and are easy prey for every predator.

The dimensions of the phenomenon of deinstitutionalization are revealed by the numbers. In 1955 there were 559,000 patients in state hospitals in the United States; today at any given time there are approximately 132,000 (Redick and Witkin 1983).

What Happened to the Patients

What happened to the chronically and severely mentally ill as a result of deinstitutionalization? In the initial years approximately two-thirds of discharged mental patients returned to their families (Minkoff 1978). The figure is probably closer to 50 percent in states such as California, which has a high number of persons without families (Lamb and Goertzel 1977). This discussion is limited to those aged 18 to 65, for those over 65 are a very different population with a very different set of problems.

In more recent years, there has been a growing number of mentally disabled persons in the community who have never been or have only briefly been in hospitals (see chapter 4). Problems in identifying and locating them make it difficult to generalize about them. But we do know they of course tend to be younger and often manifest less institutional passivity than the previous generation, who had spent many years in state hospitals.

A large proportion of the chronically mentally ill—in some communities as many as a third or more of those aged 18 to 65—live in facilities such as board-and-care homes (Lamb and Goertzel 1977). These products of the private sector are not the result of careful planning and well-conceived social policy. On the contrary, they sprang up to fill the vacuum created by the rapid and usually haphazard depopulation of our state hospitals. Suddenly many thousands of former state hospital patients needed a place to live, and private entrepreneurs, both large and small, rushed in to provide it.

"Board-and-care home" is used in California to describe a variety of facilities, many of which house large numbers of psychiatric patients. These patients include both the deinstitutionalized and the new generations of chronically mentally ill. The number of residents ranges from one to more than a hundred. Board-and-care homes are unlocked and provide a shared room, three meals a day, dispensing of medications, and minimal staff supervision; for a large proportion of long-term psychiatric patients, the board-and-care home has taken over the functions of the state hospitals of providing asylum, support, structure, and medications. And for many, the alternative to the board-and-care home would be homelessness.

There is a great deal of variability in facilities such as board-and-care homes. Generally, they could and should provide a higher quality of life than they do, and services should be made more available to their residents. Services should include social and vocational rehabilitation, recreational activities, and mental health treatment. But considering the funding available, these facilities are for the most part not bad in the sense that there is no life-threatening physical neglect or other gross abuses (Dittmar and Smith 1983).

What does stand out is the significantly higher funding for similar resources for the developmentally disabled, and the resulting increased quality in terms of location of the facility, condition of repair, general atmosphere, and staffing. For instance, as of 1984 the rate paid to operators of board-and-care facilities for the developmentally disabled in California varies from a minimum of $525 a month for easily manageable residents to $840 a month for "intensive treatment." For the mentally ill there is only one rate of $476 per month, regardless of the severity of the problem and the need for intensive supervision and care; many of the better board-and-care home operators have stopped serving the mentally ill in order to take advantage of the higher rates for the developmentally disabled. Clearly this is a gross inequity.

But facilities such as board-and-care homes and single-room-occupancy (SRO) hotels, even when adequate, often do not attract and keep the homeless (Arce et al. 1983). If they do enter one of these facilities, their stay may be brief—they drift in and out, to and from the streets. Further, these facilities are not prepared to provide the structure needed by some of the chronically mentally ill, as discussed below.

This book is, of course, concerned with those chronically mentally ill persons who live neither with family nor in board-and-care homes nor in SRO hotels nor in nursing homes nor in their own homes or apartments. Some are homeless continuously, and some intermittently. While estimates of the extent of the problem are highly variable, and there are no reliable data (see chapter 2), it seems reasonable to conclude that nationwide the homeless mentally ill number in the tens of thousands, and perhaps the many tens of thousands. They live on the streets, the beaches, under bridges, in doorways. So many frequent the shelters of our cities that there is concern that the shelters are becoming mini-institutions for the chronically mentally ill, an ironic alternative to the state mental hospitals (Bassuk in press).

The Tendency to Drift

Drifter is a word that strikes a chord in all those who have contact with the chronically mentally ill—mental health professionals, families, and the patients themselves. It is especially important to examine the phenomenon of drifting in the homeless mentally ill. The tendency is probably more pronounced in the young (aged 18 to 35), though it is by no means uncommon in the older age groups. Some drifters wander from community to community seeking a geographic solution to their problems; hoping to leave their problems behind, they find they have simply brought them to a new location. Others, who drift in the same community from one living situation to another, can best be described as drifting through life: they lead lives without goals, direction, or ties other than perhaps an intermittent hostile-dependent relationship with relatives or other caretakers (Lamb 1982).

Why do the chronic mentally ill drift? Apart from their desire to outrun their problems, their symptoms, and their failures, many have great difficulty achieving closeness and intimacy. A fantasy of finding closeness elsewhere encourages them to move on. Yet all too often, if they do stumble into an intimate relationship or find themselves in a residence where there is caring and closeness and sharing, the increased anxiety they experience creates a need to run.

They drift also in search of autonomy, as a way of denying their dependency, and out of a desire for an isolated life-style. Lack of money often makes them unwelcome, and they may be evicted by family and friends. And they drift because of a reluctance to become involved in a mental health treatment program or a supportive out-of-home environment, such as a halfway house or board-and-care home, that would give them a mental patient identity and make them part of the mental health system: they do not want to see themselves as ill.

Those who move out of board-and-care homes tend to be young; they may be trying to escape the pull of dependency and may not be ready to come to terms with living in a sheltered, segregated, low-pressure environment (Lamb 1980a). If they still have goals, they may find life there extremely depressing. Or they may want more freedom to drink or to use street drugs. Those who move on are more apt to have been hospitalized during the preceding year. Some may regard leaving their comparatively static milieu as a necessary part of the process of realizing their goals—but a process that exacts its price in terms of homelessness, crises, decompensation, and hospitalizations. Once out on their own, they will more than likely stop taking their medications and after a while lose touch with Social Security and no longer be able to receive their SSI checks. They may now be too disorganized to extricate themselves from living on the streets—except by exhibiting blatantly bizarre or disruptive behavior that leads to their being taken to a hospital or to jail.

The Question of Liberty

Perhaps one of the brightest spots of the effects of deinstitutionalization is that the mentally ill have gained a greatly increased
measure of liberty. There is often a tendency to underestimate the
value and humanizing effects for former hospital patients of simply
having their liberty to the extent that they can handle it (even aside
from the fact that it is their right) and of being able to move freely
in the community. It is important to clarify that, even if these
patients are unable to provide for their basic needs through employment or to live independently, these are separate issues from that
of having one's freedom. Even if they live in mini-institutions in
the community, such as board-and-care homes, the facilities are
not locked, and the patients generally have access to community
resources.

However, the advocacy of liberty needs to be qualified. A small
proportion of long-term, severely disabled psychiatric patients lack
sufficient impulse control to handle living in an open setting such
as a board-and-care home or with relatives (Lamb 1980b). They
need varying degrees of external structure and control to compensate for the inadequacy of their internal controls. They are usually
reluctant to take psychotropic medications and often have problems
with drugs and alcohol in addition to their mental illness. They
tend not to remain in supportive living situations, and often join
the ranks of the homeless. The total number of such patients may
not be great when compared to the total population of severely
disabled patients. However, if placed in community living arrangements without sufficient structure, this group may require a large
proportion of the time of mental health professionals, not to mention
others such as the police. More important, they may be impulsively
self-destructive or sometimes present a physical danger to others.

Furthermore, many of this group refuse treatment services of
any kind. For them, simple freedom can result in a life filled with
intense anxiety, depression, and deprivation, and often a chaotic
life on the streets. Thus they are frequently found among the homeless when not in hospitals and jails. These persons often need ongoing involuntary treatment, sometimes in 24-hour settings such as
locked skilled-nursing facilities or, when more structure is needed,
in hospitals. It should be emphasized that structure is more than
just a locked door; other vital components are high staff-patient

ratios and enough high-quality activities to structure most of the patient's day.

In my opinion, a large proportion of those in need of increased structure and control can be relocated from the streets to live in open community settings, such as with family or in board-and-care homes, if they receive assistance from legal mechanisms like conservatorship, as is provided in California. But even those who live in a legally structured status in the community, such as under conservatorship or guardianship, have varying degrees of freedom and an identity as a community member.

Some professionals now talk about sending the entire population of chronically and severely mentally ill patients back to the state hospitals, exaggerating and romanticizing the activities and care the patients are said to have received there. To some, reinstitutionalization seems like a simple solution to the problems of deinstitutionalization such as homelessness (Borus 1981; Feldman 1983). But activity and treatment programs geared to the needs of long-term patients can easily be set up in the community, and living conditions, structured or unstructured, can be raised to any level we choose—if adequate funds are made available. The provision of such community resources, adequate in quantity and quality, would go a long way toward resolving the problems of homelessness. In the debate over which is the better treatment setting—the hospital or the community—we must not overlook the patients' feelings of mastery and heightened self-esteem when they are allowed their freedom.

Criminalization

Deinstitutionalization has led to the presence of large numbers of mentally ill persons in the community. At the same time, there are limited amounts of community psychiatric resources, including hospital beds. Society has a limited tolerance of mentally disordered behavior, and the result is pressure to institutionalize persons needing 24-hour care wherever there is room, including jail. Indeed, several studies describe a "criminalization" of mentally disordered behavior (Abramson 1972; Grunberg et al. 1977; Lamb and Grant 1982; Sosowsky 1978; Urmer 1971)—that is, a shunting of mentally ill persons in need of treatment into the criminal justice system instead of the mental health system. Rather than hospitalization and psychiatric treatment, the mentally ill often tend to be subject to inappropriate arrest and incarceration. Legal restrictions placed on involuntary hospitalization also probably result in a diversion of some patients to the criminal justice system.

Studies of 203 county jail inmates, 102 men and 101 women, referred for psychiatric evaluation (Lamb and Grant 1982, 1983) shed some light on the issues of both criminalization and homelessness. This population had extensive experience with both the criminal justice and the mental health systems, was characterized by severe acute and chronic mental illness, and generally functioned at a low level. Homelessness was common; 39 percent had been living, at the time of arrest, on the streets, on the beach, in missions, or in cheap, transient skid row hotels. Clearly the problems of homelessness and criminalization are interrelated.

Almost half of the men and women charged with misdemeanors had been living on the streets or the beach, in missions, or in cheap transient hotels, compared with a fourth of those charged with felonies (p<.01, by chi-square analysis). One can speculate on some possible explanations. Persons living in such places obviously have a minimum of community supports; committing a misdemeanor may frequently be a way of asking for help. It is also possible that many are being arrested for minor criminal acts that are really manifestations of their illness, their lack of treatment, and the lack of structure in their lives. Certainly these were the clinical impressions of the investigators as they talked to these inmates and their families and read the police reports.

The studies also found that a significantly larger percentage of inmates aged 35 or older had a history of residence in a board-and-care home, compared with those under age 35 (p<.02, chi-square analysis). Obviously the older one is, the more opportunity one has had to live in different situations, including board-and-care homes. However, in talking with these men and women, other factors emerged: the tendencies of the younger mentally ill person to hold out for autonomy rather than living in a protected, supervised setting, and to resist both entering the mental health system and being labeled as a psychiatric patient, even to the extent of living in a board-and-care home.

Board-and-care homes had been repeatedly recommended to a large number of the younger persons as part of their hospital discharge plans, but they had consistently refused to go. It appeared that eventually many gave up the struggle, at least temporarily, and accepted a board-and-care placement. However, most left the homes after relatively brief periods, many to return to the streets. In some cases this living situation did not appear to be structured enough for them. In other cases, they seemed to want to regain their autonomy, their isolated life-style, and their freedom to engage in anti-social activities. Despite the fact that a high proportion of the study population had serious psychiatric problems, only eight men (out of 102) and five women (out of 101) were living in board-and-care homes at the time of arrest.

Clearly the system of voluntary mental health outpatient treatment is inadequate for this population, who are extremely resistant to it. If they do agree to accept treatment, they tend not to keep their appointments and not to take their medications, and to be unwelcome at outpatient facilities (Whitmer 1980). This is confirmed by our findings, which showed that only 10 percent of the inmates were receiving any form of outpatient treatment, such as medication, at the time of arrest, and that only 24 percent ever received outpatient treatment.

The need for mental health services in jails is apparent (Lamb et al. 1984). Even so, many mentally ill inmates will not participate in release planning and will not accept referral for housing or treatment. As a result they are released to the streets to begin anew their chaotic existences characterized by homelessness, dysphoria, and deprivation. To work with this population of mentally ill in jail is to be impressed by their need for ongoing involuntary treatment.

Conclusions

The majority of chronically mentally ill persons live with their families or in sheltered living situations such as board-and-care homes. Some live in situations such as single-room-occupancy hotels or otherwise alone. Many are in and out of hospitals. Some are continuously homeless, and some intermittently so. While a minority of the total population of chronically mentally ill are homeless at any given time, very substantial numbers of persons are involved, and homelessness of the chronically mentally ill is a critical nationwide problem.

What have we learned from our experience with more than two decades of deinstitutionalization? First of all, it has become clear that what is needed is a vast expansion of community housing and other services and a whole revamping of the mental health system to meet the needs of the chronically mentally ill. Markedly increased funding is needed to increase the quality, quantity, and range of housing and other services, improve the quality of life for this population, and meet their needs for support and stability. The availability of suitable services should make it possible to attract many of the homeless to stable living arrangements and retain them there.

Many of the chronically mentally ill are not able to find or retain such community resources as housing, a stable source of income, and treatment and rehabilitation services. The need for monitoring and treating these patients by means of aggressive case management has become increasingly apparent. Aggressive case management for all of the chronically mentally ill, given the availability of adequate housing and other resources, would probably minimize homelessness.

It is one of the injustices of deinstitutionalization that, compared to the developmentally disabled, the chronically mentally ill in the community do not fare well in terms of funding, housing, and services. Surely the mentally ill should be given equal priority. The success of deinstitutionalization for the developmentally disabled, however, does demonstrate what can be accomplished when there is determined advocacy and adequate funding and community resources.

We have learned in this era of deinstitutionalization that many of the homeless mentally ill feel alienated from both society and the mental health system, that they are fearful and suspicious, and that they do not want to give up what they see as their autonomy, living on the streets where they have to answer to no one. They may be too acutely and chronically mentally ill and disorganized to respond to our offers of help. Their tolerance for closeness and intimacy is very low, and they fear they will be forced into relationships they cannot handle. They may not want a mentally ill identity, may not wish to or are not able to give up their isolated life-style and their anonymity, and may not wish to acknowledge their dependency. Thus we are dealing with an extremely difficult and challenging population.

As with most problems, we have learned that there are no simple and universal solutions to the problems of homelessness. Let us take the shelter approach as an example. Some of the chronically mentally ill will accept food and shelter, but nothing else, and sooner or later return to the streets, despite the efforts of our most sensitive clinicians. A few will not accept simple shelter, even with no conditions attached.

Certainly we must provide emergency shelter, but we also need to be aware that this is a symptomatic approach. Instead our primary focus should be on the underlying causes of homelessness, and we should work to provide a full range of residential placements, aggressive case management, changes in the legal system, a ready availability of crisis intervention including acute hospitalization, and other crucial community treatment and rehabilitation services.

We have also learned that some of the chronically mentally ill, because of their personality problems, their lack of internal controls, and their resort to drugs and alcohol, will not be manageable, or welcome, in open settings, such as with family or in board-and-care homes, or even in shelters. Some will need more structure and control; they may need involuntary treatment in a secure inter-mediate or long-term residential setting or in the community, facil-itated by mechanisms such as conservatorship or mandatory aftercare. Such intervention should not be limited to those who can be proven to be "dangerous," but should be extended to gravely disabled individuals who do not respond to aggressive case management and are too mentally incompetent to make a rational judgment about their needs for care and treatment. In this way we can help those homeless mentally ill who are unwilling to accept our assistance and whose self-destructive tendencies, personality disorganization, and inability to care for themselves result in lives lived alternately in jails, in hospitals, and on the streets. In some cases such inter-vention is the only act of mercy left open to us.

We have learned that we must accept patients' dependency when dealing with the chronically mentally ill. And we must accept the total extent of patients' dependency needs, not simply the extent to which *we* wish to gratify these needs. We have learned, or should have learned, to abandon our unrealistic expectations and redefine our notions of what constitutes success with these patients. Some-times it is returning them to the mainstream of life; sometimes it is raising their level of functioning just a little so they can work in a sheltered workshop. But oftentimes success is simply engaging patients, stabilizing their living situations, and helping them lead more satisfying, more dignified, and less oppressive lives.

The reluctance of mental health professionals and society to fully

72   THE HOMELESS MENTALLY ILL

accept the dependency of this vulnerable group, inadequate case management systems, the preference of many mental health professionals to work with more "healthy" and "savory" patients, and an ideology that "coercive" measures should be used only in cases of "extreme danger" leave the homeless mentally ill in extreme jeopardy. If deinstitutionalization has taught us anything, it is that flexibility is all important. We must look objectively at the clinical and survival needs of the patients and meet those needs without being hindered by rigid ideology or a distaste for dependency.

References

Abramson MF: The criminalization of mentally disordered behavior. Hosp Community Psychiatry 23:101-105, 1972
Arce AA, Tadlock M, Vergare MJ, et al: A psychiatric profile of street people admitted to an emergency shelter. Hosp Community Psychiatry 34:812-817, 1983
Bachrach LL: Asylum and chronically ill psychiatric patients. Am J Psychiatry 141:975-978, 1984
Bassuk EL, Rubin L, Lauriat A: Back to Bedlam: are shelters becoming alternative institutions? Am J Psychiatry (in press)
Baxter E, Hopper K: The new mendicancy: homeless in New York City. Am J Orthopsychiatry 52:393-408, 1982
Baxter E, Hopper K: Troubled on the streets: the mentally disabled homeless poor, in The Chronic Mental Patient: Five Years Later. Edited by Talbott JA. New York, Grune & Stratton (in press)
Borus JF: Deinstitutionalization of the chronically mentally ill. N Engl J Med 305:339-342, 1981
Brill H, Patton RE: Analysis of 1955-56 population fall in New York State mental hospitals in the first year of large-scale use of tranquilizing drugs. Am J Psychiatry 114:509-514, 1957
Brown GW, Bone M, Dalison B, et al: Schizophrenia and Social Care. London, Oxford University Press, 1966
Deutsch A: The Shame of the States. New York, Harcourt Brace, 1948
Dittmar ND, Smith GP: Evaluation of board and care homes: summary of survey procedures and findings. Special briefing for Department of Health and Human Services, Denver Research Institute, 1983
Feldman S: Out of the hospital, onto the streets: the overselling of benevolence. Hastings Cent Rep 13:5-7, 1983
Fernandez J: "In Dublin's fair city": the mentally ill of "no-fixed-abode." Lecture at Conference on Homelessness, Dublin, Sept 1983
Goldman HH, Adams NH, Taube CA: Deinstitutionalization: the data demythologized. Hosp Community Psychiatry 34:129-134, 1983

Greenblatt M: The third revolution defined: it is sociopolitical. Psychiatric Annals 7:506-509, 1977

Grunberg F, Klinger BI, Grument BR: Homicide and the deinstitutionalization of the mentally ill. Am J Psychiatry 134:685-687, 1977

Johnstone EC, Owens DGC, Gold A, et al: Institutionalization and the defects of schizophrenia. Br J Psychiatry 139:195-203, 1981

Joint Commission on Mental Illness and Health: Action for Mental Health: Final Report of the Commission. New York, Basic Books, 1961

Kris EB: The role of drugs in after-care, home-care, and maintenance, in Modern Problems of Pharmacopsychiatry: The Role of Drugs in Community Psychiatry, vol 6. Edited by Shagass C. Basel, Karger, 1971

Lamb HR: Board and care home wanderers. Arch Gen Psychiatry 37:135-137, 1980a

Lamb HR: Structure: the neglected ingredient of community treatment. Arch Gen Psychiatry 37:1224-1228, 1980b

Lamb HR: What did we really expect from deinstitutionalization? Hosp Community Psychiatry 32:105-109, 1981

Lamb HR: Young adult chronic patients: the new drifters. Hosp Community Psychiatry 33:465-468, 1982

Lamb HR, Goertzel V: The long-term patient in the era of community treatment. Arch Gen Psychiatry 34:679-682, 1977

Lamb HR, Grant RW: The mentally ill in an urban county jail. Arch Gen Psychiatry 39:17-22, 1982

Lamb HR, Grant RW: Mentally ill women in a county jail. Arch Gen Psychiatry 40:363-368, 1983

Lamb HR, Peele R: The need for continuing asylum and sanctuary. Hosp Community Psychiatry (in press)

Lamb HR, Sorkin AP, Zusman J: Legislating social control of the mentally ill in California. Am J Psychiatry 138:334-339, 1981

Lamb HR, Schock R, Chen PW, et al: Psychiatric needs in local jails: emergency issues. Am J Psychiatry 141:774-777, 1984

Larew BI: Strange strangers: serving transients. Social Casework 63:107-113, 1980

Lipton FR, Sabatini A, Katz SE: Down and out in the city: the homeless mentally ill. Hosp Community Psychiatry 34:817-821, 1983

Minkoff K: A map of chronic mental patients, in The Chronic Mental Patient. Edited by Talbott JA. Washington, American Psychiatric Association, 1978

Redick RW, Witkin MJ: State and County Mental Hospitals, United States, 1979-80 and 1980-81. Mental Health Statistical Note No 165. Rockville, Md, National Institute of Mental Health, Aug 1983

Sosowsky L: Crime and violence among mental patients reconsidered in view of the new legal relationship between the state and the mentally ill. Am J Psychiatry 135:33-42, 1978

Urmer A: A study of California's new mental health law. Chatsworth, Calif, ENKI Research Institute, 1971

Whitmer GE: From hospitals to jails: the fate of California's deinstitu-
tionalized mentally ill. Am J Orthopsychiatry 50:65-75, 1980
Wing JK, Brown GW: Institutionalism and Schizophrenia. New York,
Cambridge University Press, 1970

Chapter 4

Identifying and Characterizing the Mentally Ill Among the Homeless

A. Anthony Arce, M.D.
Michael J. Vergare, M.D.

Homelessness is not a new problem. In the 19th and early 20th centuries, economic depression brought about a significant increase in the United States in the number of unemployed immigrants and destitute, uprooted, homeless persons. This period also saw the development of "skid rows" in large metropolitan areas in the U.S.

Bogue (1963) described four major needs met by a skid row. It provided the lowest cost of living, had labor markets for unskilled workers, had public welfare resources, and provided refuge for those desiring escape from the obligations of society. However, by the 1950s skid rows had started to disappear as social legislation began to take care of the needs of the indigent population. In 1958 Bogue and Schusky reported that during the preceding 50 years the skid row population in Chicago had decreased to one-fourth its original size, although the population of the city had doubled. In New York, the Department of Welfare (New York City 1965) reported a decline in the number of men served in the men's shelter from 20,003 in 1958 to 12,543 in 1965.

During the past 15 years, significant changes have taken place

Dr. Arce is executive director of the John F. Kennedy Community Mental Health–Mental Retardation Center and professor and deputy chairman of the Department of Mental Health Sciences at Hahnemann University in Philadelphia. Dr. Vergare is associate chairman of the Department of Psychiatry at Albert Einstein Medical Center, Northern Division, and associate professor of psychiatry at Temple University School of Medicine in Philadelphia.

in the composition of the homeless population. While men still outnumber women 3 to 1, women have begun to appear in growing numbers. A study in Baltimore (Walsh and Davenport 1983) disclosed that during 1981 a total of 5,000 to 6,000 women were homeless "for some reason, for some period of time," and at least half of them were accompanied by children. It was also estimated that between 3,100 and 4,200 women had been deinstitutionalized in the previous four fiscal years, and that between 875 and 1,170 would experience difficulty in obtaining and maintaining shelter during the year.

The homeless population has also become younger. Bahr (1970) reported that nearly half of the homeless Bowery men he studied were 55 or older. A 1981 study conducted by the New York State Office of Mental Health (1983) in New York City disclosed a median age of 36 for the total sample, but a median age of 32 for those who had been homeless for less than one year. Arce and associates (1983) reported that nearly 67 percent of a shelter population in Philadelphia were younger than 50 years of age.

While substance abuse, especially alcohol, continues to be a major problem among the homeless, it is no longer as prevalent as it once was among skid row men. Alcoholism formerly was a precondition for acceptance in the skid row subculture, and most investigators reported almost universal alcohol abuse or addiction. Recent studies report the prevalence of substance abuse among the homeless to be between 25 and 50 percent.

In the past 20 years, former mental patients have been added to the ranks of the homeless as a result of deinstitutionalization policies. This latter group, the mentally ill, has been the focus of so much media attention that to many people homelessness and mental illness are rapidly becoming synonymous. The purpose of this chapter is to review efforts to identify and characterize the mentally ill among the homeless and to discuss the need for further research in this area.

The Homeless

Who are the homeless? They are a cross section of American society. They are men, women, and children of all ages and all ethnic and religious backgrounds. They are single persons, couples, and families. They represent all educational levels, occupations, and professions. Their paths to homelessness are varied, but all involve increasing social marginalization as a result of inflation, unemployment, and reduced social welfare programs due to conservative fiscal policies at federal, state, and local government levels. The redevelopment and gentrification of inner cities have decreased available low-income housing and displaced many families. The deinstitutionalization of large numbers of chronically mentally ill without adequate provisions for residential and treatment programs in the community has also swelled the ranks of the homeless.

Based on information received from more than 100 agencies and organizations in 25 cities and states, Hombs and Snyder (1982) estimated that there were as many as 2.5 million homeless in the United States in 1980 and projected that the homeless population could be as high as 3 million in 1983. Such estimates are often advanced because of their shock value, but the problem of homelessness is so pervasive and visible that it can hardly escape anyone's attention. The actual magnitude of the problem—that is, the precise count of the homeless population—is difficult to establish because of insurmountable methodological barriers. Estimates generally include only those persons who are *visibly* living on the streets or in designated shelters. But the fact is that the homeless are an extremely transient population who are more dispersed than some would believe. Accurate counts cannot be made unless the living patterns of people on the street are taken into account.

Many find shelter in abandoned buildings and other locations hidden from view. The U.S. Census Bureau sent out six million forms to vacant buildings across the country with the expectation that some might be completed! Homeless families can be found camping in parks or living in makeshift accommodations in friends' apartments or in flophouses. Some homeless people are temporarily sheltered in jails, hospitals, and other institutional settings. And some who have a home today may be homeless tomorrow.

Arce and associates (1983) have concluded that people needing shelter at a given time can be grouped into three classes depending on the duration of homelessness: chronic, episodic, and situational. The chronically homeless are the so-called "street people" who regularly live on the street. The episodic homeless are those who alternate between being domiciled and being on the street, in either case for extended periods of time. The situationally homeless are those who on a particular day are undergoing an acute personal crisis, such as eviction or marital discord, that suddenly deprives them of shelter. A recognition of this taxonomy is important for program planners because the service needs for the three groups are vastly different.

Whether an accurate count of the real and potential homeless population has any utility is open to question. Certainly, given the social forces responsible for homelessness, the numbers can be expected to vary in relation to the magnitude of one or another causal factor at any particular moment.

Homelessness is a social problem that affects a broad cross section of our citizenry, including the chronically mentally ill. Homelessness and chronic mental illness are not synonymous. The solution to the problem of homelessness clearly does not lie within the purview of the mental health delivery system alone but requires interventions from other social welfare systems as well (Arce 1983).

Mental Illness Among the Homeless

Much of the early literature on homelessness focused on men living on skid rows (Bahr 1970; Bogue and Schusky 1958; Bogue 1963; Edwards et al. 1966). Many studies both here and abroad emphasized correlations between homelessness and alcoholism (Blumberg et al. 1966; Borg 1978; Edwards et al. 1968) and homelessness and criminality (Borg 1978; Edwards et al. 1968; Laidlaw 1956; Lindelius and Salum 1976; Tidmarsh and Wood 1972). Only recently has more attention been paid to the relationship between homelessness and mental illness (Arce et al. 1983; Baxter and Hopper 1981; Hopper et al. 1982; Lipton et al. 1983; Priest 1970, 1978; Segal et al. 1977).

The lack of consistency in the results reported in the above studies reflects the methodological problems encountered in studying the homeless population from almost any perspective. These problems are even more critical and complex when the focus is on characterizing the mentally ill among the homeless.

The extent of mental illness among the homeless has been studied by a variety of methods in a wide range of settings, including shelters, psychiatric units, food lines, and the open streets. Methods have included informal observation and formal interviews by trained professionals or research workers and retrospective record reviews. In some situations, attempts were made to randomize the sample using various techniques.

A number of investigators have attempted to assess the extent of mental illness among the homeless through informal observations and/or interviews in shelters, food lines, or the open streets. The most extensive and highly publicized work based on these methods is by Baxter and Hopper, in *Private Lives/Public Spaces* (1981) and its sequel, *One Year Later* (Hopper et al. 1982). They describe a survey of applicants to the Men's Shelter in New York City that suggests that half of the city's homeless suffer from serious psychiatric disorders.

Brown and associates (1983) surveyed 150 randomly selected users of two food lines in Phoenix. Interviewers spent 20 to 30 minutes eliciting answers to 54 questions and making notes on physical appearance and impressions of emotional and mental functioning. Of the 150 individuals selected, 33 (18 percent) either refused to participate or were judged unable to be interviewed. Of these, 33 percent were suspected of being psychotic.

Of the 117 interviewed, 21 percent had serious mental health problems ("actively psychotic, possibly psychotic, or severely depressed"), 22 percent were defined or defined themselves as substance abusers (usually alcohol), and 8 percent had problems adjusting to any social situation (for example, they were "con men" or habitual failures) suggestive of personality disorders. In addition, of 12 percent who had physical handicaps, three-fourths also had emotional problems.

Another group of investigators have conducted more formal psychiatric evaluations of samples drawn from shelters or treatment settings. These are studies in which the diagnostic categories used by the investigators allow comparisons between studies. They are summarized in Table 1.

In London Whiteley (1955) studied 100 male admissions to a psychiatric unit, of which 28 percent were first admissions and 72 percent readmissions. Subjects were referred by either a reception center or lodging facilities. Reception centers in England are akin to temporary shelters in this country, while lodging facilities are similar to our flop houses, with payment required for beds. Persons using either type of facility are classified as homeless because they lack a permanent home address, although clients may stay in such facilities for extended periods of time. Diagnoses included schizophrenia, 32 percent; depression, 14 percent; psychopathic personality disorder, 19 percent; alcoholism, 14 percent; paranoid state, 6 percent; and other, 15 percent.

Table 1
Studies on mental illness among the homeless[1]

Author	N	Diagnostic categories							
		Schizo-phrenia	Affective disorder	Person-ality disorder	Other psychoses	Other diagnoses	Primary substance abuse	No mental problem	Undiag-nosed or no infor-mation
Whiteley (1955)	100	32%	14%	19%	6%	15%	14%	—	—
Meyerson (1956)	101	29%	—	61%	—	—	—	—	10%
Goldfarb (1970)	200	33%	18%	38%	—	10%	—	—	—
Priest (1970)	77	32%	5%	18%	—	9%	18%	18%	—
Lodge Patch (1971)	122	15%	8%	51%	—	15%	—	11%	—
Lipton et al. (1983)	90	72%	—	11%	1%	—	9%	—	8%
Arce et al. (1983)	193	35%	5%	6%	—	8%	23%	15%	7%
Bassuk et al. (in press)	78	30%	9%	21%	—	1%	29%	9%	—
Vergare and Arce (unpublished)	193	48%	5%	11%	—	12%	12%	8%	4%

[1]Because the study settings and methodologies vary, the findings should be interpreted with caution.

Whiteley also compared the subjects based on source of referral. He found that individuals referred by the reception center were more seriously disturbed and were representative of London's "down and out" culture, while those referred by lodging facilities tended to be more stable and settled and were representative of the skid row community. The reception center group had a higher incidence of paranoid schizophrenia than the lodging facility group. This early study underscores the effect of sampling methods on the psychiatric diagnostic profile of the homeless.

Meyerson (1956) reviewed 101 cases of destitute and homeless men served at a skid row rehabilitation program. The methods used to gather data are unspecified, but the diagnoses listed include passive-aggressive personality, 55; borderline schizophrenia, 23; overt (ambulatory) schizophrenia, six; sociopathic personality–dyssocial reaction, seven; and undiagnosed, ten. Meyerson emphasized that the majority of these men "joined" skid row to make up for the loss of family relationships. Forty-nine of them became inhabitants of skid row when their wives left them and 33 when their mothers died.

By reviewing case summaries of admissions to the Manhattan Bowery Project, a treatment program for alcoholics, Goldfarb (1970) was able to construct a profile that included diagnosis. Two hundred cases were "thoroughly evaluated for psychiatric and medical illness." Schizophrenia was diagnosed in 33 percent of the group. The schizophrenic subgroups included paranoid, 10.5 percent; simple, 8 percent; chronic undifferentiated, 7 percent; catatonic, 4 percent; and pseudopsychopathic, 3 percent. Another 38 percent were thought to be suffering from personality disorders; the primary type noted was passive-aggressive personality, for 35 percent. The other main diagnostic categories were anxiety neurosis, 9 percent, and depressive reactions, 18 percent. Goldfarb also found that, besides the primary diagnosis, 36 percent had associated chronic organic brain syndrome. Alcoholic hallucinations were seen in 4.5 percent, and alcoholic paranoid reactions in 1.5 percent. Delirium tremens occurred in 2 percent. The author did not detail the exact procedures used to reach these diagnoses, but it is evident that a broad spectrum of primary psychiatric disorders was found. He concluded that there is no clear-cut evidence that persons of any one type are more likely to become homeless alcoholics.

Lodge Patch (1971) interviewed 122 men living in Salvation Army hostels. Again, a broad spectrum of psychiatric diagnoses was found:

schizophrenia, 15 percent; depression, 8 percent; personality disorders, 51 percent; organic brain syndrome, 3 percent; mental retardation, 10 percent; and no psychiatric diagnosis, 11 percent.

Priest (1970, 1976, 1978) studied the epidemiology of mental illness among homeless men. He drew attention to commonly held beliefs about the characteristics of the homeless and how these beliefs vary by country (Priest 1978). For instance, he noted that the average European psychiatrist would say that most vagabonds and tramps are simple or burnt-out schizophrenics. A typical American psychiatrist would likely assume that since the homeless are often found on skid row, they are all alcoholics. He also discussed the view, sometimes found in the literature, that these individuals are "normal," independent men who value their freedom (Orwell 1949).

Priest's work is noteworthy because he studied related samples of homeless men in an effort to identify variations among populations. For example, he compared a sample of 85 subjects from Edinburgh's common lodging houses with 50 subjects from Chicago's skid row (Priest 1970). While he was able to identify demographic similarities between these groups and demonstrate that the majority suffered from psychiatric illness, alcoholism was more prominent in the Chicago sample than in the Edinburgh sample (36 percent versus 9 percent). He also noted that schizophrenia was less frequently diagnosed in the Chicago group (18 percent versus 26 percent).

Priest (1976) also compared a representative sample (RS) of residents selected at random from three common lodging houses in Edinburgh with a clinical sample (CS) of persons who gave a lodging house as an address when admitted to inpatient or outpatient psychiatric services at a local hospital. He found that the CS patients were more likely to be unemployed, under 55, and previously married. They spent shorter time periods in the lodging houses and were more likely to be alcoholic and diagnosed as character disorders. The RS group included more chronic users of lodges and were often schizophrenic (26 percent, versus 14 percent of the CS group). On the other hand, affective disorders were present more often in the CS group (11 percent) than the RS group (5 percent). Priest also found that 54 percent of the CS group appeared more severely disturbed or psychotic as contrasted with 27 percent of the RS group.

These results provide early indication of the emergence of

subgroups of homeless persons with different clinical configurations. However, Priest's work does raise questions about the definition of homelessness, since residents of lodging houses in England are required to pay for shelter and can book beds for a week at a time.

Several studies reported in 1983 or in press are also providing more valid information on the prevalence of mental illness among the homeless. Lipton and associates (1983) studied records of 90 homeless patients treated at the Bellevue Psychiatric Hospital's emergency service. Residents of shelters were excluded. Most of the sample, 96.6 percent, had a history of prior psychiatric hospitalization. Seventy-two percent were diagnosed as schizophrenic, and 11.3 percent as having a personality disorder. Only four of the 90 (9.3 percent) were diagnosed as substance abusers or alcoholics.

An ongoing program for the homeless in New York City is the Goddard Riverside Project Reach Out (Barrow and Lovell 1983). During a nine-month period, project staff established contact to varying degrees with 238 undomiciled persons; 53 percent of them were considered to have psychiatric disability, either alone or in combination with substance abuse or medical problems. Unfortunately, the authors defined psychiatric disability as the presence of selected, observable psychiatric symptoms such as hallucinations, delusions, thought disorder, and bizarre behavior without attempting to specify diagnostic categories or differentiate between symptoms caused by functional mental illness and substance abuse. Nevertheless, the authors state that over the past two years of project operations, the proportion of psychiatrically disabled persons has remained remarkably stable.

Recently Bassuk and associates (in press) interviewed 78 homeless men, women, and children at an overflow shelter in Boston. Almost 91 percent were found to have diagnosable mental illness: schizophrenia, 30.3 percent; alcoholism, 28.9 percent; personality disorders, 21 percent; affective illness, 9.2 percent; and mental retardation, 1.3 percent. The 9 percent who were given no diagnosis included children and adolescents who were in the shelter with their parents and a few men recently arrived in Boston who expected to be working within several days.

Arce and associates (1983) reported on the psychiatric profile of 193 individuals (150 men, 43 women) admitted to an emergency shelter in Philadelphia during severe cold weather in early 1982. This homeless population came from the streets ("vent men," "bag ladies"), skid row, missions, and emergency rooms rather than from any one location. Unlike prior studies, the group included a large number of women. The sample was drawn from 600 individuals needing shelter who were screened by welfare department caseworkers for placement in alternative facilities such as private board-and-care homes or, if placements were not suitable or available, for admission to the shelter. A total of 193 were admitted directly to the shelter. Since individuals exhibiting gross psychopathology could not be placed in alternative facilities, the shelter admissions probably reflect greater overall psychiatric disability.

A total of 179 of the 193 shelter admissions received psychiatric examinations supplemented by extended observations. *DSM-III* criteria were used. Mental illness was diagnosed in 151 residents, or 78 percent. Sixty-seven residents (35 percent) had a primary diagnosis of schizophrenia, 44 (23 percent) of substance abuse, 12 (6 percent) of personality disorder, ten (5 percent) of affective disorder, nine (5 percent) of organic brain syndrome, two (1 percent) of mental retardation, and nine (five percent) of other disorders. A secondary diagnosis of substance abuse was also made for 33 (17 percent) of the subjects. Thus 77 (40 percent) had a major problem with the use of alcohol, drugs, or a combination of both.

Both of the two preceding studies (Bassuk in press; Arce et al. 1983) indicate a prevalence of 40 percent for the combined diagnoses of schizophrenia and affective disorders among the homeless who use shelters.

As noted earlier, based on the duration of the homeless episode, Arce and associates (1983) identified three subgroups in the Philadelphia sample: the chronically homeless (43 percent), who regularly lived on the street; the episodic homeless (32 percent), who alternated between being domiciled or undomiciled for extended periods of time; and the situationally homeless (13 percent), who were usually domiciled but were suddenly deprived of shelter as a result of an acute personal crisis such as eviction or family discord. No information on duration of homelessness was available for 12 percent of the subjects.

A comparison of the two principal groups in the Philadelphia study, the chronically homeless and the episodic homeless, disclosed significant differences, with major implications for treatment and management. The typical chronically homeless person emerged as a white individual over the age of 40 who had been referred by the police. He or she had a diagnosis of schizophrenia, substance abuse, or both; had a history of state hospitalization; and had a variety of health problems. The last is not surprising, given the individual's age and habitual residence on the street without adequate nutrition or health care.

Compared with the episodic homeless, the chronically homeless were more likely to require medication because of disorganized or withdrawn behavior and floridly psychotic symptoms, and to require a stay of two weeks or more in the shelter. When placed, generally in a boarding home, the chronically homeless person was more likely to be readmitted to the shelter because of voluntary return to the streets or ejection from the boarding home.

The typical episodic homeless person was under 40 years of age and black. He or she was referred by an agency or self-referred and had no history of previous hospitalization, but had sporadic contact with a variety of human services agencies. This homeless individual was more likely to be diagnosed as having a personality disorder, an affective disorder, or a substance abuse problem.

Although the episodic homeless exhibited fewer problem behaviors, they were more likely to be "agents provocateurs," disrupting shelter operations through their interactions with other residents. They stayed less than one week in the shelter, and returned to a previous residential setting or to family or friends.

In a follow-up study, Vergare and Arce (study in preparation) sampled a second set of 193 admissions to a city shelter that was opened in November 1982 as a second generation of the emergency shelter that operated from January to March 1982. This second facility was an outgrowth of recommendations made by the authors based on earlier experiences, and was developed both to shelter residents and to evaluate them for mental, medical, and social problems. It operated for eight months in conjunction with a wider range of other city and private housing alternatives for the homeless.

The preliminary analysis of the second sample showed, in comparison to the original sample, increases in the number of females (from 22 percent to 32 percent), in the number of episodically and situationally homeless (from 45 percent to 90 percent), and in length of stay. Also increased were the number of referrals from hospitals and social agencies and self-referrals. The racial and age mix of the population did not change significantly, nor did the diagnostic profile.

The findings to some extent reflect a refinement in the alternatives available in Philadelphia for the homeless. The increased duration of the program permitted a longer stay and better data collection. These factors helped in identifying residents' prior living arrangements, which reduced the number of subjects classified as chronically homeless.

However, the preliminary analysis continues to underscore the severity of psychopathology present among the homeless even after they have had the benefit of food, warmth, health care, and a place to sleep. The findings appear not to support the views of Hopper and associates (1982), who suggested that the high incidence of psychopathology among the homeless may be a reflection of hunger and sleep deprivation.

Discussion

The prevalence of psychiatric disorders among the homeless remains a controversial subject. We have reviewed the findings of numerous researchers who have attempted to identify and characterize the mentally ill among the homeless. Many types of methods have been employed in these studies, and each method has clearly exerted some influence on the data gathered. Nevertheless, most researchers have consistently identified a significant number of the homeless population who have serious psychiatric disabilities.

One of the more important issues influencing the measurement of mental illness among the homeless is the lack of a consensus about who the homeless are. For some researchers, those living in lodges or flop houses are considered homeless, even if they book beds by the week. Others have limited their studies to people living on the street or in parks. Some have focused on skid row; others have used those in food lines or soup kitchens as subjects. Most studies have excluded homeless families and children. Some recent studies have examined emergency service users with no identified addresses, yet similar studies have included emergency service users who actually have lodge or reception center addresses. Such variability in inclusion criteria ultimately affects the prevalence of mental illness identified in these groups as well as the severity of the psychopathology found.

Because of the high number of studies that have looked at boarding homes, lodges, and skid row facilities that cater primarily to males, more mentally ill homeless men than women have been found. Studies based in hospitals and emergency services have reported a much higher percentage of serious mental illness, while those that sampled skid row or flop house inhabitants have reported a high incidence of alcoholism and criminality.

Other factors besides location of sampling and inclusion criteria have an impact on the type of subject studied. For instance, the climate in which a study is done can determine who comes forward for care, and therefore evaluation. Individuals who may be able to quietly survive without notice in summer months suddenly become a source of concern (or embarrassment) during subzero weather. Studies done during severely frigid weather would therefore sample people who might go unnoticed during more temperate months.

The economic and social climate of a particular community also has an effect. For instance, if the sampling is done during a period of high unemployment or in a setting with a severe housing shortage, the subjects likely will show greater psychological integration and stability than those identified as homeless during a period of economic stability, when work and housing are plentiful. Some have suggested that this latter type of homeless individual would be more likely to choose a life on the streets or on skid row rather than have a life-style imposed.

In addition to the methods of sampling used, we have also discussed methods of examination and data review used in studies of the homeless. Most studies have not employed direct psychiatric examination. A few have attempted to employ psychological testing, as cumbersome as this might be given the setting of most of the research. Many reports have been based on impressions or observations made without case-by-case review. A few studies have indicated that subjects were evaluated over an extended period of time. Given the nature of mental illness, symptomatology may not become manifest during a brief or superficial encounter, leading to an undercounting of some diagnostic groups.

Another related issue in any research that attempts to identify the mentally ill in a population is the definition of mental illness itself. Can we assume, as some do, that if one is homeless, one is also mentally ill? None of the research reviewed in this chapter supports this assumption. Should studies focus on symptoms rather than diagnosis? Which diagnostic system should be used to adequately account for the symptoms found in the homeless? Most studies did not specify whether *DSM-I*, *DSM-II*, *DSM-III*, or the *ICD* system of diagnosis was used. Furthermore, since history of illness is critical to many psychiatric diagnoses, it must be assumed that any attempt at diagnosis of the homeless is tentative rather than definitive. Many of the studies avoided discussion of multiple diagnoses, such as schizophrenia, alcohol abuse, and drug abuse. Yet, particularly with the younger chronic patient, such a combination is reported increasingly prevalent.

In spite of all the problems that complicate research to define mental illness in the homeless, a growing collection of studies supports a prevalence of mental illness that should be cause for professional concern. It is evident that in most universes of homeless people, between 25 percent and 50 percent have serious and chronic forms of mental illness. Although the actual counting of specific diagnostic categories in a particular sample is clearly influenced by the methods employed, it is important to recognize that a variety of psychiatric subgroups are represented in any sampling of the homeless population.

References

Arce AA: Statement Before the Committee on Appropriations, in US Senate Special Hearing on Street People. Washington, US Government Printing Office, 1983

Arce AA, Tadlock M, Vergare MJ, et al: A psychiatric profile of street people admitted to an emergency shelter. Hosp Community Psychiatry 34:812-817, 1983

Bahr HM (ed): Disaffiliated Man: Essays and Bibliography on Skid Row, Vagrancy, and Outsiders. Toronto, University of Toronto Press, 1970

Barrow S, Lovell AM: Evaluation of Project Reach Out, 1981-82. New York, New York State Psychiatric Institute, June 30, 1983

Bassuk EL, Rubin L, Lauriat A: Back to Bedlam: are shelters becoming alternative institutions? Am J Psychiatry (in press)

Baxter E, Hopper K: Private Lives/Public Spaces: Homeless Adults on the Streets of New York City. New York, Community Service Society, 1981

Blumberg L, Shipley TE, Shandler IW, et al: The development, major goals, and strategies of a skid row program: Philadelphia. Q J Stud Alcohol 27:242-258, 1966

Bogue DJ: The Skid Row in American Cities. Chicago, University of Chicago Press, 1963

Bogue DJ, Schusky JW: The Homeless Man in Skid Row. Chicago, Tenants Relocation Bureau, 1958

Borg S: Homeless men. Acta Psychiatr Scand (suppl) 276:1-90, 1978

Brown CE, Paredes R, Stark L: The homeless of Phoenix: a profile, in

Homelessness in America. Washington, US Government Printing Office, 1983

Edwards G, Williamson V, Hawker A, et al: London's skid row. Lancet 1:249-252, 1966

Edwards G, Williamson V, Hawker A, et al: Census of a reception centre. Br J Psychiatry 11:1031-1039, 1968

Goldfarb C: Patients nobody wants: skid row alcoholics. Dis Nerv Syst 31:274-281, 1970

Hombs ME, Snyder M: Homeless in America: A Forced March to Nowhere. Washington, Community for Creative Non-Violence, 1982

Hopper K, Baxter E, Cox S, et al: One Year Later: The Homeless Poor in New York City. New York, Community Service Society, 1982

Laidlaw SIA: Glasgow Common Lodging Houses and the People Living in Them. Glasgow Corp, 1956

Lindelius R, Salum I: Criminality among homeless men. Br J Addict 71:149-153, 1976

Lipton FR, Sabatini A, Katz SE: Down and out in the city: the homeless mentally ill. Hosp Community Psychiatry 34:817-821, 1983

Lodge Patch IC: Homeless men in London: demographic findings in a lodging house sample. Br J Psychiatry 118:313-317, 1971

Meyerson DJ: The "skid row" problem. N Engl J Med 254:1168-1173, 1956

New York City Department of Welfare: Annual Report of the Men's Shelter, 1965

New York State Office of Mental Health: Who are the homeless? in Homelessness in America. Washington, US Government Printing Office, 1983

Orwell G: Down and Out in Paris and London. London, Penguin, 1949

Priest RG: Homeless men: a USA-UK comparison. Proc R Soc Med 63:441-445, 1970

Priest RG: The homeless person and the psychiatric services: an Edinburgh survey. Br J Psychiatry 128:128-136, 1976

Priest RG: The epidemiology of mental illness: illustrations from the single homeless population. Psychiatr J Univ Ottawa 3:27-32, 1978

Segal SP, Baumohl J, Johnson E: Falling through the cracks: mental disorder and social margin in a young vagrant population. Social Problems 24:387-400, 1977

Tidmarsh D, Wood S: Survey of a reception centre, in Evaluating a Community Psychiatric Service. Edited by Wing JK, Hailey A. London, Oxford University Press, 1972

Walsh B, Davenport D: The long loneliness in Baltimore: a study of homeless women, in Homelessness in America. Washington, US Government Printing Office, 1983

Whiteley JS: "Down and out in London": mental illness in lower social groups. Lancet 2:608-610, 1955

Chapter 5

Developing a Better
Service Delivery System
for the Homeless Mentally Ill

Stephen M. Goldfinger, M.D.
Linda Chafetz, R.N., D.N.S.

In addressing the problem of psychiatric service delivery to the homeless mentally ill, we are immediately confronted with the difficulty of defining the boundaries of this population and the types of individuals who fall within it. Some of the mentally ill have episodic shelter requirements, for not all homelessness is continuous. Similarly, even among the subgroup of the undomiciled suffering from chronic mental illness, the need for psychiatric intervention may be intermittent. Thus both homelessness and mental illness are multidimensional and subject to change over time. From this perspective, the homeless mentally ill include persons experiencing both phenomena, and requiring some sort of external psychiatric and social service supports.

The diversity of this population, and the fluidity of its boundaries, reflect the changing clinical characteristics and social situations of its members. In considering a service delivery system for this population, we must be willing to acknowledge the complexity of the task and respond with appropriate suspicion and skepticism to simple solutions. This will be a difficult posture to maintain, given the current outcry about homelessness with its attendant pressure

Dr. Goldfinger is assistant clinical professor of psychiatry at the University of California, San Francisco, and director of outpatient services at San Francisco General Hospital. Dr. Chafetz is associate professor in the Department of Mental Health and Community Nursing of the School of Nursing of the University of California, San Francisco.

for a quick or "shotgun" program or project. As Slater (1970) has observed, one facet of American pragmatism is the desire to resolve complex social problems "by gesture," often with inadequate consideration of the gesture's meaning and consequences.

To support our position, we will begin with a discussion of past service responses to the homeless, and the mentally ill among them, and of current attempts to classify the undomiciled mentally ill. We will comment on the difficulties these individuals encounter in obtaining services through conventional service systems. We will then present a set of properties or qualities we believe should be incorporated into these systems in order to address the complex and changing needs of persons for whom homelessness and psychiatric disorder coincide.

Historic Responses to the Homeless

If there is a point of absolute consensus in the literature on the homeless mentally ill, it is that they have preoccupied public authorities for centuries. The problem of indigence, in and of itself, has long concerned the public sector, for economic dependency places an unwelcome burden on the community, particularly when the dependent also present other devalued social attributes.

Reports dating back to the colonial period in this country (Carini et al. 1974; material cited in U.S. Congress 1941) note both the official resentment of the indigent and the particular burden posed by the "indigent insane," who no doubt elicited fear of their mental illness as well as irritation at their dependence.

Given the long period of contact between public officials and the homeless, it is sobering to note the limited repertoire of responses developed to deal with the problem. The most primitive response, dispersion, is also the least ambiguous in its intent. From the launching of the first ship of fools to the establishment of residency requirements for public welfare, an effective means of dealing with the unwanted has been to move them on. This tradition endures today in the passing of patients between catchment areas and in the prevalent belief that good services attract undesirables.

A rehabilitative approach to the homeless is more complex, since it attempts to dispose of behaviors rather than people. The rehabilitation response provides assistance on condition of personal change, reform, or redemption. (A variant can be seen in the charitable response, which emphasizes redemption of the giver as well as the recipient of services. However, simple charity has not prevailed as public policy since the state supplanted the church as dispenser of alms.) Early poorhouses and workhouses exchanged shelter for labor and contrition. The current debate about the function of public shelters and the risk of "promoting dependency" suggests a continuing desire to strike some kind of bargain with the destitute, and to transform indigence into productivity.

The asylum movement reflected this perspective, promising "physical and moral improvement" of the insane (Dix 1843). Mental hospitals later came to serve another function, that of containment. As they accumulated a population considered untreatable, they approached the indigent mentally ill in the manner of the prisons, from which they drew their initial patients. A different type of bargain was struck; those who could not alter their ways were obliged to cede their autonomy.

Whatever the swings of the pendulum, from dispersion to rehabilitation to containment or incarceration, we can discern two central strands. The first is a refusal to support dependence without somehow changing or isolating it. The second involves a failure to differentiate between the varied groups classed under headings such as "wandering madmen," the "indigent insane," or, lately, the "homeless mentally ill." These attitudes may have been inevitable in the distant past, because of limited psychiatric knowledge and absence of community services. Today the idea that we are dealing with a discrete population and the notion that one program or approach will dispose of the problem serve as impediments to effective service planning. The emerging literature on homeless patients and our own clinical data on these individuals indicate that large segments of the chronically mentally ill are vulnerable to loss of residence. When attempts are made to define the homeless mentally ill, what emerges is a group of people no less heterogeneous than the overall population of the chronically mentally ill to which they belong, but one whose needs are, if anything, more pressing and diverse.

Attempts to Classify the Homeless

The search for some sort of clinical typology of the homeless mentally ill is a recurring theme in the literature. Distinctions between "new" and "old" chronics, between schizophrenic disorders and non-psychotic illness, and between long-term street dwellers and the newly homeless have been proposed in an effort to specify constellations of characteristics that can be linked with treatment requirements (Arce 1983; Arce et al. 1983; Jones 1983; Reich and Seigel 1978; Schwartz and Goldfinger 1981; Spitzer et al. 1969). At the Psychiatric Emergency Service (PES) at San Francisco General Hospital, we have also tried to develop some understanding of our undomiciled patients and the possible subgroups among them.

Since the late 1970s, a consistent proportion of PES patients, approximately 25 to 30 percent, have been unable to provide a local San Francisco address at the time of their emergency contact. Initial attempts to compare these cases with the residentially stable patients identified few differences. Like the psychiatric emergency sample described by Lipton and associates (1983), they included many younger adults. So, however, did our overall patient population. The undomiciled were admitted on a voluntary basis at the same rate as other patients, and show a range of the same serious diagnoses.

A 1981 study looked more closely at the residential status of 124 representative PES cases, classifying them as homeless, transient, or residentially stable on the basis of current living situation and mobility within the past month (Chafetz and Goldfinger 1984). These groups were compared in terms of symptoms, using the Psychiatric Evaluation Form (Endicott and Spitzer 1972). The homeless and transient resembled the residentially stable except for higher ratings in the areas of social isolation and impairment in daily routine and leisure activities (both almost synonymous with homelessness in some respects). Earlier records for these patients suggest a possible explanation. Loss of residence was a recurrent, episodic event for so many that the patients in all three groups—homeless, transient, and stable—might be essentially the same patients, observed at different moments in time.

Data more recently obtained by Surber and associates (1982) support this interpretation. In the same setting they found that 30 percent of the PES patients had no local address at the time of the emergency contact. However, of the patients treated three or more times in a year, 10 percent had no address at the time of any of the contacts, but 70 percent were undomiciled at the time of at least one emergency care episode. It is difficult to determine how generalizable these figures are, since the psychiatric emergency service clientele, and particularly this high-use group, may not reflect the homeless mentally ill in a general sense. However, the magnitude of the population who are transient or undomiciled at some point in the year should at the very least alert us to the danger of attributing specific characteristics to all homeless individuals.

Impediments to Obtaining Services

In the last several years, small pilot projects, such as the St. Francis Residence in New York City and the Los Angeles Skid Row Project (Farr 1982) have been designed to serve the homeless. But there has been no consistent or coherent network of services directed to meeting their needs. In fact, one of the most significant findings in the *Report on Federal Efforts to Respond to the Shelter and Basic Living Needs of Chronically Mentally Ill Individuals* (U.S. Department of Health and Human Services 1983) was the need for "a *continuum* of residential options for this population." These patients are frequently extremely difficult to engage in treatment; previous experience with both the shelter and mental health systems have left them suspicious and distrustful of a service system that has consistently failed to address their problems (Baxter and Hopper 1981, 1982; Larew 1980; Segal and Baumohl 1980). Given their wide range of difficulties in multiple spheres and, therefore, the frequency with which they require services in multiple sites and modalities, they appear particularly vulnerable to lack of coordination, inconsistency of treatment or service philosophy, and disparity of objectives and referral protocols. Given the enormous size of the homeless population and the small number of available services, it becomes relatively easy for a shelter to ignore the specialized needs of the mentally ill or to justify their exclusion because they present behavioral problems.

Within the community mental health system, also overcrowded and underfunded, the specialized needs of the undomiciled may once again lead to their exclusion. Chafetz and Goldfinger (1984), studying the residentially unstable in an urban psychiatric emergency service, write:

> An influx of undomiciled and ill-housed clients has placed a strain on staff of this service who cannot always locate residential referrals falling short of hospital admission, at least on an emergency

basis. In the words of one clinician, "Even before you see a client, if you know he has a family and a place to live, you feel relieved. If you know he has nowhere to live, your stomach goes into a knot."

Many traditional mental health interventions are predicated on the assumption of a stable support network and permanent residence. Asking the patient to "Return home, take the medication, rest, and come back tomorrow" is a meaningless intervention when home is an alley and rest is impossible. The homeless mentally ill are viewed as unmotivated or at least ambivalent toward services; these individuals with multiple problems are frequently excluded in favor of others who are more willing and able to cooperate with the treatment offered. Few mental health sites have staff with the time, the skills, or the resources to address the residential needs of this subgroup.

In most large urban centers the homeless mentally ill are concentrated in the inner city. The agencies responsible for serving them may include the departments of social services, public health, community mental health, and housing. These disparate authorities bring to their work divergent philosophies, utilization criteria, standards for clinical accountability, and referral procedures. Such overall program planning as does exist is frequently administrative rather than clinical and suffers from the absence of a supervisory structure capable of monitoring programmatic responsiveness to identified needs. Independently functioning services lack a clear mandate to serve the homeless mentally ill, and they do not have the ability to institute interventions other than those for which they were specifically established. Agency priorities for the population they wish to serve are often set independently, and therefore the system as a whole may lack continuity or comprehensiveness. Thus homeless patients with at best tenuous links to voluntary treatment often find the barriers so difficult to overcome that they may instead choose withdrawal and its attendant hazards.

At city or county planning levels, this population's needs are often conscientiously excluded from service priorities. They may be considered as less legitimate residents of the community than those who are more residentially stable, with their lack of a local address viewed as a lack of local residence. Lumped together with migrants, tourists, and "others just passing through," their numbers are excluded from service planning and their needs ignored or left unmet (Larew 1980). Rather, they are left to shuttle between fragmented service systems faring as best they can in the complex web of requirements for service eligibility.

For example, it is possible for the homeless to be arrested for vagrancy or public inebriation and taken to jail. There they may well be deemed mentally ill and transferred to a psychiatric inpatient unit. Upon discharge, they might be placed in a short-term residential intensive treatment program, and upon discharge from that setting, although still without a place to live, they may be referred to a day treatment program. In those cities that use case management as a treatment modality, they may be lucky enough to be accompanied to the local general assistance or welfare office and receive a hotel voucher. But rare is the city with such coordinated services that the hotel is near the day treatment center. The patient, tired and confused, may end up withdrawing from treatment. With the end of treatment may come the end of medication and decompensation, behavioral problems, and eviction. The patient wends his or her way back to a public shelter, or worse, to the streets.

Even with the firm assumption of our obligation and wish to serve these clients, the path ahead remains unclear. In this post-deinstitutionalization era, the difficulties inherent in treating individuals with multiple problems in community settings are just beginning to be recognized and addressed. Our work then, must be guided by such hints as are available in the published works of those familiar with these patients and by our own experience with this population over the past several years.

Qualities of a Service System

Goldfinger and colleagues (1984) recently delineated essential qualities of any system that is to effectively serve multiproblem patients. We will enlarge here on each of the qualities, both as concepts and as manifestations of individual program elements of a system established to serve the homeless mentally ill. Specifically, we believe an effective system must be capable, comprehensive, continuous, individualized, willing and tolerant, flexible, and meaningful. We are indebted to Bachrach's discussion (1981) of the qualities of continuity of care for the conceptual framework for this presentation.

Capable. In its broadest definition, a service that is capable of dealing effectively with its clientele inherently includes all the other qualities. However, in this context, we mean an adequate physical plant, staff, and resources and the capacity to appropriately evaluate and meet the needs of the population served. Large municipal shelters are usually designed to provide housing for a modal individual; they frequently lack a sufficiently large or well-trained staff to deal with the disruptive and paranoid patient or one who, because of psychological issues, is unable or unwilling to behave according to programmatic expectations. Similarly, the mental health system has frequently excluded these patients because of their perceived unwillingness to cooperate in treatment or because their psychological problems are not defined as "treatable."

The decline of the state hospital system was based in part on its reputation of being inhumane and not providing rehabilitative treatment. Yet the state hospital does provide shelter, and, even at its worst, it provided certain aspects of treatment. The state hospital system is an expensive one, yet it may be equally expensive to provide both shelter and treatment for the homeless mentally ill in the community. Attempts have been made to treat many of these patients in less expensive settings. It is because the patients have failed there, or rather because we have failed them, that many have become dependent, high-use consumers of our most expensive services.

Homeless mentally ill patients require not only a large number of staff, but staff who are experienced, sensitive, and highly trained as well. A funding mechanism that allows for the simultaneous provision of mental health and shelter services with varied lengths of stay and intensities of intervention must be developed. Currently, for example, municipal shelters may exclude those who receive federal disability benefits. Yet these individuals may manage their money so badly that they cannot pay rent on time or otherwise provide themselves with a stable dwelling. To shift the onus of the inadequate system onto an incapable patient may serve fiscal needs but hardly addresses pressing clinical realities.

Comprehensive. As we have noted, one obstacle to adequately serving the homeless mentally ill is the administrative and fiscal split between social service and mental health agencies. The social service system in most cities clearly cannot provide the range of what is needed by the undomiciled. An ideal system might have easily accessible "crash dormitories," more structured brief-stay residences, intermediate-stay housing with both shared and private rooms, a system of access to hotel rooms payable by voucher, and, finally, adequate permanent dwellings.

It may be argued that community mental health services already provide a comprehensive network of mental health treatment modalities. For many patients with many kinds of problems, they do. But many of the homeless are unwilling or unable to engage in the bureaucratically entangled treatment system; outreach services to the places in which they congregate are needed. The aftercare system is generally based on scheduled appointments, regular attendance, and adherence to stringently enforced rules of behavior and participation. But it is difficult to keep a one o'clock appointment if you live on the street and don't own a watch. If you know that an unusually long line at a soup kitchen means missing an afternoon clinic session, you have to make the choice between following clinic rules and going hungry. Halfway houses and other brief-stay residences may on the surface provide both treatment and shelter, but by requiring patients to adjust to continual changes in locale and therapeutic staff, they hardly provide the qualities of asylum ideally present in such a system (Bachrach 1984; Minkoff 1983).

In addition to traditional mental health modalities, social, economic, and other supports must be available. But even within those rare communities where the mental health system and the social service system may each provide comprehensive care and a full range of options, the systems themselves are rarely integrated. Lacking the necessary interface, they are therefore functionally noncomprehensive.

A system designed to provide shelter for the mentally ill must have access to a full range of outreach, case management, medication, and other services. The community mental health system must be able to make referrals to low-cost housing to augment the possibility of stabilization between acute psychiatric episodes. Access of entitlements, which for many patients is the only tangible evidence of support outside the hospital, must be assured.

Services within a program or facility must be comprehensive as well; we must offer more than containment, confinement, and medication. Training in self-care, financial management, and other life skills must be accessible to those who want it, along with opportunities to discuss and improve patterns of personal and social interaction. Medical care must be made available, as the homeless suffer an extraordinarily high rate of medical and hygiene problems. Substance abuse counseling must be offered at every location.

Continuous. Even within a comprehensive range of services, discontinuities in the flow of information or in the admission criteria from one level of care to another may be manifested operationally as a lack of service (Schwartz et al. 1983). For example, a stabilized schizophrenic patient may be well known to the staff of a shelter that is open only in the evenings but that the patient has been using for years. If the patient begins to decompensate during the day and seeks services at a psychiatric emergency room, the shelter staff's knowledge of the patient's history and previous functioning might never be made available to the evaluating staff. If the patient is admitted to an acute inpatient unit, the emergency room evaluation may become the core of the data base, resulting in a total loss of this valuable source of clinical background.

When the patient is discharged from the hospital and perhaps referred to a residential treatment facility, the chain of communication is broken again. When, after a period of treatment, length-of-stay criteria mean the patient must be discharged from residential treatment, staff at that agency are probably struggling with the question of providing ongoing housing for the patient. Meanwhile, concerned staff at the shelter may well be desperately attempting to uncover the patient's whereabouts, yet they have no centralized source of information. And the patient, having told his story to four or five separate sets of intake workers, may feel misunderstood, overly burdened, and ignored, which evokes a sense of confusion, inconsistency, disillusionment, or despair.

Thus, despite the availability of a range of residential and treatment options, the very structure of the service system may ensure discontinuity of care. Although the separate elements of the continuum may be of high quality, well designed, and staffed with the best-meaning of clinicians, the absence of an effective interagency network may render their work ineffective.

The provision of service must be coordinated and monitored from a service perspective that assures delivery of integrated care across modalities and geographic boundaries. We believe that this will be accomplished only by assigning a case manager to each patient— not a nominal case manager, but someone with authority to designate and implement a service plan (Lamb 1980). Although responsibility for an individual may be placed in the hands of a single case manager or a team of case managers (Witheridge and Dincin 1981), it is essential that case management not be confined to one site. Rather, there must be a service with primary responsibility for patients regardless of where they are or how their needs will be met, to complement the separate agency-centered programs. Such case management and coordination cannot exist unless individual programs are uniformly responsible to (or at least coordinated by) a single administrative authority. As long as programs retain the option to refuse to serve specific individuals or to establish independent service plans without regard to an overall management policy, continuity of care cannot be achieved.

Individualized. Services are easiest to design when they are intended for large uniform populations. Within the system of services for the homeless, the enormity of the problem has made it extremely difficult to focus on the specialized needs of any subgroup, such as the mentally ill. Yet the mentally ill homeless are especially vulnerable and unable to protect themselves or to tolerate the intensity of stimuli at large public shelters. They are at high risk for assault from external and internal forces, both physical and psychological. Their behavior, often disruptive, may make them the target of verbal or physical abuse from other clients (Baxter and Hopper 1982), and the very sensory overload of the shelters may increase their psychological distress.

It is in many ways cruel for us to engage the homeless mentally ill to the point that they accept shelter if we do not acknowledge and address their mental health needs. It is precisely because these patients are unable to utilize existing "modal patient" services that they reappear over and over again at inpatient and emergency psychiatric facilities, cycle through our local jails, or leave the shelters provided for them. Trained mental health staff should be available at shelters and other program sites; more ideally, programs specifically designed to work with this population, and with higher staff-patient ratios, should be established. Within specially designed programs, it should be possible to provide treatment plans targeted to each patient's needs.

In providing services, we must recognize that people change over time and that treatment must reflect such change. An ongoing relationship with a single care provider or team is essential for the homeless mentally ill. Case managers must maintain enough contact with patients to recognize evidence of increased social adaptation or clinical exacerbation, and to guide patients to the services appropriate at any given time.

Willing and tolerant. The homeless mentally ill, sometimes labeled "unwilling," "untreatable," or "manipulative," often encounter anger, hostility, and rejection within the mental health system. These attitudes are as evident to the patients as they are to the referring agencies. One problem is that current services lack the four qualities listed above. Staff who might be willing to work with homeless patients under more ideal circumstances recognize the overwhelming likelihood of failure within the limits of the current system. They are often torn between the wish to meet the needs of those they treat and their institutional loyalty; institutional concerns about reimbursement or length of stay may supersede the focus on any one individual's care. One hopes that when services are specifically designed to meet the needs of the homeless mentally ill, their needs and demands will be met with more tolerance.

One of the saddest fates for these patients is the unfortunate tendency of staff to label them "manipulative." Frequently staff meet their requests with anger and a sense of being used. Perhaps as a function of heavy case load or rapid turnover, staff are unable to become acquainted enough with the patients' internal world and to recognize both the symbolic nature and significance of their requests. One explanation may be that, in a system with such high demand and inadequate resources, staff tend to view these patients as adversaries, thus avoiding the guilt of recognizing how little they can in fact offer them. Perhaps with a system that makes more resources available to staff working specifically with this population, along with the freedom and flexibility to establish both short- and long-term goals, many impediments to successful interpersonal interaction and acceptance will be overcome (Goldfinger 1981).

Flexible. Just as a given modality or program must be tailored to meet the individual's needs, the system as a whole must be flexible enough to allow for optimal utilization of its resources. Thus the barriers between the mental health residential treatment system and the social services shelter network, currently essentially impermeable, must be reduced or eliminated. For instance, when inpatient or emergency psychiatric services are overloaded, space in designated shelters might be made available for those who could be maintained with less than acute inpatient care. And residential treatment facilities might make space available at night for overflow crowds from the shelter network.

Similarly, psychiatric and medical personnel must be flexible enough to move throughout the system. Rather than remaining tied to specific sites and services, they must begin following their caseload wherever they are currently residing.

Currently many agencies use the length-of-stay guidelines built into their contracts as absolute and inflexible standards determining patients' movement regardless of clinical need or outside exigencies. In most cases, an individual who is willing to remain in a service will be kept the maximum number of days tolerated by the system. Discharge and referral plans are tied to this preset limit rather than reflecting clinical need and appropriateness.

Such a model cannot be continued in a system that hopes to have an impact on these patients. For example, we might envision a joint venture between a large shelter program and a residential treatment alternative. Admission to the residential treatment service would be independent of the patient-staff contracts currently in vogue; instead the length of stay might run from 24 hours to several months. A patient's intermittent short-term use of the service would not automatically be viewed as unwillingness to participate but rather in terms of its individual meaning. For some, it might be a clinical symptom; for others, it might express a reasonable and justifiable preference. When the structure or program of a residential treatment service becomes too intense for a patient to tolerate, he or she could live instead at a shelter and avoid the requirements of participation in the more structured program. Perhaps over time, as the services reinforce the patient's sense both of autonomy and of being helped, he or she might begin to trust the system sufficiently to become committed to a longer treatment course, and perhaps to participate more actively. Such flexibility seems essential if we are ever going to help these currently "uncooperative" patients become willing to accept and participate in our services.

Meaningful. When patients come for our services, they are rarely requesting treatment. What they come for is help, and they frequently see no correlation between what they come for, and what is offered.

To the extent that the service we offer mismatches the areas for which the patient requests help, we should understand the patient's reluctance to accept a product he or she never set out to obtain.

We may think it important for therapeutic reasons that an individual commit himself to regular appointments or a fixed length of stay. However, many patients have been spared our educational and philosophical biases. We may view an inpatient admission as a source of diagnostic evaluation, medication titration, and one-to-one psychotherapy but for many of these patients, it is the only place they can find shelter without fee and without rules. We may view the understanding that results from regular, long-term outpatient psychotherapy as the only intervention that will effect personality change, but to the person who is hungry or without shelter, a meal or a roof may be far more important. The therapist who concentrates on taking a history or interpreting relationships, disregarding the patient's explicit request for concrete help to meet physical needs, has gained little and probably lost the patient. Similarly, shelters that require residents to leave during the day may believe they are increasing the individual's sense of responsibility and avoiding institutionalism, but for those affected, who may have no daytime activities, supports, or gratifications, it is a hostile or rejecting approach. The shelter worker may consider the complexity of intake interviews, forms, and medical or psychiatric assessments necessary for an evaluation of the resident, but to someone with freezing fingers on an icy night, they are just another barrier, and an example of the system's lack of interest.

To be meaningful to those we serve, our services must offer not only what we deem useful but what they deem necessary. For many patients this means positive case management services, targeted to procuring entitlements and, if necessary, arbitrating between the patients and the world around them. The advice and interventions we offer must be relevant to the world they inhabit; it is useless to ask if a person is sleeping well if he is sleeping on the streets, or to expect a patient to follow the rules of a shelter program when he or she is responding to internal voices and not ours. In order to engage the difficult-to-treat population of the homeless mentally ill, we must begin seeing what we offer through their eyes.

Developing a Better Service System

The community mental health system was designed as a more humanized, respectful, and effective method of treating the long-term chronic patient than the state hospitals it was to replace, but it has nonetheless fallen victim to many of the same pitfalls that befell its predecessor. We would like to focus our attention on one specific element of this system's failure. Designed to be accessible to, and therapeutic for, the large mass of patients, the community mental health system has great difficulty reacting to the service needs of patient groups requiring specialized or unusual attention. For those patients who accept and are willing to work within its structures, the system has provided positive and useful treatment. But for patients who by reason of the nature or severity of their internal difficulties or overwhelming social stressors are unable to work within the existing system, it has helped to reinforce their overuse of acute services and has increased their sense of alienation, hopelessness, and rage.

In many ways, the provision of safe and protective housing for those unable to provide it for themselves has followed a course not dissimilar to that of the mental health system. The recent resurgence of interest in and recognition of the need to provide publicly funded shelter for the homeless population has likewise resulted in a system that, although probably inadequate for the total homeless population, does provide a modicum of safety and comfort to those it can serve. Much like the community mental health systems, however, the shelter system is better able to provide a transition from streets to shelters for the broad homeless population than it is to meet the needs of identified subgroups of the clientele it serves. For those willing and able to conform to its policies and protocols, a bed and a roof may in fact be guaranteed.

However, without the ability to address some of the underlying general social causes of homelessness and the psychiatric and biomedical roots of the problem, the shelter system may provide respite, but can accomplish little in terms of long-term impact. Although its clients may no longer be cold, and may be better rested and better fed, if a shelter system cannot provide access to or direct provision of treatment for the mentally ill among its clientele, it can serve only as a temporary respite but is without ameliorative value.

Bachrach (1984) and Minkoff (1983) have focused on the provision of asylum in the care of the chronic psychiatrically disturbed individual. Asylum, as we hope has become clear, is a function falling at the intersection of the provision of shelter and the provision of treatment, specifically a sense of a "safe haven." In any evaluation of a system designed to provide for the needs of the homeless mentally ill, we would do well to ask ourselves if we are providing only mental health services and shelter, or if we are also offering the asylum so desperately needed.

Rather than describing a model program designed for a given community or a given population, we would like to underscore the seven qualities enumerated above. Because geographic areas have diverse political, social, and economic concerns and unique populations and human service problems, programs to meet the needs of the homeless mentally ill must differ (chapter 2; Turner and Shifren 1979). However, we believe that the structure of any system must embody the qualities we have described.

An element of service planning not specifically addressed above is that of staff selection and training. We believe that the clinical staff entrusted to work with this group must embody a series of specific personal and professional characteristics. Some certainly must have theoretical sophistication, including familiarity with the fine points of biopsychosocial diagnosis and an understanding of both psychodynamic and social theories of personality (Borus 1978; Talbott 1980). Staff must also be able to take a practical approach to clinical problem-solving and to call upon a set of pragmatic skills, including an ability to negotiate the complications of several social welfare systems.

Finally, staff must possess what we can only describe as optimistic nihilism—a peculiar mix of intense commitment and honest detachment. It is unrealistic to work with a group that is seriously disturbed, disadvantaged, and vulnerable without acknowledging the chronicity of their illness and without recognizing that significant growth and change may be impossible. However, to become overly detached, abandoning these patients as hopeless and untreatable and ignoring the realistic, if limited and incremental, changes that can be effected is to fall victim to despair. Rather, a peculiar mixture of warmth, naturalness, and a ready openness to accept the individual as he is must be coupled with the ability to set limits, to refrain from adversive or malicious antitherapeutic or exclusionary interactions (Maltsberger and Buie 1974), and to maintain a longitudinal relationship despite disruption and frequent rejection. Like the systems in which they work, the staff must be capable, willing, tolerant, flexible, and able to find meaning both for themselves and for their patients in their work.

References

Arce AA: Statement Before the Committee on Appropriations, in US Senate Special Hearing on Street People. Washington, US Government Printing Office, 1983

Arce AA, Tadlock M, Vergare MJ, et al: A psychiatric profile of street people admitted to an emergency shelter. Hosp Community Psychiatry 34:812-817, 1983

Bachrach LL: Asylum and chronically ill psychiatric patients. Am J Psychiatry 141:975-978, 1984

Bachrach LL: Continuity of care for chronic mental patients: a conceptual analysis. Am J Psychiatry 138:1449-1456, 1981

Baxter E, Hopper K: The new mendicancy: homeless in New York City. Am J Orthopsychiatry 52:393-408, 1982

Baxter E, Hopper K: Private Lives/Public Spaces: Homeless Adults on the Streets of New York City. New York, Community Service Society, 1981

Borus JF: Issues critical to the survival of community mental health. Am J Psychiatry 135:1029-1035, 1978

Carini E, Douglas DM, Heck LD, et al: The Mentally Ill in Connecticut: Changing Patterns of Care and the Evolution of Psychiatric Nursing, 1636-1972. Hartford, Connecticut Department of Public Health, 1974

Chafetz L, Goldfinger SM: Residential instability in a psychiatric emergency service. Psychiatr Q 56:20-34, 1984

Dix DL: Address to the Massachusetts legislature: appeal on behalf of the insane in Massachusetts, 1843, in Documentary History of Psychiatry. Edited by Goshen CE. New York, Philosophical Library, 1967

Endicott J, Spitzer RL: What! Another psychiatric rating scale? the psychiatric evaluation form. J Nerv Ment Dis 154:88-104, 1972

Farr RK: Skid Row Project. Los Angeles County Department of Mental Health, Jan 19, 1982

Goldfinger S: The borderline client, in The Practice and Management of Psychiatric Emergencies. Edited by Gorton J, Partridge R. St Louis, Mosby, 1981

Goldfinger SM, Hopkin JT, Surber RW: Treatment resisters or system resisters? toward a better service system for acute care recidivists. New Directions in Mental Health Services, no 21:17-27, 1984

Jones RE: Street people and psychiatry: an introduction. Hosp Community Psychiatry 34:807-811, 1983

Lamb HR: Therapist–case managers: more than brokers of services. Hosp Community Psychiatry 31:762-764, 1980

Larew BI: Strange strangers: serving transients. Social Casework 63:107-113, 1980

Lipton FR, Sabatini A, Katz SE: Down and out in the city: the homeless mentally ill. Hosp Community Psychiatry 34:817-821, 1983

Maltsberger JT, Buie DH: Countertransference hate in the treatment of suicidal patients. Arch Gen Psychiatry 30:625, 1974

Minkoff K: Asylum as a clinical issue for chronic mental patients. Presented at the 35th Institute on Hospital & Community Psychiatry, Sept 25-29, 1983, Houston

Reich R, Siegel L: The emergence of the Bowery as a psychiatric dumping ground. Psychiatr Q 50:191-201, 1978

Schwartz SR, Goldfinger SM: The new chronic patient: clinical characteristics of an emerging subgroup. Hosp Community Psychiatry 32:470-474, 1981

Schwartz SR, Goldfinger SM, Ratener M: The young adult chronic patient and the care system: fragmentation prototypes. New Directions for Mental Health Services, no 19:23-35, 1983

Segal SP, Baumohl J: Engaging the disengaged: proposals on madness and vagrancy. Social Work 25:358-365, 1980

Slater P: The Pursuit of Loneliness: American Culture at the Breaking Point. Boston, Beacon Press, 1970

Spitzer R, Cohen G, Miller JD, et al: The psychiatric status of 100 men on skid row. Int J Soc Psychiatry 15:230-234, 1969

Surber R, Goldfinger S, Lewitter S, et al: "High-User" Patients. Department of Psychiatry, San Francisco General Hospital, 1982

Talbott JA: Medical education and the chronic mentally ill. Presented at the annual meeting of the American Psychiatric Association, May 3-9, 1980, San Francisco

Turner JEC, Shifren I: Community support systems: how comprehensive? New Directions for Mental Health Services, no 2, 1979

US Congress: Report of the Select Committee to Investigate the Interstate Migration of Citizens, Transportation of Dependents. Washington, US Government Printing Office, 1941

US Department of Health and Human Services and US Department of Housing and Urban Development: Report on Federal Efforts to Respond to the Shelter and Basic Living Needs of Chronically Mentally Ill Individuals. Washington, Department of Health and Human Services, Feb 1983

Witheridge TF, Dincin J: The Bridge: An Assertive Home-Visiting Program for the Most Frequent Psychiatric Recidivists. Summary, Final Report to the National Institute of Mental Health. Springfield, Illinois Department of Mental Health and Developmental Disabilities, 1981

Chapter 6

Shelter and Housing
for the Homeless Mentally Ill

Ellen Baxter
Kim Hopper

Attention to the crisis of homelessness across the country has grown rapidly in recent years across all levels of government, in voluntary and professional organizations, and in the print and electronic media. The problem, simply put, is that the legitimacy of our "civilized" society is strained by the evidence that millions of its citizens are lacking the basic provisions of food and shelter.

In this chapter we will combine a review of the nature and value of the developing data base on homelessness; an analysis of official postures and policies about the problem; and a discussion of the goals, standards, and strategies of advocacy, with and on behalf of homeless people, to improve their lot. It is written in the hope of reducing the dissonance between what is known about the problem and what is done about it. And it is written with full awareness of repeated official declarations in the city in which we live, New York, that far more is being done for the homeless here than elsewhere in the nation (Katz 1983; Rule 1983), and with the knowledge

Ms. Baxter and Mr. Hopper are research associates with the Community Service Society in New York City. The chapter is based on research supported in part by the Van Ameringen Foundation and the Ittleson Foundation. Portions of the chapter are also published in "Troubled on the Streets: The Mentally Disabled Homeless Poor," by Ellen Baxter and Kim Hopper, in *The Chronic Mental Patient: Five Years Later*, edited by John A. Talbott (New York, Grune & Stratton, in press).

that during the winter some 25 to 50 homeless people die on our city's streets each month (Begun 1983).

Identifying the Homeless

In a one-week period in March 1982, major news stories on the homeless poor in America appeared in *Newsweek*, *U.S. News & World Report*, and the *Wall Street Journal*. In December of that year Congress held the first hearings on the issue of homelessness since the Great Depression. Signs of the 1930s reverberated: the hardships of men, women, and children living on urban streets, in encampments on the outskirts of Sunbelt cities, and in abandoned buildings, public parks, transportation depots, and emergency shelters were reported in tragic detail. The testimony implicated as causal forces, with some regional variation in weight, persistently high unemployment, increased migration, a shrinkage of the low-cost housing market, the mental health and correctional policies of deinstitutionalization, and recent cutbacks in social service and disability programs.

A recent report to the National Governors' Association Task Force on the Homeless by Mario Cuomo (1983), Governor of New York State, cited rough estimates of the homeless population in selected cities: 60,000 in New York City, 30,000 in Los Angeles, 20,000 to 25,000 in Chicago, 12,000 to 15,000 in Baltimore, 2,500 in Denver, 2,000 in Boston, 2,000 to 3,500 in Atlanta, 7,700 in St. Louis, 8,000 in Philadelphia, 22,000 in Houston, 8,000 to 10,000 in San Francisco, and 5,000 to 8,000 in Detroit. The reliability of such estimates often becomes a focus of official and media attention, as if the precision of the estimate, rather than the obvious gravity of the situation, were the central issue. (See Hopper et al. 1982a for a discussion of definitional and planning bases for these debates.) The first direct relief provided at the federal level took the form of $150 million in emergency assistance for food and shelter, distributed nationally over the summer of 1983. As this amount served only a fraction of those in need, it exposed an even greater level of need that was formerly hidden from official view. A second federal bill allocated $40 million for winter 1983-84.

Public and private conferences, coalitions, task forces, studies, and surveys on the homeless problem have surfaced in many cities, small and large, throughout the country. Coalitions and task forces

generally categorize the homeless as a class apart and a new phenomenon, and call for statistical and demographic data on the problem,
assessments of needs for services, and the segregation of subgroups
with special needs. The prevailing assumption is that planning for
help for the homeless is a new and complex process requiring a
highly refined data base. It is also assumed that the evidence itself
will lead to appropriate public policy.

Convenient samples of the homeless population and of available
resources are commonly surveyed to gather this evidence. The surveys
generally identify a pattern of heterogeneous needs, the majority
of which remain unmet, only to be identified again by subsequent
surveyors. Planning for this range and diversity of needs becomes
ensnared in the dilemma of how to coordinate assistance among
separate departments operating only within their mandated sphere
of responsibility. And all of the departments traditionally accord
the homeless low, if any, priority.

The heightened local and national attention to the problem has
had little direct benefit for homeless people, and has hardly impinged
on the forces swelling their ranks. The needs of homeless people
are visible, severe, and urgent. Measures that would redress basic
deprivations, we will argue, are self-evident and simple. Yet policies, where they exist at all, have been meager and convoluted:
intentions are unclear, bureaucracies rigid, and interests conflicting, and in a time of fiscal austerity little is done. The artificial
barriers thrown up by the perceived need to "measure" homelessness often mean that the essential humanity of persons ravaged by
homelessness, disability, unemployment, and poverty is neglected.
Measurement, at this stage, serves little other than our own curiosity.

The Homeless Mentally Disabled

"It has been the psychiatric profession and the social survey units
of central government departments that have dominated work on
the extent of vagrancy and the social and pathological characteristics
of vagrants," Cook wrote in 1979.

It must be emphasized that the homeless population in the United
States is so heterogeneous that it defies categorization under any
single disability heading, mental or otherwise. Homeless people
today come from highly varied social, economic, and personal back-

grounds and include the young and old, single people and families, the mentally and physically disabled and the able-bodied. However, the consequences of severe deprivation and homelessness can exact a heavy toll on mental and physical status, whether frailties were formerly manifest or not. Although the subgroup of the mentally disabled homeless are separated from the larger homeless population for discussion here, the situation ultimately is one of common obstacles and solutions—primarily, the need for decent, affordable housing.

The homeless mentally ill include former state hospital patients whose precarious arrangements for living in the "community" have fallen apart or were never made and the mentally disabled who, although in obvious need of assistance, have not gained access to psychiatric inpatient care due to restrictive admissions criteria of state mental hospital systems. The proportion of the psychiatrically disabled among the homeless and their characteristics have been reported in British studies (Leach and Wing 1980; Tidmarsh and Wood 1972), Canadian studies (Freeman et al. 1979), and an increasing proliferation of American studies. Baasher and associates (1983) suggest that a marked coincidence of vagrancy and chronic mental illness is characteristic not only of the developed world but of developing countries as well. Various studies indicate that the psychiatrically disabled constitute a significant proportion of the homeless population; estimates range from a low of 20 percent to more than 50 percent in such cities as New York (Baxter and Hopper 1981; Hopper et al. 1982a; Lipton et al. 1983), Phoenix (Brown et al. 1982), St. Louis (Morse 1982a, 1982b), San Francisco (Conart House 1982; Chafetz and Goldfinger 1984), Philadelphia (Arce et al. 1983), Chicago (Chicago Task Force on the Homeless 1983), Boston (Bassuk et al. in press), and Denver (Presley 1983).

The Homeless in New York City

New York City offers a rich case for consideration of the mentally ill homeless and the responses of policy-makers to the problem. The fact that New York State was considered to be in the forefront of the nationwide deinstitutionalization movement (Scull 1977), and that it has allocated more resources to mental health services than any other state in the nation for 20 years (Begun 1983), makes its experience with the homeless particularly instructive. Examination of mental health dimensions of homelessness in New York City, on both programmatic and policy levels, should raise generic questions and proposals for most urban centers of the country.

The critical shortage of housing for the chronically mentally disabled has been officially recognized as a priority at the federal, state, and local levels for more than a decade. A recent federal document on the chronically mentally ill focuses on their shelter and other basic living needs (U.S. Department of Health and Human Services 1983). The gap, described in the report, between the extent of the need and the supply of the necessary range of residential options, has been an enduring one. The 1975 Amendments to the Community Mental Health Centers Act, the 1977 Comptroller General's Report to the Congress (U.S. General Accounting Office 1977), the 1978 President's Commission on Mental Health, the Community Support Program literature, and the HUD/HEW demonstration grants have all identified the same range of housing options as priority needs of the chronically mentally ill.

The acute shortage of housing for the chronically mentally ill in New York City and State has been reviewed by countless privately and publicly commissioned committees and studies. The dimensions of the need and the insufficiency of the supply have generated numerous recommendations (Jurow 1979; New York City 1979; New York State 1981a, 1982b; State Communities Aid Association 1982). The crux of the problem is best summarized as follows: "The single most critical factor which prevents effective service coordination and implementation of rational discharge planning is the lack of provision for adequate specialized housing for the chronically disabled" (New York State 1982a).

The dramatic shrinkage of low-income housing in New York City has intensified the problem. An example is the decrease in low-income single-room-occupancy (SRO) hotels, where many ex-patients have gravitated (New York State 1980). Between 1970 and 1982, more than 110,000 SRO units were lost in New York City, representing 87 percent of the total supply (Green 1982). (Nationwide, in the same period, 1,116,000 SRO units—or 47 percent of the total supply—disappeared.) The streets and emergency shelters have become the only remaining options for many.

City officials blame the state's policy of deinstitutionalization as the major cause of homelessness, while state officials point to the city's encouragement of conversions of SRO hotels through a tax abatement program. Valid arguments for both causes conveniently allow the blame to be shuttled back and forth. The presence of discharged psychiatric patients in the streets and shelter system first drew the attention of the public (New York State Senate 1976), the psychiatric profession (Reich and Siegel 1978), and city officials (Bellamy 1979). Mayoral charges that the state mental health system is "the shame of New York . . . vile . . . [a] travesty and disgrace" continue to date (Giordano 1983a).

State mental health officials initially retorted that only a small minority of the homeless were, in fact, mentally ill. Dr. Stanley Hoffman, director of research and evaluation for the New York City Regional Office of Mental Health, indicated that instead the homeless were "relatively well-educated, relatively well-functioning, well-traveled, middle-class dropouts, who have learned to maneuver the system and who move around" (Carmody 1981). In its 1981 Five Year Plan, the New York State Office of Mental Health (1981a, 49) disavowed a primary responsibility: "The basic needs of the 'street people'—food, shelter, bath, clothing, medical care—are the responsibility of the social welfare system." More commonly, mental health officials acknowledge the failures of deinstitutionalization (Connell 1982), assert that practices of discharge planning have improved (Haveliwala 1981), and declare that the policy of deinstitutionalization has been discontinued (Herman 1980; Sullivan 1983). Recent initiatives in the form of outreach programs and mental health assessment teams are lauded as achievements demonstrating the official commitment to the mentally ill homeless.

A report from the New York State Office of Mental Health dated March 31, 1980, shows the performance of state psychiatric hospitals in discharging patients during fiscal year 1979-80 (New York State 1980). In that year, 1,851 releases, or 23 percent, were to "unknown" living arrangements. One hospital discharged 59 percent of its patients to "unknown" destinations. Official claims that deinstitutionalization has stopped and that careful planning for placement in the community is now standard practice remain suspect.

Survey findings on the homeless, some of them generated by the mental health services themselves, have yielded much information on demographic characteristics, entitlement eligibility, mental and physical health status, histories of hospitalization, family contacts, previous place of residence, and employment histories, among many other variables. While it is evident that the findings vary according to definition of the problem, the purpose of the study, the site, the sample, and the methodology, these differences do not preclude valid inferences about the needs of homeless subgroups, specifically the mentally ill.

Assessments of 219 men in one shelter facility who were referred to an on-site mental health team for evaluation showed that 25 percent were so disturbed as to require immediate hospitalization (New York State 1981c). Examinations of 840 men and 62 women referred for evaluation from three public shelters found that 74 percent had histories of psychiatric hospitalization (over half of which took place in New York State) and that 8 percent had arrived at the shelter directly from a mental hospital. Hospitalization was the recommended "service disposition" for more than 200, or 18 percent (New York State 1981b).

A random-sample study of 107 men found that 33 percent had histories of psychiatric hospitalization, 22 percent of them in New York State facilities (New York State 1982c). These findings corroborate those of a city study of 169 "long-term" residents in one public shelter; 33 percent reported past psychiatric hospitalizations. However, 41 percent of those found to have psychiatric histories were never referred to the on-site mental health teams described above for assessment or referral (New York City 1982).

Fewer data on the mental health status of homeless women in public shelters have been compiled. This discrepancy is partly due to the fact that until 1979 only 47 beds for homeless women were available in New York City, and that applicants thought to have a mental disorder were diverted to Bellevue Hospital for a psychiatric clearance. They were granted admission to the shelter only with the written clearance in hand (Baxter and Hopper 1981). A 1975 study did find that 58 percent of the clients at this shelter had a history of at least one hospitalization (Schwam 1979). In a more recent survey of 100 first-time women's shelter applicants, 32 percent reported psychiatric hospitalizations; five had been referred to the shelter upon discharge (Vera Institute of Justice 1981).

Outreach Activities

Homeless people contacted by outreach programs are not likely to be represented in any of the above surveys conducted in the public shelter system. The experience of outreach programs consistently suggests that people remaining in the streets are more elderly and disabled than the population in the public shelters (Lovell and

Barrow, 1981). The frightening scale and Dickensian conditions of public emergency shelter facilities (Baxter and Hopper 1981; Hopper et al. 1982a) effectively exclude those most in need of a protective setting.

Three distinct mobile outreach programs funded by the New York State Office of Mental Health under the auspices of the Community Support Program—Project Reach Out, the Midtown Outreach Program, and Project HELP—provide services to homeless people who reside in the streets, subway stations, bus terminals, and parks. In some cases they make use of two voluntary drop-in centers, the Olivieri Center for Homeless Women and the First Moravian Church Coffee Pot Program (Baxter and Hopper 1981).

Project Reach Out is the oldest of the three programs; since it began operating in July 1979, it has made contact with more than 7,000 individuals (Lovell and Barrow 1981). It has been estimated that from a third to half of them are psychiatrically disabled. The Appendix lists the types of services provided to clients by Project Reach Out.

An analysis of reasons for referral to additional services for more than 1,600 Project Reach Out clients first seen in 1981 showed the largest category to be for shelter and other housing needs, followed by public assistance and substance abuse treatment (Barrow and Lovell 1982). An examination of referral outcomes found that less than one-third of all incomplete referrals resulted from clients' failure to follow through, whereas more than two-thirds were incomplete for such reasons as lack of space or exclusionary admitting criteria. The poor referral outcomes are attributed to time-consuming processes, the inadequate supply of shelter and housing, and complications in or failures of public assistance processing, all of which may result in many referrals per person—as high as 26 referrals in one case.

While almost 500 of Project Reach Out's new clients during 1981 were assessed as psychiatrically disabled, the staff made only 26 referrals to mental health services. Similarly, during the first six months of operation, the Midtown Outreach Program made only 33 such referrals, or 2.2 percent of their contacts. Barrow and Lovell (1983) studied another outreach sample to determine the variables influencing the low percentages of referrals for mental health services. Table 1 shows the study's central finding, namely, highly significant associations between referral to mental health services and referral for housing and public assistance. While the

Table 1
Relationship of mental health referrals to referrals for
housing and public assistance from an outreach program
for the homeless[1]

	Mental health referral			
	Referred		Not referred	
	N	%	N	%
Housing referral[2]				
Yes (N = 39)	24	62	15	38
No (N = 53)	3	6	50	94
Public assistance referral[3]				
Yes (N = 36)	23	64	13	36
No (N = 43)	4	9	39	91

[1]Source: Barrow S, Lovell A: The Referral of Outreach Clients to Mental Health Services: Progress Report for 1982-1983. New York, New York State Psychiatric Institute, 1983
[2]$\chi^2 = 31.19$, df = 1, p ≤ .0001
[3]$\chi^2 = 25.58$, df = 1, p ≤ .0001

idea of causal relationship must be viewed with caution, interviews with outreach program staff "strongly suggest that stable housing and income are almost invariably secured before mental health referrals can be realistically undertaken" (Barrow and Lovell 1983).

The importance of securing income supports has been severely hampered by the increasing difficulty of establishing Supplemental Security Income (SSI) eligibility for the chronically mentally ill, thus increasing their reliance on local public assistance benefits. Reporting for 1981-82, Barrow and Lovell (1982) say that beginning November 1981, *all* Project Reach Out clients applying to SSI on the basis of psychiatric eligibility were turned down, regardless of severity of their disability.

Project HELP is the third of the mobile outreach programs in New York City, instituted in the fall of 1982 with special authority to transport individuals for psychiatric evaluation on an involuntary basis (Project HELP 1983). In more than ten months of operation, 2,218 evaluations of 574 individuals (some were evaluated several times) resulted in only ten (1.7 percent) being judged at sufficient imminent risk of harming themselves or others to warrant involuntary hospitalization. Some 16 percent of the contacts resulted in voluntary referrals to hospitals, shelters, and detoxification programs. The majority remained on the streets.

Outreach and referral for the homeless mentally ill are described by most front-line workers in New York City as processes requiring time, engagement, and building of trust. Similar emphases on time and trust in the successful approach to homeless people have emerged in a Boston study (Bassuk et al. in press), in the activities of the Philadelphia Committee for the Homeless, and in work with homeless people in a San Francisco hospital system (Chafetz and Goldfinger 1984). The latter observe that "to consider both environmental stressors and intrinsic illness process, the time constraints of a usual emergency contact must often be relaxed."

Repeated contacts with homeless individuals and the passage of time often result in varying degrees of engagement and trust. But once engagement has been secured, repeated failure to meet the expressed needs of the homeless can jeopardize the credibility of the outreach effort. More time is lost, and rewards are too few: the distribution of sandwiches, hygiene kits, and blankets may assist with sheer survival, but it hardly constitutes much in terms of achieving mental health goals or minimal standards of care. To some homeless people, who have withstood years of accumulated institutional and social neglect, outreach efforts appear benign at best. To others who are willing to risk some hope for assistance once they have been approached, an artificial response by society is self-deceptive and cruel.

Current Attitudes and Policies

The evidence from survey data and evaluations of mental health outreach programs raises fundamental questions about the responsibilities of policy-makers and service providers. Improved case management and a sophisticated system of coordinated services aimed at linking the homeless individual to the larger service delivery system, along the model of the Community Support Program, is the most common recommendation offered (Bassuk et al. in press; New York State 1981a). Yet the experience of New York City— where thousands of homeless mentally ill cases are managed by three outreach programs, mental health evaluation and referral teams, and two Community Support System teams in the public shelters— has shown limited substantive returns. Most individuals remain on the streets or in emergency shelters indefinitely. During two years of operation, a Community Support System team in the Men's

Shelter assessed several hundred chronically mentally ill persons, but succeeded in placing only 15 men in residences off the Bowery (Hopper et al. 1982b).

The problem is not primarily large, unwieldy caseloads, but rather that very little can actually be done in the absence of supportive shelter or housing resources. Linkage to services holds virtually no meaning when immediate survival remains under constant threat. This is not to say that services are not needed, but to suggest that the value of rehabilitative or therapeutic efforts is so grossly undermined by the reality of life on the streets or in emergency shelters that an alternative approach is warranted.

Mental health professionals commonly adhere to the notion that mentally ill homeless people are noncompliant, are "hard to reach," and shun offers of assistance. While this may be true for a small minority, the bulk of homeless mentally ill identified by outreach programs and shelter staff are most willing to avail themselves of whatever is offered. The demand made on all shelters, drop-in centers, soup kitchens, and outreach programs by the chronically mentally ill far exceeds program capacities.

To focus on the few homeless who are resistant to services does not absolve responsibility toward the remaining majority. A genuinely responsible mental health policy must entail the provision of a decent place to live, complemented by an appropriate level of service. A residence is the base from which social and clinical needs can be addressed simultaneously. Supportive housing is the basic missing mental health provision without which outreach, assessment, and case management simply cannot function effectively.

For several years, the New York State Office of Mental Health has contracted with not-for-profit agencies to establish community residence programs. Since 1980 several Five Year Plans issued by the state (New York State 1981a, 1982b) have indicated that approximately 6,000 community residence beds are needed to accommodate the mentally ill in New York City. As of October 1983 there were 1,300 community residence beds available. However, admission standards and rigid programmatic requirements categorically exclude most mentally ill homeless persons. Only one 24-bed community residence program in the city is known to consider homeless applicants. Moreover, many potential not-for-profit sponsors of such residences cannot withstand the extensive site review procedures and arduous contract negotiations involved, in most cases lasting for more than two years.

The growing public and professional call for reinstitutionalization of the obviously disturbed homeless on the streets can be viewed as regressive and shortsighted. The choice need not be limited to mental hospitalization or a life on the streets. Community housing models abound (Carling and Perlman 1980). The regularity with which mentally disabled homeless people express a strong preference for getting by as they do rather than submitting to hospitalization, where a bed and three meals are assured, says much about human resistance to institutionalization.

A New York State Supreme Court justice refused to appoint a committee of the person for an elderly "shopping bag lady," who had resided on the streets for nine years, as a preparatory step to having her institutionalized as incompetent (Fox 1982). The court saw the effort, by the deputy commissioner of social services, as an attempt to remove a political embarrassment from "the closeness of City Hall," where the woman had lived for years. The court paid particular attention to the woman's adamant refusal to be institutionalized that resulted from her earlier "terrifying experiences in the clinical discipline of hospitals." Such fears, the decision said, are "not based on either illusion or delusion."

To confirm the homeless person's fears of being hospitalized or rehospitalized, after enduring a harsh life outside, strains one's conscience as a mental health professional. To be sure, isolated cases may offer no other recourse. The exception, however, is no basis for a sound mental health policy.

At this time a critical opportunity exists to recover the original goals of community care and to invest in the foundation of this care through housing in the community. Only when rhetorical and service commitments to the chronically mentally ill are capitalized in this way can the future of community care be assured. If housing for the chronically mentally ill is to be developed, direct responsibility lies with the mental health community: no other entity can be expected to assume responsibility for this population. The private and public housing markets are traditionally geared to family units, and are becoming more sensitive to the growing housing needs of single people with higher incomes. The mentally disabled homeless will hardly be afforded priority.

Strategies of Advocacy

Advocacy with and on behalf of homeless mentally ill persons is often vexed by varying conceptualizations of the nature of the problem and by competing interests of advocates themselves. Moreover, advocacy is often carried out on a piecemeal or ad hoc basis, reactive to immediate crisis. To confuse matters further, advocacy has become a legitimizing catchword for virtually anything done in the best interests of "clients."

Conceptualizing Advocacy

When advocacy efforts are directed only toward procuring benefits or services, advocacy becomes nearly synonymous with case management. This conception may be an unnecessary restriction on the proper domain of advocacy. Advocacy in the form of case management may assist some mentally disabled individuals, but it cannot be relied upon to resolve the multitude of broader problems encountered by the mentally disabled or to help reformulate faulty policies. At the same time that advocacy on behalf of the mentally ill homeless must demand the improvement and expansion of present mental health and social services, it must insist upon a reconceptualization of the problems of disability and dependency and, in turn, of the appropriate public response to them. Campbell (1969, 410) proposes the following:

"One simple shift in political posture which would reduce the problem is the shift from the advocacy of a specific reform to the advocacy of the seriousness of the problem, and hence to the advocacy of persistence in alternative reform efforts should the first one fail."

The meaning of rights and entitlements is central to the practice of persistent advocacy. Yet no constitutionally based right to subsistence exists in this country; all "welfare rights" are established by state and local statutes. Moreover, to assert a right is not only to make a principled claim but to insist upon the material resources necessary to implement that right. Acknowledgment of rights commits a society to constructive action toward their fulfillment; limited resources offer no excuse.

Legal Advocacy in New York State:
The Right to Shelter

Legal advocacy is contrained by what is formally embodied in administrative codes, statutes, and constitutions. Interpretations of what is written, procedural maneuvering, ingenious use of legal principles and reasoning, citation of precedents, and, very important, success in implementation, monitoring, and enforcing legal rulings will influence the outcomes of legal efforts to redress fundamental deprivations of rights of the mentally disabled.

The courts in New York have proven to be a useful means of last resort to press for the rights of homeless people and to generate activity from an otherwise intransigent public, but persistence has been necessary. While critics admonish that the courts are not well suited to make shelter policy (Main 1983), the history of the litigation suggests that without such intervention even less would have been accomplished (Hopper and Cox 1982). In this effort the homeless mentally ill have joined to the larger homeless poor population, not on the basis of disability but of their common needs for shelter.

In 1979 *Callahan v. Carey*, a class-action suit filed in the New York State Supreme Court on behalf of homeless men, resulted in a court order, issued on Christmas Eve, establishing the right to shelter for all who applied (Callahan 1979). At that time the city provided homeless men a total of 1,700 beds in flophouses along the Bowery or at Camp Laguardia, a facility located two hours north of the city; the overflow, up to 250 men a night, languished on plastic chairs and on the floor of the "Big Room" at the central processing station of the Municipal Shelter. The plaintiffs' arguments for additional shelter drew on the State Constitution, the New York State Social Services Law, and the New York City Municipal Code, in which provision of the bare necessities of life to the destitute, including shelter, is explicitly mandated.

Ten days following the ruling, the city administration opened a new facility to accommodate men formerly denied shelter for lack of space. Ironically, the building selected was an empty structure within the state mental hospital complex on Wards Island, certified to hold 180 men. By winter's end, more than 600 men were quartered there each night. Again court action was sought; the plaintiffs' objections to the severe overcrowding there, as well as in the flophouses and at Camp Laguardia, resulted in a consent decree, signed in August 1981. The decree reaffirmed the right to shelter and also set minimal physical standards that all public shelters would have to meet.

Within six weeks of signing the decree, the city had run out of available beds, and the court ordered the establishment of 400 new beds within 24 hours. An abandoned school building in Brooklyn was opened the next day. Within a month, that shelter was also full beyond capacity, men were being quartered in the office spaces and lobby of the central intake facility, and the city found itself back in court. An armory was opened the following day. The court proved to be the indispensable prod in the opening of the two other armories in the winter of 1982. Court-motivated preparations for the winter of 1983 included a fourth armory and the use of Creedmoor State Hospital buildings, with a projected capacity for 500 to 1,000 men.

The city refused to voluntarily extend the right to shelter and the terms of the *Callahan* consent decree to homeless women. Another suit, *Eldredge v. Koch*, was filed on behalf of an estimated 6,000 homeless women, and the court ruled in favor of the plaintiffs (Eldredge 1982). Remarkably, the city appealed the decision. The city was told that the case "is so meritorious that it hardly warranted discussion" by the presiding judge, but is continuing the appeals process.

Throughout the expansion of public shelter facilities, the city has claimed that shelter capacity is sufficient to meet the demand and that conditions within shelters are adequate. Translating judicial recognition of a formal right to shelter into actual provision of relief has been a protracted, contested affair. City policy toward the homeless is best described as one that lurches from court order to court order. Practically speaking, since the litigation began, the number of shelter beds for homeless men has increased from 1,700 to 6,000, and the number of shelter beds for homeless women from 47 to more than 700. The annual operating budget for the shelter system rose from $7 million in 1979 to a projected $50 million in 1984.

While shelter conditions have improved somewhat in the wake of the litigation, the shelters remain crowded, desolate, barren, unsafe, and often lacking in adequate shower and toilet facilities. The Fort Washington Armory, for example, shelters more than 960 men on a single drill floor; the hallucinations and bizarre behaviors of the mentally disturbed among them can hardly be quelled by the seven to 12 staff members on a shift. Attention to the ten available showers does not prevent their breaking down either. Chaos prevails.

Many homeless people in the city understandably find the shelters too large, frightening, and degrading, and elect instead to stay on the streets. The elderly and mentally disabled, in particular, are vulnerable prey in public shelters. Outreach programs, in good conscience, can only rarely propose that their clients leave the streets for the city's dole.

Besides affording some homeless people relief from the streets, the litigation has served as a focal point for public scrutiny of the government's policies toward the homeless. The litigation has received continued coverage from the New York media, and both city and state governments have been called upon repeatedly by the press, legislative bodies, and a growing cross section of the general public to improve their care of the homeless.

The limitations of the legal effort are evident upon sight of the public shelters. Men and women simply should not be forced to live, seemingly indefinitely, in a state of emergency. The protracted time and cost of litigious advocacy are other serious limitations, particularly when weighed against such compromised outcomes. The hazards of implementation are rooted in judicial reluctance to "fine tune" the relief ordered, which allows the defendants full discretion over the terms and conditions of shelter. And although emergency shelters may be a necessary, palliative first step, they are no answer to homelessness—homes are.

In May 1982 a class-action suit, *Klostermann v. Carey*, was filed on behalf of homeless men and women with histories of psychiatric hospitalization or current debilitating mental disorders, with the goal of securing housing more appropriate to their special needs (Klostermann 1982). The suit seeks to enforce plaintiffs' statutory, common-law, and constitutional right to minimal housing as part of their right to treatment for mental illness, "to *some residence* more suited to the needs of the mentally ill than a cardboard box, or a park bench."

In response to the suit, state mental health defendants blamed the homeless mentally ill for failing to take "any responsibility for meeting their own needs in the community" and stated that the homeless mentally ill plaintiffs must "join hundreds of thousands of other low-income persons in New York City who must endure inadequate housing." Whatever else the right to treatment includes, statutory law mandates—in accordance with common sense—that it cover, at the very minimum, a place to live. The State Mental Hygiene Law describes obligations to provide least restrictive alternatives and discharge planning, to include "a specific recommendation of the type of residence in which the patient is to live and a listing of the services available to the patient in such a residence" (Mental Hygiene Law 29.15[g]).

The suit was initially dismissed by a judge who referred the mentally ill homeless plaintiffs to "the voting machine as the ultimate public remedy against poor government management (Wallach 1982). A first appeal by plaintiffs was denied. The state's highest court of appeal, which accepts only about 2 percent of cases submitted to it, agreed to hear the case in January 1984.

Other Advocacy Strategies

The limitations of legal advocacy require that other strategies of reform be simultaneously pursued. Legislative efforts, public education, and not-for-profit housing development offer mechanisms for change on a number of levels. Cost-effective arguments are important elements of these approaches.

New York City officials have repeatedly stressed that economies of scale make large, warehouse-type shelters the most cost-effective option. A closer analysis of current shelter policies and their attendant costs makes such a claim suspect. According to a memorandum of the New York City Human Resources Administration dated May 20, 1983, the projected per capita shelter operating costs for fiscal year 1984 range from $18.60 to $39.34 per diem. Variation in costs is a function of the scale of the facility, levels of staffing and services, capital improvements, and payment of rent at certain sites. To illustrate: the projected costs of the Fort Washington Armory, a 950-bed dormitory, are $21.39 per diem. This amounts to more than a half a million dollars monthly. Were each homeless man to be given the per diem equivalent, or $641 per month, many might well secure independent housing and services far superior to the city's dole. The Bushwick Shelter, a most overcrowded and substandard facility for women with an average year-round census of 160, costs $39.34 per diem, or $2.3 million annually. Were equivalent dollars available to the women directly, each would receive $1,180 per month to secure housing and services—hardly a negligible sum.

Obviously, a simple transfer of funds to individuals is not the point. Rather, serious consideration must be given to the return on investment in costly emergency shelter settings. The city's "crisis management" policies both corrode the stability of the individuals served and are self-perpetuating, in that they drain funds away from more permanent solutions.

Given the scarcity of low-cost housing in the city and the inadequate levels of public assistance payments, most individuals are relegated to the costly emergency settings indefinitely. Were homeless people able to move out of shelters to permanent housing, the potential cost savings would be great. Not-for-profit housing and service agencies, such as the St. Francis Friends of the Poor and the West Side cluster, have demonstrated that good-quality permanent housing can be established at a significantly lower cost. The St. Francis Residence, with 100 private rooms, was developed at half the capitalization cost and is run at two-thirds the operating cost of the city's shelters, and residents are provided with private rooms rather than a dormitory bed. The Travelers Hotel, with 27 rooms for 36 women, operates at $16 per diem, or 41 percent of the cost of public women's facilities.

The great majority of tenants in both St. Francis and the Travelers are selected on the basis of having extensive psychiatric histories and no other housing options. It would be reasonable to expect the service costs for this particularly needy subgroup to be higher than for the general homeless population, yet they are not. Permanent housing for homeless people capable of independent functioning would cost even less.

Harvests of waste rather than economies of scale are reaped when crisis management becomes the modus operandi of housing and social service agencies. Two unassailable facts of urban life must be faced squarely: first, emergency shelter, no matter where and how it is provided, will never repair fundamental defects in the structure of the housing market itself, and second, once massiveness of scale and the lure of profit have been removed as sine qua nons of housing for the dependent poor, both cost-efficiency and humanity are served.

Advocacy must pay attention and give priority to the views and direct participation of homeless people themselves. Cook (1979, 81) warns that "the homeless person's vulnerability is such . . . that they fear any 'militant' action on their part may remove the tenuous foothold they presently hold in society." To the extent that advocates make this foothold somewhat more secure, the possibility for direct participation by homeless people gains some strength.

The Homeless Caucus associated with the Central City Shelter Network in San Francisco has emerged as a leader in this regard, as has an organized group in Sacramento that encamped at the doors of a county administrative building in the fall of 1983, in a successful bid for more emergency beds. The Homeless Peer Review in Phoenix has also had direct success: savings from deposits on return cans and bottles were used to rent a small house that has now served more than 100 different individuals. Those who find employment are required to pay rent. When they accumulate savings, they must move on, creating space for others.

Control over one's basic rights and daily activities is an important condition from which to challenge paternalism and the institutional inertia of authorities and the psychiatric profession (Scull 1977; Estroff 1981). The punitive history of care for the chronically mentally disabled in this country is cause enough for the ongoing concern about reform efforts on their behalf.

The Basic Need for Housing

Homelessness today is not fundamentally a social service or mental health problem. It is a state of deprivation defined by the absence of a primary element of civilized life—a home. That said, it must be emphasized that emergency shelters are not homes.

Given the enormous scale of need and the slow rate at which mental health agencies appear to be able to develop housing, there is little doubt that thousands of mentally disabled people will continue to reside on the streets and in emergency shelters for many years to come, unless other types of less costly facilities emerge. The November 1983 opening of an emergency shelter at Creedmoor State Hospital, with a projected capacity of 500 to 1,000 beds, and the 800-bed Keener Shelter in the Manhattan Psychiatric Center on Wards Island may well be signs of things to come. Ironically, the selection of these sites stoked controversy among psychiatric authorities, who alleged that the proximity of the homeless would harmfully impact on their care of psychiatric inpatients. The Board of Visitors of Manhattan Psychiatric Center brought suit in federal district court opposing the Keener Shelter, but the judge determined that the homeless did not pose any danger to the patients (Seide 1982). Officials now claim that the "integrity" of Creedmoor as a mental institution is threatened in ongoing considerations of alternative uses (Rule 1983).

A proposal currently under discussion by a blue-ribbon commission in New York State would shelter 600 homeless mentally ill individuals in dormitory settings of 200 beds each. One, called a domiciliary care facility (DCF), would hold those determined to be in need of hospitalization. Mentally ill residents of DCFs and of shelters would be guaranteed none of the rights (that is, right to treatment, right to a minimum wage for labor performed, and rights related to commitment and discharge) that have been won by patients' advocates in recent years. These rights have been legally limited, in most cases, to inpatients. The conversion of state hospital buildings, as proposed, would require modest cost and staffing levels. The ominous feature is that residents would be as isolated from the community as are inpatients, and yet legally and statistically would be considered to reside in a "community-based" structure.

Some homeless mentally ill will in all likelihood be relegated to the criminal justice system. Others have already arrived there (U.S. General Accounting Office 1979, 1980). According to a study by the Department of Corrections, 10 percent of prisoners in New York City jails are either former psychiatric patients or are in need of hospitalization for severe psychoses (Giordano 1983b).

Mental health professionals occasionally argue that the advocates' position, to meet basic survival needs before providing therapeutic services, minimizes the extent of service needs of the homeless (Begun 1983, Jones 1983). The point merits clarification. Despite the foregoing evidence of the limitations of outreach programs and emergency-shelter psychiatric care, it cannot be concluded that these mental health initiatives have no value. Clearly, unknown thousands of homeless mentally ill in the nation's cities are in desperate need of care. Any attempt to help them, whatever its limitations, must be credited. In the past four years, several thousand homeless mentally ill people in New York City alone have been assisted in some way, or at least have been made known to outreach programs.

Mental health professionals and workers are sometimes the only people who maintain regular contact with and who talk directly and kindly with the homeless mentally ill. They also offer food, equipment for survival outside, shelter beds when available, emergency room attention, assistance with entitlements, and, on rare occasions, a housing placement. Moreover, most voluntary and public agencies sheltering the general homeless population welcome the support of mental health services. The agencies are often ill prepared to meet the special needs and manage the sometimes disruptive behaviors of the mentally ill among their clients. Added staff, treatment expertise, and, particularly, back-up support for crises are important kinds of mental health assistance.

A Taxonomy of Housing Needs

The advocates' position is not to oppose the delivery of much-needed services, but to insist that basic survival needs must be met before therapeutic efforts can have a chance of success. That said, it must be recognized that to expose the outcome limitations of the outreach and assessment initiatives is to confront a deeply ingrained "more services" mentality in the field. Again, the issue is not the value of services in themselves, but the context of their effective deployment. It is only in this way that social and clinical needs—deeply intertwined—can be met. Advocates argue for the necessary extension of mental health care for the homeless—decent shelter and housing—to greatly ease the delivery of services. For the foreseeable future, outreach work to make initial contact with those floundering in fear on the streets will be needed. A legacy of abandonment and mistreatment is not immediately undone.

With respect to the range of shelter needed, we suggest a three-tiered approach:

> *Tier 1:* basic emergency shelters, made as undemanding and accessible as security and hygiene considerations allow, which provide clean bedding, three meals, and adequate security and supervision. In addition, regular clinical attention should be available. Virtually any structure with a roof and walls, such as armories, church basements, and school buildings, can be turned into a shelter.
>
> *Tier 2:* transitional accommodations, a step up from emergency shelters in demands made of residents and services provided, which address differentiated needs of homeless individuals. Intensified efforts to secure entitlements as well as necessary clinical linkages should be made. Placement in tier 2 should be followed by implementation of an individualized plan for permanent housing.
>
> *Tier 3:* long-term supportive residences in the community where privacy and independence are afforded residents and where assistance in obtaining services in times of need is assured.

Shelter and housing models along this graduated continuum, accommodating the mentally ill along with other homeless people, do exist. Rosie's Place and the Pine Street Inn in Boston, Mercy's Hospice in Philadelphia, Emergency Shelter, Inc., in Richmond, the Open Door Community in Atlanta, and the Dwelling Place (among several others) in New York City have demonstrated success in assisting the chronically mentally ill. That they do so by default rather than by design is testament both to the dedication of the workers and to the relative simplicity of the resources needed; quality of concern weighs far more significantly than quantity of space, equipment, and professional time. The Burnside Consortium in Portland, Oregon, and the St. Francis Residence and the Travelers Hotel in New York City provide evidence of the cost-effectiveness and humanity of not-for-profit sponsorship and operation of permanent residences. If each mental health initiative included the development of such shelter and housing programs, the interests of both the homeless mentally ill and the mental health providers would be furthered.

Testing the Right to Shelter

The success of legal advocacy in establishing emergency shelters is not based on the uniqueness of New York state and city law; laws mandating care for the destitute are on the books of most states and municipalities across the country. As of early 1984 the only state other than New York in which the right to shelter had been tested was West Virginia. In February 1983 the West Virginia Supreme Court, citing the Social Services Act, ordered the State Department of Public Welfare to provide emergency shelter and "other appropriate services" to homeless men and women. In early 1984 courts were considering the right to shelter in Hartford, Connecticut, and legal papers related to that right were in preparation in Los Angeles, Philadelphia, and Elizabeth, New Jersey.

Some of this work has been assisted by the National Coalition for the Homeless, headquartered in New York City. The coalition is a federation of individuals, agencies, and organizations representing more than 40 cities and committed to a single principle: decent shelter is a fundamental right in a civilized society. The coalition provides legal counsel to groups in jurisdictions throughout the country who have demonstrated that responsible state and local officials will not extend adequate emergency relief voluntarily.

Experience has shown that the threat of a suit may itself be sufficient to move officials forward—as in the opening of 1,000 new
beds in San Francisco in the winter of 1982.

City officials throughout the country generally view the New
York experience with dread, and often defend their resistance on
the grounds that were shelter provided, their city would become
the mecca for the nation's homeless. These parochial fears are usually
not warranted: studies of homeless populations in several states,
including New York, have found that the majority are indigenous.
In other areas—the Sunbelt and the West Coast—a higher proportion of recent arrivals has been recorded. But it strains credulity to
think that shelters themselves will prove the decisive factor in
attracting people from other regions.

The Public Conscience

To go beyond judicial mandates for assistance for the homeless
means ultimately relying on the public conscience. Sometimes
viciousness toward homeless people is starkly evident, as embodied
in the proposal of a Fort Lauderdale deputy commissioner to spray
trash cans with poison to "get rid of the vermin" searching for
food. Sometimes it receives majority consent, as in the passage of
ordinances in Phoenix prohibiting lying down in public places and
declaring garbage to be city property; thus the act of foraging through
garbage is considered a misdemeanor, subject to jail or fines.

Exploitation or trivialization of the homeless phenomenon in "bag
lady" fashion advertisements for designer bags and lighthearted
images of "bag people" in commercial films and network television
is more and more frequent. A "Street Couture" promotion at
Bloomingdale's in New York City featured mannequins with ban-
daged legs and feet among racks of torn, wrinkled clothing designed
to have a "layered look." A window display at Tiffany & Company
on New York's Fifth Avenue depicted a homeless man and woman
as a backdrop for a $50,000 diamond necklace; the display was
captioned "Enhance your life."

It should not be concluded, however, that hostility and callous-
ness are the prevailing public attitudes. Increasingly, public curiosity, sympathy, and genuine concern are aroused by the sight of
men and women suffering so visibly. The press and electronic media
have also generally proven to be worthy allies in their recent cover-

age of the problem. And many of the public, especially as they go to work or take public transportation, routinely are exposed to the homeless poor. Regular contact with the same homeless person may generate curiosity and interest, which upon reflection may stimulate a feeling of obligation toward that individual or those in similar straits.

Evidence of a progressively better organized and more favorable community response to the homeless is also amassing. In New York City, churches and synagogues, business and civil organizations, universities and seminaries, professional organizations, and thousands of ordinary citizens all take part in various efforts aimed at redressing the plight of the homeless, as do countless coalitions and task forces across the country. Their activities are often determined by the nature of their contact with the homeless as well as by the resources available to them; thus they encompass distant study, bureaucratic meandering, direct service, indignation and outrage, and lobbying and other kinds of advocacy.

Still, resources for housing, shelter, and mental health care for the homeless are so scarce nationwide that, even assuming positive outcomes for these efforts, the prognosis remains bleak. And as fewer and fewer housing, legal, and social service resources are being made available to the poor, the ranks of the homeless are growing rapidly. A backlash "bootstrap" philosophy, more evident during poor economic times, that the poor should fend for themselves threatens to leave more of the poor and the mentally disabled in its wake. The newer Supplemental Security Income review procedures, for example, have resulted in some 350,000 people losing their disability entitlements since the fall of 1981 (Mental Health Law Project 1982). Mental disability has been found to be overrepresented by a factor of three in cases in which benefits are discontinued, and nearly a third of the people whose benefits are discontinued are mentally impaired.

Conclusions

Policies for the mentally ill homeless should be framed to meet the predominant needs of the bulk of this population. To focus on the exceptions—those who allegedly refuse assistance—will mean further rounds of official and professional dithering, will incite objections from civil libertarians, and will leave the majority unaided. It does not require mental health expertise to know that security and stability of environment promote stability of mind. Many of the homeless' fears and unusual behaviors must be first understood as reactions to conditions none of us could bear.

Meeting basic needs is essentially a political question, one of social justice, whereas the provision of services commonly becomes a technical or administrative problem. The domain of mental health practice cannot be restricted to the latter: decades of research have demonstrated intimate relationships between poor social environments and mental instability. Mental health service providers cannot be expected to compensate for elemental scarcities in resources, but they can join a growing constituency in organized efforts to challenge the official priorities that have created homelessness and that continue to swell its ranks.

Appendix
Types of services provided by Project Reach Out to clients[1]

Concrete
Showering
Delousing
Transportation to home
Money (when welfare check was late)
Loans (when food stamps were late)
Money (daily allowance until client was put on welfare)
Grooming articles
Clothes (e.g., thermal underwear, shoes, coat, sweater, socks)
Blanket
Plastic bags
Food
Meals
Cigarettes
Items for housing (clock, radio, hotplate)
Carfare
Magazines, newspapers
Miscellaneous: provision of mailing address: photocopying of legal papers; Christmas gift or birthday party

---

[1]Source: Barrow S, Lovell A: Evaluation of Project Reach Out, 1981-1982. New York, New York State Psychiatric Institute, 1982

Clinical
Engagement and trust-building (talking with client, etc.)
Crisis intervention
Supportive interpretation of delusions
Social-medical counseling (before operation, after radiation treatment, etc.)
Psychological counseling
Family counseling
Orientation to alcoholism programs
Counseling after victimization (mugging, etc.)
Contacting "network" members (sister, cousin, former roommate, friend, etc.)
Job counseling
Counseling on finding housing

Case management
Making appointments
Helping client keep appointments
Escorting to new program
Escorting to appointments
Discussion, liaison with other Community Support System program workers
Preparation for and accompaniment to housing intake appointments
Discussion of relapse with psychiatric social worker
Negotiating with hotel manager about handling of funds
Persuading private shelter to keep client until public assistance check arrives
Negotiating with super (e.g., to fix broken lock, replace broken window, fumigate)
Representing client in welfare hearing
Arranging transfer of client to hospital closer to his home
Getting attention for client in emergency room
Advocating for client with doctor
Persuading shelter to shower and delouse client

Socialization
Opening savings account for client
Showing client how to do banking
Teaching management and budgeting of funds
Supervising funds

Taking client to Thrift Shop
Helping client move into room
Supervising maintenance of client's room
Counseling client about living conditions
Explaining importance of showering
Explaining importance of delousing
Helping client keep calendar (time orientation)
Preparing client for interview (job, housing intake, etc.)
Preparing client for court case

Housing
Providing room
Looking for alternative housing (before eviction, hotel closing, etc.)
Explaining tenants' rights
Discussing housing possibilities (adult home, SRO, etc.)
Explaining rent, dispossession notice, etc.

Public assistance/economic
Filling out forms
Writing letters of referral, introduction
Re-opening closed case
Tracking down lost check
Advising about lost check
Helping client prepare for fair hearing
Accompanying client to welfare office and advocating for client
Interpreting regulations

References

Arce AA, Tadlock M, Vergare MJ, et al: A psychiatric profile of street people admitted to an emergency shelter. Hosp Community Psychiatry 34:812-817, 1983

Baasher T, Elhakim ASED, El Fawal K, et al: On vagrancy and psychosis. Community Ment Health J 19:27-41, 1983

Barrow S, Lovell A: Evaluation of Project Reach Out, 1981-1982. New York, New York State Psychiatric Institute, 1982

Barrow S, Lovell A: The Referral of Outreach Clients to Mental Health Services: Progress Report for 1982-1983. New York, New York State Psychiatric Institute, 1983

Bassuk E, Rubin L, Lauriat A: Is homelessness a mental health problem? Am J Psychiatry (in press)

Baxter E, Hopper K: Private Lives/Public Spaces: Homeless Adults on the Streets of New York City. New York, Community Service Society, 1981

Begun M: Misconceptions of homelessness. Presented to the Metropolitan Council, American Jewish Congress, Mar 10, 1983, New York City

Bellamy C: From County Asylums to City Streets. Office of the New York City Council President, July 1979

Brown C, Paredes R, Stark L: The Homeless of Phoenix: A Profile. Phoenix South Community Mental Health Center, 1982

Callahan v Carey, New York State Supreme Court, index no 42582/79

Campbell DT: Reforms as experiments. Am Psychol 24:409-429, 1969

Carling P, Perlman L (eds): Readings in Housing and Mental Health. Prepared for a HUD-HHS technical assistance workshop, Demonstration Program for Deinstitutionalization of the Chronically Mentally Ill. Rockville, Md, National Institute of Mental Health, 1980

Carmody D: New York is facing crisis on vagrants. New York Times, June 28, 1981

Chafetz L, Goldfinger S: Residential instability among a psychiatric emergency service clientele. Psychiatr Q 56:20-34, 1984

Chicago Task Force on the Homeless: Homelessness in Chicago. Oct 1983

Conart House. San Francisco Support Services: A Comprehensive Approach to Services for the Chronically Mentally Ill. San Francisco, 1982

Connell S: Letter to the editor. New York Times, Oct 27, 1982

Cook T (ed): Vagrancy: Some New Perspectives. New York, Academic Press, 1979

Cuomo M: 1933/1983: Never Again: A Report to the National Governors' Association Task Force on the Homeless. Albany, New York State Executive Chamber, 1983

Eldredge v Koch, New York State Supreme Court, index no 41494/82

Estroff S: Making It Crazy: An Ethnography of Psychiatric Clients in an American Community. Berkeley, University of California Press, 1981

Fox M: Ruling on Homeless Women. New York Law Journal, Oct 13, 1982

Freeman SJ, et al: Psychiatric disorder in a skid-row mission population. Compr Psychiatry 20:454-462, 1979

Giordano M: City giving 2.6 million to mental clinics. New York Daily News, Nov 22, 1983a

Giordano M: 10% of city inmates mentally ill, study finds. New York Daily News, Jan 30, 1983b

Green CB: Housing single, low-income individuals. Presented at the Conference on New York State Social Welfare Policy, Oct 1-2, 1982, New York

Haveliwala Y: Community help for the homeless (letter). New York Times, Oct 8, 1981

Herman R: New York City psychiatric wards overflow as Albany changes its mental health role. New York Times, Dec 8, 1980

Hopper K, Cox S: Litigation in advocacy for the homeless: the case of New York City. Development: Seeds of Change 2: 1982

Hopper K, Baxter E, Cox S, et al: One Year Later: The Homeless Poor in New York City, 1982. New York, Community Service Society, 1982a

Hopper K, Baxter E, Cox S: Not making it crazy: the young homeless patients in New York City. New Directions for Mental Health-Services, no 14:33-42, 1982b

Jones RE: Street people and psychiatry: an introduction. Hosp Community Psychiatry 34:807-811, 1983

Jurow GL: Financing long-term care of the chronically mentally impaired in New York State: an issue analysis. Presented at the State Communities Aid Association's Institute on Care of the Mentally Impaired in the Long-Term Care System, June 4, 1979, New York City

Katz S: NBC Channel 4 interview by Gabe Pressman with the New York State commissioner of mental health, Dec 23, 1983

Klostermann v Carey, New York State Supreme Court, index no 11270/82

Leach J, Wing J: Helping Destitute Men. London, Tavistock Publications, 1980

Lipton FR, Sabatini A, Katz SE: Down and out in the city: the homeless mentally ill. Hosp Community Psychiatry 34:818-821, 1983

Lovell A, Barrow S: Psychiatric disability and homelessness: a look at Manhattan's Upper West Side. Presented at the Conference on the Community Support Population: Designing Alternatives in an Uncertain Environment, Syracuse, NY, Nov 19, 1981

Main T: New York City's lure to the "homeless." Wall Street Journal, Sept 12, 1983

Mental Health Law Project: Arbitrary Reductions of Disability Roles. Washington, Mar 3, 1982

Morse G: A Conceptual Paper to Develop a Comprehensive System of Care for Chronically Mentally Disturbed Homeless Persons in St Louis, Missouri. St Louis, Community Support Program, 1982a

Morse G: Homeless Men: A Study of Service Needs, Predictor Variables, and Subpopulations. St Louis, University of Missouri, Department of Psychology, 1982b

New York City Human Resources Administration: Chronic and Situational Dependency: Long-Term Residents in a Shelter for Men. New York, May 1982

New York City Office of the Comptroller. Performance Analysis of Programs of New York State Assistance to New York City Agencies Serving Deinstitutionalized Psychiatric Patients, Sept 21, 1979

New York State Department of Social Services: Final Report of the SRO Project: Survey of the Needs and Problems of the Single Room Occupancy Hotel Residents on the Upper West Side of Manhattan, New York City. New York, May 7, 1980

New York State Office of Mental Health: Memo from Policy Planning and Program Development Division, Oct 29, 1980, with report dated Mar 31, 1980

New York State Office of Mental Health: Five Year Comprehensive Plan for Mental Health Services. Albany, 1981a

New York State Office of Mental Health: Shelter Outreach Project: Statistical Report, February to June, 1981. New York City, Regional Office of Mental Health, 1981b

New York State Office of Mental Health: Who Are the Homeless Mentally Ill? This Month in Mental Health, Apr 1981c

New York State Office of Mental Health: Committee Report to the Commissioner of Mental Health. Albany, Jan 1, 1982a

New York State Office of Mental Health: Five Year Comprehensive Plan for Mental Health Services. Albany, 1982b

New York State Office of Mental Health: Who Are the Homeless? A Study of Randomly Selected Men Who Use the New York City Shelters. Albany, May 1982c

New York State Senate, Senate Democratic Task Force on the City of New York: Shelter Care for Men. Albany, 1976

President's Commission on Mental Health: Report to the President. Washington, 1978

Presley A: Health problems of homeless people in the Denver metro area. Presented at the American Public Health Association meeting, Dallas, Nov 15, 1983

Project HELP: Summary Report October 30, 1982, to August 31, 1983. New York State Community Support Services, Gouverneur Hospital, New York City, 1983

Reich R, Siegel L: The emergence of the Bowery as a psychiatric dumping ground. Psychiatr Q 50:191-201, 1978

Rule S: 2,000 more beds for the homeless planned in city. New York Times, Nov 24, 1983, pp A1,B9

Schwam K: Shopping Bag Ladies: Homeless Women. New York, Manhattan Bowery Corp, 1979

Scull AT: Decarceration: Community Treatment and the Deviant: A Radical View. Englewood Cliffs, NJ, Prentice-Hall, 1977

Seide v Prevost, 81 Civ 6205 SD New York, Mar 19, 1982

State Communities Aid Association: Housing for the Chronically Mentally Ill. New York, Feb 1982

Sullivan R: The homeless: officials differ on the causes. New York Times, Nov 24, 1983

Tidmarsh D, Wood S: Psychiatric aspects of destitution: a study of the Camberwell Reception Centre, in Evaluating a Community Psychiatric Service: The Camberwell Register 1964-1971. Edited by Wing JK, Hailey AM. New York, Oxford University Press, 1972

US General Accounting Office: Returning the Mentally Disabled to the Community: Government Needs to Do More. Washington, US Government Printing Office, 1977

US General Accounting Office: Prison Mental Health Care Can Be Improved by Better Management and More Effective Federal Aid (GGD-80-11). Washington, 1979

US General Accounting Office: Jail Inmates' Mental Health Care Neglected:

State and Federal Attention Needed (GGD-81-5). Washington, 1980

US Department of Health and Human Services and US Department of Housing and Urban Development: Report on Federal Efforts to Respond to the Shelter and Basic Living Needs of Chronically Mentally Ill Individuals. Washington, Department of Health and Human Services, Feb 1983

Vera Institute of Justice: First Time Users of Women's Shelter Services: a preliminary analysis. New York, 1981

Wallach RW: Klosterman v Carey. Decision no 11270/82, New York State Supreme Court, Aug 20, 1982

Chapter 7

Shelter Is Not Enough: Clinical Work With the Homeless Mentally Ill

Robert E. Drake, M.D., Ph.D.
David A. Adler, M.D.

A substantial number of homeless individuals have chronic psychotic illnesses and histories of psychiatric hospitalization (Arce et al. 1983; Freeman et al. 1979; Lipton et al. 1983; Segal and Baumohl 1980). However, studies of the homeless frequently ignore or minimize the clinical difficulties of providing care for these patients (Baxter and Hopper 1981, 1982; Gershberg 1983; Larew 1980). Along with the lay literature, these studies imply that the availability of low-cost housing and social services would remedy the problem of homelessness. When patients' refusal of services is cited, caregivers are sometimes severely rebuked for suggesting that anyone would decline services offered in a dignified manner.

Although low-cost housing and social services would help a large proportion of the homeless mentally ill, our clinical experience tells us that a number of these individuals present a more formidable challenge. We therefore believe that an exclusive focus on services must be tempered by several clinical realities. Linking the homeless mentally ill with available resources is, in practice, an enormously

Dr. Drake is instructor in the Department of Psychiatry at Harvard Medical School and co-director of ambulatory community services at the Cambridge-Somerville Mental Health Center in Cambridge, Massachusetts. Dr. Adler is associate professor in the Department of Psychiatry at Tufts University School of Medicine and associate chief of the Division of Adult Psychiatry of the New England Medical Center in Boston. The authors wish to acknowledge the assistance of Randy Bailey, R.N., Lori Jannen, and Bill Salton in the preparation of this chapter.

difficult task. Caregivers who work with this population daily confront the paradox that extremely needy individuals reject a variety of services offered with good will and make choices that do not appear to be in their own best interests. Denying rather than understanding these facts only impedes progress in helping the homeless.

In this chapter we will describe some of the practical problems that caregivers face in attempting to help these patients. The discussion begins with case histories of four typical patients who have been homeless in the Boston area. The first patient is an intermittent shelter user; the second has been banned from shelters and lives on the streets; the third is a regular resident of a shelter for actively drinking alcoholics; and the fourth is a patient who was rescued from the streets.

Case Examples

Case 1: The Intermittent Shelter User

"I can't stand any place I am!"

Mr. M is a 54-year-old man with chronic schizophrenia. He first became psychotic at age 20 and has been continuously psychotic for 34 years. He currently takes antipsychotic medications and attends a community day program for deinstitutionalized patients. He receives Social Security assistance and a Veterans Administration pension. His living situation alternates between a hotel of his choice, two shelters for the homeless, and a community mental health center inpatient unit.

Mr. M denies any psychiatric disorder. He insists that his problem is only "storms," which occur frequently and interfere with his capacity to think and function. He evidences loose associations, bizarre thoughts, and a shifting delusional picture, with occasional auditory hallucinations and thought blocking. At his best he is socially inappropriate, agitated, and distant. As his "storms" get worse, he becomes increasingly paranoid, frightened, hallucinatory, agitated, and bizarre. His life plans are unrealistic, and he has little motivation to change.

Mr. M's history includes more than 40 psychiatric hospitalizations in the VA and community mental health systems. Since deinstitutionalized into a supervised community living situation, he has never stayed in one place for long. During the past four years, he has lived in two community residences, a board-and-care home, a halfway house, three nursing homes, a veterans' home, one hotel (recurrently), three shelters for the homeless, and the CMHC inpatient unit. After a brief stay in any of these places, Mr. M typically says, "I can't stand this place any longer. The storms are all around me. Can't you get me into something else?" If hospitalization or other housing is not arranged, he leaves anyway. He often requests a return to a previous placement, and he consistently blames the mental health system for not providing adequate housing.

Case 2: Banned From Shelter

"This is no place for an intellectual."

Mr. K is a 27-year-old single man who carries the diagnosis of chronic schizophrenia. He first became psychotic while attending college in Boston, had one brief remission of symptoms, and has now been continuously psychotic for five years since college graduation. He has a case manager but refuses treatment, including medications, with the exception of demanding that forms be filled out for welfare. He receives Supplemental Security Income and spends the money entirely on expensive radio equipment, which he then uses for barter in the streets. For the past five years he has lived almost entirely on the streets of Boston, New York, and San Francisco.

Although continuously paranoid, delusional, and hallucinatory, Mr. K does not physically threaten himself or others and is able to care for himself. He therefore rarely spends time in hospitals. He has had only four brief admissions during several years of illness. He not only denies mental illness but also insists that he is superior to other patients and staff. He treats all caregivers with contempt. Mr K spends most of his time hanging around a local university with which he has a delusional affiliation. Passing himself off as an academic, he uses his caustic wit to keep people at a distance. During the winter he regularly sleeps in the ducts of the university heating system. Following angry confrontations with university authorities, he turns to shelters for food and a bed.

When he does seek shelter, Mr. K clearly finds it a humiliating experience and verbally abuses clients as well as staff. He insists that staff are part of a plot to control him and typically escalates his verbal assaults until he is asked to leave. After a series of such incidents, he is temporarily banned from one shelter after another. He has also been asked to leave two halfway houses for constant verbal harassment of clients and staff. On the streets he appears much calmer. He takes great pride in his independence and ability to survive without help. He claims to prefer the streets to shelters and other housing.

Case 3: The Regular Shelter Resident

"At least on the streets I'm free."

Mr. P is a 38-year-old single man with chronic schizophrenia and alcoholism. He began to drink alcoholically in early adolescence and was first noted to be psychotic after sobering up in detention at age 17. He currently attends a social club for patients, attends Alcoholics Anonymous daily, takes antipsychotic medications, maintains a good alliance with his case manager of three years, and receives Supplemental Security Income. Nevertheless, he continues to drink daily, and when not in a detoxification center, hospital, or jail, he lives on the streets and sleeps in a shelter for actively drinking alcoholics.

Mr P worries about his inability to control his drinking. He spends most of his money on alcohol and is usually a pleasant drinker, but periodically comes to the attention of police because of violent outbursts. Currently he is on probation for charges of drunken and disorderly conduct, destruction of property, assaulting a police officer, and public loitering. When Mr. P sobers up in jail, hospital, or detoxification center, he experiences frightening hallucinations and believes that his thoughts are broadcast aloud. These symptoms have never been controlled by medications, but they become tolerable if Mr. P stays slightly intoxicated.

Thus for the past ten years, he has not gone for more than three days outside an institution without drinking. Drinking eventually initiates again the cycle of violent behavior, arrest, jail or transfer to a hospital, detoxification, and psychosis. Despite more than 30 hospital admissions, several jail terms, and innumerable detoxifications, Mr. P has not achieved sobriety outside an institution for nearly 20 years.

Mr. P believes that he will be institutionalized permanently when he develops Korsakoff's disease and can no longer care for himself.

For now he prefers to live on the streets and sleep in a shelter. He dislikes the confinement of institutions, the homosexual demands in jails, the intolerable psychotic symptoms when sober, and the lack of freedom in detoxification centers. The freedom he values so highly may be only the opportunity to drink; no treatment has diminished his thirst for alcohol. Meanwhile Mr. P is slowly killing himself in the community.

Case 4: A Treatment Success

"I just want to be a rock star."

Ms. L is a 30-year-old single woman who carries the diagnosis of chronic schizophrenia. She first became psychotic at age 17 and spent ten years on the streets before responding to treatment. She currently lives in a structured halfway house, attends a social club for patients, takes antipsychotic medications, receives Supplemental Security Income, and maintains regular contact with her case manager and her therapist.

In adolescence Ms. L began experiencing auditory hallucinations, paranoia, ideas of reference, and grandiose delusions centering on her identity as a famous rock star. After her initial psychotic break, she lived on the streets or in shelters for almost ten years, interrupted only by brief hospitalizations. Almost 30 hospitalizations were terminated after a few days when she signed out against medical advice. She was never on any medications long enough to determine whether she would respond.

During the years of living on the streets and in various shelters, Ms. L used illicit drugs and alcohol, was often abused, was occasionally violent toward others, and formed no close relationships. She bore two illegitimate children, who were given up for adoption. As part of denying her illness, she consistently refused offers of help from caregivers in shelters and hospitals. She declined welfare money and housing. When her grandiosity or delusions were questioned in any of these settings, she became violent or fled.

This pattern was interrupted two and a half years ago when Ms. L destroyed her parents' home in a violent outburst and was court-committed to the state hospital for one year on the grounds of dangerousness. During the first five months of hospitalization, she continued to resist treatment and to be preoccupied with her delusional world. For the first time, however, Ms. L did take antipsychotic medications on a regular basis and met consistently with one staff member whom she began to trust. After six months she began to relate to other staff, including the community case manager with whom she had refused involvement during her years on the streets. Her paranoia, ideas of reference, and auditory hallucinations began to diminish.

At the end of her year's commitment, Ms. L elected to stay in the hospital and to plan an appropriate discharge. She was transferred soon thereafter to a community hospital. She began working with a new therapist who would follow her regularly after discharge and continued to meet with her community case manager. Supplemental Security Income was applied for, and Ms. L was accepted into a halfway house. The main condition for placement was her controlling the violent outbursts, and they decreased steadily. Over five months she slowly made the transition to a social club during the days and the halfway house at nights. Her mental status and ability to control her behavior continued to improve slowly. Discharge from the hospital occurred without problems.

At this time Ms. L has lived in the community for more than a year. She continues to make steady progress in developing social skills and behavioral control, even though she remains delusional much of the time. She is forming some friendships, participates regularly in all treatments offered, and feels hopeful about the future.

Recognizing Clinical Realities

These four patients in many ways exemplify some of the more difficult problems among the homeless mentally ill in Boston. Their case histories provide a realistic view of the psychopathology, housing problems, and treatment difficulties that caretakers confront. In the first place, they exhibit serious, chronic, and refractory psychopathology. Chronic psychotic illness and substance abuse produce withdrawn, fearful, and help-rejecting behaviors. These patients typically deny illness, seek interpersonal distance, and retreat into a delusional world of paranoia, grandiosity, or disorganized oblivion. In addition, they often manifest difficult behaviors—violence, substance abuse, or just boisterous unruliness. Life on the streets, with its realistic dangers, reinforces their paranoia and exacerbates their other problems.

These patients spend relatively little time in hospitals. When hospitalized, they behave well enough to exercise their right to refuse treatment and leave after brief admissions. They are either "young chronics" (Pepper and Ryglewicz 1982) who have never had significant institutionalization and deny their illnesses, or older, chronically hospitalized patients who have now been "deinstitutionalized" but not successfully placed in the community (Borus 1981).

As the cases above illustrate, even when low-cost housing is available, these patients often gravitate toward a disorganized, isolated life-style in the streets. Many have been evicted from their own homes, several apartments, halfway houses, and rooms because of their difficult and "unacceptable" behavior. They sometimes settle into shelters, but even shelters have limits on behavior so that they often spend time on the streets. Life on the streets and in shelters, while dangerous, affords them freedom, anonymity, and interpersonal distance. In congruence with their paranoid delusions, they often develop a counterculture identity that glorifies the independence of street life.

Because life on the streets is so difficult and so foreign to most of us, its adaptive significance is often missed. Just as earlier researchers had difficulty understanding that many patients liked hospitals and preferred them to the community (Drake and Wallach 1979), researchers today often fail to appreciate the attraction of life in the shelters and on the streets. Individuals with a chronic psychosis simply do not see the world in the same way as professional caregivers. They frequently make choices for themselves about living situations, relationships, and treatment that are different from those that caregivers would make for them. They typically refuse medications and psychotherapy. They form attachments slowly and mistrust caretakers, who threaten not only their need for interpersonal distance but also their denial, delusional rationalizations, and countercultural values and identity. They sometimes even refuse housing and welfare money. Their attempts to cope with chronic mental illness involve a complex interaction of many forces (Adler et al. 1984).

A cross-sectional view of the homeless mentally ill based on interviews can mislead us in several respects. Patients who have migrated to the anonymity of street life are reluctant to reveal their histories. In addition, denial, psychotic distortion, and projection are psychological coping mechanisms that grossly misrepresent reality. Patients often deny much of their behavior as well as their illness. The same patient who appears docile and compliant today may have a history of many episodes of violence. Past failures may be denied or rationalized. The paranoia attributed to street life is often present—or even exacerbated—in other living situations. For psychiatric patients, as for nonpatients, attitudes are poorly correlated with behaviors (Ajzen and Fishbein 1977). What people say they want in their lives is often inconsistent with how they actually lead their lives and the behavioral choices they actually make.

Conclusions

These case studies, which provide a longitudinal perspective, illustrate some of the practical difficulties caretakers encounter in trying to help psychotic patients in shelters and on the streets. The problems are much more complex than inaccessibility of low-income housing and social services. Even when these services are available, patients often migrate toward the crevices of the cities. Engaging them in treatment, particularly when their psychopathology and disruptive behavior cannot be contained, is sometimes an impossible task. Given these clinical realities, what can we recommend?

First, we must *avoid blame*. Blaming the patients for choosing an unstable life-style is obviously not helpful. But blaming caregivers is equally misguided. Chronic psychotic illness, alcoholism, and the other serious disorders from which these patients suffer are poorly understood. Our treatments, even under ideal circumstances, are often grossly inadequate. This was true when these patients were largely contained in hospital settings, and it remains true now that they are in the community. Furthermore, treating seriously disturbed patients living in the streets is a task for which we have relatively little experience and no established guidelines.

Second, we must *understand how chronic psychopathology interacts with community pressures* outside of institutions to push people toward disorganized, isolated lives in the inner cities. A lack of resources, particularly housing, is of course important. The above cases illustrate, however, that even when resources and community caseworkers are available, treatment in the community can be highly problematic. Many of these patients are headed on inexorably self-destructive courses.

Third, as a corollary of the second point, we must *be prepared for the inevitable conflicts between need and acceptance of services*, and between patients' and caregivers' perspectives. Even when services are offered in the most sensitive and dignified manner, they may be refused. Linking patients with resources was easier during the early waves of deinstitutionalization, when released patients had less severe psychopathology and before the arrival of a new generation of patients with chronic illness who have never been institutionalized. The clinical task now becomes exceedingly complex; these patients do not make an easy or rapid adjustment to having mental illness. Without the experience of prolonged hospitalization, they learn to recognize and manage their illnesses more slowly. While living outside of hospitals has enormous advantages for some patients, others inevitably flounder. Like diabetic patients who have not learned to control their illness, they suffer the consequences of living with an illness that controls them.

Reclaiming patients from the streets is exceedingly difficult. The successes that we have had, like Case 4 above, are often based on a traditional model of forced confinement and treatment. After several months of containment of destructive behavior, adequate antipsychotic medications, and caring treatment, some patients begin to emerge from psychosis. At that point, they make different choices for themselves and use the treatment alliance to further their gains. However, most patients on the streets do not meet the criteria for a forced long-term confinement and do not choose it for themselves. Even when they do prefer hospitalization, they are often discharged rapidly. Given the present constraints, we will not be successful in attracting all patients into treatment.

Finally, our responsibility as clinicians is to *advocate for patients' health*. Economic, political, and legal decisions that channel patients onto the streets and potentially toward early deaths should be resisted. The wisdom of allowing patients to make decisions that are based in psychosis and clearly self-destructive must be questioned. As stated above, some patients cannot be treated effectively without containment. Their health—and even survival—depends upon the use of long-term hospitalization (Group for the Advancement of Psychiatry 1982) or highly structured alternatives in the community (Lamb 1980).

This chapter describes only homeless patients with chronic psychosis. These remarks should not be generalized to other homeless groups, but we believe they are relevant to a substantial minority of the homeless. We have described the clinical dilemmas of treating these patients but not some of the innovative treatment approaches. They are presented in other chapters.

Although the homeless mentally ill are themselves a heterogeneous group, we can summarize several general points. These patients typically have severe psychopathology characterized by poor reality testing. Because of recent shifts in social policy and the commitment laws, they spend little time in hospitals. Their psychopathology and concomitant difficult behaviors are contained less well outside the hospital so that placement in low-income housing is problematic, even when such housing is available. Many of these patients have histories of failure in numerous living situations. They clearly need much more than housing and social services before their psychiatric illness is treated. Furthermore, without structure and containment their psychopathology often interacts with the pressures of street life to produce a vicious pattern of treatment refusal and slow self-destruction.

References

Adler D, Drake R, Stern R: Viewing chronic mental illness: a conceptual framework. Compr Psychiatry 25:192-207, 1984

Ajzen I, Fishbein M: Attitude-behavior relations: a theoretical analysis and review of empirical research. Psychol Bull 84:888-918, 1977

Arce AA, Tadlock M, Vergare MJ, et al: A psychiatric profile of street people admitted to an emergency shelter. Hosp Community Psychiatry 34:812-816, 1983

Baxter E, Hopper K: Private Lives/Public Spaces: Homeless Adults on the Streets of New York City. New York, Community Service Society, 1981

Baxter E, Hopper K: The new mendicancy: homeless in New York City. Am J Orthopsychiatry 52:393-408, 1982

Borus JF: Deinstitutionalization of the chronically mentally ill. N Engl J Med 305:339-342, 1981

Drake R, Wallach M: Will mental patients stay in the community? a social psychological perspective. J Consult Clin Psychol 47:285-294, 1979

Freeman SJ, Formo A, Alampu AG, et al: Psychiatric disorder in a skid-row mission population. Compr Psychiatry 20:454-462, 1979

Group for the Advancement of Psychiatry: The Positive Aspects of Long Term Hospitalization in the Public Sector for Chronic Psychiatric Patients. New York, Mental Health Materials Center, 1982

Gershberg J: Homeless in New York. The Pharos, 7-10, Fall 1983

Lamb HR: Structure: the neglected ingredient of community treatment. Arch Gen Psychiatry 37:1224-1228, 1980

Larew RI: Strange strangers: serving transients. Social Casework 63:107-112, 1980

Lipton FR, Sabatini A, Katz SE: Down and out in the city: the homeless mentally ill. Hosp Community Psychiatry 34:817-821, 1983

Pepper B, Ryglewicz H (eds): The Young Adult Chronic Patient, New Directions for Mental Health Services, no 14, 1982

Segal S, Baumohl J: Engaging the disengaged: proposals on madness and vagrancy. Social Work 25:358-365, 1980

Chapter 8

Constructing Support Systems for Homeless Chronic Patients

Frank R. Lipton, M.D.
Albert Sabatini, M.D.

The delusional schizophrenic who used to anoint his followers on the back wards of state mental hospitals now anoints passersby on the streets, in subways, and in the public spaces of society. The chronic mentally ill were once cared for in asylums that provided refuge and custodial care. Many are now left to their own devices, scavenging through the garbage to find a meal and panhandling on the streets to obtain money, wearing layer upon layer of dirty, tattered clothes and rags to protect themselves from the elements. Muttering to themselves, finding warmth over street grates, or carting their meager possessions in shopping bags, the homeless mentally ill have become blatant manifestations of our society's failure to care for those who cannot care for themselves.

In certain respects it is somewhat disconcerting that this Task Force report must still be written. For the past ten to 15 years, mental health professionals have been describing the plight of the chronic mental patient and denouncing the consequences of poorly planned and implemented deinstitutionalization policies. They have been calling for the development of a comprehensive network of community services that would be capable of caring for the chronic

Dr. Lipton is director of emergency services at Bellevue Psychiatric Hospital in New York City and assistant clinical professor of psychiatry at New York University School of Medicine. Dr. Sabatini is medical director at Bellevue Psychiatric Hospital and associate professor of clinical psychiatry at New York University School of Medicine.

mentally ill living in the community. Yet the insights, recommendations, and pleas of these professionals have essentially gone
unheeded. The plight of chronic patients living in the community
has grown more desperate, and homelessness is a reflection of their
increasingly extreme predicament. The time has come to stop
squabbling over percentages, to stop pointing the finger of blame,
and to begin to tackle the problems engendered by homelessness
among the mentally ill.

We will discuss deinstitutionalization as it relates to the homeless,
describe characteristics that the homeless mentally ill share with
other groups of psychiatric patients, and outline the service needs
of homeless patients. In the major part of the chapter we will describe
eight specific types of services and supports that should be offered
to the homeless mentally ill, starting with contact services and shelter and ranging through residential, financial, psychiatric, and rehabilitative services to "connecting links" and governmental and societal
supports.

Two Flaws in Deinstitutionalization

In examining the concept of deinstitutionalization and the policies
associated with its enactment, two major flaws emerge. The first is
apparent in the conceptual framework upon which deinstitutionalization was based. The "traditional" biomedical model that held
preeminence in the first half of the 20th century viewed the development of chronic impairment as a phenomenological manifestation
of the natural course of schizophrenia. This concept was reflected
in Kraepelinian and Bleulerian approaches to diagnosis.

Increasing attention to psychosocial variables brought this view
into question. Eventually the idea evolved that the marked dependency, social isolation, and low levels of functioning seen in the
chronic mental disorders could be minimized, if not totally prevented,
by providing more humane care within the community as opposed
to long-term-care institutions. This view was reflected in Goffman's
concept (1959) of "institutionalism" and Gruenberg's initial
descriptions (1967) of the "social breakdown syndrome." This philosophical and ideological shift in thinking was not adequately vali-
dated, yet it became one of the major conceptual bases for moving
the locus of care into the community. Coincidentally, it also shifted
the burden of fiscal responsibility from the state to the federal

government, and the burden of clinical responsibility to the local government.

The second major flaw is evident in the manner in which deinstitutionalization was implemented. Conceptually inherent in the policy of deinstitutionalization was the development of a network of community services that would facilitate the reintegration of chronic patients into the community. However, the network has rarely been adequately developed. The partial dismantling of the state hospital system has left a massive void in the delivery of mental health care. With the locus of care shifting from large, isolated state hospitals, which provided at least custodial care, to carelessly developed, poorly coordinated, and inadequately funded community-based services, the chronic psychiatric patient has fallen by the wayside. Homelessness is in part a consequence of the failure to develop sufficient social supports for a population that suffers from severe intrinsic impairment.

These two flaws are interrelated. The notion that chronic handicap would vanish with the dissolution of institutions for the mentally ill permitted policy-makers to neglect the development of the necessary network of services. The high incidence of homelessness among the mentally ill (Arce et al. 1983; Bassuk in press; Lipton et al. 1983), the criminalization of the chronically impaired (Lamb and Grant 1982), the high rates of recidivism among chronic patients (Goldfinger et al. 1984), and the apparent emergence of a new category of young adult chronic patients (Pepper et al. 1981; Schwartz and Goldfinger 1981) are the sequelae of a poorly conceptualized and inadequately implemented policy. Deinstitutionalization not only altered the face of our mental health care system; it markedly altered the career and life-style of the chronic mental patient.

Common Characteristics

The similarities and relationships between the homeless mentally ill and several other groups described in the psychiatric literature are not surprising. A significant proportion of the homeless mentally ill fall into the category of "young adult chronic patients" and vice versa (Lamb 1982; Pepper et al. 1981). Lamb, describing patients living in the community, emphasizes their low levels of functioning, high levels of dependency, and marked social isolation (Lamb 1979; Lamb and Goertzel 1977). Wing (1978), exploring the roots of chronicity, describes two groups of patients; one he labels the "new long stay in hospital," and the other the "chronically disabled outside hospital."

Wing describes the former group as follows: "Nearly all were socially isolated, unmarried, out of touch or at odds with their families or friends, and had few occupational skills. Many required continued treatment of various kinds but the overriding need was for sheltered residential accommodation, providing care and supervision which could only be given by experienced staff" (p. 182). In describing patients with chronic disability living in the community, he emphasizes the similarity between the groups in the area of marked social isolation and says, "The fact that they were 'living in the community' did not mean that they had made social contact with it" (p. 185). Chafetz and Goldfinger (1984) have pointed to the high incidence of homelessness among a group of recidivist patients and repeated emergency room users in San Francisco.

Synthesizing these descriptions, it becomes apparent that one of the common characteristics of the homeless patient, the young adult chronic patient, and the recidivist patient, as well as the chronic patient in general, is their lack of a social network. The homeless lack what Segal and others (1977) have called a "social margin," which refers to "the set of resources and relationships an individual can draw on either to advance or survive in society." A social network, which has been defined as "the set of concrete interpersonal relationships linking individuals with other individuals," has been shown to be markedly depleted for chronic patients (Lipton 1981). The various factors that have contributed to this depletion have been delineated elsewhere. However, numerous investigators have emphasized the importance of providing the chronic schizophrenic with a new network, an active support system that can enhance the patient's social margin (Beels 1979; Cohen and Sokolovsky 1978; Lipton et al. 1981; Tolsdorf 1976).

The term "homeless" is actually a catchword, a misnomer that focuses our attention on only one aspect of the individual's plight: his lack of residence or housing. In reality the homeless often have no job, no function, no role within the community; they generally have few if any social supports. They are jobless, penniless, functionless, and supportless as well as homeless.

Service Needs: General Considerations

It must be acknowledged that the long-term handicap intrinsic in chronic mental illness has persisted in spite of the shift to community care. Chronic disability places patients at a social disadvantage and hampers their ability to compete and function within society. The present gaps and barriers within our system of mental health care compound the patient's intrinsic deficits, further impeding his ability to adapt to community living. Depriving the chronic patient of food, shelter, and clothing, thus subjecting him to the vicissitudes of the elements, undoubtedly contributes to his deterioration and repeated decompensations. Our present system of mental health care, which provides few humane residential alternatives, is a breeding ground for the destitution, recidivism, and criminalization associated with mental illness.

Simple, low-stress, supportive social structures can facilitate the reintegration of chronic patients into the community. Mosher and Keith (1980), among others, have put forth such a concept. Patients suffering from a schizophrenic episode in newly developing countries have significantly better outcomes than patients in more developed countries. The presence in the emerging countries of supportive, extended-kinship networks that buffer the patient from stress is posited as a possible explanation. This concept is in keeping with observations that some patients can be maintained outside the hospital when adequate interpersonal support is provided.

Numerous approaches to providing the chronic patient with support have been tried. There are indications that foster families, halfway houses, psychosocial rehabilitation centers, aftercare clinics, and day centers, to name but a few, are effective modalities for improving social adjustment, decreasing rates of recidivism, and enhancing employment. A number of "model" programs have shown that if sufficient social support is provided to patients, it is possible to alter the patient's functional ability and his adaptation to community living (Greenblatt and Budson 1976).

It is unrealistic to think that the homeless mental patient will be able to negotiate the complex bureaucratic systems that presently exist to provide financial, housing, and medical assistance. Many homeless individuals lead extremely isolated, solitary lives, avoiding contact with others. Their experiences with traditional services have generally been frustrating and rejecting, leading to still further

alienation and disenfranchisement. Consequently they are often wary
of the system's willingness to help them. Their states of psychosis,
disorganization, and paranoia make it difficult for them to seek out,
let alone obtain services from, existing providers. Barriers inad-
vertently built into many existing bureaucracies are catch-22s for
this population.

To further complicate the problem, the existing service systems
are inadequately developed and organized to meet the needs of this
population. Care often comes from multiple public and private
providers who are mutually antagonistic and competitive. This creates
a system that is poorly coordinated, fragmented, and unable to
provide continuous care. Patients are shuffled from one agency to
the next. No one is held responsible or accountable. The patient
"falls through the cracks" (Segal and Baumohl 1980).

We must give up trying to fit square pegs into round holes, and
accept the fact that many of the homeless chronically mentally
disabled do not fit into our present system of mental health care
delivery. Our goal should not be to reshape the patient to fit into
an ineffective system, but rather to focus on and accommodate the
needs of this handicapped group in innovative ways. A well-coor-
dinated network of community services that has the capacity to
designate responsibility and accountability and that is able to provide
integrated, comprehensive treatment must be developed (Talbott
1983).

The general characteristics of systems targeted to care for the
chronic mentally ill have been clearly delineated by Bachrach (1980b).
In chapter 2 of this report she notes that such features as linkage
with other community resources, provision of integrated and
comprehensive services, liaison with hospital services, and flexibility that permits the development of individualized treatment plans
are common traits of effective service systems for this population.
In chapter 5 Goldfinger and Chafetz discuss the qualities of an
effective service system for homeless chronic patients, emphasizing
the need for such services to be capable, comprehenisve, continuous, individualized, willing and tolerant, flexible, and meaningful.

A foundation of services that will provide for the residential,
financial, vocational, social, medical, and psychiatric needs of this
population must be constructed. In each of these dimensions a
spectrum of programs must be available. For example, available
living situations should range from highly structured and supervised settings to more autonomous living arrangements. Psychiatric

services should include crisis centers; community mental health clinics; acute, intermediate, and long-term-care facilities; day treatment programs; and outreach programs. Financially, a variety of entitlement programs that take into consideration patients' functional levels, residential requirements, and living costs must be developed. A graduated range of vocational programs must be available, including sheltered workshops, transitional job programs, and independent employment as well as programs that train patients in the activities of daily living.

Using such an approach, one develops a matrix with multiple cells. Discussing this type of multifaceted approach, Bachrach (1980a) states: "Such a multidimensional approach is exceedingly difficult to summarize verbally or even graphically and its complexities may at first glance appear forbidding. But this kind of thinking is in fact used whenever truly appropriate placements are made—whenever caregivers focus on people instead of places and consider individual patients' complex needs." For each patient we are developing a relatively stable social support system that can promote adjustment to community living by providing the patient with a larger social margin.

Service Needs: Specific Considerations

We now turn to a discussion of the specific types of services and supports that should be developed for the homeless mentally ill.

Contact Services

"Contact services form the first stage in the process of rehabilitation and resettlement and should be provided in all areas known to be inhabited by destitute or homeless individuals" (Leach and Wing 1980, 167). As previously noted, the homeless chronic patient is often unable to effectively use existing services because of his disability, disorganization, or paranoia. Contact services are essential in engaging this fearful, resistant, often frustrated population.

Drop-in centers, soup lines, outreach programs, emergency shelters, and multiservice centers are all means of opening the system's doors to the homeless chronic mental patient. Through such services staff can make contact with the homeless on a regular basis in an informal, nondemanding, and noncritical manner, hoping to gradually develop enough trust to allow the patient to accept more formal and comprehensive services. Patients who are seriously ill medically or considered to be dangerous to themselves or others may require involuntary treatment. Mobile outreach teams such as Project Reach Out, Project HELP, and the Midtown Outreach Program in New York City have demonstrated their effectiveness in initiating contact with the homeless and eventually connecting some of them with necessary service providers.

The best staffing for such programs is multidisciplinary teams capable of assessing the multiple needs of the homeless. These teams can be composed of a variety of professional and paraprofessional staff including internists, psychiatrists, social workers, nurses, and nurse practitioners as well as workers from housing, employment, and other relevant human service agencies. Close linkages with hospitals, residential facilities, and entitlement agencies facilitate the functioning of contact services. Case managers must be available to help the patient carry out the prescribed treatment plan. The concept of case management has gained widespread support as a means of providing more integrated and comprehensive care for the chronic mental patient, and should also prove effective for the homeless chronic patient if there is access to a sufficient network of community resources.

Shelter as an Approach to Contact

In response to the growing numbers of homeless across the nation, an intricate shelter system is being established in major urban centers. The shelters vary in their size, quality, source of funding, programmatic aims, levels of staffing, and ability to provide services. Most are ill equipped to provide anything beyond food, clothing, and temporary shelter. Some have liaisons or linkages with medical services and social service agencies, but few if any are able to provide for the homeless chronic patient in a sufficiently comprehensive or aggressive manner. Most shelters are incapable of assessing the biopsychosocial needs of their clients, let alone of implementing any integrated treatment plan, and most communities have limited resources to which shelters can refer patients for longer-term placements.

The establishment of massive shelters in which homeless individuals are warehoused is of questionable therapeutic value. And while emergency shelters are essential in order to provide the homeless with food, clothing, and shelter, they are only stopgap measures and must not be viewed as permanent solutions. The overcrowding, oppressiveness, and squalid conditions existing in many shelters, emergency or otherwise, are as unacceptable as the conditions that once existed in some state hospitals. Present-day shelters are reminiscent of the almshouses or poorhouses of colonial America that were used to "care for" the aged, the destitute, the criminals, the deranged, and other socially undesirable groups. Let us not forget that it was in response to inhumane conditions in these facilities that state hospitals were born.

Primary shelters should house limited numbers of individuals for limited periods of time until transitional and/or long-term placement can be achieved. Individuals requiring greater protection, supervision, structure, or medical or psychiatric care should be temporarily placed in more sophisticated shelters that can provide greater degrees of support and care. They should be staffed by enough trained workers to assess each client's needs and develop long-term, individualized treatment plans. On-site teams of workers from multiple disciplines and agencies are highly desirable. When on-site teams are not available, the shelters must have strong linkages with a variety of community services, including medical and psychiatric facilities, Social Security offices, welfare facilities, vocational rehabilitation programs, socialization programs, and alcohol rehabilitation programs, to name but a few. Only programs capable of providing such a full range of services will ensure that shelters do not become permanent fixtures of society nor mini-institutions replacing state hospitals (Bassuk in press).

Residential Supports

The cornerstone of any service system for the homeless chronic patient is a foundation of community residential facilities. The lack of a sufficient number and variety of residential accommodations is one of the major deficiencies in our present service system, as well as one of the leading contributors to homelessness among the chronic mentally ill. A recent federal report identified the lack of adequate housing as "perhaps the major unmet need of the chronically mentally ill" (U.S. Department of Health and Human Services 1983). A report to the New York State commissioner of mental health notes that "the single most critical factor which prevents effective service coordination and implementation of rational discharge

planning is a lack of provision for adequate housing for the chronically disabled" (New York State Office of Mental Health 1984).
As a result many mentally ill reside in board-and-care homes, single-
room-occupancy hotels, shelters, and other dilapidated settings in
addition to the streets and public interstices of society.

There have been multiple barriers to the development of community residential supports. For one, the types and the quality of
programs are so diverse that no standard nomenclature exists. Terms
like halfway house, hostel, board-and-care home, and group home
have different meanings for different providers and researchers.
The lack of a standard nomenclature confounds the development
of residential programs, and the use of ill-defined jargon makes
research cumbersome and replication of programs difficult. The
American Psychiatric Association's task force report on community
residences (1982) outlined a continuum of residential settings, ranging from independent living arrangements to nursing home care.

Budson (1981) defines ten types of residential facilities including
transitional halfway houses, long-term group residences, cooperative apartments, lodge programs, total rural environments, foster
or family care, crisis centers, nursing homes, board-and-care homes,
and hotels. He emphasizes that such programs should have a rehabilitative focus rather than merely serving a custodial function, and
highlights the need for a reevaluation of building codes and zoning
regulations to facilitate the development of such settings. Licensing
is also of utmost importance to ensure a reasonable quality of care,
he says.

Whatever the nomenclature chosen, it becomes apparent that
community residential settings must be described by a set of variables including size, types and numbers of on-site staff, clinical
linkages, capacity for and mode of providing a variety of nonresidential services, levels of disability of patients, lengths of stay,
location, and goals and objectives. The type and characteristics of
a setting chosen for an individual patient will depend on his needs
for support, structure, and supervision in a variety of areas. Settings
should facilitate the resident's attainment of his highest adaptive
capacity without being overly demanding. In this regard, it should
be made clear that certain residential facilities will be therapeutic
environments; others will be more supportive than rehabilitative,
helping the patient maintain his present level of functioning; and
still others will be custodial or protective. Some will protect the
individual, and others society.

Certain general features of effective residential programs have been elucidated. Residential settings that provide a place to live and little else are generally ineffective or undesirable. The likelihood that such arrangements will end up resembling the back wards of state hospitals has been commented on previously. The provision of social, rehabilitative, and recreational activities in conjunction with a residential program promotes more effective community adjustment and integration. The availability of psychiatric aftercare services as well as medical services facilitates medication and treatment compliance, decreasing the chance of decompensation and the need for hospitalization. As Meyerson and Herman (1983) stated, "It seems clear that humane environments linked with holistic care and treatment programs are justified."

In reviewing existing effective programs, two general approaches emerge. The first approach is on-site provision of services; social, recreational, rehabilitative, medical, and other human services are provided within the residence itself under the supervision of trained interdisciplinary staff. The second approach is off-site provision of a similar array of nonresidential services through strong linkages with other community resources; patients attend day centers, psychosocial rehabilitation programs, psychiatric aftercare clinics, socialization groups, or sheltered workshops elsewhere in the community. The approaches vary depending on the patient's level of disability and potential for rehabilitation as well as the provider's goals, objectives, and resources.

The present emphasis many local authorities put on the funding and development of subsidized housing programs is a step in the right direction and must be expanded. But residential support is not the final solution. It is but one of the bricks necessary to build social support for the homeless chronic patient.

Financial Supports

If residential support is the cornerstone of a community service system, then financial support is the mortar with which the system is constructed. However, existing income maintenance, health insurance, and food stamp programs often seem designed to thwart or turn away the truly needy. Eligibility criteria are frequently too rigid and unrealistic to permit the chronically disabled to gain access to these benefits. Requirements that applicants have proof of a place of residence, a limited amount of funds in a bank account, a mailing address, and so on are ludicrous when applied to the homeless. The bureaucratic barriers built into many federal, state, and local agencies are so frustrating and obstructionist that one can only assume that their aim is to turn people away rather than provide assistance.

There is no acceptable or reasonable explanation for why every homeless patient is not receiving some form of financial support. Their levels of disability would indicate that most, if not all, are eligible for either Supplemental Security Income or Social Security Disability Insurance. While several studies and reports indicate that a significant number of the homeless are veterans, few are receiving the benefits they are entitled to (City of New York 1982). National cutbacks in Social Security programs, accompanied by increasingly arbitrary review criteria, must be viewed as a major contributor to the growing incidence of homelessness among the mentally ill.

Patients who are not eligible for Social Security benefits warrant some general form of relief. In addition, the amount of money alloted to individuals through many of these programs often borders on the poverty level. If we are to have any degree of success in helping the homeless patient, it is mandatory that the government review the financial needs of these patients and provide more realistic allowances. In many cases it will be necessary to designate a payee to receive a patient's checks and help him manage his monies.

Health insurance is another major form of financial support. A majority of the homeless mentally ill do not have any kind of health insurance, be it Medicaid, Medicare, veterans' benefits, or other equivalents (Bassuk in press; Lipton and Micheels 1983). This deficiency must be remedied immediately, as many voluntary and private facilities reject the uninsured. Providing patients with adequate insurance coverage would make treatment of the chronic mental patient more attractive to these organizations and open up a vast network of existing services.

Methods for reimbursing those who provide care in the community must be equitable, and must take into account the multiple services, medical and nonmedical, that are required. Residential treatment programs, vocational rehabilitation programs, socialization activities, and day centers must all be accounted for when devising fair reimbursement schedules.

The range of services required by the homeless mentally ill cuts across agency boundaries. One approach would be for health and human service agencies to designate and pool funds for the homeless and to form a distinct agency or commission to fund programs and arbitrate disputes among service providers. Through such an arrangement, the financial support needed to cement together an adequate artificial network might well become available.

Hospital and Psychiatric Supports

Many of the homeless chronically mentally ill are in need of periods of acute psychiatric hospitalization, either brief or longer term. In one study in which 90 homeless patients presenting to a municipal psychiatric emergency service were examined, more than 50 percent required hospitalization in an acute care facility (Lipton et al. 1983). Of the 47 admitted to the hospital, 93.6 percent were admitted on an involuntary, emergency basis as being dangerous to themselves or others. This percentage was exceedingly high in comparison with the overall hospital population.

The homeless patient often needs brief periods of acute hospitalization for purposes of stabilization. In many urban areas the shortage of acute care beds has resulted in overly stringent admitting criteria that require a patient to be seriously decompensated or dangerous to himself or others before hospitalization is possible. Bed shortages have also resulted in limits on lengths of stay, leading to premature discharge with inadequate dispositional planning. This pattern is an irresponsible, perhaps negligent, manner of providing care for the chronically mentally ill. Is it surprising that hospitalized patients who are discharged into a community that provides inadequate housing, little money on which to survive, and a paucity of aftercare services should soon reappear in our admitting offices in a decompensated state? It may well be in the patient's best interest *not* to comply with our treatment recommendations after discharge, as the hospital provides for all his needs; no other place within the community can offer as much.

The pressure on the acute care system in many major urban centers has reached crisis proportions. It is compounded by many state hospitals' rigid and exclusionary admitting criteria. The lack of intermediate and chronic care facilities further exacerbates the situation. In New York City patients often wait in psychiatric emergency rooms for several days until an acute care bed becomes available. The catchment-area concept is ludicrous when applied to the homeless patient. It has become a device through which hospitals can transfer responsibility at the cost of patient care.

The need for increased numbers of intermediate and chronic care beds as well as acute care beds, at least temporarily, cannot be denied. Some homeless patients require varying periods of hospitalization until discharge into the community is feasible. We must accept our own deficiencies, realizing that there will remain a group of patients who cannot be cared for in the community, no matter how flexible or comprehensive our approach, no matter how receptive the community. Long-term hospitalization will remain a necessity for some patients.

Equally important is the construction of other, non-hospital-based psychiatric services. Chronic patients must have ongoing contact with a psychiatrist who can regularly monitor their psychiatric status, evaluate their progress or deterioration, and prescribe appropriate pharmacological treatment. The importance of psychotropic medications for the chronic patient cannot be minimized; the role of drugs in controlling pathological symptoms and behavior and preventing relapse has been well documented.

Psychiatric monitoring can be made available through clinics, private practitioners, or psychiatrists on-site at community residential settings. In this regard, there is a need to train more psychiatrists to care for the chronic patient. Residency programs should be encouraged, through financial inducements, to emphasize the care and treatment of the chronic mental patient in their curriculum.

Rehabilitative Supports

Placing homeless chronic patients in a "noninstitutional" community residential setting and providing them with funds to live on as well as adequate psychiatric care is merely part of a comprehensive therapeutic program; rehabilitation is an intrinsic component. The social incompetence and residual impairment of many homeless chronic patients make it difficult for them to interact socially, to carry out basic activities of daily living, or to get and maintain a job. Service programs must offer the patient the opportunity to develop the necessary skills around which a functional identity may begin to crystallize and a social network may begin to emerge.

The principles of psychiatric rehabilitation have been intensively reviewed by Anthony (1977), who emphasizes the importance of assessing a patient's functional skills and deficits in a variety of environmental settings, including work, living, and social situations. On the basis of such an assessment an individualized treatment program can be formulated. For patients who are unable to perform such basic activities as maintaining personal hygiene, caring for their living quarters, cooking, and managing money, training in skills of daily living is essential. For patients who can carry out these basic functions but lack the requisite social or vocational skills, social clubs, socialization groups, day treatment centers, psychosocial rehabilitation programs, and activity programs within the residence can foster the development of interpersonal relationships and encourage patients to engage in social activities. For patients capable of working if they can acquire rudimentary skills or practice existing skills, vocational training programs that are flexible in their work expectations should be available. A graduated system of volunteer work programs, sheltered workshops, and transitional employment will allow patients to begin at an appropriate level and move into more structured work settings as they acquire needed skills.

Few would argue that many chronically impaired individuals are working successfully in jobs in which they perform simple tasks with limited demands placed on them. However, with the present levels of employment, the available jobs generally require high levels of expertise or training. Inducements for private industry to develop low-level jobs that are open to those with chronic impairment must be expanded.

Connecting Links

The various types of support enumerated above form the basis of a patient's support system, but they must be coordinated into a cohesive treatment plan if the patient is to receive integrated and continuous care. Ideally such linkages would be built into a unified service delivery system, but the current system is discontinuous and fragmented. In a fragmented care system it becomes necessary to designate someone to connect the patient with the appropriate service providers and to coordinate his care among these providers. Each patient requires a case manager, who becomes the connecting link or "continuity agent" (Granet and Talbott 1978) to ensure continuity of care over space and time.

It is questionable whether we need to train a whole new breed of mental health workers to perform the function of case management. Many homeless mentally ill patients continue to have sporadic contact with their family and friends, who may be an invaluable extension of the more formal support system. Family members, friends, and coworkers as well as professionals and paraprofessionals are all capable of providing case management. Interdisciplinary and interagency meetings often accomplish the task of coordinating care. The use of members of existing formal or informal networks to provide case management should be encouraged.

Patients suffering from chronic psychiatric illnesses often place substantial emotional and financial burdens on their families, which can be buffered to some extent by providing the family with appropriate supports. Educating the family in methods of coping with chronic illness and pathological behavior can be extremely useful in engaging them in the patient's treatment. Financial inducements to families of chronic patients may also permit them to become more active participants in the patient's care and treatment. The reintegration of patients into their natural social networks can provide a means through which they can receive many of the necessary supports discussed elsewhere in this chapter.

Governmental and Societal Supports

The ideas, concepts, and programs described thus far are not new. The question is why they have not been implemented. Several interrelated barriers stand out most prominently. A lack of leadership in the formulation of national policy, deficiencies in funding, and community opposition have all obstructed the development of a unified, comprehensive network of community-based services.

Underlying these barriers is the fact that homeless chronic mental patients lack political clout. They do not form a political constituency. No one need respond to those who cannot be heard. Family organizations such as the National Alliance for the Mentally Ill and community groups such as the Community Service Society in New York City and the Coalition for the Homeless have been advocates for this population and must continue their efforts. The psychiatric profession must become increasingly involved in lobbying for the needs of the homeless mentally ill.

The stigma, apprehension, and fear associated with mental illness make communities resistant to accepting patients into their midst. As noted by Segal and Baumohl (1980), "Negative public attitudes effectively inhibit the social integration of former mental patients." Some investigators have concluded that the handicaps of many mental patients are partly attributable to public attitudes of rejection and avoidance (Rabkin 1974). Susan Sontag's *Illness as Metaphor* (1977) is as applicable to mental illness as it is to cancer. Public misconceptions must be torn down. A nationwide educational campaign to alter negative public attitudes would be beneficial. It is only when the community is willing to accept chronic patients that they will be able to lead a humane existence outside of institutions.

Insufficient funding has made it almost impossible to effectively implement deinstitutionalization policy. In many areas of the country, the funds that supported patients in state hospitals have not been rechanneled into community services. Major portions of many state mental health budgets continue to go to maintaining state hospital services despite a massive decline in hospital census. In New York State only 37 percent of the $850 million mental health budget for 1982 went to community mental health services, while 63 percent went to state hospital services. Reallocation of funding remains an essential objective if community treatment is ever to be viable in large urban centers.

While it is seldom stated directly, a major impetus to the enactment of deinstitutionalization policy was the anticipated financial savings. Those with a short-sighted view envisioned it would be less costly to maintain patients in the community than in state facilities. They saw only the savings that would accrue by dismantling state hospital systems, but failed to acknowledge the cost of constructing comprehensive community treatment networks and the escalating costs of maintaining unionized staffs in decaying hospitals. It was relatively inexpensive to empty out the state hospitals. It was and will be costly to develop an adequate community service system to care for the chronic mental patient. The longer we procrastinate, the greater will be the cost both financially and in terms of human hardship.

Funding of programs and services is contingent upon a well-formulated policy and plan. The lack of such a policy is a result of governmental resistance to taking responsibility in an era of fiscal restraint. No one agency at any level of government has been given sufficient authority, funds, or resources to singlehandedly develop multifaceted programs to serve the homeless chronic mental patient. Many questions remain unanswered. Who will be responsible for the development and funding of social, medical, rehabilitative, residential, and entitlement programs? What funding mechanisms can and should be used? Who will be accountable for their functioning?

Who will be designated to deliver the necessary services? Who will coordinate and monitor such an intricate network of services? These are complex questions that require complicated answers.

The federal government, which in essence legislated deinstitutionalization policy, is responsible for answering these questions, setting new policy directions, and ensuring that they are appropriately implemented. The chronic mentally ill, including the homeless, must be given highest priority by those formulating policy, designing services, and delivering care. Funding mechanisms must encourage service delivery to the chronically disabled patient. Economic policies that focus on slowing inflation and simultaneously promote military spending do so at the cost of human service programs. The homeless chronic mental patients are the victims of such a philosophy.

The appropriate federal, state, and local agencies must work together, pooling their vast resources, to develop integrated policies that foster the development of comprehensive service systems. If monies from these governmental departments were pooled, it would be possible to begin to finance treatment programs capable of meeting the diverse needs of a multidimensionally deprived population.

The delivery of services by private and voluntary sectors is encouraging and deserves to be fostered as long as they provide for sufficient monitoring of services and promote flexibility and variability. Funding of any one form of service at the expense of another is likely to result in stereotyping of services and warehousing of patients, with a recurrence of the same types of problems encountered in the state hospital system. The work of religious organizations and private foundations in the delivery of essential services to the homeless chronic mental patient has been exemplary in many areas of the country. Economic inducements should be granted to such groups to encourage them to continue their work.

Society and its leaders can no longer look the other way. The homeless are a phenomenon for all to see. In whatever direction we turn, they stand before us as blatant manifestations of unmet need in a society so affluent it can afford massive budgetary deficits under a government so wealthy it can grant huge industrial bureaucracies guaranteed loans to prevent them from falling into bankruptcy. Where are the loans for the homeless mentally ill? The government spends billions of dollars constructing nuclear warheads. Where are the dollars to feed, house, and clothe the mentally ill? How many homeless must die in the cold of winter beneath the flimsy protection of a cardboard box before the plight of the chronically ill is addressed?

References

American Psychiatric Association Task Force on Community Residential Services: A Typology of Community Residential Services. Washington, APA, 1982

Anthony WA: Psychological rehabilitation: a concept in need of a method. Am Psychol 32:658-662, 1977

Arce AA, Tadlock M, Vergare MJ, et al: A psychiatric profile of street people admitted to an emergency shelter. Hosp Community Psychiatry 34:812-817, 1983

Bachrach LL: Is the least restrictive environment always the best? sociological and semantic implications. Hosp Community Psychiatry 31:97-103, 1980a

Bachrach LL: Overview: model programs for chronic mental patients. Am J Psychiatry 137:1023-1031, 1980b

Bassuk EL, Rubin L, Lauriat A: Back to Bedlam: are shelters becoming alternative institutions? Am J Psychiatry (in press)

Beels CC: Social networks and schizophrenia. Psychiatr Q 51:209-215, 1979

Budson RD: Community residential care, in The Chronic Mentally Ill. Edited by Talbott JA. New York, Human Sciences Press, 1981

Chafetz L, Goldfinger S: Residential instability among a psychiatric emergency service clientele. Psychiatr Q 56:20-34, 1984

City of New York, Office of the Comptroller, Research and Liaison Unit: Soldiers of Misfortune: Homeless Veterans in New York City, Nov 11, 1982

Cohen C, Sokolovsky J: Schizophrenia and social networks. Schizophr Bull 4:546-560, 1978

Goffman E: The moral career of the mental patient. Psychiatry 22:123-142, 1959

Goldfinger SM, Hopkin JT, Surber RW: Treatment resisters or system resisters? toward a better service system for acute care recidivists. New Directions for Mental Health Services, no 21:17-27, 1984

Granet RB, Talbott JA: The continuity agent: creating a new role to bridge the gaps in the mental health system. Hosp Community Psychiatry 29:132-133, 1978

Greenblatt M, Budson R: A symposium: follow-up studies of community care. Am J Psychiatry 133:916-921, 1976

Gruenberg EM: The social breakdown syndrome: some origins. Am J Psychiatry 123:1481-1489, 1967

Lamb HR: The new asylums in the community. Arch Gen Psychiatry 36:129-134, 1979

Lamb HR: Young adult chronic patients. Hosp Community Psychiatry 33:465-468, 1982

Lamb HR, Goertzel V: The long-term patient in the era of community treatment. Arch Gen Psychiatry 34:679-682, 1977

Lamb HR, Grant RW: The mentally ill in an urban county jail. Arch Gen Psychiatry 39:17-22, 1982

Leach J, Wing J: Helping Destitute Men. London, Tavistock Publications, 1980

Lipton FR, Micheels P: Down and out in New York: the homeless patient. Presented at the annual meeting of the American Psychiatric Association, New York, 1983

Lipton F, Cohen C, Fisher E, et al: Schizophrenia: a network crisis. Schizophr Bull 7:144-151, 1981

Lipton F, Sabatini A, Katz S: Down and out in the city: the homeless mentally ill. Hosp Community Psychiatry 34:818-821, 1983

Meyerson AT, Herman GS: What's new in aftercare? a review of recent literature. Hosp Community Psychiatry 34:333-342, 1983

Mosher LR, Keith SJ: Psychosocial treatment: individual, group, family, and community support approaches. Schizophr Bull 6:10-41, 1980

New York State Office of Mental Health: Committee Report to the Commissioner of Mental Health. Albany, Jan 1, 1984

Pepper B, Kirshner MC, Ryglewicz H: The young adult chronic patient: overview of a population. Hosp Community Psychiatry 32:463-469, 1981

Rabkin J: Public attitudes toward mental illness: a review of the literature. Schizophr Bull, no 10, 9-33, 1974

Schwartz SR, Goldfinger SM: The new chronic patient: clinical characteristics of an emerging subgroup. Hosp Community Psychiatry 32:470-474, 1981

Segal SP, Baumohl J: Engaging the disengaged: proposals on madness and vagrancy. Social Work 25:358-365, 1980

Segal SP, Baumohl J, Johnson E: Falling through the cracks: mental disorder and social margin in a young vagrant population. Social Problems 24:387-400, 1977

Sontag S: Illness as Metaphor. New York, Farrar, Strauss & Giroux, 1977

Talbott JA (ed): Unified mental health systems: utopia unrealized, in New Directions for Mental Health Services, no 18:107-111, 1983

Tolsdorf CC: Social networks, support, and coping: an exploratory study. Fam Process 15:407-418, 1976

US Department of Health and Human Services and US Department of Housing and Urban Development: Report on Federal Efforts to Respond to the Shelter and Basic Living Needs of Chronically Mentally Ill Individuals. Washington, Department of Health and Human Services, Feb 1983

Wing JK: Who becomes chronic? Psychiatr Q 50:178-188, 1978

Chapter 9

Service Programs for the Homeless Mentally Ill

Irene Shifren Levine, Ph.D.

They languish in doorways, on streets, and in alleys. They wait
. . . for a hot meal, for a warm bed, for a few coins for cigarettes
or coffee. They are herded into overcrowded shelters that are understaffed, devoid of privacy, and often physically isolated from the
larger society. They are deprived of a sense of belonging, of their
own belongings, and of security and freedom from violence and
assault, and are even deprived of the necessities to maintain personal
hygiene and minimal standards of health. As a final assault, they
are stripped of any vestiges of dignity and self-esteem (Coleman
1983). Even among the homeless, there is nothing lower than a
"homeless psycho."

Yet there are relatively few service programs that have been
specifically developed to meet the needs of the homeless mentally
ill. In fact, the population bears the cross of a dual disenfranchisement from society and its agents of service delivery: the mentally
ill are often excluded from programs designed to serve the homeless, and those who are homeless are typically screened out from
receiving services designed for the chronically mentally ill.

In most communities, there is no clear focal point for responsi-

Dr. Levine is coordinator of the Program for the Homeless Mentally Ill of the
National Institute of Mental Health in Rockville, Maryland. The views expressed
in this chapter are those of the author and do not reflect official policy of the
National Institute of Mental Health or the Public Health Service.

bility for the homeless mentally ill. Responsibility for the population is fragmented among a labyrinth of agencies whose funding, administration, and monitoring cuts across health, housing, and human service agencies, across layers of government, and across the public and private sectors. At federal, state, and local levels, mental health and housing authorities vociferously argue that someone else should have major responsibility for providing services to the homeless mentally ill; in most instances, each wishes to abrogate its responsibility because of insufficient resources. This confusion has resulted in a disorganized nonsystem of services that is highly inconsistent from locality to locality in appropriateness, availability, acceptability, and quality. Because the "system" is a de facto one, there are no real standards for programs or established credentials for staff.

This chapter describes several programs that have emerged to respond to the shelter, food, treatment, and other basic life survival needs of the homeless mentally ill in local communities. They were selected to illustrate some of the important principles of program design and service delivery that are the subject of other chapters in this report.

There is no agreed-upon typology or classification of service programs for the homeless mentally ill; the categories used here are emergency shelters, outreach programs, drop-in centers, crisis housing, transitional housing, and long-term housing. Although some principles of program design cut across these categories, each type of program coupled with different supportive services combines to form a unique profile that has salient and defining characteristics.

Emergency Shelters

Because the homeless mentally ill are not adequately served by the existing network of generic mental health, housing, and social service programs, emergency shelters are often the only alternative to the streets. Of course, the quality of life in these facilities varies greatly, as do their auspices, physical plants, and programs. Many of the shelters started during the Depression and grew out of the altruistic traditions of rescue missions and church groups. Increasingly, municipalities and private social service agencies are establishing new shelters to meet the growing demands for a place of last resort for homeless people who don't quite fit any place else.

Shelter capacities range in size from less than ten beds to several hundred; as their size increases, shelters become more anonymous, and their high client-staff ratios make it exceedingly difficult to personalize services to residents or, as they are sometimes called, "guests." Because large shelters usually house heterogeneous populations with multiple problems, staff are often unable to establish the intensive one-to-one relationships necessary to build trust and support with the chronically mentally ill.

Most shelters are night operations; because of a variety of factors (which may include budget limitations, staffing constraints, a strong work ethic, and community resistance to residents remaining during the day), they evict their guests after breakfast in the early morning. Such shelters provide a temporary bed off the streets, and are generally available on a first-come, first-serve basis after they open in the evening. Since demand invariably outstrips capacity, residents cannot be assured of a bed in the same shelter, let alone the same bed, on successive nights. Only a few shelters, like Columbus House in New Haven, Connecticut, permit guests to reserve rooms for successive nights. Some shelters provide lockers, but generally accommodations are such that there is no place to store possessions and few opportunities to establish connections.

The "spirit" of different shelters (Baxter and Hopper 1981) also varies widely with differences in management philosophies and staff attitudes. While some shelters are operated in a fashion characteristic of a total institution, many others are mission-oriented and strive, even if only for one night, to provide a sense of caring, respect, and dignity for their guests. While some staff are authoritarian, condescending, and invasive of the personal privacy of residents, other staff are there to listen, provide comfort, and assist when asked.

Because of large censuses and transient guests, social services efforts at intake may be quite limited (Reich and Siegel 1978); ironically, large municipal shelters may solicit data on individual guests, but only for "management" purposes. Gathering some background data can be extremely valuable; unless shelter staff are available to sensitively obtain some information, it may be difficult to arrange linkages with social service and entitlement programs (J. Johnson, personal communication, 1984).

While some shelters are set up to provide referrals for psychiatric treatment, only a few have the staff capability to provide mental health or rehabilitative services on site. Similarly, there are often insufficient staff to help guests find appropriate alternative living situations. As a result, chronically mentally ill persons often become long-term shelter users. Moreover, this situation creates a great deal of occupational stress among shelter staff, who must deal with untenable, and often seemingly hopeless, circumstances (C. Kennedy, personal communication, 1983).

At minimum, shelter staff should be trained to identify major psychiatric disorders among shelter residents, to intervene appropriately in times of crisis, to provide supportive counseling, and to help plan and assure follow-through of linkages with requisite treatment and social services. It is also desirable to have on-site psychiatric consultation for prescription and administration of psychotropic medications for shelter residents who need them.

Because of limited budgets and the unwillingness of many professionals to work with the homeless population, shelters frequently lack staff who have either professional training or experience to deal with the overwhelming mental health needs of their resident population (P. Lawrence, personal communication, 1983). In the District of Columbia, the Mental Health Support Services Project of Lutheran Social Services is an innovative program providing mental health consultation to public and private shelter and day program providers, operating under contract to the District's Mental Health Services Administration. The project provides professional staff consultation about mental health issues of daily shelter management, case consultation to assist staff in working with individual residents, and observation and screening services to identify residents who should be referred to community mental health treatment programs. A consulting psychiatrist is also available to work with clients and serve as a staff resource.

With the growing numbers of chronically mentally ill persons entering the shelters, shelters are being dubbed "microcosims of the former state hospital system" (Reich and Siegel 1978) and "alternatives to the old mental institutions" (Bassuk 1983). In describing the Keener Shelter, housed in a former state hospital facility in New York, Baxter and Hopper (1981) note:

> Men lounge around in various stages of undress, in contact with an assortment of realities; some of them are former hospital patients. By a stroke of grim irony, these ex-patients have come full circle back to the institution which had originally discharged them—this time for shelter, not treatment (p. 55).

Bassuk conducted 78 interviews of persons residing at the city-operated Shattuck Shelter in Boston (Dietz 1983). She estimated that 40 percent of the emergency shelter population was clearly psychotic and that an astounding 91 percent had "definable psychological problems." She noted that "although shelters provide only a minimal standard of care, some people believe they are preferred by policymakers because shelters are less costly than either hospitals or community facilities" (Bassuk 1983).

Pine Street Inn (Boston)

When all the residences and shelter beds in Boston's city center are filled, there is always room for one more at the Pine Street Inn, even if it means that someone will be sleeping in the lobby or a hall. The Inn has no exclusionary policies (except in cases of violence) and accepts alcoholics, the mentally disabled, and other street people.

Founded in 1916 as the Dawes Hotel for men, through the years the Inn has provided services under different auspices and management. It is currently operated by a nonprofit corporation, Pine Street Inn, Inc., which receives some city funds under contract. In April 1980 the Inn relocated to new and more spacious quarters and expanded its services to women.

> Over the years, Pine Street's purpose has been a simple one: to ensure survival for its Guests. The men and women who come to our doors are assured of the most basic needs—food in their stomachs, adequate clothing, clinic care, a shower and warm bed—while they are here. The philosophy which guides us as we provide these essentials is also simple: acceptance and respect for each and every individual (Pine Street Inn Newsletter 1982, 1).

The doors of the Inn open at 4:30 p.m.; there are beds for 300, which are assigned on a nightly basis. Each day 1,100 meals are served by volunteers from various religious and civic groups in the community. The premises are strikingly clean and well kept given the numbers who utilize these facilities each day. Guests are screened for infection, and showers are required before bed; clothing is sorted, sanitized, and deloused in a specially designed, 180-degree, gas-heated "hot room." When necessary, new or recycled clothing is available from a clothing distribution room that receives donations from school projects, department store clearances, rummage sales, and similar initiatives. A work-rehabilitation program affords opportunities for guests to become live-in staff.

Counselors are both well trained and committed to their work. They are on duty and make rounds throughout the night; they stop and talk and have warm, caring relationships with their guests. Since violence is endemic to any facility housing large numbers of persons with various social problems, a policeman remains on duty at the Inn during afternoon and evening hours to provide security for both staff and residents. Because of the number and calibre of available staff, most disputes are resolved "without resort to the sticks, threats of retaliation, or abuse so common in public shelters" (Baxter and Hopper 1981).

Staff provide residents with information and referral services for alcohol and drug rehabilitation programs, psychiatric facilities, nursing homes, Social Security and welfare offices, Veterans Administration services, housing and work opportunities, and a myriad of other community services. When necessary, staff provide van transportation for guests to their appointments. Student volunteers from a variety of academic training programs complement the in-house staff, and each evening a volunteer nurses' clinic tends to the immediate health needs of guests. If more intensive medical care is needed, guests are referred to the city hospital outpatient clinic or emergency room.

Baxter and Hopper (1981) note that in addition to the comprehensiveness of the services provided by the Inn, the manner in which they are provided is unique and exceptional.

> To take a surface indicator: rituals of courtesy figure prominently in the Inn's relations with its guests. All the men are addressed by "mister"; inquiries are regularly made as to how one's day has gone; and guests are asked, not ordered, to cooperate when something needs to be done (p. 111).

With changes in the economy and in social policy, the client population of the Pine Street Inn has changed greatly over the years. At present, it is estimated that 50 percent of the males and 90 percent of the females are mentally disabled (Pine Street Inn overview 1983, 2). The state mental health agency provides one psychiatric nurse, who works with counselor staff and initiates referrals for mental health treatment or makes arrangements for more appropriate or more permanent living quarters.

The emphasis of our referral work is to try and get as many of our guests resituated as we can. Such emphasis is rooted in the feeling that our shelter is not a proper "home" for anyone while it still always stands ready to "shelter," for as long as necessary, those whose placement is difficult and complex (Pine Street Inn program description 1983, 2).

Long Island Shelter (Boston)

At the end of a promontory that juts into Boston Harbor is Long Island; here one finds an old, seemingly abandoned hospital campus dotted with institutional-type buildings owned by the city. A few are vacant; others still house the indigent terminally ill from the city's municipal hospitals. Each night homeless persons wait their turn to be bused from Boston City Hospital to the emergency shelter established at the Tobin Building on Long Island; it is physically removed from and out of the sight of the local citizenry. (In New York buses also carry the homeless to distant or removed sites, such as Camp Laguardia in Chester, New York, and the Keener Shelter on Wards Island, off Manhattan.)

With the support of both the health and the addiction services departments of Boston, the Long Island Shelter was opened in January 1983. It serves homeless women, men, and occasionally children; its guests can stay as many nights as necessary. If a guest requests case management services or has a physical problem, he or she may remain for the day and meet with a caseworker or student. But for the vast majority of guests, breakfast immediately precedes their bus ride back to the city. During the first seven months of the shelter's operation, 1,150 persons spent the equivalent of 17,500 nights at the facility (Bassuk 1983).

The program is unique in that it is staffed by former street people and directed by someone who spent more than 20 years on the streets. There are no regular mental health clinicians at the shelter. A psychiatrist-researcher with an interest in the facility makes occasional visits and tries to reach the most disturbed guests.

Creedmoor Shelter (Queens Village, New York)

Since the beginnings of deinstitutionalization, there has been a great deal of resistance to the development of community residences for the mentally disabled. Many citizens do not oppose the theory of community care for the mentally ill, but when faced with the reality, they often oppose the siting of such facilities near their own business or residence; in fact, for every community residence that surmounts that resistance, three potential residences do not (Scott and Scott 1980). Communities at large are equally resistant to the development of residences for the homeless; opposition to new shelters seems to be related to such factors as the size of the planned facility, the nature and timing of the announcement to the community, and the specific location (that is, residential or commercial). Because of this resistance, many citizens are advocating that homeless persons be returned to the vacant buildings that remain on the grounds of state institutions.

> We have witnessed the horror of increasing numbers of mentally ill and physically ill-nourished, filthy, and frequently abusive and abused persons who by no stretch of the imagination will ever be "self-directed human beings." . . . In the light of these facts, Community Board 9 in Manhattan, which covers the area between West 110th and West 155th Streets, has unanimously approved a resolution which calls for "the mentally ill among the homeless to be housed and supervised in reopened state institutions organized in small cottage-type facilities" (Dutka 1983, 30).

Creedmoor Psychiatric Center is a state hospital located in a middle-class suburban community in Queens Village, New York. Unlike the area governed by Community Board 9, low population density and other circumstances of its location have militated against the appearance of large numbers of homeless persons in the community surrounding Creedmoor. The hospital still serves 1,450 mentally ill inpatients and some 3,500 outpatients (Floral Park Bulletin 1983). But with deinstitutionalization, many of the buildings on the tree-lined campus of the hospital have been emptied. Since 1974 a building that was once a nurses' dormitory has been leased (at a dollar per year) to a private corporation providing halfway house services to the mentally disabled. Another unit, with attached houses in which psychiatric residents formerly lived, is also leased to that program and provides transitional apartments as a graduated step from the halfway house.

In November 1983 city and state officials announced a plan to establish two shelters to provide emergency housing for up to 800 homeless men in another vacant building on the hospital grounds (Leahy 1983). Included was a proposal to erect a fence around the shelters to keep the homeless from bothering hospital patients or the local community. Shortly afterward the first shelter received more than 160 homeless persons who came in vans from locations in other parts of the city, including the West Side of Manhattan.

The new shelter evoked the wrath of Community Board 13, which represents the area surrounding the hospital. A town meeting at a local church drew 800 angry community leaders and other citizens. Protests were made on behalf of the Creedmoor patients, the local neighborhood, and the homeless themselves. Most of the complaints centered on the incompatibility of the two populations (the homeless and the mentally ill) and cited the plan as a violation of the purposes and function of a state institution for the mentally disabled. Advocates for the homeless criticized the scale of the plan and urged that smaller shelters be set up in consultation with the surrounding community. A local legislator sought a court order to bar the opening of the facility, a request that was ultimately dismissed.

Many weeks of negotiation resulted in the decision to reduce the size of the planned shelters and to use them exclusively for the homeless mentally ill (Treaster 1984). As of early 1984 one wing of the building will provide temporary shelter for approximately 200 persons, referred by Office of Mental Health staff, placed in other New York City shelters; a second wing will become the city's first long-term residence for homeless mentally ill persons. Psychiatric and social services for both facilities will be provided through a contract with Catholic Charities, Inc. Although funded by the state, the day-to-day shelter operation will either remain under the auspices of the New York City Human Resources Administration or be transferred to a voluntary agency.

Adams-Morgan Hispanic Shelter (Washington, D.C.)

In many cities racial and ethnic minorities are overrepresented among the homeless. Recently the District of Columbia government and representatives of the local Hispanic community developed a 50-bed emergency shelter for homeless Hispanics. The planners also aim to meet the social service needs of its residents by linking them with social services programs, public assistance, and mental health clinics (Slacum 1984). The project is staffed by bilingual volunteers who hope to eliminate some of the cultural and language barriers faced by its residents in more traditional shelter programs. Hispanic churches and construction companies have contributed volunteers and materials to the project.

Outreach Programs

On January 27, 1982, a 61-year-old former psychiatric patient (and college valedictorian) was found dead in her cardboard-box "home" in a New York City street. She had been living in the box for eight months, since her public assistance benefits had been revoked in May of 1981 for "failure to appear for certification." She had rebuffed the efforts of various agencies to relocate her. She died of hypothermia just hours before a court order directing her removal to a hospital for evaluation was secured (Project HELP 1983).

Chronically mentally ill persons often do not seek out the assistance of mental health or human service professionals on their own, because of either the lack of motivation or the lack of ability to establish and sustain rapport with such helpers (Test and Stein 1979; Turner and TenHoor 1978; Turner and Shifren 1979). Among the homeless, the mentally disabled are probably least able to know where to find agencies, programs, and resources and are most vulnerable to the pressures created by too many questions, too many forms, and long waits. Therefore, the mentally ill, along with other frail and vulnerable populations, often never reach the doors of shelter, food, and service programs. To address these needs, both New York State and the City of New York have provided support for outreach efforts aimed at the homeless mentally ill.

The clients targeted by outreach programs are those who are disaffiliated, reject the services offered by traditional mental health clinics or social services offices, and require a flexible, patient approach. In fact, even when first approached by outreach staff, they may resist offers of assistance and help. Outreach teams have identified a sequence of techniques for gradually engaging the hardest-to-reach, most resistant clients (Barrow and Lovell 1981). They include offering a "brown bag" food snack; providing "minimal material services," such as food and clothing; using multiple, repeated contacts to establish familiarity and trust; and providing assessment, referral, and supportive counseling and other services.

Project Reach Out (New York)

> He was sitting disheveled and apparently disoriented, on a bench
> on the traffic island at 91st Street and Broadway. . . . Sam Evans
> approached the man and introduced himself . . . and told him
> that he was part of "Project Reach Out" (Schwartz 1979).

In April 1979 the Goddard Riverside Community Center, on the
West Side of Manhattan, began an innovative program called Project Reach Out to aggressively "reach out" to the growing numbers
of homeless people roaming the streets. The catchment area served
by the project was seeing a rapid and steady decline in the number
of low-rent single-room-occupancy units (SROs), which were being
converted into hotels, and a steep increase in street people, many
of whom had at one time been discharged from Manhattan Psychiatric Center to the SROs. The project was designed to provide
special assistance to the street population that was so disenfranchised that they would be unable or unlikely to obtain needed
services on their own.

The project began with a $100,000 start-up grant from the New
York State Office of Mental Health, provided under the auspices
of the Community Support System. Initially using a van as a mobile
office, project staff cruised a 50-block area west of Central Park
and attempted to make contact with the homeless, sometimes by
offering a cup of coffee and a brief respite from the cold (J. Berry,
personal communication, 1982). In May 1981 the "Park team" was
added to permit expansion of services into Central Park, where
there is a large concentration of mentally disabled homeless persons
(Barrow and Lovell 1982). Because the need for baths, food, and
other facilities was obvious, a camper was added to the mobile fleet.
In March 1982 services were again expanded, to night and weekend
hours.

The program makes direct contact with approximately 40 persons
(both domiciled and undomiciled) per day; it has contacted more
than 2,000 persons during its first three years of operation. A "direct
contact" is defined as "an interaction with a client in which a worker
is able to assess the client's needs, identify significant changes in
the client's situation, and/or initiate or continue action aimed at
meeting the client's needs" (Barrow and Lovell 1981, 19). Although
the majority of total clients seen by the project staff were not mentally
disabled, those contacted most frequently *were* mentally disabled.

For example, of those clients contacted by the teams during the first eight months of the program's second year, 28.8 percent were psychiatrically disabled. Of those with whom staff had two direct contacts, 42.2 percent were psychiatrically disabled; of those with whom staff had seven or more contacts, the proportion rose dramatically to 76.8 percent. The overlap between the mentally disabled and the homeless was considerable; 53 percent of the homeless seen by the project were mentally disabled (Barrow and Lovell 1981).

Initially the outreach team was composed of an M.S.W. project director and four paraprofessional aides. With experience, and expansion of the program, there was a shift toward professionalization and specialization; the team grew to 24, including a driver and specialists in the areas of mental health, alcoholism, drug abuse, and income maintenance. The staff are also multilingual, to meet the needs of immigrants and other non-English-speaking clients.

While the original intent of the project was to link individuals with existing agencies and programs to meet their needs, the outreach team found they needed to supply concrete assistance (for instance, food, clothing, money for transportation), and to provide ongoing case management services for weeks, or even months, in order to procure shelter and mental health services, obtain entitlements, establish Medicaid eligibility, and so on. In some cases, clients were incapable of scheduling appointments for themselves, and staff had to do it. In other instances, when clients were unlikely to follow through on their own, staff actually escorted them to appointments.

A social worker and caseworker conduct client assessments and work with clients to develop a service plan. Both the particular outreach techniques and the linkages utilized for a given client depend on a host of variables including the client's willingness to accept assistance, the nature of the client's problems, and the available resources of the service delivery system (Barrow and Lovell 1982). Data from the project reveal that although Project Reach Out has been able to provide counseling and an array of concrete services, 43 percent of referrals made by the teams have been "incomplete." In describing this limitation, the report noted, "While Project Reach Out can itself provide a range of concrete services to initiate the process of meeting clients' needs, and can offer support and counseling to assist clients in accepting basic life supports, the lack of such supports (especially housing) combined with system breakdown in the delivery of services (for example, public assistance) can jeopardize both the willingness and the ability of many clients to pursue further referrals" (Barrow and Lovell 1981).

Although an effective outreach effort cannot compensate for a fragmented, incomplete system of services, it can link the homeless mentally ill with existing programs. To further meet the needs of this population, the project has developed a number of adjunct programs including a six-room emergency shelter; a pilot program for financial entitlements in which the project serves as payee and provides the address for receipt of the entitlement; a prereferral socialization program at the offices of the project; and a weekly music workshop in collaboration with another agency (Barrow and Lovell 1982).

Manhattan Bowery Corporation's Midtown Outreach Program (New York)

Manhattan Bowery Corporation's Midtown Outreach Program operates in the area around Times Square, between 30th and 59th streets, on weekdays between 8 a.m. and midnight. The project is funded by the New York City Department of Mental Health, Mental Retardation, and Alcoholism Services (with state Community Support System dollars) and has two component programs: street outreach teams and a mobile psychiatric outreach team (Midtown Outreach Program 1984).

The two street outreach teams each have two master's-level social workers who cruise the service area looking for individuals who appear to be homeless and chronically mentally ill. In addition to its mental health efforts, the program also identifies alcoholics on the verge of convulsions or delirium tremens (City of New York 1983). When a team identifies a prospective client, a social worker approaches the individual on foot and offers concrete assistance—food, a beverage, or clothing, from a large canvas shopping bag carried by each outreach worker. The worker may suggest a hot meal at a church or at the Antonio Olivieri Center (described elsewhere in this chapter), or a bed at a public or private shelter. If the person is not interested in help (and in no grave danger), the team member offers a flyer with a phone number of the program for consideration at another time (Midtown Outreach Program 1984). The two teams see between 2,500 and 4,000 persons a year to whom they "extend resources and the invitation to live indoors" (M. Martin, personal communication, 1984).

The program's mobile psychiatric outreach team provides on-site medical and psychiatric services at shelters, drop-in centers, and voluntary programs serving the homeless. Its two part-time psychiatrists, who work with nurses, a psychiatric aide, and a driver, can initiate the involuntary transport of an individual who is dangerous to himself or herself or others. (Street teams also use this approach on occasion.) In the last four months of 1983, the team had one or more direct contacts with 510 different individuals. Although the long-term goal of the Midtown Outreach Program is to move clients toward permanent residence, staff recognize the need for a patient approach that may require repeated contacts over months and even years.

Drop-in Centers

> There is not a woman on the street who does not want shelter. It's just that they are afraid. . . . One woman used to ring the doorbell but would refuse to come inside. We used to give her food on the doorstep. Eventually, she agreed to come in and sit on the bench in the foyer. Three months later, she came up the stairs and slept in a chair in the living room. Now she sleeps in a bed. . . . It's a matter of gaining their trust (Baxter and Hopper 1981, 73).

Use of the generic term "drop-in centers" seems to convey a philosophy or an attitude rather than a specific physical structure or type of program. Drop-in centers are often distinguished from more formal programs by their zealous commitment to helping meet the survival needs of their "guests" while respecting the dignity and worth of each as an individual. As implied by their title, they require no commitment or formal affiliation for a night's respite from the streets (F. Depp, personal communication, 1983). In fact, when one such "survival center" opened (Rosie's Place in Boston), women were informed of its opening by signs tacked up around the neighborhood. It was thought its use might be discouraged if women heard about it from an "agency" (Slavinsky and Cousins 1982).

Drop-in centers generally are small and personal, and based in a locale where street people congregate or have easy access; frequently they occupy storefront space. They may offer day programs, evening programs, housing, or a combination; they may serve men, women, or both sexes. Their appeal is their accessibility and acceptability to the homeless mentally ill who are fearful of government and institutions. Characteristically, the staff of many of these programs are both caring and sensitive; they do not counsel or preach, make few demands, and encourage self-help and peer support.

Downtown Women's Center (Los Angeles)

The Downtown Women's Center is located in a storefront near the missions, shabby hotels, and vacant buildings that line the stretch called Skid Row in Los Angeles. The center provides meals and a daytime base for homeless women who have given up on bureaucracy and more traditional services for fear that they will again be institutionalized. The director of the center, a former Department of Public Social Services worker, doesn't ask any questions, doesn't require any forms, and doesn't try to change people. As she reports:

> A friend helped me to realize that while I should call this the Downtown Women's Center, it was in fact a mental health clinic. I certainly didn't have the mental health background at the time. What I did understand was the need for socialization. I wanted to create a sense of community. As we went along, I discovered that's one of the essentials in providing mental health care too (Overend 1983).

The director started the center with her own private savings and doesn't rely on any public source of funds. The center does benefit from contributions of goods, professional services, and other donations; the operation ran on a $40,000 budget in 1983 (Overend 1983). The Los Angeles County Department of Mental Health supports the weekly visit of a psychiatrist to help the women deal with some of their concrete problems and to prescribe medication. He estimates that during a one-year period some 500 women have come to the center, a sizable proportion suffering from chronic mental illness. Many are too frightened to enter the male-dominated shelters or to seek services from traditional mental health agencies (R. Farr, personal communication, 1982).

> It has taken months to establish credibility with them. We talk about how to avoid being raped, how to stay free of lice, what to eat. Eventually, we want to help these people understand the nature of their illness (Farr 1982, 3).

Antonio Olivieri Center (New York)

The Antonio Olivieri Center remains open 24 hours a day, seven days a week, and is located in the vicinity of the New York City Port Authority. It is supported by a combination of city and state funds, and since it is not licensed as a shelter, many of its guests sleep on chairs or mats. The center, which accepts only women, serves an average of 105 persons every day (City of New York 1983). Although a few of its guests live in nearby dilapidated single-room-occupancy hotels, most are homeless mentally ill persons who are fearful of public shelters. The center appears to serve a portion of the homeless population that would remain untouched by other service programs (J. Berry, personal communication, 1983).

A woman can take a shower, get deloused, and obtain a referral for psychiatric or medical assistance. She is not required to give her name, provide any identification, or use available services. The overcrowded storefront resembles a back ward of a mental hospital, with severely disabled persons sitting idly against the walls of one large room. Hopper and colleagues (1982) note, "Tolerant, warm, and nondemanding treatment by staff make this overcrowded, understaffed, and occasionally chaotic setting a secure haven for many women."

St. Vincent's Hospital provides back-up medical and psychiatric services, and the involvement of the local welfare office speeds up the processing of entitlements. The city's Department of Human Resources provides van services from the center for those who wish to move to an evening shelter; many of the clientele could not make it to the shelters on their own.

Arch Street Drop-In Center (Philadelphia)

The strengths of drop-in programs (their freedom, informality, and inner-city locale) can pose management problems and conflict, particularly for mentally ill persons who are vulnerable to intimidation. The City of Philadelphia, through a contract with the nonprofit Diagnostic and Rehabilitation Center, funded the Arch Street Drop-in Center as the first tier of a multitiered system designed to assist the city's homeless by moving them toward opportunities for more permanent residence. When the second tier of the system, the 50-bed backup transitional tier, was closed because of fiscal conflicts between the municipal government's health and social services departments, it placed even greater demands on the Arch Street Center's already strained capacity. Last winter 150 people a night sat in the downstairs waiting room, while 60 others were offered beds, warm showers, and food (I. Shandler, personal communication, 1984).

Those conditions bred frustration and turned volatile. In November 1983 several dozen frustrated guests at the center picketed and alleged "inhumane" treatment (Kaufman 1983). Center management maintained that the center had become overwhelmed with young to middle-aged unemployed men and that the situation was driving away the chronic street people (including the elderly, women, the physically handicapped, and the mentally ill) that it was designed to help. To resolve the fierce competition for beds, the city eventually arranged for permanent free housing for 50 young men at the YWCA, providing that they promised not to return to the Arch Street Center (Kaufman and McMillan 1983).

Crisis Housing

Many mentally disabled persons experience periods of acute stress requiring intensive treatment and closely supervised care; most commonly, these functions are performed in costly inpatient settings. Although there are some alternatives to hospitalization, few of them have focused on the concomitant treatment and housing needs of the homeless mentally ill.

Fenwood Inn/Massachusetts Mental Health Center (Roxbury)

> Although it has been clear that many patients on inpatient services need acute intensive psychiatric treatment, a large number primarily require a place to sleep, asylum from the rigors of a world with which they have difficulty coping, and a place where they can improve their social adjustment. That virtually all public mental institutions have been hospitals has meant that everyone who needs the services of a public mental institution becomes an inpatient (Gudeman et al. 1983, 750).

The Massachusetts Mental Health Center has developed an innovative model that enables undomiciled patients who are in crisis to receive assistance in a stable environment on the center's premises.

Supported by the state mental health authority, the center provides a broad continuum of services designed to meet a range of supportive and rehabilitative needs of the mentally disabled. These services include two day hospitals, a 24-hour intensive care unit, and a dormitory facility. Screening and evaluation take place at the day hospital; the intensive care unit helps provide stabilization for those who are dangerous to themselves or others.

The dormitory is called the Fenwood Inn and operates on weekends and weekday evenings. The Inn is actually a large gymnasium that has been lined with army-style cots; cafeteria meals are provided for approximately 30 persons. During the day, patients are encouraged to get up, get dressed, and participate in the day hospital program. During the evening, they sleep at the Inn. It serves as a transitional residence until appropriate longer-term housing arrangements can be made.

In a study of day hospital patients comparing data before and after the organization of this new service configuration, it was found that the proportion of patients needing inpatient care decreased from 76 to 28 percent, and that 35 percent of the sample were able to benefit from residence at the Inn. Clearly the combination of the day hospital and the Inn represents a new mix of services for mentally disabled persons who require shelter (Gudeman et al. 1983).

Transitional Housing

> Alone on the streets, with no place to turn to. A warm bed and hot food feel wonderful at first. But after a few days or weeks in an emergency shelter, you wonder, "What next?" (Friends of Ruth Newsletter 1983, 3).

Because of the nature of their mental disabilities and the paucity of appropriate residential options, it is often impossible to make permanent living arrangements for the homeless mentally ill during the short stay permitted at an emergency shelter. For this reason, emergency shelters need to be complemented by temporary residences that allow time for the homeless to receive assistance in making the physical and emotional transition from shelter to long-term housing.

House of Ruth (Washington, D.C.)

The ceiling leaks, the plaster is chipping, and the couch sags so much that it almost reaches the floor. But there's hot coffee on the stove, people who care, and a special warmth that makes it feel like a home. Before 1976 there was no shelter for destitute, abused, and homeless women in the nation's capital. Since then, the House of Ruth, a nonprofit agency, offers women in the District of Columbia both emergency and transitional shelter 24 hours a day, seven days a week; no one is ever turned away.

The emergency shelter is a renovated school owned by the District government; it has four dormitories (about 16 beds in each), and a kitchen, dining room, and pantry that can provide two meals a day. Upon arrival, women receive clean linens, nightclothes, and personal toiletries. While at the shelter, clients can obtain help in making and keeping appointments that will lead to entitlements, jobs, and permanent housing.

The "rules" of the program seem to be imbued with flexibility to permit responsiveness to the needs of its residents. For example, there are 65 beds, but there is always room for someone to sleep on a couch or sit up on a chair. The average stay is ten days, but women are permitted to remain at the shelter up to 30 days; on occasion, if there is nowhere else to go, they stay longer (J. Johnson, personal communication, 1984). More than 2,000 women a year are guests at the shelter (House of Ruth brochure 1983).

A recent study of 65 persons in the shelter on a winter day revealed that almost two-thirds (65 percent) of the residents had a history of psychiatric care, while almost half (47 percent) had sufficient self-reported symptoms to indicate need for psychiatric treatment (Depp and Ackiss 1983). When indicators of previous treatment were combined with staff assessments of need for treatment, almost all residents (94 percent) met both criteria. Clearly the program serves a substantially impaired population, and the House of Ruth staff have found that a significant proportion of the women leaving the shelter will need a low-rent living situation with some degree of ongoing support, supervision, and advocacy.

To meet this need, the House of Ruth provides 34 transitional, or second-stage, beds at three residences. The women may stay in the residences as long as a year while staff help them make more permanent housing, psychiatric, and financial arrangements. In a family-like rooming-house situation, residents share living room and kitchen privileges. They are assisted in managing the house themselves and are taught the skills necessary for truly independent living. They buy and cook food, take care of laundry, and perform other household chores. Staff also help residents become motivated to move out on their own.

Increasing numbers of women in the second-stage housing program have long histories of incapacitating mental disabilities; many of them are so disabled that there are no other alternatives for long-term permanent housing. Some of them have had lengthy stays at St. Elizabeths Hospital, the federal hospital in the District of Columbia; others have received treatment at outpatient clinics. Although the women in second-stage housing would greatly benefit from professional supervision, the program receives no mental health support from the District government and operates on a shoestring budget.

In essence, the House of Ruth has filled a gap in the community mental health treatment system and provides a humane and caring environment, but the program operates without the necessary psychiatric and other professional backup that is needed for persons seriously impaired by mental illness. This situation is paralleled in many communities in which religious and charitable organizations are struggling to provide for the survival needs of the mentally ill with limited, and insufficient, resources.

Long-Term Housing

Due to the nature of their illness, chronically mentally ill persons may require brief, and occasionally extended, periods of hospitalization to recover from an acute episode. If the chronic patient is living in a residential treatment program with a long waiting list, the patient's bed may be given to someone else when he or she enters the hospital. If the patient has finally acquired an apartment, a loss of benefits may mean giving up that residence while hospitalized. These disruptive life situations often exacerbate the psychiatric problems of the mentally disabled.

For the chronically ill, rules governing length of stay in residential settings coupled with their inability to secure conventional housing at reasonable rents often propel them into a transient life-style, and they often end up on the streets. Yet both housing advocates and mental health professionals agree that long-term permanent housing, linked to supportive services, is an essential component of a continuum of appropriate services for the homeless mentally ill.

St. Francis Residence (New York)

A gray-bearded man with shaggy hair stood in a narrow hall shifting slowly from foot to foot and moving his lips as if talking to himself. He was like the many homeless men in New York City who are avoided by the rest of the world, inhabiting doorways or dingy Bowery hotels. But the scene around this man was different. The hallway was newly painted and brightly lit. Others in the hall did not avoid him; some smiled as they passed, or touched his arm in friendship, even though he did not seem to respond. The man was in the St. Francis Residence. . . . Were there more such facilities, many of the homeless would undoubtedly put down their belongings and stay (Bird 1981, 32).

In the late summer of 1980, a group of Franciscan friars and lay people purchased and renovated a 100-bed single-room-occupancy hotel located near Lexington Avenue and 24th Street in Manhattan. How did Franciscans become landlords? Not long after the stock market crash of 1929, the St. Francis Breadline was founded; the line grew to more than 5,000 persons per day who came from surrounding doorways, parks, and storefronts seeking sandwiches and coffee. There were "no questions asked, no red tape, just the concrete filling of an evident human need" (St Francis program description 1983, 2).

Over the years, the Franciscans noticed that the presence of chronically mentally disabled persons on the line was growing. Moreover, a nearby SRO hotel, the Aberdeen, housed almost 200 released mental patients who were receiving meager services at high rents. In 1970, with leadership from the Franciscans, a number of agencies combined their resources to provide for the residents of the Aberdeen. They included the St. Francis of Assisi Church, Crisis Intervention Services of the city's Human Resources Administration, New York University Medical Center, Bellevue Hospital Center, the New York State Department of Health, the Visiting Nurse Service of New York, and the Hudson Guild Counseling Center of St. Vincent's Hospital and Medical Center of New York.

When the residents of the Aberdeen were threatened with eviction to make way for a luxury hotel, the St. Francis of Assisi Church raised enough money (primarily through mail solicitation of small donations totaling approximately $500,000) to purchase another nearby hotel and renovate it from top to bottom. Although the residence required a sizable initial capital investment, its continued operation is totally supported by rental income. In an evaluation of the residence conducted by New York City (New York City 1983) the importance of the ownership status of the SRO is noted: "Not-for-profit ownership, where management and program staff are both interested in the complete welfare of the tenants such as in the case of the St. Francis, is of obvious benefit. It provides for a living environment where the human needs of permanent housing, recreation, health, and psycho-social services are met under one roof" (p. 4).

The broad goal of the program is to provide a humane and dignified home for the mentally disabled and others. The sole admission criterion is the presence of a chronic mental disability. There are 75 men and 25 women at the residence: of those, 57 meet the eligibility criteria of the New York State Community Support System project, based upon "history of prior hospitalization and chronic functional psychiatric disability" (New York City 1983,7). Because the residence is permanent, openings are rare, and usually signify the death of a tenant.

The residence provides food, clothing, medical and psychiatric care, linkages with vocational and rehabilitation programs, assistance in securing entitlements, and help with money management in addition to a stable, long-term residence. Room rents range between $35 and $50 a week, meals between 25 and 50 cents. A residents' council sets house policies and resolves problems between residents. There is a regular paid maintenance crew; however, as part of a work preparation program, residents assist with the upkeep of common areas (which include an office, a recreation room, a kitchen, and a dining area) and receive a small stipend. The residence also offers numerous organized trips to social and cultural events.

Tenants have free access to staff; there is no need to wait in line or make an appointment. Staff of the residence help clients make appointments for outside services, including day programs and outpatient mental health services, and serve as advocates with the numerous agencies utilized by residents. Bellevue Hospital provides on-site medical, psychiatric, and activities therapy staff to residents twice a week; the New York City Human Resources Administration provides a full-time social worker for crisis intervention. Approximately 40 tenants receive psychotropic medications daily.

> The residents visit one another in hospitals, shop for or bring
> food to those who are ill, and inform the staff of the absence or
> problems of others. A high degree of unusual behavior and/or
> appearance is tolerated. Second, third, and fourth chances are
> given to those having difficulty. Birthdays are remembered and
> celebrated. To people with years of their lives spent behind mental
> hospital walls or on the streets, such decency is well-deserved and
> met with excitement and gratitude (St. Francis program descrip-
> tion 1983, 10).

Although only a limited number of residents at the St. Francis
have been street people, the residence provides a model for long-
term permanent housing for the chronically mentally ill who are
now homeless; it is also very likely that the St. Francis has provided
many of its present residents with an alternative to the streets.

Conclusions

The fact that there are so many homeless mentally ill persons on
the streets of so many of our cities calls attention to the glaring
inadequacy of the human service system for the chronic mental
patient. The homeless mentally ill are the "casualties of a 'system'
whose promise far outstrips its capacity to deliver" (Baxter and
Hopper 1981, 106). An adequate and appropriate system for the
chronically mentally ill needs to provide an array of housing
arrangements linked to supportive services and must address both
the basic and the specialized needs of the population. Elsewhere in
this report, Bachrach, Goldfinger and Chafetz, and Lipton and
Sabatini describe essential principles for designing and planning
service systems for mentally ill individuals. If these resources were
available, the need for emergency "survival programs" for the
homeless mentally ill would be substantially reduced.

The Appendix, from the National Plan for the Chronically Mentally
Ill (U.S. Department of Health and Human Services 1980), presents
a review of both the basic and the specialized needs of the chronically mentally ill. Basic needs include food, shelter, clothing, income,
meaningful activities, and transportation; specialized needs include
general medical, mental health, habilitation and rehabilitation,
vocational, and social services. Finally, certain integrative services

are also necessary to assure coordination and continuity.

Borus (1981, 342) notes that deinstitutionalization "has shown that without sufficient resources, simply changing the locus of bad care will not create good care." Although there are some programs and other opportunities for long-term supportive housing for the chronically mentally disabled, such beds do not exist in sufficient number to serve the population of persons who have been either discharged or diverted from institutions as a result of deinstitutionalization policy. Additionally, for a variety of reasons, the mentally disabled are often precluded from accessing an insufficient and diminishing stock of low-income housing slots.

Realistically, we must acknowledge that in our less-than-utopian society, we will never be able to fully meet the needs of those who will reside outside the walls of hospitals and other institutions; despite our best efforts there will always be some chronically mentally ill persons on the streets. While shelters are a necessary first step in bringing the homeless mentally ill in from the streets to connect them with more appropriate services and facilities, shelters cannot serve as long-term solutions for the problems of the mentally ill. Moreover, as we improve the "system" of community-based care, the need for emergency placements can and should be substantially reduced.

Outreach programs and drop-in programs for the homeless mentally ill offer the potential to "engage the disengaged" (Segal and Baumohl 1980). A growing body of literature points to a "young chronic," "chronic recidivist," or "urban nomad" population that, in contrast to other mentally disabled persons, is more likely to be mobile, disaffiliated, and resistant to traditional treatment approaches (Appleby et al. 1982; Bachrach 1982; Chafetz and Goldfinger 1984; Lamb 1982; Pepper et al. 1981). This subgroup of the mentally ill needs the flexibility, informality, and noninvasiveness of these approaches to move toward longer periods of more stable residence. A variety of transitional housing programs can help bridge the gap between hospital and community and between residential instability and permanent housing.

Thus the continued efforts of mental health planners, policymakers, and providers must have two thrusts: 1) improving the community mental health and generic human service systems so that they comprehensively address both the basic and the specialized needs of the chronically mentally ill (including long-term housing) in order to prevent homelessness; and 2) working with other citizens and advocates to improve the emergency and transitional shelter network so that it provides appropriate mental health supports and linkages for those who are mentally disabled and least able to sustain life on the streets.

Appendix
Basic and specialized needs of the chronically mentally ill[1]

Basic needs/opportunities
  Shelter
    Protected (with health, rehabilitative, and/or social services provided on site)
      Hospital
      Nursing home
      Intermediate care facility
      Crisis facility
    Semi-independent (linked to services)
      Family home
      Group home
      Cooperative apartment
      Foster care home
      Emergency housing facility
      Other board-and-care home
      Independent apartment (access to services)
  Food, clothing, and household management
    Fully provided meals
    Food purchase/preparation assistance
    Access to food stamps
    Homemaker service
  Income/financial support
    Access to entitlements
    Employment
  Meaningful activities
    Work opportunities
    Recreation
    Education
    Religious/spiritual
    Human/social interaction
  Mobility/transportation

[1]Source: U.S. Department of Health and Human Services: Toward a National Plan for the Chronically Mentally Ill. Washington, 1980

Special needs/opportunities
   Treatment services
      General medical services
         Physician assessment and care
         Nursing assessment and care
         Dental assessment and care
         Physical/occupational therapy
         Speech/hearing therapy
         Nutrition counseling
         Home health services
      Mental health services
         Acute treatment services
         Crisis stabilization
         Diagnosis and assessment
         Medication monitoring (psychoactive)
         Self-medication training
         Psychotherapies
         Hospitalization: acute and long-term care
   Habilitation and rehabilitation
      Social/recreational skills development
      Life skills development
      Leisure time activities
   Vocational
      Prevocational assessment counseling
      Sheltered work opportunities
      Transitional
      Job development and placement
   Social services
      Family support
      Community support assistance
      Housing and milieu management assistance

Integrative services
   Client identification and outreach
   Individual assessment and service planning
   Case service and resource management
   Advocacy and community organization
   Community information
   Education and support

References

Appleby L, Slagg MS, Desai PN: The urban nomad: a psychiatric problem. Curr Psychiatr Ther 21:253-261, 1982

Bachrach LL: Young adult chronic patients: an analytical review of the literature. Hosp Community Psychiatry 33:189-197, 1982

Barrow S, Lovell AM: Evaluation of Goddard Riverside's Project Reach Out. New York, New York State Psychiatric Institute, June 30, 1981

Barrow S, Lovell AM: Evaluation of Project Reach Out, 1981-1982. New York, New York State Psychiatric Institute, June 30, 1982

Bassuk EL: Addressing the needs of the homeless. Boston Globe Magazine, Nov 6, 1983, pp 12, 60ff

Baxter E, Hopper K: Private Lives/Public Spaces: Homeless Adults on the Streets of New York City. New York, Community Service Society, 1981

Bird D: Wanderers find shelter and a new life. New York Times, Apr 21, 1981

Borus JF: Deinstitutionalization of the chronically mentally ill. N Engl J Med 305:339-342, 1981

Chafetz L, Goldfinger SM: Residential instability in a psychiatric emergency setting. Psychiatr Q 56:20-34, 1984

City of New York: Efforts by the City of New York to Assist the Homeless. Mayor's Office, 1983

Coleman JR: Diary of a homeless man. New York Magazine, Feb 21, 1983, pp 5-14

Depp FC, Ackiss V: Assessing needs among sheltered homeless women. Presented at the Conference on Homelessness: A Time for New Directions, Washington, DC, July 19, 1983

Dietz J: Psychiatrist decries shelter for the homeless. Boston Globe, June 22, 1983, p 19

Dutka AB: Reopen institutions for the mentally ill (letter). New York Times, Nov 2, 1983

Farr RK, in Street People: Whose Problem? Washington, DC, Hillenbrand Report, Mar 29, 1982

Floral Park Bulletin (Queens Village, NY): Leffler seeks homeless solution in vacant buildings, Dec 22, 1983

Friends of Ruth Newsletter (Washington, DC): What next? second stage housing, Mar 1983

Gudeman JE, Shore, MF, Dickey B: Day hospitalization and an inn instead of inpatient care for psychiatric patients. N Engl J Med 308:749-753, 1983

Hopper K, Baxter E, Cox S, et al: One Year Later: The Homeless Poor in New York City, 1982. New York, Community Service Society, 1982

House of Ruth (Washington, DC): Brochure, 1983

Kaufman M: Stormy times for city shelter. Philadelphia Inquirer, Nov 22, 1983, pp 1B, 2B

Kaufman M, McMillan J: The new poor: demands of young indigents straining shelters. Philadelphia Inquirer, Dec 27, 1983, pp 1B, 4B

Lamb HR: Young adult chronic patients: the new drifters. Hosp Community Psychiatry 33:465-468, 1982

Leahy J: Slam homeless shelters. Newsday, Nov 30, 1983

Midtown Outreach Program (New York): Program Description, 1984

New York City Department of Mental Health, Mental Retardation, and Alcoholism Services: A community support systems on-site rehabilitation program, June 1983

Overend W: Mentally ill overtaking alcoholics on skid row. Los Angeles Times, Dec 30, 1983, View Section, pp 1-3

Pepper B, Kirshner MC, Ryglewicz H: The young adult chronic patient: overview of a population. Hosp Community Psychiatry 32:463-469, 1981

Pine Street Inn (Boston): An Overview, 1983

Pine Street Inn Newsletter (Boston): Fall 1982

Pine Street Inn (Boston): Program Description, 7-3:00 Shift, 1983

Project HELP Summary, October 30, 1982–August 31, 1983. New York State Community Support Services, New York, 1983

Reich R, Siegel L: The emergence of the Bowery as a psychiatric dumping ground. Psychiatr Q 50:191-201, 1978

St Francis Residence (New York): Program Description, 1983

Schwartz T: Homeless given help on streets. New York Times, Sept 1, 1979, pp M21-22

Scott NJ, Scott RA: The impact of housing markets on deinstitutionalization. Administration in Mental Health 7:210-222, 1980

Segal SP, Baumohl J: Engaging the disengaged: proposals on madness and vagrancy. Social Work 25:358-365, 1980

Slacum MA: District opening special shelter for Hispanics. Washington Post, Jan 6, 1984

Slavinsky AT, Cousins A: Homeless women. Nursing Outlook 30:358-362, 1982

Test MA, Stein LI: Practical guidelines for the community treatment of markedly impaired patients. New Directions for Mental Health Services, no 2, 1979

Treaster JB: Long-term residence planned for mentally ill. New York Times, Jan 29, 1984

Turner JC, Shifren I: Community support systems: how comprehensive? New Directions for Mental Health Services, no 2, 1979

Turner JC, TenHoor WJ: The NIMH Community Support Program: pilot approach to a needed social reform. Schizophr Bull 4:319-348, 1978

US Department of Health and Human Services: Toward a National Plan for the Chronically Mentally Ill. Washington, 1980

US Department of Health and Human Services and US Department of Housing and Urban Development: Report on Federal Efforts to Respond to the Shelter and Basic Living Needs of Chronically Mentally Ill Individuals. Washington, Department of Health and Human Services, Feb 1983

Chapter 10

Implications of Biological Psychiatry for the Severely Mentally Ill: A Highly Vulnerable Population

Charles A. Kaufmann, M.D.

The origins of homelessness are myriad. Economic and social factors such as unemployment, unavailability of low-cost housing, and mass deinstitutionalization combine with interpersonal stressors—loss of income, eviction, withdrawal of family support, and lack of after-care—in biologically and psychologically vulnerable individuals (Baxter and Hopper 1981). Such public policy and personal precip-itants of homelessness are considered elsewhere in this book. In this chapter, we shall focus on the third element in the formula for disenfranchisement: individual vulnerability. We contend that many of the mentally ill homeless suffer from chronic and severe psychi-atric disorders, that often such disorders are, in part, biologically based, and that they render the individual continually susceptible to environmental stress, both during and between acute episodes of illness. Let us consider each of these contentions in greater detail.

In the discussion that follows, we assume that mental illness among the homeless appears in its most pernicious form. To our knowledge, comparisons with appropriate control populations have not been made. In the absence of such definitive data, we extend the "drift hypothesis" of Faris and Dunham (1939), that under-privileged urban areas attract individuals with the most severe of

Dr. Kaufmann is a senior staff fellow in the Adult Psychiatry Branch of the Intramural Research Program of the National Institute of Mental Health at St. Elizabeths Hospital in Washington, D.C.

mental illnesses, schizophrenia; we hypothesize that impoverished areas and fragmented life-styles attract individuals with more severe forms of *all* major psychiatric disorders.

By psychiatric disorders, we mean primary psychiatric disorders, those that theoretically antedated the individuals' homelessness and caused or contributed to it, rather than psychiatric disorders that appeared later, as a consequence of being homeless. Thus homelessness and extreme poverty may result in chronic malnutrition, which may be associated with acute psychotic illnesses and such chronic disturbances as apathy, retardation, lability, and memory impairment (Helweg-Larsen et al. 1952). Chronic malnutrition also may be accompanied by specific deficiencies in thiamine, nicotinic acid, folic acid, and vitamin B_{12}, which in turn may be associated with memory impairment, delirium, dementia, and paranoid psychosis, respectively (DeWardener and Lennox 1947; Lishman 1978). Moreover, homelessness may result in sleep deprivation, associated with memory impairment or delirium (Hartmann 1980), or in hypothermia, which in its early stages may be linked with delirium. Some of the mentally ill whose hypothalamic temperature regulation is impaired—alcoholics or schizophrenics on neuroleptic medication—may be especially susceptible to hypothermia (Dalton and Robertson 1982; Hultgren 1975).

While such secondary disorders may produce considerable disability in otherwise psychiatrically healthy individuals, and while they may compound preexisting psychopathology, they will not be the focus of this discussion. Rather, we shall highlight three major psychiatric disorders—schizophrenia, alcoholism, and bipolar disorder—that are frequent among the homeless. For example, they represented 37 percent, 25 percent, and 6 percent of primary diagnoses among residents of an emergency shelter in Philadelphia (Arce et al. 1983). In their more severe forms they can result in chronic disability and vulnerability not only to further episodes of illness, but to social isolation and economic instability.

In this chapter we intentionally narrow our focus by considering these mental illnesses primarily as biological *diseases*. This approach certainly runs the risk of being reductionistic. Thus the seemingly aimless wandering of the "bag lady" certainly could be understood at the most elemental biological level as the motor hyperactivity that accompanies lesions of the posterior orbital prefrontal cortex (Meyer and McLardy 1948). But at a more complex psychological level, it may be understood as a defensive flight from anxiety-laden interpersonal relations, and at a still more complex sociological level, it may be understood as the consequence of economic and hence residential instability.

The multidimensional problems of the homeless may best be considered, in light of systems theory (von Bertalanffy 1968), as hierarchical, running from simpler to more complex. Each level within this hierarchy is, at the same time, both a whole unto itself and a part of more complex levels. Moreover, levels within the hierarchy interact with one another. Stressors—losses, frustrations, conflicts—interact with individual adaptational capacities to produce psychopathology (Marsella and Snyder 1981). Family and community supports may buffer these stressors and reduce medical and psychiatric morbidity (Caplan 1974). Other chapters in this book deal with the influence of the family (chapter 13), community (chapter 5), and society (chapters 12 and 14) on the homeless. Ultimately, however, all individual experience and behavior is mediated through the nervous system. Disordered brain structure and function, with associated cognitive and behavioral disturbance, will be the subject of this chapter, despite the obvious limitations of the approach.

Finally, we shall briefly consider the *morbid* aspects of psychiatric illness (for example, the paranoia of the schizophrenic, the irritability of the intoxicated alcoholic, or the impropriety of the manic) with their acknowledged disruptive effects on social functioning. In addition, and perhaps more important, we shall consider the less recognized *intermorbid* aspects of these illnesses. The behavioral and cognitive deficits that we maintain are less reversible (spontaneously or with treatment) are more highly correlated with chronicity and poor outcome, and are thus more relevant to the lot of the severely mentally ill who are numbered among the homeless.

We turn now to three disorders: schizophrenia, alcoholism, and bipolar illness. In actuality, each disorder is a heterogeneous group of conditions, varying in clinical presentation, prognosis, and treatment. Despite this variety, schizophrenia, alcoholism, and possibly bipolar illness all may be associated with a similar morbid outcome, a dementia resulting from damage to the prefrontal cortex. After describing the disorders themselves, we shall consider this relatively irreversible "prefrontal syndrome" and discuss the psychological deficits and behavioral vulnerability it produces. Lastly, we shall make broad treatment recommendations that both recognize and attempt to compensate for the unique impairments of the severely mentally ill.

Schizophrenia

Schizophrenia is not a unitary disease but a syndrome (Kety 1980). It refers to a group of disorders of diverse etiology with shared characteristics: psychosis at some stage of the illness and a chronic, deteriorating course. These two aspects of the illness, that is, its cross-sectional phenomenology and longitudinal course, have each been used diagnostically since Kraepelin first differentiated "dementia praecox" from manic-depressive insanity (Kraepelin 1919). Thus Kraepelin focused on course and prognosis of illness, while Bleuler (1911) shifted his focus from outcome to symptomatology.

These two diagnostic approaches tap into different features of the schizophrenic illness: florid, potentially reversible symptoms and less obvious but probably irreversible symptoms that affect outcome. Florid symptoms have received much attention, probably because they are effectively treated by neuroleptics. (The introduction of neuroleptics led to an emptying of the back wards of state hospitals [Davis 1980].) We submit, however, that more subtle deficit symptoms, although less acknowledged, are more specific and may have greater bearing on the course of severe mental illness.

Bleuler himself recognized the differences between accessory symptoms (delusions, hallucinations, and catatonic symptoms) and primary or fundamental symptoms (dissociation of thinking, weakening of the will, emotional flattening, and ambivalence). Similarly, Berze (1914) felt that deficit symptoms (lack of will and spontaneity) resulted from permanent organic damage, were primary, and in turn resulted in overactivity or excitement due to disinhibition. Langfeldt (1956) differentiated schizophrenia into process and reactive or schizophreniform dimensions; the latter, with precipitating factors, acute onset, and paranoid coloring, had a better prognosis at five- to 15-year follow-up. More recently, Lilliston (1970, 1973) showed that schizophrenics on the process end of this dimension had less affective response, were more likely to be disoriented, and had more evidence of brain damage on such measures as the Bender-Gestalt, Graham and Kendall's memory-for-design test, and Reitan's trail-making test.

Type I Versus Type II

One current formulation of schizophrenia is that of Crow (1980), who has contended that the fundamental defect in chronic schizophrenia may differ from that underlying acute schizophrenia. Type

I, acute schizophrenia, is characterized by "positive" symptoms: delusions, hallucinations, thought disorder, and Schneider's first-rank symptoms. Type II, deficit state schizophrenia, is characterized by "negative" symptoms: affective flattening and poverty of speech. These different dimensions of illness can be distinguished on the basis of phenomenology, prognosis, family history, and treatment response, and may have different pathogenesis.

Phenomenology. Type I symptoms are, in reality, not only symptoms of schizophrenia but of psychosis in general. Thus among 18 studies of well-validated cases of manic-depressive illness, 20 to 50 percent of manic and depressed patients showed such typically "schizophrenic" symptoms as persecutory delusions, ideas of reference, loosening of associations, auditory hallucinations, catatonic symptoms, and even delusions of passivity (Pope and Lipinski 1978). This last symptom is among those "first-rank" symptoms described by Schneider (1959); he believed that if a first-rank symptom was "undeniably present," one could make "the decisive clinical diagnosis of schizophrenia."

Further evidence of the nonspecificity of positive symptoms is provided by longitudinal observation of bipolar patients. Such patients pass through stages of classic "manic" symptoms (euphoria, hyperactivity, pressure of speech, grandiosity, hostility, and sleeplessness) into a state of extreme dysphoria and "schizophrenic" symptoms (bizarre and idiosyncratic delusions, ideas of reference, and hallucinations) and then, with or without somatic treatment, return through classically "manic" symptoms before obtaining full remission (Carlson and Goodwin 1973).

Type II symptoms appear to be more specific to schizophrenia, and are not found among manic-depressive patients in full remission. Moreover, unlike Type I symptoms, Type II symptoms seem to be associated not only with personality deterioration but with intellectual decline. Thus patients without positive symptoms and, even more strikingly, patients with negative symptoms show impairment on the Withers and Hinton test of the sensorium and the Inglis Paired Associate Learning Test (Johnstone et al. 1978b). Intellectual dysfunction (associated with Type II symptoms) may not improve despite symptomatic (Type I symptom) improvement (Depue et al. 1975). The specific intellectual deficits and particular vulnerability of chronic schizophrenics will be discussed more fully below.

Prognosis. Positive and negative symptoms have different courses: positive symptoms (hallucinations and delusions) are often present early in the course of the disease and are frequently the reason patients are first brought to medical attention (Pfohl and Winokur 1982). In chronically hospitalized schizophrenics such symptoms may be less frequent after the first decade (Bridge et al. 1978), while flat affect develops late and persists (Pfohl and Winokur 1982). Thus while Type I symptoms may remit or progress to Type II symptoms, it seems to be very unusual for Type II symptoms, once present, to disappear (Crow et al. 1982). In accord with their lack of specificity for differentiating schizophrenia (as an ingravescent illness) from bipolar disorder (as a relapsing, remitting illness), Type I symptoms are not good predictors of long-term outcome (Bland and Orn 1980; Brockington et al. 1978). Conversely, negative symptoms and associated intellectual impairment may be better predictors of poor long-term outcome (Crow et al. 1982; Tsuang 1982).

There is further indirect evidence of the differential prognostic implications of positive and negative symptoms. Neuroleptic treatment appears to affect short-term but not long-term prognosis of schizophrenia (Pritchard 1967; Scarpiti et al. 1964), suggesting that prognosis is related to a treatment-insensitive aspect of the disease. As discussed below, negative symptoms are less responsive than positive symptoms to neuroleptic treatment and may thus constitute this treatment-refractory aspect.

Family History. Thirty to 40 percent of poor-prognosis (that is, unrecovered or Type II) schizophrenics have relatives with schizophrenic illness. In relatives of patients with good-prognosis (recovered or Type I) schizophrenia, the disease is much rarer, 0 to 15 percent, whereas affective illness may be more common (Pope and Lipinski 1978).

Treatment Response. Neuroleptic treatment is overwhelmingly more effective than placebo in both the treatment of schizophrenic symptoms (Klein and Davis 1969) and the prevention of relapse (Davis 1975). Type I symptoms (hallucinations, paranoid ideation, and incoherent speech) seem especially responsive to neuroleptic treatment (National Institute of Mental Health 1964) yet such drugs have less effect on the symptoms of chronic schizophrenics than of acutely ill patients (Prien and Klett 1972). In fact, some studies have failed to show any advantage of neuroleptic drug over placebo for chronic schizophrenics (Hughes and Little 1967; Letemendia and Harris 1967; Prien and Cole 1968; Prien et al. 1969). This paradox can be understood by the finding of Angrist and others (1980) that positive symptoms, not negative symptoms, account for most of the change seen in Brief Psychiatric Rating Scale scores for acute and chronic schizophrenic patients following one to six weeks of neuroleptic treatment.

Similarly, Johnstone and others (1978a) showed that positive symptoms (incoherence, hallucinations, and delusions) but not negative symptoms (flattening of affect and poverty of speech) improved with administration of the active neuroleptic alpha-fluphenthixol in comparison with its inactive isomer, beta-fluphen-thixol, or with placebo. Cognitive deficits associated with negative symptoms also may not be neuroleptic-responsive, as Dupue and others (1975) found; the NIMH collaborative study (1964) likewise showed little effect of neuroleptics on symptoms like disorientation and memory deficit. This is an important finding to which we will return later.

Additional evidence that Type II symptoms may be relatively neuroleptic-refractory was provided by Weinberger and others (1980); they found that only ventricular enlargement, a feature associated with Type II symptoms, could discriminate neuroleptic responders from nonresponders among 20 chronic schizophrenics well matched for age, duration of illness, drug dose, and plasma level and treated for two months. Neuroleptic drugs work principally by antagonism of central dopamine receptors (Carlsson and Lindqvist 1963); not only are negative symptoms unresponsive to neuroleptics, but they may be effectively treated with dopamine agonists like amphetamine (Angrist et al. 1982) and dopamine precursors like levodopa (Gerlach and Luhdorf 1975; Ogura et al. 1976), which may have the opposite effect of stimulating such receptors. The effectiveness of dopamine receptor stimuation may be understood in terms of the hypodopaminergic theory of negative symptoms, to be discussed below.

Pathogenesis: Type I

The dramatic response of positive symptoms to neuroleptic medication (dopamine antagonists) has suggested that increased dopamine function (transmitter turnover, receptor sensitivity, or both) might underlie such symptoms. It is worth emphasizing that such mechanisms might account for the florid psychotic symptoms seen in schizophrenia but not necessarily for the other (dementing) aspects of the disease. Some laboratory studies support the notion of increased dopamine function. Increases in dopamine metabolites have been reported in the frontal cortex of schizophrenics on postmortem examination (Bacopoulos et al. 1978). However, such increases are not found consistently in other brain areas (for example, the nucleus accumbens) thought relevant to schizophrenia (Bird et al. 1979; Kleinman et al. 1980); they may not be matched by increases in cerebrospinal fluid levels of dopamine (Gattaz et al. 1983) or its metabolites (Persson and Roos 1969); and they may be a consequence of previous neuroleptic exposure.

Other studies suggest increased dopamine receptor sensitivity, as assessed with radio-labeled butyrophenone binding techniques (Lee et al. 1978; Owen et al. 1978). Similarly Post and others' (1975) finding of decreased dopamine turnover in remitted schizophrenics versus actively psychotic schizophrenics and manic controls suggests trait-related receptor supersensitivity, with feedback inhibition of dopamine turnover. Other investigators have questioned if this increase in receptor sensitivity may be an artifact of previous neuroleptic treatment (Mackay et al. 1982).

Pathogenesis: Type II

A number of converging research findings suggest that structural brain damage may underlie negative symptoms. Other data implicate selective damage to dopamine-containing neurons, resulting in hypodopaminergic function, as opposed to hyperdopaminergic function found with Type I symptoms. With regard to the former, there is evidence for both diffuse impairment and specific damage to the prefrontal cortex. Evidence for diffuse damage ranges from postmortem neuropathological studies through *in vivo* studies of brain structure (by pneumoencephalography and computerized axial tomography) and brain function (by electroencephalography and the presence of neurological soft signs). Evidence for localized damage appeared with the advent of topographic imaging techniques of brain function (regional cerebral blood flow, positron emission tomography, and brain electrical activity mapping) and is supported by studies of specific neurologic impairment such as deviant eye tracking.

Evidence for Diffuse CNS Damage

Neuropathology. The most consistent neuropathological finding in schizophrenia is that of cerebral atrophy (Colon 1972; Tatetsu 1964). Factors such as diet, institutionalization, and treatment (neuroleptics and convulsive therapy) might artifactually produce such atrophy (Trimble and Kingsley 1978); however, the presence of cortical abnormalities in patients who never received somatic treatment and their absence in patients who had various convulsive therapies (Tatetsu 1964) argue against atrophy as merely an artifact of previous treatment. Supporting an atrophic process are findings of gliosis in the periventricular structures of the diencephalon, the basal forebrain (Stevens 1982), and the brainstem (Fisman 1975) of schizophrenics. Recent postmortem findings of reduction of the neuropeptides cholecystokinin and somatostatin in limbic regions (amygdala and hippocampus) of the brains of schizophrenics who had a predominance of Type II symptoms (Ferrier et al. 1983) further support an atrophic process.

Pneumoencephalography (PEG). Pneumoencephalography is an x-ray technique involving injection of air into the ventricular system. More than 30 PEG studies of schizophrenics have found brain abnormality (Weinberger et al. 1979): 25 to 70 percent of chronic schizophrenic patients manifest cerebral atrophy (ventricular enlargement and cortical atrophy) on PEG. The highest percentages are found in studies of the most severely ill, chronically hospitalized patients, perhaps those most comparable to homeless schizophrenics. The degree of intellectual and personality disintegration (that is, negative symptoms) correlates with the severity of atrophy, especially of the ventricular system (Haug 1962).

Not surprisingly, in light of the association of negative symptoms and prognosis, PEG abnormalities are associated with unfavorable outcome (Huber et al. 1975). In some individuals worsening clinical course (affective blunting, social decay, and decreased intellect) is associated with increasing PEG abnormalities (Haug 1962); in others, PEG abnormalities, once present, remain static (Lemke 1936). In either case, data from studies of patients with organic brain disease suggest that increased PEG-assessed ventricle size may correlate with the degree of overall adaptive impairment, social and work impairment, and poor neuropsychological test performance (Seidman 1983).

Computerized axial tomography (CT scan). CT scan, another radio-logic technique, uses an x-ray source that rotates in a horizontal plane and scans a thin cross section of the head in combination with a computer that constructs an image ("slice") representing the distribution of radiodensities within the cross section. It represents a vast improvement over PEG as it is not invasive and provides better resolution; it can discriminate structures down to .3 mm.

More than 25 CT scan studies in schizophrenic patients have almost uniformly found enlarged ventricles and cortical atrophy, as well as cerebellar atrophy and reversed cerebral asymmetry (Seidman 1983). Ventricular enlargement is the most common abnormality, occurring in 20 to 35 percent of schizophrenics. The finding that the entire distribution of ventricular sizes in schizophrenics is shifted upward in relation to controls suggests that the abnormality is not the province of a distinct subgroup. Moreover, the finding that 20 percent of first-episode patients demonstrate ventricular enlargement argues against its being an exclusive characteristic of chronic, Type II patients (Weinberger et al. 1982). Nonetheless, it would appear that an especially high incidence of CT scan abnormalities, approaching 50 percent, occurs in chronic inpatients with substantial neuropsychological deficits (Donnelly et al. 1980; Golden et al. 1980; Johnstone et al. 1976) and with a predominance of negative symptoms such as alogia, affective flattening, avolition, and anhedonia (Andreasen et al. 1982). Ventricular enlargement seems to be associated with a poor response to neuroleptic drug treatment (Weinberger et al. 1980).

Electroencephalography (EEG). EEG and other neurophysiologic measures like sensory evoked potentials have been used in hundreds of studies of schizophrenic patients. About 25 percent of the patients show EEG abnormalities, even in studies with careful diagnosis, control for treatment effects, and rigorously quantified EEG interpretation (Itil 1977; Seidman 1983). Although a variety of "nonspecific" EEG abnormalities have been found, Mirsky (1969) has noted diffuse slowing, poor response to light stimulation, and little or no alpha activity in patients with a predominance of negative symptoms. Fenton and others (1980) also noted increased delta slowing in chronic inpatient schizophrenics compared with chronic outpatient schizophrenics, acute schizophrenics, and controls; one might assume the inpatients had a predominance of deficit symptoms. Ambulatory EEG studies have also demonstrated greater delta slow activity in schizophrenics (Stevens et al. 1982). This unresponsive "hyperstable" EEG record is associated with poor prognosis (Pincus and Tucker 1978).

Neurological soft signs. "Soft" signs of neurological dysfunction, such as right-left disorientation, extinction on double simultaneous stimulation, and impaired graphesthesia, are no more equivocal than "hard" signs like motor weakness, sensory impairment, or pathologic reflexes. Rather, unlike localizing hard signs, they reflect diffuse dysfunction of the nervous system (Pincus and Tucker 1978). Thirty-five to 75 percent of schizophrenics demonstrate such soft signs (Seidman 1983); schizophrenics show a higher frequency of soft signs than other psychiatric patients or normal controls. The presence of soft signs correlates with negative symptoms, poor performance on neuropsychological testing, and poor prognosis (Quitkin et al. 1976).

Evidence for Localized Prefrontal Damage

Regional cerebral blood flow (CBF). Regional cerebral blood flow in the brain correlates highly with local metabolism (glucose and oxygen consumption) and function (Sokoloff 1977). Changes in regional CBF can therefore be used as an index of specific neuronal activity. To monitor the flow, the movement of radioactive xenon[133], an inert gas that has been injected intra-arterially or inhaled, is followed with gamma detectors on the surface of the head, and "functional landscapes" of hemispheric blood flow are constructed.

Studies comparing regional CBF of schizophrenics and normal controls have found significant reductions in frontal blood flow in the former (Ingvar 1976). Schizophrenics showed low frontal activity, or "hypofrontality," both at rest and during cognitive stimulation, unlike normals, who demonstrated a "hyperfrontal" pattern. In fact, schizophrenics may actually suppress frontal blood flow in response to abstracting tests, like the Wisconsin Card Sort, that ordinarily activate frontal flow in normals (Berman et al. 1984). The hypofrontal response to visual stimulation was especially noted in older schizophrenic patients, with a predominance of negative symptoms.

Positron emission tomography (PET scan). As noted, local glucose utilization in the brain closely parallels neuronal activity. In recent

studies deoxyglucose, an analog of glucose, is labeled with a posi-
tron-emitting radioisotope, ^{18}F; extracranial detection of positron
emission and computer reconstruction depicts regional differences
in glucose metabolism and thus neuronal function. PET scan studies of schizophrenic patients, although preliminary, again suggest
lower (dorsolateral) frontal activity in relation to normal controls
(Buchsbaum et al. 1982; Farkas et al. 1980).

Brain electrical activity mapping (BEAM). Another innovative
research tool, BEAM, makes a computer-assisted tomographic map
from EEG and evoked potential data derived from 20 or more scalp
electrodes. BEAM studies in drug-free, neuroleptic-resistant schizophrenic patients have demonstrated more low-frequency activity
(delta, 0 to 3.5 Hz) bilaterally in frontal regions than in normal
controls matched for age, gender, and handedness. This abnormality persisted despite neuroleptic treatment. In addition, in medicated subjects a large bifrontal abnormality was seen late in the
visual evoked potential, further evidence of frontal dysfunction
(Morihisa et al. 1983). As mean EEG frequency may correlate with
cerebral blood flow (Ingvar et al. 1976), this finding of frontal
slowing is consistent with the regional CBF and PET scan findngs
of "hypofrontality" discussed above.

Deviant eye tracking. Diefendorf and Dodge reported an association between schizophrenia and impaired smooth-pursuit eye
movements (using a pendulum as stimulus) as early as 1908. More
recent work by Holzman and Levy (1977) has reaffirmed these
findings: schizophrenics, especially chronic patients, are most likely
to be impaired, with 50 percent to 80 percent of patients showing
abnormalities versus only 8 percent of normal controls. Abnormalities do not seem to be artifactually related to voluntary factors
or lack of motivation. Deviant eye tracking may be associated with
CT scan signs of cerebral atrophy (Weinberger and Wyatt 1982)
and, although attributed to brainstem or cerebellar dysfunction, it
can be found in patients with hemispheric lesions (Mayuzumi and
Tsutsui 1974). A core, nonvoluntary, attentional deficit may be
involved (Holzman et al. 1973).

Evidence for Selective Hypofunctionality of Dopaminergic Systems

In addition to gross damage to the prefrontal cortex, a growing body of evidence indicates that chronic (Type II) schizophrenics have selective damage to dopamine-containing neurons (Chouinard and Jones 1978; Lecrubier et al. 1980; Wyatt 1983). Such selective damage may be related to more general findings of prefrontal dysfunction, as this region has the highest dopamine concentrations of all cortical areas (Berger 1981) and is the major terminus for mesocortical dopamine neurons. Evidence for selective hypofunctionality of dopaminergic systems comes from clinical, neurochemical, neuroendocrinological, and neuropharmacological studies. Moreover, added support is provided by preclinical studies of selective dopamine lesions in laboratory animals.

Clinical evidence. Deficit symptoms of schizophrenia strongly resemble the apathy, lack of spontaneity, and impaired concept formation seen in Parkinson's disease (Javoy-Agid and Agid 1980), a disorder in part related to brain dopamine deficit. Negative symptoms also are similar to the "psychic torpor" seen as a sequel to encephalitis lethargica (Economo 1931), a disorder marked by profound (20-fold) loss of dopaminergic nerve cell bodies in the mesencephalon (Bogerts et al. 1983). Further, Type II symptoms are comparable to the akinesia that may occur as a side effect of neuroleptic (dopamine antagonist) treatment. This latter syndrome is marked not only by diminished motor activity but by alterations in nonmotor behavior like apathy, lack of goal-directedness, and alogia (Klein et al. 1980). Parenthetically, neuroleptic-induced akinesia may therefore compound the deficit syndrome in schizophrenia, which complicates its pharmacotherapy.

Neurochemical evidence. Bowers (1974) found lower accumulation of the dopamine metabolite homovanillic acid in the cerebrospinal fluid of poor-prognosis (perhaps Type II) schizophrenics. More recently, van Kammen and others (1983) have found decreased homovanillic acid concentrations in cerebrospinal fluid of drug-free schizophrenic patients with ventricular enlargement and cortical atrophy. Similarly, Kaufmann and others (1984) have found decreased concentrations of another metabolite, dopamine sulfate, in cerebrospinal fluid of treatment-refractory chronic schizophrenic patients.

Neuroendocrinological evidence. Dopamine agonists inhibit prolactin secretion and stimulate secretion of growth hormone in man
and laboratory animals. Dopamine has a less clear role in the release
of luteinizing-hormone-releasing hormone (LHRH) and hence
luteinizing and follicle-stimulating hormones. Neuroendocrine studies
in poor-prognosis schizophrenics with progressive deterioration reveal
reduced levels of follicle-stimulating, luteinizing, and growth
hormones (Bambrilla et al. 1979), consistent with dopamine deficiency. The finding of slightly elevated serum prolactin levels in
medicated schizophrenics also is consistent with such a deficit (Meltzer
and Fang 1976). The existence of diminished dopamine function
is further supported by blunted growth hormone response of
apathetic, withdrawn, unmedicated schizophrenics to insulin challenge (Bambrilla et al. 1975) and of chronically ill, neuroleptic-
refractory schizophrenics to challenge with the dopamine agonist
apomorphine (Meltzer et al. 1981).

Neuropharmacological evidence. Preliminary data for the effectiveness of dopamine agonists and precursors in the treatment of
certain negative symptoms, discussed above, support the existence
of a hypodopaminergic substrate for such symptoms. Evidence also
comes from the relative resistance of large-ventricle patients to the
psychosis-exacerbating effects of the dopamine agonist apomorphine (Jeste et al. 1983) and the resistance of chronic schizophrenic
patients to the dopamine-releasing agent dextroamphetamine
(Kornetsky, 1976). Finally, indirect evidence for dopamine hypo-
function underlying *hypo*frontal cerebral blood flow in Type II
schizophrenics is provided by the finding of *hyper*frontal blood flow
(up to a 100 percent increase) in a case of amphetamine intoxication
with paranoid (Type I) symptoms (Berglund and Risberg 1980).

Preclinical studies. A number of animal models for the cognitive
deficits that accompany gross lesions of the prefrontal cortex have
been developed. Delayed-response tasks are particularly sensitive
to such lesions. In rhesus monkeys not only surgical removal of
dorsolateral prefrontal cortex but selective depletion of dopamine
with the neurotoxin 6-hydroxydopamine impairs delayed-response
performance. This behavioral deficit can be reversed by the dopamine precursor levodopa and the dopamine agonist apomorphine
(Brozoski et al. 1979). The prefrontal cortex receives dense recip-
rocal projections from diencephalic structures (like the mediodorsal

thalamic nucleus and anterior striatum), which in turn receive projections from mesencephalic dopaminergic (A_{10}) neurons. Six-hydroxydopamine injections in rat striatum (Dunnett and Iversen 1979) or mesencephalon (Simon et al. 1980) also disrupt delayed-response tasks.

Thus a growing body of data supports the idea that selective loss of neurons at critical stations in dopaminergic pathways can produce the characteristic cognitive disturbances associated with prefrontal dysfunction. Neuronal loss has been noted in the mediodorsal nucleus of the thalamus (Hempel and Treff 1960), and to a lesser extent in the mesencephalic dopamine-containing cell groups in schizophrenics, half of whom had a predominance of Type II symptoms (Bogerts et al. 1983). Atrophy of microneurons in the striata of catatonic schizophrenics has also been described (Dom et al. 1981).

Summary

In sum, schizophrenia appears to be a heterogeneous disorder, characterized at various times or in various individuals by a predominance of productive symptoms (hallucinations, delusions, thought disorder, Schneiderian first-rank symptoms) or deficit symptoms (flat affect, alogia, avolition, anhedonia, and cognitive deficits). While the former symptoms may be neuroleptic-responsive, the latter are relatively refractory to such treatment (may even be exacerbated through side effects like akinesia) and are associated with poor prognosis and social decline. Epidemiologic studies among the mentally ill homeless have not specifically addressed the prevalence of positive versus negative symptoms, or of cognitive disruption; such studies are clearly necessary. Nonetheless, anecdotal accounts suggest that Type II symptoms predominate.

Recent work in the fields of clinical brain imaging, neuropathology, neurophysiology, neurochemistry, neuroendocrinology, and neuropharmacology support the view that Type II schizophrenia is a frontal lobe disease resulting from gross structural damage or selective damage to dopaminergic neurons. Frontal lobe dysfunction results in a specific constellation of behavioral and cognitive disturbance that renders the chronic schizophrenic vulnerable to stress-induced exacerbations of illness (Zubin 1980) and that presents clear implications for treatment.

A fuller discussion of neruopsychological disturbance in frontal lobe disease (including chronic schizophrenia) follows. But first we shall briefly discuss two other disorders found among the mentally ill homeless—alcoholism and bipolar illness—that in their more severe forms can also produce cognitive disruption and chronic social disability.

Alcoholism

While alcoholism as a primary diagnosis may be waning among the mentally ill homeless, secondary alcohol abuse continues to be a major problem, with possibly more than 40 percent of residents of emergency shelters manifesting primary or secondary alcohol abuse (Arce et al. 1983). As in schizophrenia, it is useful to separate reversible from relatively irreversible behavioral and cognitive dysfunction. Reversible disturbances include acute intoxication and withdrawal (each associated with a unique disruption in cognition), alcohol withdrawal delirium (delirium tremens), alcohol hallucinosis, and a related organic delusional syndrome. In addition, medical complications of prolonged alcohol abuse including hepatic encephalopathy and Wernicke's encephalopathy (associated with thiamine deficiency and characterized by a global confusional state with ophthalmoplegia, ataxia, and peripheral neuritis) produce organic mental disorders that are potentially reversible.

Irreversible disturbances include other disorders possibly related to nutritional deficiency: alcohol amnestic disorder, also known as Korsakoff's psychosis; Marchiafava-Bignami disease, a rare disorder that in its slowly progressive form may present with dementia and spastic paralysis; and central pontine myelinolysis, an acute fatal disorder associated with confusion, quadriplegia, and loss of pain sensation in the limbs and trunk. Irreversible disturbances also include a dementia associated with alcoholism (Horvath 1975; Lishman 1978). In the discussion that follows, we shall highlight, somewhat arbitrarily, the cognitive disturbances seen in acute intoxication, withdrawal, and Korsakoff's psychosis. We shall then discuss, in greater depth, the behavioral and cognitive dysfunction associated with alcoholic dementia, drawing parallels to the dysfunction in schizophrenic dementia where appropriate.

Acute Intoxication

Alcohol intoxication produces subjective exhilaration, excitement, and loquacity, or, if more severe, irritability and loss of restraint.

In addition, alcohol has a direct, dose-dependent disruptive effect on short-term memory. It would appear that both alcoholic and matched nonalcoholic subjects are susceptible (Parker et al. 1974). Alcohol, even at relatively moderate doses, produces defects in free-recall learning (Weingartner and Faillace 1971). Intoxicated alcoholics and normals show similar impairment in information registration and recall; however, alcoholics show greater impairment in a third aspect of memory, category clustering, which is related to abstracting ability (Parker et al. 1974). The memory loss is anterograde, resulting in difficulty in retaining new information received during the time of amnesia, known colloquially as a blackout (Goodwin et al. 1970). Because remote (previously encoded) memory remains intact, the individual may be able to perform complicated acts and may appear normal to the casual observer (Goodwin et al. 1969). Despite this normal appearance, the maladaptiveness of severe memory impairment is obvious.

Alcohol Withdrawal

Withdrawal from chronic use of alcohol precipitates a syndrome that appears within 12 to 24 hours, peaks at 48 to 72 hours, and usually disappears within five to seven days. In addition to symptoms such as insomnia, irritability, restlessness, weakness, and tremor, as well as the more severe psychological states of hallucinosis and delirium, the withdrawal syndrome may be associated with more subtle deficits in attention and sustained concentration, resembling what Lipowski (1975) describes as a "subacute amnestic-confusional state." Thus alcoholics may show impairment in continuous-performance tasks in which experimenter-paced arithmetic problems are presented either visually or orally; errors of commission and omission are noted (Portnoff and Dougan 1983).

While physiologic symptoms of alcohol withdrawal subside within the first week, attentional disturbances may not peak until the second week following withdrawal. Withdrawal symptoms may be associated with bursts of slow waves on EEG (Isbell et al. 1955). Not surprisingly, given the association between mean EEG frequency and cerebral blood flow, noted above, average cerebral blood flow may be reduced up to 20 percent during withdrawal (Berglund and Risberg 1981). Decreased blood flow appears to be especially related to the severity of confusion. Attentional disturbances rapidly improve as detoxification continues (Burdick et al. 1970). Yet, as we shall see below, deficits in short-term memory, visuoperceptual analysis, and abstracting ability may persist for some time.

Korsakoff's Psychosis

As noted, alcohol has some disruptive effect on anterograde memory among all long-term users. It is usually reversible. However, a certain subgroup, especially those who have suffered episodes of Wernicke's encephalopathy (Victor et al. 1971) go on to develop relatively irreversible anterograde amnesia. New information, both verbal and nonverbal, is rapidly forgotten. This phenomenon appears to be secondary to difficulty encoding all aspects of stimuli at the time of storage. While some superficial physical or semantic attributes of a stimulus may be encoded, temporal and spatial contexts are lost; Korsakoff patients may therefore recognize a stimulus as familiar but be unable to recall when or where they experienced it (Butters 1981). Difficulties with encoding make these patients especially susceptible to proactive interference from previously learned materials, which is apparent in free-recall tasks. Conversely, retrieval techniques that reduce interference (for example, cuing patients with the first two letters of words to be recalled, thereby limiting the number of words that might interfere with the target word) result in relatively normal recall (Warrington and Weiskrantz 1970).

Furthermore, while encoding of specific, data-based information (declarative information) may be defective, acquisition of procedural information, like perceptual-motor and pattern-analyzing skills, may remain intact. Patients may preserve the ability to "know how" to do something while losing the ability to "know that" something is so (Cohen and Squire 1980). Korsakoff patients also retain the ability to be classically conditioned, while not remembering the conditioning itself (Weiskrantz and Warrington 1979). Impaired recall of declarative information underscores the need to minimize novelty in the Korsakoff patient's environment; nonetheless, intact procedural memory and conditioning suggest that some "learning" may be possible.

In addition to anterograde amnesia, patients with Korsakoff's psychosis usually suffer from some retrograde amnesia, or difficulty retrieving from long-term memory events that occurred before the onset of illness. While a tendency to compensate for such memory impairments by confabulation is often cited as characteristic of the disorder, it is an inconstant finding, usually most marked during the acute stages of the illness and less noticeable as the more chronic patient adjusts to his deficits.

Beyond amnesic symptoms and despite normal verbal, performance, and full-scale IQ scores, Korsakoff patients, like other chronic alcoholics, often have neuropsychologic deficits involving visuospatial and concept formation. They may be associated with significant personality change, including apathy and lack of spontaneity. Damage to diencephalic structures (mamillary bodies and dorsomedial nucleus of the thalamus), found at autopsy, appears to underlie amnesic symptoms (Victor et al. 1971). Antemortem CT scan studies (Carlsson et al. 1979), showing dilation of the third ventricle, also suggest degeneration of midline thalamic nuclei. Other cognitive as well as behavioral deficits, which superficially resemble deficits associated with frontal lobe dysfunction in Type II schizophrenia, may relate to cortical atrophy (Butters 1981).

Korsakoff's syndrome and alcoholic dementia thus probably represent poles in a spectrum of disorders, with amnesic syndromes predominant in the former and cognitive deficits predominant in the latter. The etiology of Korsakoff's syndrome remains obscure. While thiamine deficiency may be important, other evidence implicates a direct toxic role for alcohol itself; Wernicke's encephalopathy can occur in the absence of alcoholism, but Korsakoff's syndrome is almost universally associated with prolonged alcohol abuse. Moreover, mice fed ethanol-containing but nutritionally controlled liquid diets for several months still show impairment on a variety of learning tasks (Freund 1973).

Alcoholic Dementia

Progressive, largely irreversible impairment in intellectual function, memory, and social behavior is not an uncommon complication of alcoholism. Perhaps 10 percent of chronic alcoholics are demented (Wilkinson et al. 1971). The incidence of dementia increases with age and is relatively higher in women. Fully one in three alcoholic women in their seventh decade are demented (Horvath 1975). Dementia is associated with a longer history of drinking and heavier alcohol consumption than uncomplicated chronic alcoholism. It is frequently preceded by episodes of delirium tremens, Wernicke's encephalopathy, or head trauma.

As noted above, alcoholic dementia is not synonymous with Korsakoff's psychosis: in addition to memory impairment, demented alcoholics show difficulty in visuospatial abstracting (analyzing complex visual stimuli) (Jones and Parsons 1972), and possibly in verbal abstracting (Parker et al. 1974), concept formation, and concept shifting (Tartar, 1975). Impaired abstracting ability (as demonstrated, for example, on the categories test of the Halstead-Reitan battery) has been found comparable to that in brain-damaged controls (Jones and Parsons 1971) and suggests mild to moderate dysfunction of the prefrontal cortex. Frontal lobe damage may also underlie the personality changes seen in chronic alcoholism. As with alcoholic amnestic symptoms, cognitive deficits may appear along a continuum, with alcoholic dementia being an extreme, but lesser degrees of impairment correlating with the amount of alcohol consumed even by sober social drinkers (Parker et al. 1983).

Cognitive impairment may have significant prognostic implications. At follow-up at two and a half to five years, Berglund and others (1977) found that alcoholics with more cognitive impairment during treatment were less likely to improve their drinking habits. Similarly, Abbott and Gregson (1981), using stepwise multiple linear regression and discriminate function analysis, found that the degree of cognitive dysfunction measured during treatment significantly predicted outcome—relapse versus abstinence or controlled drinking—at one-year follow-up. Thus cognitive dysfunction is both a consequence of prolonged alcohol consumption and a cause of further cycles of abuse.

Cognitive deficits associated with long-term alcohol abuse resemble those seen in normal senescence and Alzheimer's disease, prompting Ryan and Butters (1980) to hypothesize that alcohol accelerates normal age-related declines in cognitive functioning. However, alcoholic dementia may not completely mimic normal senescence: several components of sensory evoked potentials may be aberrant in alcoholics but not in aged normals (Porjesz and Begleiter 1982).

As in chronic schizophrenia, neuroanatomic changes may underlie the cognitive and behavioral disturbance in chronic alcoholism. Courville (1955) recorded atrophy, especially of the dorsolateral aspects of the prefrontal cortex, at postmortem in alcoholics. Pneumoencephalography revealed some abnormality, especially cortical atrophy and ventricular enlargement, in 70 percent of chronic alcoholics, all under age 60 (Brewer and Perrett 1971; Haug 1968). Duration of alcohol abuse and quantity consumed were related to the degree of cortical atrophy; this in turn was closely associated with deficits on psychometric testing (Brewer and Perrett 1971). More recent CT scans of long-term alcoholics have confirmed prefrontal atrophy (Kroll et al. 1980).

Some of this cortical atrophy may be reversible with short-term abstinence (Carlen et al. 1978). This reversal may be associated with improvement of alpha slowing on EEG (Carlen et al. 1977) and of psychometric testing performance (Carlen 1979). Short-term memory defects appear to be especially reversible with prolonged abstinence. However, certain cognitive impairments—for example, in learning novel associations or analyzing complex visual stimuli— may persist even after seven years of continuous sobriety (Brandt et al. 1983).

Conclusions

There are several similarities between the dementia of chronic alcoholism and that of chronic schizophrenia. Prefrontal dysfunction is evident in both and is supported by data from neuropathological, neuroradiological, and neurophysiological studies. This dysfunction produces specific behavioral and cognitive disturbances that interfere with adaptive functioning. There is a loss of ability to process novel and complex information, to filter distractions, and to plan. These deficits persist in the absence of more florid symptoms of either disorder and are associated with a poor prognosis.

Bipolar Disorder

Course and Outcome

Investigators since the time of Kraepelin have stressed that bipolar disorder, unlike schizophrenia, was associated with a relatively favorable course and outcome: some patients were noted to recover, while others had a variable number of manic or depressive episodes between which there was medical and social remission (Lundquist 1945). Recent studies suggest that this initial assessment may have been overly optimistic (Welner et al. 1977). Tsuang and others (1979) provided a 30- to 40-year follow-up of 100 patients with mania and compared them with 200 patients with schizophrenia and 160 controls (surgical patients who were free of psychiatric symptoms). Manic patients fared significantly better than schizophrenics; nonetheless, 19 percent never married, 25 percent had incapacitating symptoms, 12 percent were chronically hospitalized, and 21 percent were unable to work because of mental illness. The control subjects had much lower rates of disability on those variables, from 0 to 5 percent.

Longitudinal studies of bipolar illness have demonstrated a progressive increase in the frequency of cycling and a decrease in the well-intervals between episodes, as a function both of age and of number of previous episodes (Goodwin 1983). This progression occurs despite pharmacotherapy. In fact, treatments like tricyclic antidepressants may convert some patients from intermittently to continuously ill, without intervening well-intervals (Kukopulos et al. 1980). In addition, lithium may increase the frequency of recurrence among individuals with a "depression-mania-well-interval" pattern of illness (while providing prophylaxis for patients with a "mania-depression-well-interval" pattern). Once episodes increase to greater than four per year, lithium may lose its effectiveness (Dunner and Fieve 1974).

It has been suggested that frequent episodes of affective illness may facilitate ever more rapid recurrence of illness through an underlying sensitization process. Animal models of limbic system "kindling," in which repeated intracerebral electrical stimulation renders neuronal pathways (and associated behavior) more susceptible to reactivation, may account for this phenomenon (Post and Ballenger 1979). The anticonvulsant carbamazepine, especially effective in inhibiting limbic system excitability in kindling models, has been shown to provide prophylaxis in rapidly cycling bipolar patients who are lithium-resistant, decreasing the number, duration, and severity of episodes (Post et al. 1983)

Bipolar Dementia?

Thus it would appear that some patients with bipolar disorder—perhaps a quarter to a third—have a progressive course with poor outcome (Welner et al. 1977). We have seen that poor prognosis in schizophrenia and alcoholism may be associated with structural brain damage, evidenced by neuroradiological, neurophysiological, and neuropsychological studies. CT scan studies in manics reveal lateral ventricular enlargement, with approximately 30 percent of manics exceeding a control mean by two standard deviations (Nasrallah et al. 1982). PET scan studies in patients with affective illness, as with schizophrenia, suggest hypofrontality (Buchsbaum et al. 1983). Cerebral blood flow studies of bipolar patients in depressed or manic phases suggest they have slightly decreased flow to the nondominant hemisphere compared with controls (Rush et al. 1982). Neuropsychological testing of bipolar patients similarly suggests nondominant hemispheric dysfunction (Taylor et al. 1981). Tests of abstraction—for example, the categories test of the Halstead-Reitan battery—suggest greatest impairment in processing spatial information, again implicating the nondominant hemisphere. Impairment in bipolar depressed patients exceeds that in unipolar depressed patients or controls; deficits in older bipolars often exceed that expected in brain-damaged subjects (Savard et al. 1980).

On the basis of the above-mentioned longitudinal studies, we might expect such older bipolar patients to be a more continuously ill group. However, detailed correlational studies of biological markers and treatment response-prognosis have not been undertaken in bipolar illness as they have in schizophrenia and alcoholism. Studies that have addressed outcome have found little association between errors on neuropsychological tests (for aphasia screening) and response to somatic treatment (Taylor and Abrams 1981). If anything, neurophysiological abnormalities (nonspecific slowing on EEG), which might be associated with structural brain abnormalities, were moderately associated with *good* treatment outcome (Taylor and Abrams 1981).

To our knowledge, no study assessing outcome in bipolar patients with normal versus abnormal CT scans has been published. Nonetheless, we might hypothesize, by way of analogy with schizophrenia and alcoholism, that bipolar disorder in some individuals might be associated with progressive neuropsychiatric dysfunction, structural brain damage, accumulating cognitive impairment, treatment refractoriness, and susceptibility to relapse. Clearly more extensive research is indicated.

The Prefrontal Syndrome

Several converging lines of evidence suggest specific dysfunction of the prefrontal cortex in chronic (Type II) schizophrenia, alcoholic dementia, and possibly poor-prognosis bipolar disorder. The prefrontal cortex, while phylogenetically recent, represents more than 25 percent of the mass of the human cerebrum. It may be divided, on the basis of connections and functions, into two major components, lying dorsolaterally and ventromedially. The prefrontal cortex receives a variety of inputs related to the general drive state or arousal of the organism, to its internal needs, and to the motivational significance of external stimuli in gratifying those needs. In turn, it is responsible for forming cohesive behavioral schemes to obtain these goals.

Studies in laboratory animals suggest that simple, well-established behavioral patterns can be executed without the prefrontal cortex. More complex, novel behaviors, especially those discontinuous over time (that is, with long delays interposed) demand the involvement of the prefrontal cortex: the prefrontal cortex is necessary to bind individual elemental behaviors into a gestalt, an organized whole whose meaning transcends that of its component behaviors, to include the relation of these elements one to another (their timing and order) and to the overall goal.

In forming temporal gestalts, the prefrontal cortex embraces four functions, two apparently localized in its dorsolateral and two in its ventromedial (orbital) components. The dorsolateral prefrontal cortex is involved in the prospective function of *anticipation* or foresight, preparing the sensory and motor apparatus for a range of possible environmental cues relevant to the goal, thereby optimizing reception and compensating for expected movement. It is also involved in the retrospective function of *provisional memory*, allowing for the referral of any event in a behavioral sequence to preceding events or to the original scheme. The ventromedial prefrontal cortex is involved in *suppressing interference*, be it irrelevant external stimuli or internal drives or affects (Fuster 1980). It may also be involved in *maintaining cortical tone* (Luria 1973), evident in the vasodilation of cerebral blood vessels and increase in EEG fast-wave activity (desychronization) that accompany voluntary attention. Lesions to the prefrontal cortex result in characteristic deficits in motor, language, cognitive, and affective functioning.

Motor Disorders

Dorsolateral lesions (involving anticipation) affect the spontaneity and purposefulness of behavior. Severe lesions result in what Luria has called the "apathico-akinetico-abulic syndrome": behavior is not initiated but can be provoked (for example, an individual will not speak spontaneously but may respond automatically when a neighbor is questioned). Less extensive lesions produce fragmented responses, either aimless restlessness or irrelevant perseverative stereotypies. In either case, reference to a goal-oriented scheme is lost.

Language Disorders

Impaired motor behavior finds a counterpart in impaired speech. Severe lesions result in poverty of content: speech lacks spontaneity in what Luria has called "frontal dynamic aphasia" (Luria 1970). Posterior lesions, near Broca's area, affect the syntactic component of language, governing the relation between words (for example, subject, verb, and object). More anterior lesions affect the discourse component of language, governing the manner in which sentences are combined to construct an idea or story. This latter component appears to be especially disrupted in schizophrenia (Andreasen 1982). Furthermore, as dorsolateral lesions interfere with provisional memory, language loses its primacy over behavior. The individual may recall instructions and intend to comply with them but lack the capacity to compare ongoing actions with these instructions. The capacity to verify actions, to check them against the original cognitive scheme and notice mistakes, is lost.

Cognitive Disorders

Ventromedial lesions result in characteristic cognitive disturbances: an inability to sustain attention and to suppress irrelevant stimuli. Familiar but random behaviors (stereotypies) that superficially resemble goal-oriented behaviors break through, disrupting the intended gestalt; for example, when asked to light a candle, the individual may strike a match correctly but proceed to place the candle in his mouth, as if to smoke it (Luria 1973). Impaired suppression also affects the ability to analyze complex stimuli. Considered interpretations are replaced by impulsive, fragmentary guesses based on irrelevant details.

Attentional deficits can be measured by continuous-performance tasks (CPT), as noted in our discussion of alcohol withdrawal. CPT deficits have been most thoroughly investigated in cases of schizophrenia (Chapman 1979). More than 40 percent of patients with chronic schizophrenia show deficits in CPT performance (Orzack and Kornetsky 1966), which may persist despite clinical remission

(Wohlberg and Kornetsky 1973). Neuroleptic treatment apparently reduces such deficits (Kornetsky and Orzack 1978). Attentional deficits may underlie the characteristic "overinclusive" thought disorder of schizophrenics (Cameron 1946). Interestingly, this thought disorder may also be neuroleptic-responsive (Chapman and Knowles 1964).

Several theoretical models have been advanced to explain the attentional deficits in schizophrenia, including segmental set (Shakow 1962) and excessive arousal (Venables 1964). These models implicate dysfunction of the brainstem reticular activating system. We have seen how such deficits might also result from selective damage to the prefrontal cortex.

Disorders of Affect

Damage to the prefrontal cortex may produce specific disorders of affect. Dorsolateral lesions result in profound indifference and blunted affect. Ventromedial lesions reduce inhibition of instinctual drives. Individuals may inappropriately express euphoria or sexual or aggressive impulses (Rylander 1939).

Treatment

The homeless are not all mentally ill, and the mentally ill homeless do not all suffer from chronic, disabling, dementing diseases. Certainly many do, and any effective treatment approach must be sensitive to their unique vulnerability and needs. But if our clinical descriptions have shown anything, it is the heterogeneity of symptoms, treatment responses, and outcomes among the chronically psychiatrically ill.

First and foremost, treatment of this patient group must be flexible. Such flexibility depends on accurate diagnostic assessment, not only of manifest psychopathology but of more subtle neuropsychological deficits. We have repeatedly seen that measures of cognitive impairment have significant prognostic value; they should be an integral part of epidemiological surveys as well as individual evaluations. Beyond diagnosis, treatment of the mentally ill homeless may involve environmental interventions, rehabilitation, psychosocial approaches, and, in the case of chronic schizophrenia, pharmacotherapy.

The "Prosthetic Environment"

Individuals with largely irreversible prefrontal dysfunction have a need for ongoing compensatory interventions, what Lindsley (1970) has called a "prosthetic environment." Difficulties with anticipation and planning suggest the importance of active case management (Lamb 1980) and aggressive outreach. Without these, the symptoms of the mentally ill and their lack of goal-directedness will deny them continuous access to the very treatment they need.

Stein and Test (1980) have reported on the beneficial effects of an intensive community-based treatment program. They found that chronically disabled psychiatric patients provided with ongoing monitoring and outreach and a highly behavioral approach to acquiring skills for community living (Test and Stein 1976) were more likely to be employed, living independently, and free of productive psychotic symptoms (paranoia, thought disorder, agitation) than were hospitalized counterparts at 14-month follow-up. It should be noted, however, that the presence of deficit symptoms (withdrawal and retardation) did not differ between experimental and control groups, and that improvements in employment status, living situation, and productive symptomatology did not persist one year after the aggressive community program was replaced by more traditional programming. It would appear that ongoing, active involvement was necessary to compensate for the persisting deficit (prefrontal) symptoms. In its failure to effect permanent changes, this work provides a clear message: cognitive dysfunction may be largely irreversible, and commitment to intervention may life-long. Nonetheless, the authors suggest that community-based treatment, however intensive, may be less expensive than recurrent hospitalization (Weisbrod et al. 1980).

Deficits in filtering stimuli suggest the importance of individualized treatment. Vast public shelters are disruptive for neurologically intact individuals, let alone for the psychiatrically ill with impairments in sustaining attention. Intensive sociotherapy in the absence of medication may present comparable risk. A failure to control disruptive stimuli may account for the high relapse rate among neuroleptic-free chronic schizophrenics who receive intensive social casework (Hogarty et al. 1974a) as well as among those who return to overinvolved families with a high level of expressed emotion (Vaughn and Leff 1976). Neuroleptic drugs, as noted above, improve attention, may normalize autonomic arousal, and enable the schizophrenic to cope with added environmental stimulation. Social withdrawal may reduce the stimuli themselves, and for that reason may not be entirely undesirable (Falloon and Liberman 1983).

Unfortunately, social withdrawal also limits relationships based on reciprocity. The mentally ill individual relinquishes important social supports (Lipton et al. 1981). Moreover, people originally close to him simultaneously withdraw, fearful that they will fall beneath the shadow of stigma surrounding the mentally ill (Goffman 1963). A network of complex social supports no longer shields the chronic patient from life's stressors. Contacts that remain are less complex, members of such social networks being connected only to the impaired individual and not to each other. Such "unsupported" connections are easily disrupted—for example, by hospitalization—further limiting the individual's supports (Hammer 1981). Conversely, chronic patients with larger social networks are less likely to be rehospitalized (Sokolovsky et al. 1978). Moreover, they appear to be more satisfied and better functioning, especially if social contacts remain casual and unintrusive (Lehmann 1980).

Environmental interventions aimed at restoring social networks are clearly needed. Family work based on education and support may help some individuals, especially relatively early in the course of illness. Others may benefit from drop-in centers, which provide accessible, "supported" social groups—persisting even without individual initiative—and which tolerate optimal social distance. The need for flexibility, continuity, individualization, support, and tolerance in the treatment of the mentally ill is discussed in chapter 5.

Rehabilitation and Psychosocial Approaches

We have referred to the relative irreversibility of cognitive deficits and associated symptoms of the prefrontal syndrome. Yet lest we succumb to therapeutic nihilism, it is important to note, with Carlen (1979), that some intermediate stages of alcoholic dementia may be reversible with continuing sobriety, and, with Snyder and Harris (1976), that other dementias may improve with resolution of drug toxicity, medical illness, environmental stressors, and secondary depression. Moreover, recent work in the nascent field of "cognitive retraining" suggests that impaired individuals can, with extensive practice, be taught new strategies for carrying out psychological tasks. As Luria (1963) suggests, undamaged cortical function systems may be recruited to perform activities ordinarily performed by damaged areas. Cognitive retraining has helped victims of cerebro-vascular disease to overcome deficits in memory, attention, visuo-spatial perception, and problem-solving (R.M. Reitan, personal communication, 1983).

That this retraining may truly involve functional reorganization of the brain is suggested by a case report of alexia following infarc-tion in the left angular gyrus. One year after the stroke, the patient was able to read, albeit slowly. Serial regional cerebral flow studies before and after recovery revealed a novel redistribution of blood flow to the right temporal and occipital regions, suggesting that these areas had partially taken over the disturbed function (Demeu-risse et al. 1983). We can hope that, as the field develops, such cognitive retraining will come to supplement environmental inter-ventions in the rehabilitation of the severely mentally ill.

Individual and family psychotherapy may also have important roles in the treatment of the chronic mentally ill. While neither approach alone is as effective as pharmacotherapy in the manage-ment of chronic schizophrenia (Goldstein 1978; Grinspoon et al. 1972; May 1968), both approaches may enhance neuroleptic treat-ment. Thus Hogarty and others (1974a, 1974b) found that individ-ual "major role" therapy, a problem-solving, psychosocial technique, reduced relapse rates and improved social adjustment in neurolep-tic-maintained patients at two-year follow-up. Similarly, Leff (1979) has advocated working with families of medicated schizophrenics in multifamily groups. Overinvolved parents interact with less involved parents to learn more adaptive ways of dealing with their patient-offspring. Unfortunately, most studies of individual and family psychotherapy for the chronic mentally ill have not adequately considered diagnostic heterogeneity, have not controlled for neuro-leptic medication, and have not provided appropriate outcome measures. Future studies, it is hoped, will address these method-ologic issues (Mosher and Keith 1980).

Medication

Neuroleptic medication has been shown to be effective for a wide range of symptoms in acutely ill schizophrenic patients. Moreover, maintenance treatment with antipsychotic drugs offers protection from relapse for many chronic patients. Nonetheless, pharmaco-therapy in schizophrenia has not proven the panacea it was once thought to be. Approximately 30 percent of patients relapse within one year despite neuroleptic treatment. This significant relapse rate persists even when medication compliance is guaranteed with long-acting depot fluphenazine decanoate (Schooler et al. 1980). Neuroleptics (dopamine antagonists) may produce side effects like akinesia that mimic the deficit symptoms of schizophrenia (presumably due to hypofunctionality of dopamine systems). It is therefore not surprising that neuroleptics become less effective against deficit symptoms (retardation, indifference, disorientation) with prolonged use, while remaining effective against productive symptoms (hostility, paranoid delusions) (Goldberg et al. 1967).

These limitations should not detract from the enormous value of neuroleptics: they are still a mainstay of treatment, are clearly indicated for the control of productive symptoms, and obviously prevent relapse in more patients than not. What these limitations should indicate, however, is that antipsychotic drugs are not equally effective against all symptoms, that more is not always better, and that schizophrenics with predominant deficit symptoms may warrant a reduction in dose, a trial of anticholinergic medication, or even cautiously administered dopamine agonist treatment. Moreover, as continuous neuroleptic maintenance may not prevent relapse in all cases and may increase the risk of tardive dyskinesia, alternate drug treatment strategies are needed.

One such strategy, low-dose treatment (1.25 to 5 mg of fluphenazine decanoate biweekly), apparently results in a high relapse rate, but does not preclude rapid restabilization in the community (Kane 1983). Moreover, relatively young schizophrenics treated with this regimen appear less withdrawn and demonstrate fewer signs of dyskinesia. It should be emphasized that these patients received intensive follow-up. Nonetheless, if such follow-up can be provided, low-dose treatment may afford a reasonable approach to maintaining patients in the community while minimizing cumulative neuroleptic dose (Kane 1983).

A second strategy, intermittent or targeted treatment, involves following patients drug-free until prodromal signs of impending relapse appear. Medication is then provided to abort the impending episode, and discontinued following restabilization. Patients receiving targeted medication fare no worse, in terms of psychopathology ratings, number of hospitalizations, or days in hospital, than those receiving continuous drug treatment; moreover, cumulative neuroleptic exposure is diminished by 60 percent (Carpenter and Heinrichs 1983). Once again, it bears mentioning that the success of this approach lies partly in intensive follow-up—with individual, group, and family therapies and, when necessary, active environmental manipulation to reduce stress.

Conclusions

The homeless mentally ill suffer from diverse disorders of varying severity that call for a flexible approach to treatment. Neuropsychological impairments, when present, require environmental interventions including active case management, outreach, and stimulus reduction. Recent studies suggest that some impairments may be partly reversible with cognitive retraining. Neuroleptic medication, of limited value by itself, plays an integral role in the comprehensive treatment of schizophrenia. Newer treatment strategies, including low and intermittent dosing, may provide adequate prophylaxis against relapse of productive symptoms while minimizing deficit symptoms and cumulative drug exposure. These pharmacological approaches are most successful when combined with psychosocial interventions. Only through such individualized, comprehensive treatment can the needs of this highly vulnerable population be met.

References

Abbott MW, Gregson RAM: Cognitive dysfunction in the prediction of relapse in alcoholics. J Stud Alcohol 42:230-243, 1981

Andreasen NC: The relationship between schizophrenic language and the aphasias, in Schizophrenia as a Brain Disease. Edited by Henn FA, Nasrallah HA. New York, Oxford University Press, 1982

Andreasen NC, Olsen SA, Dennert JW, et al: Ventricular enlargement in schizophrenia: relationship to positive and negative symptoms. Am J Psychiatry 139:297-302, 1982

Angrist B, Rotrosen J, Gershon S: Differential effects of amphetamine and neuroleptics on negative versus positive symptoms in schizophrenia. Psychopharmacology 72:17-19, 1980

Angrist B, Peselow E, Rubinstein M, et al: Partial improvement in negative schizophrenic symptoms after amphetamine. Psychopharmacology 78:128-130, 1982

Arce AA, Tadlock M, Vergare MJ, et al: A psychiatric profile of street people admitted to an emergency shelter. Hosp Community Psychiatry 34:812-817, 1983

Bacopoulos NC, Spokes ES, Bird ED, et al: Antipsychotic drug action in schizophrenic patients: effects on cortical dopamine metabolism after long-term treatment. Science 205:1405-1407, 1978

Bambrilla, F, Guerrini A, Rovere C, et al: Growth hormone secretion in chronic schizophrenia. Neuropsychobiology 1:267-276, 1975

Bambrilla F, Scarone S, Ponzano M, et al: Catecholaminergic drugs in chronic schizophrenia. Neuropsychobiology 5:185-200, 1979

Baxter E, Hopper K: Private Lives/Public Spaces: Homeless Adults on the Streets of New York City. New York, Community Service Society, 1981

Berger PA: Biochemistry in schizophrenia: old concepts and new hypotheses. J Nerv Ment Dis 169:90-99, 1981

Berglund M, Risberg J: Regional cerebral blood flow in a case of amphetamine intoxication. Psychopharmacology 70:219-221, 1980

Berglund M, Risberg J: Regional cerebral blood flow during alcohol withdrawal. Arch Gen Psychiatry 38:351-355, 1981

Berglund M, Leijonquist H, Horlen M: Prognostic significance and reversibility of cerebral dysfunction in alcoholics. J Stud Alcohol 38:1761-1770, 1977

Berman KF, Zec RF, Weinberger DR: Impaired frontal cortical function in schizophrenia, I: rCBF evidence, in Abstracts, 39th Annual Meeting, Society of Biological Psychiatry, Los Angeles, 1984

Berze J: Primary Insufficiency of Psychic Activity. Vienna, Deuticke, 1914

Bird ED, Crow TJ, Iversen LL, et al: Dopamine and homovanillic acid concentrations in the postmortem brain in schizophrenia. J Physiol 293:36-37, 1979

Bland RC, Orn H: Schizophrenia: Schneider's first-rank symptoms and outcome. Br J Psychiatry 137:63-68, 1980

Bleuler E: Dementia praecox or the group of schizophrenias (1911). Translated by Zinkin J. New York, International Universities Press, 1950

Bogerts B, Hantsch J, Herzer M: A morphometric study of the dopamine-containing cellgroups in the mesencephalon of normals, Parkinson's patients, and schizophrenics. Biol Psychiatry 18:951-969, 1983

Bowers MB: Central dopamine turnover in schizophrenic syndromes. Arch Gen Psychiatry 31:50-54, 1974

Brandt J, Butters N, Ryan C, et al: Cognitive loss and recovery in long-term alcohol abusers. Arch Gen Psychiatry 40:435-442, 1983

Brewer C, Perrett L: Brain damage due to alcohol consumption: an air-encephalographic, psychometric, and electroencephalographic study. Br J Addict 66:170-182, 1971

Bridge TP, Cannon HE, Wyatt RJ: Burned-out schizophrenia: evidence for age effects on schizophrenic symptomatology. J Gerontol 33:835-839, 1978

Brockington IF, Kendell RE, Leff JB: Definitions of schizophrenia: concordance and prediction of outcome. Psychol Med 8:387-398, 1978

Brozoski TJ, Brown RM, Rosvold HE, et al: Cognitive deficits caused by regional depletion of dopamine in prefrontal cortex of rhesus monkey. Science 205:929-932, 1979

Buchsbaum MS, Ingvar DH, Kessler R, et al: Cerebral glucography with positron tomography: use in normal subjects and patients with schizophrenia. Arch Gen Psychiatry 39:251-259, 1982

Buchsbaum MS, Holcomb HH, DeLisi LE, et al: PET in schizophrenia and affective illness, in New Research Abstracts, 136th Annual Meeting, American Psychiatric Association, New York, 1983. Washington, APA, 1983

Burdick JA, Johnson LC, Smith JW: Measurement of change during alcohol withdrawal in chronic alcoholics. Br J Addict 65:273-280, 1970

Butters N: The Wernicke-Korsakoff syndrome: a review of psychological, neuropathological, and etiological factors, in Currents in Alcoholism, vol 8. Edited by Galanter M. New York, Grune & Stratton, 1981

Cameron NS: Experimental analysis of schizophrenic thinking, in Language and Thought in Schizophrenia. Edited by Kasanin JS. Berkeley, University of California Press, 1946

Caplan G: Support Systems and Community Mental Health. New York, Behavioral Publications, 1974

Carlen PL: Reversible effects of chronic alcoholism on the human central nervous system: possible biological mechanisms, in Cerebral Deficits in Alcoholism. Edited by Wilkinson DA. Toronto, Addiction Research Foundation 1979

Carlen PL, Blair RDG, Singh R, et al: Improvement from alcoholic organic brain syndrome: early EEG changes predict degree of psychologically and clinically assessed recovery. Can J Neurol Sci 4:224, 1977

Carlen PL, Wortzman G, Holgate RC, et al: Reversible cerebral atrophy in recently abstinent chronic alcoholics measured by computed tomography scans. Science 200:1076-1078, 1978

Carlson GA, Goodwin FK: The stages of mania: a longitudinal analysis of the manic episode. Arch Gen Psychiatry 28:221-228, 1973

Carlsson A, Lindqvist M: Effect of chlorpromazine and haloperidol on formation of 3-methoxy-tyramine and normetanephrine in mouse brain. Acta Pharmacol Toxicol 20:140-144, 1963

Carlsson C, Claesson L-E, Karlson K-T: Clinical psychometric and radiologic signs of brain damage in chronic alcoholism. Acta Neurol Scand 60:85-92, 1979

Carpenter WT Jr, Heinrichs DW: Early intervention, time-limited, targeted pharmacotherapy of schizophrenia. Schizophr Bull 9:533-542, 1983

Chapman LJ: Recent advances in the study of schizophrenic cognition. Schizophr Bull 5:568-580, 1979

Chapman LJ, Knowles RR: The effects of phenothiazine on disordered thought in schizophrenia. J Consult Psychol 28:165-169, 1964

Chouinard G, Jones BD: Schizophrenia as dopamine-deficiency disease. Lancet 2:99-100, 1978

Cohen NJ, Squire LR: Preserved learning and retention of pattern-analyzing skill in amnesia: dissociation of knowing how and knowing that. Science 210:207-210, 1980

Colon EJ: Quantitative cytoarchitectonics of the human cerebral cortex in schizophrenic dementia. Acta Neuropathol 20:1-10, 1972

Courville CB: The Effects of Alcohol on the Nervous System of Man. Los Angeles, San Lucus Press, 1955

Crow TJ: Molecular pathology of schizophrenia: more than one disease process? Br Med J 280:66-68, 1980

Crow TJ, Cross AJ, Johnstone EC, et al: Two syndromes in schizophrenia and their pathogenesis, in Schizophrenia as a Brain Disease. Edited by Henn FA, Nasrallah AH. New York, Oxford University Press, 1982

Dalton J, Robertson M: Cold injury caused by psychiatric illness: six case reports. Br J Psychiatry 140:615-618, 1982

Davis JM: Overview: maintenance therapy in psychiatry, I: schizophrenia. Am J Psychiatry 132:1237-1245, 1975

Davis JM: Antipsychotic drugs, in Comprehensive Textbook of Psychiatry, 3rd ed. Edited by Kaplan HI, Freedman AM, Sadock BJ. Baltimore, Williams & Wilkins, 1980

Demeurisse GL, Patte MJ, Verhas MJ: Bilateral cerebral functional reorganization after stroke in a patient with alexia without agraphia. Clinical Neuropsychology 5:179-180, 1983

Depue RA, Dupicki MD, McCarthy T: Differential recovery of intellectual associational and physiological functioning in withdrawn and active schizophrenics. J Abnorm Psychol 84:325-330, 1975

DeWardener HE, Lennox B: Cerebral beri beri (Wernicke's encephalopathy). Lancet 2:11-17, 1947

Diefendorf AR, Dodge R: an experimental study of the ocular reactions of the insane from photographic records. Brain 31:451-489, 1908

Dom R, DeSaedeleer J, Bogerts J, et al: Quantitative cytometric analysis of basal ganglia in catatonic schizophrenics, in Biological Psychiatry. Edited by Parris C. Struwe G, Jansson B. Amsterdam, Elsevier North Holland, 1981

Donnelly EF, Weinberger DR, Waldman IN: Cognitive impairment associated with morphological brain abnormalities on computed tomography in chronic schizophrenic patients. J Nerv Ment Dis 168:305-308, 1980

Dunner DL, Fieve RR: Clinical factors in lithium carbonate prophylaxis failure. Arch Gen Psychiatry 30:229-233, 1974

Dunnett SB, Iversen SD: Selective kainic acid (KA) and 6-hydroxydopamine (6-OHDA) induced caudate lesions in the rat: some behavioral consequences. Neurosci Lett (Suppl) 3:207, 1979

Economo CF: Encephalitis Lethargica: Its Sequelae and Treatment. Edited and translated by Neuman KO. London, Oxford Univeristy Press, 1931

Falloon RH, Liberman RP: Interactions between drug and psychosocial therapy in schizophrenia. Schizophr Bull 9:543-554, 1983

Faris REL, Dunham HW: Mental Disorders in Urban Areas. Chicago, University of Chicago Press, 1939

Farkas T, Reivich M, Alavi A, et al: The application of ^{18}F-deoxy-2-

fluoroglucose and positron emission tomography in the study of psychiatric conditions, in Cerebral Metabolism and Neural Function. Edited by Passonneau JV, Hawkins RA, Lust WD, et al. Baltimore, Williams & Wilkins, 1980

Fenton GW, Fenwick PBC, Dollimore J: EEG spectral analysis in schizophrenia. Br J Psychiatry 136:445-455, 1980

Ferrier IN, Roberts GW, Crow TJ, et al: Reduced cholecystokinin-like and somatostatin-like immunoreactivity in limbic lobe is associated with negative symptoms in schizophrenia. Life Sci 33:475-482, 1983

Fisman M: The brain stem in psychosis. Br J Psychiatry 126:414-422, 1975

Freund G: Chronic central nervous system toxicity of alcohol. Annu Rev Pharmacol 13:217-227, 1973

Fuster JM: The Prefrontal Cortex: Anatomy, Physiology, and Neuropsychology of the Frontal Lobe. New York, Raven Press, 1980

Gattaz WF, Riederer P, Reynolds G: Dopamine and neuroadrenalin in the cerebrospinal fluid of schizophrenic patients. Psychiatry Res 8:243-250, 1983

Gerlach J, Luhdorf K: The effect of L-dopa on young patients with simple schizophrenia treated with neuroleptic drugs: a double-blind crossover trial with madopar and placebo. Psychopharmacologia 44:105-110, 1975

Goffman E: Stigma. Englewood Cliffs, NJ, Prentice-Hall, 1963

Goldberg SC, Schooler NR, Mattsson N: Paranoid and withdrawal symptoms in schizophrenia: differential symptom reduction over time. J Nerv Ment Dis 145:158-162, 1967

Golden CJ, Moses JA, Zelazowski MA, et al: Cerebral ventricular size and neuropsychological impairment in young chronic schizophrenics: measurement by the standardized Luria-Nebraska Neuropsychological Battery. Arch Gen Psychiatry 37:619-623, 1980

Goldstein MJ, Rodnick EH, Evans JR, et al: Drug and family therapy in the aftercare of acute schizophrenics. Arch Gen Psychiatry 35:1169-1177, 1978

Goodwin FK: The natural course of manic-depressive illness, in Neurobiology of Mood Disorders. Edited by Post RM, Ballenger JC. Baltimore, Williams & Wilkins, 1983

Goodwin DW, Crane JB, Guze SB: Phenomenological aspects of the alcoholic "blackout." Br J Psychiatry 115:1033-1038, 1969

Goodwin DW, Othmer E, Halikas JA, et al: Loss of short-term memory as a predictor of the alcoholic "blackout." Nature 227:201-202, 1970

Grinspoon L, Ewalt JR, Shader RI: Schizophrenia: Pharmacotherapy and Psychotherapy. Baltimore, Williams & Wilkins, 1972

Hammer M: Social supports, social networks, and schizophrenia. Schizophr Bull 7:45-57, 1981

Hartmann EL: Sleep, in Comprehensive Textbook of Psychiatry, 3rd ed. Edited by Kaplan HI, Freedman AM, Sadock BJ. Baltimore, Williams & Williams, 1980

Haug JO: Pneumoencephalographic studies in mental disease. Acta Psychiatr Scand 38 (suppl 165):1-104, 1962

Haug J: Pneumoencephalographic evidence of brain damage in chronic alcoholics. Acta Psychiatr Scand (suppl 204):135-143, 1968

Helweg-Larsen P, Hoffmeyer H, Kieler J, et al: Famine disease in German concentration camps: complications and sequels. Acta Psychiatr Neurol Scand (suppl 83):1-460, 1952

Hempel K-J, Treff WM: Be steht eine korrelation zwischen nervenzellausfall und den schwundzellveranderungen bei der katatonie? J Hirnforsch 4:479-485, 1960

Hogarty GE, Goldberg SC, Schooler NR, et al: Drug and sociotherapy in the aftercare of schizophrenic patients, II: two year relapse rates. Arch Gen Psychiatry 31:603-608, 1974a

Hogarty GE, Goldberg SC, Schooler NR, et al: Drug and sociotherapy in the aftercare of schizophrenic patients, III: adjustment of non-relapsed patients. Arch Gen Psychiatry 31:609-618, 1974b

Holzman PS, Proctor LR, Hughes DW: Eye tracking patterns in schizophrenia. Science 181:179-181, 1973

Holzman PS, Levy DL: Smooth pursuit eye movements and functional psychoses: a review. Schizophr Bull 3:15-27, 1977

Horvath TB: Clinical spectrum and epidemiological features of alcoholic dementia, in Alcohol, Drugs, and Brain Damage: Proceedings of a Symposium: Effects of Chronic Use of Alcohol and Other Psychoactive Drugs on Cerebral Function. Edited by Rankin JG. Toronto, Alcoholism and Drug Addiction Research Foundation of Ontario, 1975

Huber G, Gross G, Schuttler K: A long-term follow-up study of schizophrenia: psychiatric course of illness and prognosis. Acta Psychiatr Scand 52:49-57, 1975

Hughes JS, Little JC: An appraisal of the continuing practice of prescribing tranquilizing drugs for long-stay psychiatric patients. Br J Psychiatry 113:867-873, 1967

Hultgren HN: Hypothermia, in Medicine for Mountaineering, 2nd ed. Edited by Wilkerson JA. Seattle, Mountaineers, 1975

Ingvar DH: Functional landscapes of the dominant hemisphere. Brain Res 107:181-197, 1976

Ingvar DH, Sjolund B, Ardo A: Correlation between dominant EEG frequency, cerebral oxygen uptake, and blood flow. Electroencephalogr Clin Neurophysiol 41:268-276, 1976

Isbell H, Fraser HF, Wickler A, et al: An experimental study of etiology of "rum fits" and delirium tremens. Q J Stud Alcohol 16:1-33, 1955

Itil TM: Qualitative and quantitative EEG findings in schizophrenia. Schizophr Bull 3:61-79, 1977

Javoy-Agid F, Agid Y: Is the mesocortical dopamine system involved in Parkinson's disease? Neurology 30:1326-1330, 1980

Jeste DV, Zalcman S, Weinberger DR, et al: Apomorphine response and subtyping of schizophrenia. Prog Neuropsychopharmacol 7:83-88, 1983

Johnstone EC, Crow TJ, Frith CD, et al: Cerebral ventricular size and cognitive impairment in chronic schizophrenia. Lancet 2:924-926, 1976

Johnstone EC, Crow TJ, Frith CD, et al: Mechanism of the antipsychotic effect in the treatment of acute schizophrenia. Lancet 1:848-851, 1978a

Johnstone EC, Crow TJ, Frith CD, et al: The dementia of dementia praecox. Acta Psychiatr Scand 57:305-324, 1978b

Jones B, Parsons OA: Impaired abstracting ability in chronic alcoholics. Arch Gen Psychiatry 24:71-75, 1971

Jones B, Parsons OA: Specific versus generalized deficits of abstracting ability in chronic alcoholics. Arch Gen Psychiatry 26:380-384, 1972

Kane JM: Low dose medication strategies in the maintenance treatment of schizophrenia. Schizophr Bull 9:528-532, 1983

Kaufmann CA, Weinberger DR, Linnoila M, et al: CSF monoamines and schizophrenic subtypes, in Abstracts, 39th Annual Meeting, Society of Biological Psychiatry, Los Angeles, 1984

Kety SS: The syndrome of schizophrenia: unresolved questions and opportunities for research (the 52nd Maudsley Lecture). Br J Psychiatry 136:421-436, 1980

Klein DF, Davis JM: Diagnosis and Drug Treatment of Psychiatric Disorders. Baltimore, Williams & Wilkins, 1969

Klein DF, Gittelman R, Quitkin A (eds): Diagnosis and Drug Treatment of Psychiatric Disorders: Adults and Children. Baltimore, Williams & Wilkins, 1980

Kleinman JE, Bridge TP, Karoum F, et al: Biochemical abnormalities in postmortem brain, in Perspectives in Schizophrenia Research. Edited by Baxter C, Melnechuk T. New York, Elsevier, 1980

Kornetsky C: Hyporesponsivity of chronic schizophrenic patients to dextroamphetamine. Arch Gen Psychiatry 33:1425-1428, 1976

Kornetsky C, Orzack MH: Physiological and behavioral correlates of attention dysfunction in schizophrenic patients. J Psychiatr Res 14:69-79, 1978

Kraepelin E: Dementia Praecox and Paraphrenia (1919). Translated by Barclay RM, Robertson SM. New York, Krieger, 1971

Kroll P, Seigel R, O'Neill B: Cerebral cortical atrophy in alcoholic men. J Clin Psychiatry 41:417-421, 1980

Kukopulos A, Reginaldi D, Laddomada P, et al: Course of the manic-depressive cycle and changes caused by treatment. Pharmakopsychiatria Neuro-psychopharmakologie 13:156-167, 1980

Lamb HR: Therapist-case managers: more than brokers of service. Hosp Community Psychiatry 31:762-764, 1980

Langfeldt G: The Prognosis of Schizophrenia. Copenhagen, Munksgaard, 1956

Lecrubier Y, Puech AJ, Widlocher D, et al: Schizophrenia: a bipolar dopaminergic hypothesis, in Proceeding of the 12th CINP Congress, Goteburg. Prog Neuropsychopharmacol, supplement, 1980

Lee T, Seeman P, Tourtelotte WW, et al: Binding of ^{3}H-neuroleptics and ^{3}H-apomorphine in schizophrenic brains. Nature 274:897-899, 1978

Leff JP: Developments in family therapy of schizophrenia. Psychiatr Q 51:216-232, 1979

Lehmann S: The social ecology of natural supports, in Community Mental Health: A Behavior-Ecological Perspective. Edited by Jeger A, Slotnich RW. New York, Plenum Press, 1980

Lemke R: Untersuchungen uber die social prognose der schizophrenie unter besonderer beruksichtisung des encephalographischen befundes. Archiv fur Psychiatrie 104:89-136, 1936

Letemendia FJJ, Harris AD: Chlorpromazine and the untreated chronic schizophrenic: a long-term trial. Br J Psychiatry 113:950-958, 1967

Lilliston L: Tests of cerebral damage and the process reactive dimension. J Clin Psychol 26:180-181, 1970

Lilliston L: Schizophrenic symptomatology as a function of probability of cerebral damage. J Abnorm Psychol 82:377-381, 1973

Lindsley OR: Geriatric behavioral prosthetics, in New Thoughts on Old Age. Edited by Kastenbaum RJ. New York, Springer, 1970

Lipowski ZJ: Organic brain syndromes: an overview and classification, in Psychiatric Aspects of Neurologic Disease. Edited by Benson DF, Blumer D. New York, Grune & Stratton, 1975

Lipton FR, Cohen CI, Fischer E, et al: Schizophrenia: a network crisis. Schizophr Bull 7:144-151, 1981

Lishman WA: Organic Psychiatry: The Psychological Consequences of Cerebral Disorder. Oxford, Blackwell Scientific, 1978

Lundquist G: Prognosis and course in manic-depressive psychoses: a follow-up study of 319 first admissions. Acta Psychiatr Scand (suppl)35:1-96, 1945

Luria AR: Restoration of Function After Brain Injuries. London, Pergamon, 1963

Luria AR: Traumatic Aphasia. The Hague, Mouton, 1970

Luria AR: The Working Brain: An Introduction to Neuropsychology. Translated by Haigh B. New York, Basic Books, 1973

Mackay AVP, Iversen LL, Rossor M, et al: Increased brain dopamine and dopamine receptors in schizophrenia. Arch Gen Psychiatry 39:991-997, 1982

Marsella AJ, Snyder KK: Stress, social supports, and schizophrenic disorders: toward an interactional model. Schizophr Bull 7:152-163, 1981

May PRA: Treatment of Schizophrenia. New York, Science House, 1968

Mayuzumi K, Tsutsui J: Abnormalities of pursuit eye movement and visual field in hemispherical brain damage. Acta Societatis Ophthalmologicae Japonicae 78:1059-1065, 1974

Meltzer HY, Fang VS: The effect of neuroleptics on serum prolactin in schizophrenic patients. Arch Gen Psychiatry 33:279-286, 1976

Meltzer HY, Busch D, Fang VS: Hormones, dopamine receptors, and schizophrenia. Psychoneuroendocrinology 6:17-36, 1981

Meyer A, McLardy T: Posterior cuts in prefrontal leucotomy: a clinico-pathological study. Journal of Mental Science 94:555-564, 1948

Mirsky AF: Neuropsychological bases of schizophrenia. Annu Rev Psychol 20:321-348, 1969

Morihisa JM, Duffy FH, Wyatt RJ: Brain electrical activity mapping (BEAM) in schizophrenic patients. Arch Gen Psychiatry 40:719-728, 1983

Mosher LR, Keith SJ: Psychosocial treatment: individual, group, family, and community support approaches. Schizophr Bull 6:10-41, 1980

Nasrallah HA, McCalley-Whitters M, Jacoby CG: Cerebral ventricular enlargement in young manic males: a controlled study. J Affective Disord 4:15-19, 1982

National Institute of Mental Health, Psychopharmacology Service Center, Collaborative Study Group: Phenothiazine treatment in acute schizophrenia: effectiveness. Arch Gen Psychiatry 10:246-261, 1964

Ogura C, Kishimoto A, Nakao T: Clinical effect of l-dopa on schizophrenia. Current Therapeutic Research 20:308-318, 1976

Orzack MH, Kornetsky C: Attention dysfunction in chronic schizophrenia. Arch Gen Psychiatry 14:323-326, 1966

Owen F, Cross AJ, Crow TJ, et al: Increased dopamine receptor sensitivity in schizophrenia. Lancet 2:223-226, 1978

Parker ES, Alkana RL, Birnbaum IM, et al: Alcohol and the disruption of cognitive processes. Arch Gen Psychiatry 31:824-828, 1974

Parker DA, Parker ES, Brody JA, et al: Alcohol use and cognitive loss among employed men and women. Am J Public Health 73:521-526, 1983

Persson T, Roos BE: Acid metabolites from monoamines in cerebrospinal fluid of chronic schizophrenics. Br J Psychiatry 115:95-98, 1969

Pfohl B, Winokur S: The evolution of symptoms in institutionalized hebrephrenic catatonic schizophrenics. Br J Psychiatry 141:567-572, 1982

Pincus JH, Tucker GJ: Behavioral Neurology. New York, Oxford University Press, 1978

Pope HG, Lipinski JF: Diagnosis in schizophrenia and manic-depressive illness: a reassessment of the specificity of "schizophrenic" symptoms in the light of current research. Arch Gen Psychiatry 35:811-828, 1978

Porjesz B, Begleiter H: Evoked brain potential deficits in alcoholism and aging. Alcoholism: Clinical Experimental Research 6:53-63, 1982

Portnoff LA, Dougan DR: Disturbances of attention in alcohol withdrawal syndrome. Int J Neurosci 18:183-190, 1983

Post RM, Ballenger JC: Models for the progressive development of behavioral psychopathology: sensitization to electrical, pharmacological, and psychological stimuli, in Handbook of Biological Psychiatry, part 4. Edited by van Praag HM, Lader MH, Rafaelson OJ. New York, Marcel Dekker, 1979

Post RM, Fink E, Carpenter WT Jr, et al: Cerebrospinal fluid amine metabolites in acute schizophrenia. Arch Gen Psychiatry 32:1063-1069, 1975

Post RM, Uhde TW, Ballenger JC, et al: Prophylactic efficacy of carbamazepine in manic-depressive illness. Am J Psychiatry 140:1602-1604, 1983

Prien RF, Cole JO: High dose chlorpromazine therapy in chronic schizophrenia. Arch Gen Psychiatry 18:482-495, 1968

Prien RF, Klett JC: An appraisal of the long-term use of tranquilizing medication with hospitalized schizophrenics: a review of the drug discontinuation literature. Schizophr Bull 5:64-73, 1972

Prien RF, Levine J, Cole JO: High dose trifluoperazine therapy in chronic schizophrenia. Am J Psychiatry 126:305-313, 1969

Pritchard M: Prognosis of schizophrenia before and after pharmacotherapy. Br J Psychiatry 113:1345-1359, 1967

Quitkin F, Rifkin A, Klein DF: Neurologic soft signs in schizophrenia and character disorders: organicity in schizophrenia with premorbid asociality and emotionally unstable character disorders. Arch Gen Psychiatry 33:845-853, 1976

Rush AJ, Schlesser MA, Stokely E, et al: Cerebral blood flow in depression and mania. Psychopharmacol Bull 18:6-8, 1982

Ryan C, Butters N: Learning and memory impairments in young and old alcoholics: evidence for the premature-aging hypothesis. Alcoholism 4:288-293, 1980

Rylander G: Personality Changes After Operations on the Frontal Lobes. London, Oxford University Press, 1939

Savard RJ, Rey AC, Post RM: Halstead-Reitan category test in bipolar and unipolar affective illness: relationship to age and place of illness. J Nerv Ment Dis 168:297-304, 1980

Scarpiti FR, Lefton M, Dinitz S, et al: Problems in a homecare study for schizophrenia. Arch Gen Psychiatry 10:143-154, 1964

Schneider K: Clinical Psychopathology. Translated by Hamilton MW. New York, Grune & Stratton, 1959

Schooler NR, Levine JR, Brauzer D, et al: Prevention of relapse in schizophrenia: an evaluation of fluphenazine decanoate. Arch Gen Psychiatry 37:16-24, 1980

Seidman LJ: Schizophrenia and brain dysfunction: an integration of recent neurodiagnostic findings. Psychol Bull 94:195-238, 1983

Shakow D: Segmental set: a theory of the formal psychological deficit in schizophrenia. Arch Gen Psychiatry 6:1-17, 1962

Simon H, Scatton B, LeMoal M: Dopaminergic A_{10} neurones are involved in cognitive functions. Nature 286:170-171, 1980

Snyder BD, Harris S: Treatable aspects of the dementia syndromes. J Am Geriatr Soc 24:179-183, 1976

Sokoloff L: Relation between physiologic function and energy metabolism in the central nervous system. J Neurochem 29:13-26, 1977

Sokolovsky J, Cohen C, Berger D, et al: Personal networks of ex-mental patients in a Manhattan SRO hotel. Human Organization 37:5-15, 1978

Stein LI, Test MA: Alternative to mental hospital treatment, I: conceptual model, treatment program, and clinical evaluation. Arch Gen Psychiatry 37:392-397, 1980

Stevens JR: Neuropathology of schizophrenia. Arch Gen Psychiatry 39:1131-1139, 1982

Stevens JR, Livermore A: Telemetered EEG in schizophrenia: spectral analysis during abnormal behavior episodes. J Neurol Neurosurg Psychiatry 45:385-395, 1982

Tartar RE: Psychological deficit in chronic alcoholics: a review. Int J Addict 10:327-368, 1975

Tatetsu S: A contribution to the morphological background of schizophrenia: with special reference to the findings in the telencephalon. Acta Neuropathol 3:558-571, 1964

Taylor MA, Abrams RC: Prediction of treatment response in mania. Arch Gen Psychiatry 38:800-803, 1981

Taylor MA, Redfield J, Abrams R: Neuropsychological dysfunction in schizophrenia and affective disease. Biol Psychiatry 16:467-478, 1981

Test MA, Stein LI: Practical guidelines for the community treatment of markedly impaired patients. Community Ment Health J 12:72-82, 1976

Trimble M, Kingsley D: Cerebral ventricular size in chronic schizophrenia. Lancet 1:278-279, 1978

Tsuang MT: Schizophrenic syndromes: the search for subgroups in schizophrenia with brain dysfunction, in Schizophrenia as a Brain Disease. Edited by Henn FA, Nasrallah HA. New York, Oxford University Press, 1982

Tsuang MT, Woolson RF, Fleming JA: Long-term outcome of major psychoses, I: schizophrenia and affective disorders compared with psychiatrically symptom-free surgical conditions. Arch Gen Psychiatry 39:1295-1301, 1979

Van Kammen DP, Mann LS, Sternberg DE, et al: Dopamine-beta-hydroxylase activity and homovanillic acid in spinal fluid of schizophrenics with brain atrophy. Science 220:974-976, 1983

Vaughn CE, Leff JP: The influence of family and social factors on the course of psychiatric illness. Br J Psychiatry 129:125-137, 1976

Venables PH: Input dysfunction in schizophrenia. Prog Exp Pers Res 1:1-47, 1964

Victor M, Adams RD, Collins GH: The Wernicke-Korsakoff Syndrome. Philadelphia, Davis, 1971

Von Bertalanffy L: General Systems Theory. New York, Braziller, 1968

Warringtron EK, Weiskrantz L: Amnesic syndrome: consolidation or retrieval? Nature 228:628-630, 1970

Weinberger DR, Wyatt RJ: Cerebral ventricular size: a biological marker for subtyping chronic schizophrenia, in Biological Markers in Psychiatry and Neurology. Edited by Hanin PI, Usdin E. New York, Pergamon, 1982

Weinberger DR, Torrey EF, Neophytides AN, et al: Lateral cerebral ventricular enlargement in chronic schizophrenia. Arch Gen Psychiatry 36:735-739, 1979

Weinberger DR, Bigelow LB, Klein JE, et al: Cerebral ventricular enlargement in chronic schizophrenia: association with poor response to treatment. Arch Gen Psychiatry 37:11-14, 1980

Weinberger DR, DeLisi LE, Perman GP, et al: Computed tomography in schizophreniform disorder and other acute psychiatric disorders. Arch Gen Psychiatry 39:778-783, 1982

Weingartner H, Faillace A: Alcohol and state-dependent learning in man. J Nerv Ment Dis 153:395-406, 1971

Weisbrod BA, Test MA, Stein LI: Alternative to mental hospital treatment, II: economic benefit-cost analysis. Arch Gen Psychiatry 37:400-405, 1980

Weiskrantz L, Warrington EK: Conditioning in amnesic patients. Neuropsychologia 17:187-194, 1979

Welner A, Welner Z, Leonard MA: Bipolar manic-depressive disorder: a reassessment of course and outcome. Compr Psychiatry 18:327-332, 1977

Wilkinson P, Kornaczewski A, Rankin JG: Physical disease in alcoholism: initial survey of 1,000 patients. Med J Aust 1:1217-1223, 1971

Wohlberg GW, Kornetsky C: Sustained attention in remitted schizophrenics. Arch Gen Psychiatry 28:533-537, 1973

Wyatt RJ: The dopamine hypothesis: variations on a theme. Presented at the American College of Psychiatrists, New Orleans, 1983

Zubin J: Chronic schizophrenia from the standpoint of vulnerability, in Perspectives in Schizophrenia Research. Edited by Baxter C, Melnechuk T. New York, Elsevier, 1980

Chapter 11

Medical Aspects of Homelessness

Philip W. Brickner, M.D.
Thomas Filardo, M.D.
Michael Iseman, M.D.
Richard Green, M.D.
Barbara Conanan, R.N.
Alexander Elvy, M.S.W.

The physical disorders of the homeless are all the ills to which flesh is heir, magnified by disordered living conditions, lack of heat and protection from the elements, lack of sleeping accommodations, and overcrowding in shelters. These factors are exacerbated by stress, psychiatric disorders, and the consequent sociopathic behavior patterns of many of the people. The problems of alcoholism and drug abuse are added to this picture.

To be specific, we are dealing with the consequences of trauma, both major and petty; the problems of infestation with scabies and lice, and the skin infections that ensue; the problems of peripheral vascular disease, cellulitis, and leg ulcers, which stem from the fact that these men and women are required to keep their legs in dependent positions day after day; plus all the standard medical disorders,

Dr. Brickner is director of the Department of Community Medicine at St. Vincent's Hospital and Medical Center of New York, in New York City. Dr. Filardo is assistant professor in family practice at the University of Illinois College of Medicine at Urbana/Champaign. Dr. Iseman is associate professor of medicine in the Division of Pulmonary Sciences at the University of Colorado School of Medicine in Denver. Dr. Green is an associate attending physician in dermatology at New York University Medical Center in New York City. Ms. Conanan is director of the SRO/Homeless Program in the Department of Community Medicine at St. Vincent's Hospital and Medical Center of New York. Mr. Elvy is a social worker and community organizer in the Department of Community Medicine at St. Vincent's Hospital and Medical Center of New York.

including cardiac disease, diabetes mellitus, hypertension, acute and chronic pulmonary disease, and tuberculosis.

Defining the Homeless

Our concern is those men and women living on the streets of our cities or gathered into shelters. They are skid row people, present in every large city, and noted by sociologists since the Civil War era (Bahr and Caplow 1973; Blumberg et al. 1978); patients deinstitutionalized from mental hospitals in the last two decades; and the newly homeless, people without jobs alienated from their families.

In addition, for this discussion we must add those who are living isolated lives in marginal housing, such as rooming houses and single-room-occupancy (SRO) hotels. In cities where the phenomenon of gentrification is taking place, SRO residents are at risk of homelessness. Furthermore, the similarities of personal conduct, sociopathy, and illness between the truly homeless individuals and those in marginal housing are striking. The discussion of tuberculosis, below, makes the point.

Treating Chronic Illness in the Homeless

Management of patients with chronic illness is a difficult task for health workers in the most favorable of circumstances. The ability of people living normal lives to cooperate with complex medical regimens, dietary restrictions, and other compromises to an unfettered style of life is often poor, and yet we feel that adherence to these therapeutic plans is essential to disease control and recovery. By adding homelessness as a factor, the entire treatment structure becomes vastly more complex.

Chronic diseases are those that necessitate, for successful management, continued involvement by the patient and steady, persistent monitoring by health workers. Diabetes mellitus, for instance, often fails to produce significant symptoms, even when control is poor. By the time patients with this disorder become acutely aware of symptoms, a medical emergency may exist.

Hypertension is the classic silent disease, which can announce its presence by a life-threatening or lethal catastrophe. Hypertension is present in 40 to 50 percent of homeless people studied (Brickner and Kaufman 1973; work in progress at St. Vincent's Hospital, New York City). This disorder is ranked as the fourth most commom ambulatory care diagnosis in the United States (National Ambulatory Medical Care Survey 1980). While we recognize a parallel incidence of this disorder in the homeless and the population at large, distinctions exist as well. Among them is the well-established fact that blacks have an increased incidence of high blood pressure, and that blacks are overrepresented in the homeless group.

Homeless patients are usually the poorest of the poor, the most destitute of the disenfranchised in our complex world. We live in a society that demands much of healthy people, and considerably more of those burdened with even a minor and self-limiting disease. Poverty prevents patients from acquiring medicines unless they have the motivation to make the bureaucracy of the welfare system work for them. Where there is cash available for medicines, priorities of homeless people for spending may differ from those of health care providers. Often shelter, food, or substances of abuse come first.

Once medicines are obtained, storage may present a problem. Bottled pills or capsules must be kept dry, and subjecting them to constant motion in a pocket may in many cases mill them to a powder. Insulin is an obvious example of storage difficulty for the homeless person, since refrigeration is rarely if ever available. In the winter, freezing is a problem, not only for insulin but for any medication in liquid form. Establishment of a sterile injection site presents obvious problems for diabetics. Possession of hypodermic supplies adds significant risk in the violent, drug-abusing environment of the typical homeless diabetic. The alcohol used to cleanse the skin and the vial top are also subject to confiscation by stronger members of the social group. In addition, any medication is subject to sale or barter.

Dietary issues are significant in the treatment of chronic illness, and clearly the homeless have an unfavorable situation. Lack of cooking facilities virtually eliminates the possibility of the sort of caloric and sodium intake control that treatment of diabetes and hypertension requires. In the most destitute, who may eat refuse, nutrient intake is completely random. When some money is available for food and is so expended, fast foods are often the choice. Fast food shops are less likely to evict poorly attired and unwashed customers, and offer relatively cheap food in an impersonal atmosphere. Soup kitchens and other charity establishments may or may not offer the controlled diets needed.

Winnick (1983) analyzed the constituents of the monthly menu prepared by the Human Resources Administration of New York City for use in the shelter system. He found that the diet fulfilled the standard daily nutrient requirements that have been accepted for the general population of the country. He pointed out, however, that the diet included large quantities of potato chips, pickled beets, sauerkraut, sour pickles, luncheon meats, franks and beans, and cheese, all heavily loaded with sodium. This sort of food intake, on a regular basis, has harmful implications for people at risk of hypertension and hypertensive cardiovascular disease.

Let us focus on the course of diabetes mellitus in patients who are insulin-dependent. Scheduling of meals and insulin injections presents a significant burden even to people with the stability of a home. Homeless individuals are far less likely to be able to coordinate scheduling of food intake with insulin dosage.

With poor control of serum glucose among these individuals, renal and ocular damage ensue, infections become more common, and hospitalization rates increase. Once ocular disease progresses to the point of diminished vision or blindness, the victim of diabetic microangiopathy is constrained to a narrow corridor of human potential and, if homeless, will soon be unable to compete in a terribly harsh environment.

Stress, that vaguely defined but omnipresent magnifier of disease processes, is particularly relevant to the two disorders we have just touched upon. Hypertension is well known to be aggravated by stress. The consequences in diabetes mellitus are similar, since glucose levels shift upward under conditions identified by the patient as stressful. Life on the streets or in the various makeshift shelters is replete with stressors of a magnitude that are hard to imagine by those of us who return each day to a stable home.

Treatment of chronic illness in homeless people is cost-effective compared to the alternative of ignoring the problem. Outpatient maintenance with insulin costs a few dollars a week, hospitalization a few hundred dollars a day. Hypertension, like diabetes, costs relatively little to control in most cases. The drugs, although at times rather expensive relative to other medications, are cheaper than dealing with the sequelae of uncontrolled elevated blood pressure: stroke, myocardial infarction, and end-stage renal disease.

Major Clinical Problems

Organized information about the nature, extent and distribution of medical disorders in the homeless is sparse. The available data indicate that, in addition to the chronic illnesses noted above, major problems exist in the areas of infestations, peripheral vascular disease, trauma, and pulmonary tuberculosis (Brickner and Kaufman 1973; Brickner et al. 1972; Kelly 1983; Noble 1983).

Infestations: Scabies and Lice

Scabies. Scabies is a highly contagious condition caused by a mite and manifested clinically as an intensely itchy cutaneous disease. This disorder is a common clinical problem in homeless people congregated in shelters (Felman and Nikitas 1980; Green 1983; New York City Department of Health 1983), and is nearly intractable in terms of control. Human scabies is caused by the host-specific mite *Sarcoptes scabiei*, which is white, eyeless, and oval, with small brown spines and eight short legs. The male mite is .2 mm in length, the female .3 mm.

The scabies mite is an obligate parasite and can survive for only two to three days away from the human skin, where it completes its entire life cycle in 30 days. The female mite, after being fertilized on the surface, excavates a burrow on the outermost layer of the skin. Here it lays ten to 25 eggs before dying. The eggs hatch within three to four days, and the emerging larvae mature on the skin surface. Common locations of colonization are the hands, wrists, armpits, feet, waist, breasts, and male genitalia. The giveaway lesion is a burrow, the tunnel that the female mite excavates while laying her eggs. Burrows are commonly observed on the hands, especially in the webs of the fingers and on the ventral surface of the wrists.

Other lesions include excoriations, vesicles, indurated nodules, and eczematoid dermatitis. Complications derived from secondary bacterial infection include abcesses, pyelonephritis, pyogenic pneumonia, and septicemia (New York City Department of Health 1983).

The diagnosis of scabies is made by the clinical presentation of intense pruritis in association with the lesions described above. A history of contact with infested patients also supports the diagnosis. It can be verified by scraping suspicious areas on the skin surface and identifying the organism or its eggs under the microscope. Skin biopsy specimens, of course, also can show the organism.

Scabies is usually considered a sexually transmitted disease. The act of sexual intercourse, however, is of secondary importance. The primary means of transmission are the acts of people sleeping together or sharing clothing.

The itching and skin eruption that accompany scabies are not caused by the organism, but rather by an allergic response. This reaction usually takes four to six weeks to develop. Hence one can have scabies for up to that period of time without clinical symptoms, an important fact for management of the condition.

Treatment of scabies is both simple and effective. The most widely used agent is gamma benzine hexachloride, or lindane. A 1% lotion or cream is applied to the entire body surface except the head and left on overnight. The next day the medication is washed off. The clothes the patient wore on the preceding day and the bed linens are washed in very hot water. Although the medication is lethal to the organism, pruritis can persist for one to two weeks, until the mite antigens are sloughed off with the dead skin layers.

The great difficulty in treating scabies in homeless people is that we cannot simultaneously control all their contacts. In a normal situation, if a patient has scabies, everyone in the household is treated at the same time. The homeless have temporary shelters and are moving from place to place. Today's cure becomes tomorrow's reinfection.

Lice. Let us now picture an elderly man with a generalized dermatitis lying beneath a sheet on the examination table in the emergency room of a hospital, shivering and scratching. Almost all of his skin is red and scaly. There are many scratch marks, with dried blood, but no primary lesions to help you make a diagnosis. An intern asks you to examine his ragged dirty clothing draped over a chair in the room. You notice a movement near the seams. On closer inspection you find that the clothing is alive with hundreds of tiny elongated white bodies. You spear one with a needle, place it on a slide for inspection under a microscope, and find a small moving insect. This is a louse.

Three species of lice affect humans. *Phthiris pubis*, commonly known as the crab or pubic louse, affects the pubic area and other hairy parts, including the eyelashes. These lice are spread primarily by sexual relations and are uncommon in the homeless. *Pediculus capitis*, head lice, are moderately common in the homeless and are found on the scalp or the back of the neck. They are usually associated with body lice. *Pediculus corporis*, body lice, cause severe skin eruptions in the homeless, and are those found in the clothing of the man in the emergency room. These lice spend most of their life cycle in garments worn by infested people.

Lice are small, flattened, wingless insects with three pairs of conspicuous legs ending in a claw. The female, after being fertilized, lays eggs at the base of the hairs or, in the case of body louse, on rough fibers of clothing, especially around the seams. The egg, together with a substance that attaches the egg to the hair or fibers, is called the nit. The eggs hatch in five to ten days, and the larvae quickly mature to an adult form. Lice spend their entire life cycle on or close to human skin and can live without feeding for only three to four days. The egg, however, can survive up to six weeks.

Lice have a stylet for piercing the skin and a tube-like structure to draw in blood. They also deposit saliva in the wound they create, and it is the saliva that causes the inflammatory response. Pubic lice are approximately 1 mm in size. Head and body lice are 3 to 4 mm, are readily seen, and are easy to diagnose. Sometimes one sees only the nits in the scalp or pubic areas. They also are readily diagnostic.

Body lice spread among the homeless through exchange of clothing, or when people are huddled together on the streets or in shelters. Complications of infestation that occur especially in this group of people are bacterial infections from scratching and poor hygiene.

Eradication of lice presents the same problem for homeless people in shelters as does the control of scabies. Reinfestation is almost inevitable. Treatment of individuals is effective, through the use of lindane and the fumigation of clothing.

Trauma

The few existing studies of health problems in the homeless indicate that injury is a common cause for which they seek medical attention. Table 1, compiled from a 1973 study at a free clinic in New York City, indicates that trauma was a major complaint in close to 20 percent of patients seen (Brickner and Kaufman 1973).

Kelly, in his 1983 analysis of this issue in San Francisco, notes the vulnerability of the homeless to trauma:

> Without safe refuge, [the homeless] are vulnerable to criminal acts such as robbery, assault, and rape. People whose faculties

Table 1
Presenting medical diagnoses in 434 homeless patients seen in a free clinic in New York City

Diagnosis		N[1]
Acute or chronic alcoholism		160
Drug use, intravenous or subcutaneous		102
Trauma		80
Assault	32	
Accidental	38	
Burns	10	
Respiratory infection		76
Active pulmonary tuberculosis		6
Cardiovascular disease		54
Leg ulcer, cellulitis		41
Acute gastrointestinal disease		22
Seizure disorder		16
Jaundice or ascites		15
Venereal disease		7
Gonorrhea	5	
Primary lues	2	
Osteomyelitis		2

[1]Several patients had multiple diagnoses.

are impaired by alcoholism and mental illness are particularly susceptible to injury. Their recovery may be hampered by inadequate wound care, poor nutrition, and exposure (Kelly 1983).

Immediate care of serious injuries is often excellent, because patients are commonly brought to hospital emergency rooms for treatment. However, the requisite follow-up frequently fails because of the situations of these people. Obstacles to follow-up care are the low priority the patients assign to such care; patients' confusion due to psychiatric illness, organic brain syndrome, and/or alcoholism; and the negative attitude of health workers.

In Kelly's study, the records of all patients entering the inpatient services of San Francisco General Hospital in the first three months of 1983 were reviewed. Three hundred and forty homeless patients were admitted (6.7 percent of total admissions); 50 (14.7 percent) suffered from major trauma.

The homeless major trauma victims included men and women of all ages, but were typically males from 20 to 39 years of age. They suffered a great variety of trauma, including stab wounds, fractures, head injuries, blunt trauma, multisystem trauma, gunshots, suicide attempts, burns, and bites. Injuries included complex facial fractures, hip fractures, pneumothoraces, and lacerations of the face, eyelids, neck, chest, liver, large and small bowel, and tendons of the hands. Stab wounds and fractures predominated and accounted for 64% of injuries (Kelly 1983).

Peripheral Vascular Disease, Cellulitis, and Leg Ulcers

Homeless people suffer from lower-leg disorders to a disproportionate degree because they are often denied the opportunity to lie down at night. If the legs always remain in a dependent position, edema and loss of venous valve competence occur, followed by decrease in microvascular circulation to the skin. Inflammation, chronic phlebitis, infection, and ulceration are the consequences. Treatment of these disorders is a slow, painstaking process, often difficult for homeless patients to accept, as the following case report indicates.

A 65-year-old man was induced to come for treatment of a massive leg ulcer due to venous stasis, trauma, and neglect. The patient had visited the emergency rooms and outpatient departments of local hospitals but had always refused hospital admission and did not keep clinic appointments. The ulcer involved the entire anterior and lateral surface of the left leg below the knee. Exuberant granulation tissue made the circumference three times that of the right leg. When the patient was first seen, purulent, foul-smelling drainage was marked, despite any benefits rendered by the maggots found in the lesion.

Treatment lasted for ten months and consisted of warm antiseptic soaks (up to five times per week), sterile dressings, and oral antibiotics. Although the patient was persuaded to visit the clinic daily, he often refused soaks and antibiotics. Improvement was slow.

When reepithelialization was almost complete and drainage minimal, the patient refused to return to the clinic. When outreach staff visited him, he would not discuss his leg, which was seen to be reinfected; the newly formed skin had been destroyed, and gross purulent drainage was present.

When staff made another visit to the patient, he was semicoma-

tose on the floor. The leg was gangrenous. The patient was removed
to the hospital (Brickner et al. 1972).

Cellulitis is a common complaint (see Table 1). In another study
Noble (1983) reviewed 75 urgent admissions to the emergency overnight shelter at Boston City Hospital during the first nine months
of 1983. Of these, 20 were patients with cellulitis of a severity
requiring immediate care. Some were straightforward streptococcal
cellulitides; others involved deep infection of tissues. Nine of the
20 had leg ulcers in addition.

Frostbite may be a significant contributing factor in peripheral
vascular diseases among homeless people during very cold weather.
This, of course, is a consequence of exposure to cold, but the
problem is aggravated by damp clothing, which can freeze, and by
the effects of ethanol intoxication and poor nutrition, which lead
to failure of thermoregulatory mechanisms (Goldfrank and Kirstein
1982). Eight of Noble's 75 emergency admissions in Boston had
frostbite.

As Mulcare (1983) points out, a normal individual empties the
venous system in the legs through standard forms of muscular action.
In a person with incompetent venous valves, however, constant
back pressure inhibits emptying. The critical factor in prevention
and treatment is elevation of the legs. This practice minimizes the
initial threat of risk to the valves. If valve damage has occurred, it
permits venous emptying via the effects of gravity.

The use of external compression through elastic stockings is another
means of counteracting elevated venous tension. Encouraging dry
feet and socks minimizes the likelihood and harmful consequences
of skin breakdown.

An effective treatment regimen for leg ulcers that is easy, safe,
and inexpensive includes simple cleansing with soap and water,
application of a dry dressing, and wrapping with an ace bandage.
Antibiotic ointments are expensive, greasy, and can lead to allergic
reactions. They should be avoided.

A more complex procedure, the use of the Unna boot, may sometimes be necessary. This is a gauze roll impregnated with substances
including gelatin and zinc oxide, wrapped around the leg over the
ulcerated area. The boot serves as a source both of external support
and of antisepsis. However, Unna boots are fairly expensive, require
regular changing, and present some risk, because they are circum-
ferential dressings, which may occlude the arterial circulation.

Tuberculosis

From 1947 to 1952, when isoniazid, streptomycin, and para-aminosalicylic acid were discovered, tuberculosis (TB) went from a disease with a less than a 50 percent five-year survival rate to merely another infectious disorder that was curable in almost every instance. In the modern era of tuberculosis chemotherapy, TB sanitoria have been closed, specialty clinics have been curtailed, and long-term inpatient care has been abandoned in favor of ambulatory treatment.

Unfortunately these changes have resulted in a substantially worse outcome in many cases. The public no longer perceives tuberculosis as an ominous disease, and both professional and lay concern have substantially diminished. Through lack of interest, lack of resolve, and/or lack of resources, few public health officers consistently enforce the statutes related to TB. And as chemotherapy has shifted to the outpatient setting, many patients have either abandoned treatment or taken their medications so erratically that treatment failures or relapses ensue, frequently with drug-resistant organisms (Leff et al. 1981). The homeless mentally ill, who have a poor record of compliance with treatment for any disorder, are among those most unlikely to be engaged in a tuberculosis treatment regimen, and most likely to drop out.

In relation to tuberculosis, the homeless in America are in double jeopardy: not only is it unlikely that, once they are afflicted, they will receive curative chemotherapy, but they are at high risk of developing tuberculosis.

Groups at Risk

We inherited from Europe a 500-year cycle of epidemic tuberculosis, which has substantially receded in this century; such circumstances as improved nutrition, more hygenic housing, the sanitorium movement with patient isolation, and chemotherapy are responsible for the decline. However, this reduction has left behind pools of residual infection and encapsulated mini-epidemics within defined groups in America, including the elderly, minorities, recent immigrants, and substance abusers. These groups contribute substantially to the ranks of the homeless.

The elderly have a strikingly increased risk for tuberculosis, which is substantially related to the aftermath of the above-mentioned epidemic. Since TB was rampant in the first decades of this century, the vast majority of today's elderly were exposed to it in childhood. At the turn of the century more than half of the urban high school graduates had a positive tuberculin skin test, evidence of tuberculosis infection. Most have remained free of overt tuberculous disease until their sixth, seventh, and eighth decades. Now a variety of factors, such as the stresses of inadequate housing and nutrition that many older people experience, have combined to diminish their immunological defenses and tip the balance in favor of the mycobacterium. U.S. Public Health Service data for 1980 indicate the following age-group prevalence rates, expressed as cases of disease per 100,000 persons per year: overall prevalence, 12.3; 20 to 34 years, 9; 35 to 44 years, 14; 45 to 54 years, 18; 55 to 64 years, 20; and over 65 years, 31 (Iseman 1983).

Many members of minority groups have recently come from regions where tuberculosis is still epidemic. A small percentage arrive in the United States with active disease. A vastly greater number arrive infected but without overt disease; subsequently, under the stresses associated with the immigrant life-style, they develop active tuberculosis. Under either circumstance, there is a great risk for communication of the disease to others. Extraordinarily crowded housing or transient sleeping quarters promote spread of this infection, which under ordinary circumstances is only minimally contagious. Data from Colorado, which are typical of national statistics, indicate

Table 2
Preliminary results of tuberculosis screening program in shelters and SRO hotels in New York City

Outcome	Shelters (N = 355)	SROs (N = 117)	Total (N = 472)
PPD reactors[1]	128 (36%)	58 (50%)	186 (39%)
PPD nonreactors	177 (50%)	52 (44%)	229 (49%)
Noncompliers with PPD testing[2]	50 (14%)	7 (6%)	57 (12%)
Cases of active TB	18 (5%)	3 (2.5%)	21 (4.5%)

[1]Residents with a positive reaction to the test antigen PPD (purified protein derivative), indicating tuberculosis infection but not necessarily active disease
[2]These individuals refused to have skin tests.

strikingly disparate rates of tuberculosis among various racial or ethnic groups. Expressed as cases per 100,000 population per year, the rates are whites, 4; blacks, 12; whites with Spanish surnames, 15; American Indians, 75; and Southeast Asians, approximately 1,000 (Iseman 1983).

Another pool of tuberculosis in America exists among substance abusers. By far the most prominent group here is alcoholics. For a variety of reasons, there is a strong association between tuberculosis and alcohol abuse. Exact prevalence data are difficult to obtain. However, estimates of tuberculosis case rates in unaffiliated or homeless urban alcoholics range as high as 500 per 100,000 per year.

Hard data are also difficult to obtain for TB case rates among the other large group of substance abusers, heroin addicts. Nevertheless, limited surveys indicate a high level of both tuberculosis infection and tuberculosis disease among this group.

Current Studies on TB Among the Homeless

Analyses carried out among homeless people and SRO residents in New York City in the last several years provide information on tuberculosis prevalence among these groups. In 1980 a preliminary

Table 3
Relation of length of stay in shelters and SRO hotels to positive PPD reaction (positive tuberculin skin test)

Length of stay	Shelters (N = 355) N	Positive PPD reactors	SROs (N = 117) N	Positive PPD reactors	Total (N = 472) N	Positive PPD reactors
1 month	50	13 (26%)	2	1	52	6 (27%)
1–3 months	35	9 (26%)	5	1	40	10 (25%)
3–6 months	57	18 (32%)	3	1	60	19 (32%)
6 months–1 year	67	27 (40%)	4	1	71	28 (39%)
1–2 years	39	19 (49%)	18	7 (39%)	57	26 (46%)
2–4 years	32	15 (47%)	22	13 (62%)	54	28 (52%)
4 or more years	75	39 (52%)	63	33 (53%)	138	72 (52%)

Table 4
Rates of positive PPD reaction (positive tuberculin skin test) among residents in shelters and SRO hotels, by race and ethnic distribution

Race or ethnic group	Shelters (N=355)		SROs (N=117)		Total (N=472)	
	Distri-bution	Positive PPD reactors	Distri-bution	Positive PPD reactors	Distri-bution	Positive PPD reactors
White	82 (23%)	27 (33%)	62 (47%)	23 (37%)	144 (34%)	50 (35%)
Black	227 (64%)	89 (39%)	44 (42%)	31 (71%)	271 (54%)	120 (44%)
Hispanic	14 (13%)	16 (36%)	11 (11%)	6 (54%)	57 (12%)	22 (39%)

Table 5
Rates of positive PPD reaction (positive tuberculin skin test) among residents in shelters and SROs, by age group

Age group	Shelters (N = 355)		SROs (N = 117)		Total (N = 472)	
	Distri-bution	Positive PPD reactors	Distri-bution	Positive PPD reactors	Distri-bution	Positive PPD reactors
19–30	139 (39%)	31 (22%)	3 (3%)	2 (67%)	142 (30%)	33 (23%)
31–40	99 (28%)	41 (41%)	28 (24%)	10 (36%)	127 (27%)	51 (40%)
41–50	67 (19%)	24 (36%)	19 (16%)	9 (47%)	86 (18%)	33 (38%)
51–60	35 (10%)	17 (49%)	29 (25%)	22 (76%)	64 (14%)	39 (61%)
61–70	11 (3%)	5 (45%)	22 (19%)	16 (73%)	33 (7%)	21 (64%)
71–80	4 (1%)	4 (100%)	11 (9%)	4 (36%)	15 (3%)	8 (53%)
80 and up	0		5 (4%)	0	5 (1%)	0

study (Sherman et al. 1980) was conducted by the Department of Community Medicine at St. Vincent's Hospital in New York City in three characteristic SROs. Tuberculin skin tests were administered to 191 of the 250 people living in the three hotels, following protocols established by the American Thoracic Society (1980). Of the 191, a total of 98 (or about 50 percent) had positive tuberculin skin tests. According to the protocol, 44 of the 98 required either chemoprophylaxis or treatment for tuberculosis. Of the 191 people screened, 13 (or 8 percent) had positive cultures for tuberculosis.

As a consequence of this preliminary work, a major analysis of the prevalence of tuberculosis in the homeless population at major shelter sites and SROs in New York City has been started (Brickner 1983; Glicksman et al. in press). As Table 2 shows, of 472 residents screened in the shelter-SRO system to date, 186 (39 percent) were PPD reactors—that is, had a positive tuberculin skin test, indicating tuberculosis infection but not necessarily active disease. A total of 21 (4.5 percent) proved to have active pulmonary tuberculosis.

The length of time that people live in this system appears to have a direct relation to the development of tuberculosis, as measured by percentage of positive skin tests, indicating infection. As Table 3 indicates, for people in the system one month or less, 27 percent were positive PPD reactors. For those in the system four years or more, the percentage rose to 52. Tables 4 and 5 present data about the distribution, by race and ethnic group and by age group, of the positive PPD reactors.

These data show that individuals in shelters and single-room-occupancy hotels are at risk of serious illness with tuberculosis. They pose a potential public health problem as well. Many of the people now temporarily housed in shelters will ultimately return in an infected state to their home or other living quarters, to the work place, and elsewhere in the community.

References

American Thoracic Society and Center for Disease Control: Guidelines for short-course tuberculosis chemotherapy. Am Rev Respir Dis 121:611, 1980, and Morbidity Morality Weekly Report 29:97, 1980

Bahr HM, Caplow T: Old Men Drunk and Sober. New York, New York University Press, 1973

Blumberg LU, Shipley TE, Barsky SF: Liquor and Poverty: Skid Row as a Human Condition. New Brunswick, NJ, Rutgers Center of Alcohol Studies, 1978

Brickner PW: Health issues. Presented at United Hospital Fund of New York's Conference on Health Issues in Care for the Homeless, New York, Oct 27-28, 1983

Brickner PW, Kaufman A: Case finding of heart disease in homeless men. Bull NY Acad Med 49:475-484, 1973

Brickner PW, Greenbaum D, Kaufman A, et al: A clinic for male derelicts: a welfare hotel project. Ann Intern Med 77:565-569, 1972

Felman YM, Nikitas JA: Scabies. Cutis 25:32-42, 1980

Glicksman R, Brickner PW, Edwards D: Tuberculosis screening and treatment of New York City homeless people. Ann NY Acad Sci (in press)

Goldfrank LR, Kirstein R: Hypothermia (the shiver), in Toxicologic Emergencies: A Comprehensive Handbook in Problem Solving, 2nd ed. Edited By Goldfrank LR. New York, Appleton-Century-Crofts, 1982

Green R: Infestations. Presented at United Hospital Fund of New York's Conference on Health Issues in Care for the Homeless, New York, Oct 27-28, 1983

Iseman M: Tuberculosis. Ibid

Kelly JT: Trauma. Ibid

Leff AR, Leff DR, Brewin A: Tuberculosis chemotherapy practices in major metropolitan health departments in the United States. Am Rev Respir Dis 123:176-180, 1981

Mulcare RJ: Peripheral vascular disease, cellulitis, leg ulcers. Presented at United Hospital Fund of New York's Conference on Health Issues in Care for the Homeless, New York, Oct 27-28, 1983

New York City Department of Health: City Health Information 2, no 37, 1983

Noble J: Infections. Presented at United Hospital Fund of New York's Conference on Health Issues in Care for the Homeless, New York, Oct 27-28, 1983

Sherman MN, Brickner PW, Schwartz MS, et al: Tuberculosis in single-room-occupancy hotel residents: a persisting focus of disease. New York Medical Quarterly 39-41, Fall 1980

US National Center for Health Statistics: National Ambulatory Medical Care Survey: 1977. Public Health Service, Hyattsville, Md, 1980

Winnick M: Nutrition. Presented at United Hospital Fund of New York's Conference on Health Issues in Care for the Homeless, New York, Oct 27-28, 1983

Chapter 12

The Legal System and the Homeless

Roger Peele, M.D.
Bruce Gross, Ph.D., J.D.
Bernard Arons, M.D.
Mokarram Jafri, M.D.

Over the past two decades many legislative and judicial actions have directly and adversely affected the homeless mentally ill. These legal developments have limited the actions that the family, the police, and psychiatric professionals can take in relation to mentally ill individuals, which in turn have reduced their ability to provide needed care for the seriously mentally ill.

In reviewing the impact of legal developments on the homeless mentally ill, we will first address the characteristics of the court system, which often do not serve the best interests of the homeless mentally ill. Next we will briefly review current trends and philosophy in relation to advocacy, the principle of least restrictive alternative, malpractice and civil liability, commitment laws, the right to treatment, and the right to refuse treatment; we believe that many of these trends have contributed to homelessness. Other legal considerations related to the homeless are briefly discussed, including the potential resources of guardianships/conservatorships and

Dr. Peele is chair of the Department of Psychiatry at St. Elizabeths Hospital in Washington, D.C., and clinical professor of psychiatry at George Washington University. Dr. Gross is acting director of the Institute of Psychiatry, Law, and Behavioral Science at the University of Southern California School of Medicine in Los Angeles. Dr. Arons is director of the Dixon Implementation Office at St. Elizabeths Hospital and associate clinical professor of psychiatry at George Washington University. Dr. Jafri is commissioner of Broome County Mental Health Services in Binghamton, New York.

interstate pacts for transfer of patients. The chapter ends with some suggestions on what changes might be made in the legal-psychiatric interface to help the population of homeless mentally ill.

Characteristics of the Court System

At the heart of the court system is a procedural style and a system of values that can be at cross-purposes with the needs of the homeless mentally ill.

Services for the chronically mentally ill must be provided through a cooperative process in which a variety of people or agencies work together to provide the constellation of programs that patients need. Yet the judiciary values an adversary process, not a collaborative one. To make certain factual determinations about the mentally ill requires an intricate understanding of the interplay of social, psychological, and biological factors that comes with years of training. Yet the court system operates on facts determined by juries and judges who have no background in dealing with problems facing the mentally ill. In working with the chronically mentally ill, one often needs to make a variety of decisions, which must change frequently as treatment needs change. Yet the judiciary perceives decisions as the end-point, and as fixed and final, and the system is not geared to monitoring the changing needs of the mentally ill. In monitoring services for the chronically mentally ill, a review procedure that focuses on the *results* of the work is needed. Yet the judiciary's appellate review of its own efforts is focused on reviewing *process*, not results.

Further, the most basic value of those treating the chronically mentally ill is to protect the individual from serious harm or to protect society from him. Thus clinicians believe it is better that ten persons be hospitalized unnecessarily than one suffer serious harm unnecessarily. The judiciary believes, however, that it is better for ten people to go free than for one "innocent" person to be confined. In other words, when facing uncertainty about an individual, medicine increases its supervisory and observational vigilance, whereas the judiciary tends to free the individual.

The severely chronically mentally ill usually need long-term care and attention from others to improve their functioning and welfare. However, the judiciary's main impetus is not directed toward providing care but toward enjoining, fining, or imprisoning. Thus, for example, the judiciary may commit a person who is mentally ill to a hospital, but it has no system to monitor treatment.

Despite the inherent difficulties of the judiciary in providing the kinds of actions that the chronically mentally ill need, the power of the court remains an important element in serving the chronically mentally ill. The ideal role for the judiciary in serving the mentally ill would be as an instrument for making a fixed decision when such a decision is needed.

Advocacy

Over the past 15 years, lawyers representing the mentally ill before the courts have become more assertive in representing the patient's expressed wishes. There is nothing in the ethical canons stating that an attorney must represent the patient's best interests (Stone 1975); the patient's stated wishes may be contrary to his health and welfare. Brooks (1980) has stated that "Lawyers stress physical liberty and individual autonomy, the freedom to move around, to be in the community, to not be institutionalized, and to have the right to make choices without decisions being imposed by others." Thus releasing the patient—whether the patient will be well served or not—is the goal if that is the patient's wish.

This more aggressive advocacy not only directly increases the number of patients who will be released prematurely, in the judgment of their psychiatrists, but also creates a climate in which psychiatrists decide to release some patients prematurely because they believe they will probably lose in a court hearing, and because the time "wasted" in court can be better spent on patients amenable to treatment. When the patient is discharged according to legal criteria even though he is still not well, the attorney has helped enforce his client's civil liberties, but has not always served his client's nor society's best interests.

Least Restrictive Alternative

A major legal development that has implications for care of the homeless mentally ill is the "least restrictive alternative" doctrine. It was first enunciated in 1960 in a nonpsychiatric case before the U.S. Supreme Court, *Shelton v. Tucker:* "Even though the government purpose be legitimate and substantial, that purpose cannot be pursued by means that broadly stifle fundamental personal liberties when the end can be more narrowly achieved" (Shelton 1960). The *Shelton* standard was applied in *Lake v. Cameron* (1966), in which a U.S. court of appeals ruled that a patient could not be involuntarily hospitalized if an alternative that infringed less on his right to liberty (a community placement) could be found, and was applied in subsequent cases.

Many argue that mental hospitals can provide more freedom for some patients than available community alternatives (Bachrach 1980; Brooks 1980; Peele and Keisling 1983), and some mental health professionals have argued that the goal should not be the least restrictive alternative but the most optimal setting for the patient (Bachrach 1980; Perr 1978). But generally the concept of least restrictive alternative has encouraged legislation, judicial decisions, and executive branch regulations that consider psychiatric hospitals the most restrictive setting for all mental patients.

Malpractice and Civil Liability

Professional liability and civil liability have had some indirect impact on the homeless mentally ill. While concerns about professional liability (malpractice) tend to encourage responsible and effective treatment, concerns about civil liability tend to encourage a rapid discharge of the patient. Paragraph 1983 of Title 42 of the United States Code states that any public official who deprives a person of his constitutional rights is personally liable for damages. This liability received considerable publicity in the *O'Connor v. Donaldson* case, which went to the Supreme Court in 1970. (O'Connor 1975). As part of the issues in the case, a Florida psychiatrist was sued personally for damages for maintaining the involuntary hospitalization of Mr. Donaldson. The fact that the courts had ruled affirmatively 30 times on the need for hospitalization of Mr. Donaldson did not exempt the psychiatrist from liability.

Especially for psychiatrists working in public settings in which staffing was inadequate for delivering satisfactory treatment, the implications of the Donaldson case were disquieting. The easiest way for public institutions to avoid both professional liability for inadequate treatment, on the one hand, and civil liability for deprivation of liberty, on the other hand, was to avoid being responsible for the patient in the first place, by discouraging admissions or effecting rapid discharge.

Avoiding being responsible for the severely mentally ill in the first place is also a way to avoid liability for a patient's violent acts. The *Tarasoff* decision in California a decade ago (Tarasoff 1974) and the *Hedlund* case, also in California, in 1983 (Hedlund 1983) are disquieting for clinicians. The *Tarasoff* case moved liability for a mentally ill person's violent acts away from the hospital. Tarasoff was a woman killed by a clinic patient who had made threats in treatment to kill her. The California Supreme Court held that the clinician could be held liable for not warning or taking some other action to protect the potential victim. *Hedlund* reaffirmed *Tarasoff* on the duty to warn a potential victim. Assuming responsibility for the mentally ill who are homeless, particularly those who have any potential for violence, is not made attractive by these decisions.

Trends in Commitment Laws

In the early 19th century there were virtually no legal standards for involuntary psychiatric treatment. As a result of concern about inappropriate or even vengeful involuntary hospitalization, many states in the late 19th century developed legal procedures that included jury trials as a necessary part of involuntary commitment. In the first half of this century, the pendulum swung back toward an informal commitment process, with vague standards, that avoided the public humiliation of open court jury trials. Because of renewed concern about the civil rights of the mentally ill, the pendulum swung again in the early 1960s to more extensive procedures and narrow admission criteria. Standards emphasizing that for commitment a patient must be dangerous as well as mentally ill, limitations on the loss of rights of patients, mandatory times of judicial review, and an increase in procedural safeguards became prominent in the standards legislated in the 1960s and 1970s. While some states still consider the need for psychiatric treatment an adequate criterion for involuntary treatment, by and large state legislation requires that the individual be not only mentally ill but also likely to harm others, likely to harm himself, or likely to be harmed if not hospitalized.

After patients are involuntarily admitted, judicial review takes place within a specified period. In some states, such as California, indefinite commitment has become a thing of the past (Lamb et al. 1981). In California suicidal patients cannot be hospitalized involuntarily for longer than 31 days; those dangerous to others and those who are gravely disabled can be held much longer, but only if many legal criteria are met along the way.

Workable civil commitment laws are not easily drawn. If such laws are drafted in more general terms, to easily permit hospitalization of the mentally ill, they may become subject to abuse. On the other hand, narrow commitment criteria emphasizing the autonomy of individuals make it impossible to commit persons who, according to many psychiatrists, should be committed. In short, narrow commitment criteria ignore the treatability of mental illness and the effects of mental illness on free will and meaningful autonomy.

Narrowly drawn commitment laws have taken on particular importance in relation to the homeless mentally ill. These individuals have typically chosen not to seek psychiatric treatment either through hospitalization or through local community mental health centers. While some professionals believe that they would receive and accept treatment provided in a nonthreatening, accessible location, in fact many of the homeless mentally ill, because of their mental illness, refuse all treatment. Psychiatrists who have worked in shelters and in the community have seen many individuals who could be treated successfully if they would accept treatment; instead they choose to live a despondent and shelterless life. While the controversy over involuntary treatment has not yet been resolved, it is clear that the homeless mentally ill have been affected in significant ways.

Beyond the legal hurdles themselves, the impact of legal trends of the 1960s and 1970s on the clinicians' daily work dissuaded them from wanting to serve the involuntary patient. The increase in procedures has placed psychiatrists in the position of testifying in court against their patients, a situation that sometimes affects their ability to work effectively with the patients. Moreover, the paperwork and testimony divert clinical resources away from treatment activities, often in settings that are already thinly staffed. In Washington, D.C., in the mid-1960s these trends led almost all the private hospitals to change their policy from serving involuntary patients to serving only voluntary patients.

Another area of civil commitment that limits psychiatrists' ability to help the homeless mentally ill has been the inflexibility of civil commitment laws; in most jurisdictions a person is either involuntarily committed to an institution or is totally free. Intermediate alternatives, such as outpatient commitment, typically are not available; when they are available, they generally are not used. In many cases the homeless mentally ill may not need acute psychiatric hospitalization but do need assessment, diagnostic review, and initiation of medications or other therapy, which could be provided in an outpatient setting.

There is a move toward statutory provision for compulsory outpatient treatment; about 20 states now permit a court to order outpatient treatment in place of hospitalization for patients in the civil commitment process (R. D. Luskin, personal communication, 1984). Outpatient commitment has been successful in the District of Columbia, and reports are available on its use in North Carolina (Hiday and Goodman 1982; Miller and Fiddleman 1984). But in general it is an untapped potential for dealing with the chronically mentally ill who are reluctant to seek treatment.

Besides involuntary outpatient treatment, commitment to other alternatives such as open wards, day hospitals, and halfway houses could be utilized to provide a more meaningful balance between the right to freedom and the need for treatment. Sometimes the availability of a secure environment with food and housing can remove the stresses that brought about the acute psychiatric manifestations of a chronic psychotic illness. (Again, it is not easy to impose a sense of security that a severely mentally ill person does not welcome.) However, commitment to noninstitutional settings is a difficult process to develop in a legal system that allows only two choices: involuntary hospitalization or totally voluntary treatment.

In attempts to produce more workable and reasonable civil commitment laws, more psychiatrists are involving themselves in the legislative process (Victoroff 1977; Weitzel 1976). They have begun to push for a role in the commitment procedures that will enable them to apply their specific expertise, the diagnosis of mental illness; they are suggesting expansion of commitment criteria to allow commitment of individuals who are clearly afflicted with diagnosable mental illness and whose free will and judgment are substantially impaired, even if they are not physically dangerous (Chodoff 1976; Stone 1975).

In summary, the effort to make commitment laws more attentive to the rights and freedom of individuals has made it increasingly difficult to provide treatment for those who need it yet refuse it, and thereby to reduce such problems as homelessness among the mentally ill.

Right to Treatment

In 1960 Morton Birnbaum, a lawyer and physician, proposed that a legal "right to treatment" for the mentally ill should be recognized (Birnbaum 1960). While such a right could have focused on providing access to treatment to those not in the health system, it has evolved to focus on the adequacy of the treatment for those already in the system, especially in the public mental hospital. The first judicial decision reflecting this principle was handed down in *Rouse v. Cameron* in 1966 in Washington, D.C. (Rouse 1966); it did not directly consider the right to treatment but pointed in the direction of either treating or releasing the patient. The case involved a St. Elizabeths Hospital patient who had been found not guilty by reason of insanity; the court stated that the patient must receive treatment or must be released.

The next landmark decision, *Wyatt v. Stickney* in 1971, and subsequent related decisions focused on Alabama's state mental hospitals. The court said that patients had a constitutional right to treatment, which it tried to achieve by setting very specific staffing, facility, and policy standards (Wyatt 1971, 1972). One way Alabama tried to meet specific employee-to-patient ratios of the staffing standards was by reducing the number of patients being treated. Concerns arose that *Wyatt* and similar decisions meant that many of the mentally ill were being discharged into the community where there were no services for them.

This concern was addressed in the Willowbrook case in 1973 (New York State Association 1973) in which it was held not only that the retarded patients at Willowbrook State School must be placed in the community but that adequate community resources must be developed. Later, in Washington, D.C., in *Dixon v. Weinberger* (Dixon 1975), a federal district court ruled that many of the patients at St. Elizabeths Hospital must be placed in the least restrictive alternative in the community, and that adequate community services must be developed.

Although *Wyatt* addressed the need to develop adequate treatment in the institution, and Willowbrook and *Dixon* addressed the need to develop alternatives in the community, none of these decisions have fully accomplished the stated goal. The right-to-treatment thrusts have undoubtedly helped some patients get better hospital and community treatment, but the suits have decreased the accessibility of treatment for others. This diminished accessibility has been a contributing factor to homelessness. Moreover, the focus on right to treatment has meant no care for some. Patients whose response to treatment is limited are especially likely to be ignored.

Right to Refuse Treatment

Another major impact the legal system has had on the homeless mentally ill is the recognition of the right to refuse treatment. Over the past decade this right has evolved to the point that in some settings patients, including involuntary or committed patients, cannot be required to take medications. A survey of the 50 states and the District of Columbia in 1983 found that in 25 states all patients have a right to refuse medication, in six states they have no right to refuse medication, and in the other 20 states the right depends on the patient's competency or voluntary status (Callahan and Longmire 1983). In states in which all patients have a right to refuse medication, this right can be overruled in emergency situations, and in all but ten states other conditions that allow the patient's refusal to be overruled are specified.

Many psychiatrists believe that a physician should be in charge of treatment—that the physician knows best how to treat the patient, has only the patient's best interests in mind, and should be allowed to decide whether a patient should be required to obtain treatment. Proponents of this approach would consider that the homeless mentally ill need treatment and have no right to refuse it when it has the potential for increasing their functioning and reducing symptomatology, including the symptomatology that resulted in homelessness. The alternative view is that the patient's expressed wishes, regardless of how irrational or misguided, must be respected, and that the right to refuse treatment is absolute.

Most psychiatrists and civil libertarians recognize that neither of these extreme positions provides the proper response to all situations. While often a physician would not force treatment against the patient's will, there are also times when involuntary administration of treatment is life-saving, or is so vital for restoring full health that there should be some mechanism by which a physician can override refusal of treatment. However, agreement about when a patient should or should not be able to refuse treatment has not been reached.

The legislatures and courts are still attempting to find a satisfactory answer to the paradox of allowing involuntary admission but not involuntary medication. Several models have been suggested: court approval of the decision to medicate, determination of medication by the patient's physician, an outside-the-hospital review, an inside-the-hospital clinician review, approval by an "independent" clinician, or resolution of the issue of the patient's involuntary medical treatment at the point of admission. The American Psychiatric Association has proposed that one of the criteria for involuntary hospitalization (though not a sufficient criterion by itself) be the finding that the "person lacks capacity to make an informed decision concerning treatment" (Guidelines 1982).

The Plight of the Homeless Mentally Ill

For some time the legal responses to the problems and plight of the mentally ill reflected the attitude of much of society, that the best way to deal with mental illness is to ignore it and hope it goes away. However, in the 1960s and 1970s, the legal system became increasingly involved in mental health issues. Unfortunately, in the areas of the commitment laws, the right to treatment, and the right to refuse treatment, the system's impact on the practice of psychiatry has contributed to the plight of the homeless mentally ill. Today many of the homeless mentally ill who clearly need treatment do not meet the new requirements for commitment; in a number of states, even if they are admitted on involuntary status, they are considered to have the right to refuse treatment. In addition, the lack of community support programs for the mentally ill has complicated the plight of the homeless mentally ill. Many who could be served in nonhospital settings go without any care and treatment.

Remedies should include revisions of commitment laws to allow for more flexibility in sites and methods of providing treatment so that homeless mentally ill in need of treatment could receive it in open wards, halfway houses, and community mental health centers, or in the shelters or on the streets when necessary and appropriate. In addition, the right to treatment should be expanded to include the right of the homeless mentally ill to receive treatment appropriate to their needs. In regard to the right to refuse treatment, society must decide whether the rights and freedom of individuals are being appropriately balanced with the opportunity for better functioning and less suffering that treatment generally offers, and with the societal need to reduce the impact of homelessness on our communities.

Guardianships and Conservatorships

Theoretically guardianships and conservatorships are important resources for the mentally ill that could preclude homelessness under many circumstances. Unfortunately in many states their effectiveness remains theoretical, as the authority available through the guardianship laws is often inadequate and the procedures are discouraging. The usefulness of guardianships and conservatorships varies state by state, and the topic is almost always intertwined with the commitment laws.

In California, conservatorship provides for continuous control and monitoring of patients who need social controls while at the same time retaining adequate legal safeguards. Under conservatorship, granted by the court for one-year renewable periods, patients can be hospitalized when necessary and for an indefinite period, their money can be managed when they cannot manage it themselves, and they can be compelled to live in a suitable community residential facility that meets their needs for care and structure. Such a facility can be a board-and-care home or, when needed, a locked skilled nursing facility with special programs for psychiatric patients, as exists in California (Lamb 1980).

Why is greater use not made of conservatorship? Bureaucratic obstacles and the inertia of the system are among the greatest problems, even when mental health professionals recognize the need for ongoing controls of patients who are in the community. What is needed is a treatment philosophy recognizing that external controls, such as conservatorship, can be a positive and often crucial therapeutic modality for those who lack the internal controls to deal with their impulses and to organize themselves to cope with life's demands (Lamb and Grant 1982). Such external controls can often interrupt a self-destructive life on the streets that is frequently interspersed with crises, hospitalization, and time in jail, and can help patients achieve some measure of order and security in their lives.

Interstate Transfer of Patients

The mentally ill can be homeless partly because they are no longer in their home state. Generally it is easier to establish eligibility for entitlements for a patient who is living in his state of legal residence; also, the patient who is in his home state is more likely to have family or other supports or resources. Some states have agreements for transfer of the mentally ill from one state to another. Unfortunately the provisos of these agreements often preclude a transfer because the illness affects the patient's understanding of why such a transfer would be useful, and an involuntary transfer is more difficult. And sometimes there is no pact at all between two specific states. The lack of an effective interstate transfer mechanism for the mentally ill contributes to the number of patients who are homeless.

Contact With the Police

In many locales, because of the barriers to hospitalization or the inaccessibility of hospitalization, the police have no choice but to put a seriously disturbed homeless person in jail (see chapter 3). Even when there is a choice between hospitalization and jail, the police's frustration with the mental health system can lead to the criminalization of a patient. For example:

> Mr. A has been admitted to a public mental hospital many times. He responds quite well to haloperidol or fluphenazine decanoate so his hospitalizations have been short, but he does not keep his clinic appointments or take his medication, and so deterioration sets in after several weeks. When his voices and delusions return, he strips off all his clothes and attempts to direct traffic at the same corner in downtown Washington. He is brought to the hospital by the police, admitted, and treated. Within days he improves and is returned to the community, but he fails to attend the clinic or take his medication, and the cycle is repeated. After a half-dozen of these traffic-directing episodes—behavior that is danger-

ous to him and dangerous to others, as he is a distraction to drivers—the police became frustrated at the brevity of time between them. Thus they have resorted to filing criminal charges to increase the time between episodes.

Competency to Stand Trial

When the homeless mentally ill do not find their way into the mental health system directly, they often find their way into the criminal justice system (see chapter 3). Being found incompetent to stand trial places the defendant in the hands of mental health professionals.

Competency to stand trial is a legal determination of whether the defendant has sufficient ability to consult with his lawyer with a reasonable degree of rational understanding, and whether he has "a rational as well as factual understanding of the proceedings against him"(Dusky 1960). Conversely, the question is whether the defendant has a mental illness of such magnitude that he is unable to cooperate with his attorney, or is unable to understand the nature of the charges against him or the possible penalties. Whether an individual is competent is a court decision, usually based on the testimony of a psychiatrist and sometimes of members of other disciplines. Once the question of competency has been raised, it is usually the prosecutor's responsibility to prove that the patient is competent.

Competency to stand trial is the most frequent competency examination a psychiatrist carries out. "Incompetent to stand trial" is a far more frequent court finding than "not guilty by reason of insanity." Since the homeless mentally ill are among psychiatrists' sickest patients, they are often found incompetent to stand trial. Their inability to cooperate with their attorney and their inability to comprehend the material relating to the alleged crime are the relevant factors.

If the defendant is found incompetent by the court, the usual consequences are confinement to a hospital, delay of trial, and denial of bail. Hospitalization, theoretically, is to continue until the defendant returns to competency. Thus in the past individuals who were found incompetent to stand trial were not likely to join the ranks of the homeless mentally ill. This changed somewhat with the 1972 Supreme Court decision in *Jackson v. Indiana;* the court held that a person could not be held indefinitely while awaiting restoration of competency. If the trial court concludes that the patient will never be competent, then "the state must either institute the customary civil commitment procedures or release the defendant" (Jackson 1972).

Under those circumstances, the defendant is given a "Jackson hearing" to determine if he can return to competency. If it is determined that he cannot, further involuntary hospitalization depends on whether he meets the civil standards for involuntary hospitalization in that state. If not, then the defendant must be released or can be hospitalized voluntarily. The important point is that *Jackson v. Indiana* moves the patients who are permanently disabled into the civil commitment process, and civil procedures often lead to a relatively quick release. Thus *Jackson* contributes to an increase in the number of patients who are released, some of whom will join the homeless mentally ill.

Alcoholism

Although substance abusers, including alcoholics, are not the focus of this report, many of the psychotic homeless have the additional problem of alcoholism or other substance abuse. The law's views of alcoholism and addiction cast additional light on the legal system's approach to mental illness.

Through three federal cases in the 1960s—*Easter v. the District of Columbia* (1966), *Driver v. Hinnant* (1966), and *Powell v. Texas* (1968)—there evolved the legal principle that alcoholism is a disease and that one cannot be punished for that disease. (The three men named in these cases were typical of the homeless of the 1960s.) When the courts adhere to this principle, a defendant can be found guilty of acts committed while drunk, but not of signs and symptoms of drunkenness per se. In *Powell* Supreme Court Justice White touched on the issue of homelessness when he stated that the defendant should not be found guilty of a crime if "it was not feasible for him to have made arrangements to prevent his being in public when drunk" (Powell 1968).

As a result of the federal decisions, alcoholism is increasingly considered the responsibility of the mental health system, not the criminal justice system. It is not clear whether the increased tendency to define alcoholism as an illness rather than a crime has increased or decreased the number of homeless mentally ill. Some point out that 90 days in a workhouse kept patients off the streets longer than five days in a detoxification center, and thus the current legal trend might increase the number of homeless. (In the 1950s some of the homeless of Washington, D.C., used the workhouse as their mailing address because they knew they would return there often.) And some suspect that because of the court decisions, the police have less interest in arresting alcoholics.

It is hoped that the judicial decisions have resulted in more effective and more humane management of alcoholics, and in a fewer number of severe alcoholics among the homeless. However, not many observers are impressed with how well the public services are able to deal with alcoholism among the homeless.

Conclusions

Although there are no clear-cut answers, there are several directions that the law-psychiatry interface should explore in order to reduce the tragedy of the homeless mentally ill. The options for the homeless mentally ill should not simply be jail or the streets—criminalization or abandonment. Facilitating the options for care and treatment for the severely mentally ill should include these steps:

—Involuntary commitment laws should be made more humane so that they ensure prompt return to active inpatient treatment for patients whose exacerbated illness renders their lives in the community chaotic, unsafe, and unbearable.

—Involuntary treatment laws should include the category of gravely disabled—that is, unable to take care of one's own basic needs for food, clothing, and shelter—as one criterion for commitment.

—Involuntary treatment laws should facilitate adequate treatment through a determination on admission of whether the patient is capable of making treatment decisions. That step would preclude the legal system's paradox of permitting involuntary hospitalization for treatment but not involuntary treatment during hospitalization.

—Involuntary treatment laws should provide for high-quality care for involuntarily treated patients. For example, at one point the American Psychiatric Association took the position that involuntary hospitalization should take place only in an institution accredited by the Joint Commission on Accreditation of Hospitals.

—Involuntary treatment laws should be revised to allow the option of outpatient civil commitment; in states that already have provisions for such treatment, that mechanism should be more widely used. While outpatient commitment is not a possibility for all patients, for many patients it could obtain the treatment they need.

—The legal system should allow for ongoing asylum for those patients whose mental disability is enormous and whose personal resources are slim.

—Conservatorship and guardianship status should be easier to obtain for the mentally ill who are gravely disabled and/or have impaired judgment that renders them unable to care for themselves in the community.

—Interstate transfer laws to facilitate the return of the mentally ill to their home states should be more widely adopted.

—Comparative studies of state laws on the hospitalization and treatment of the mentally ill should be undertaken to help move the issue of effective and humane prevention of homelessness among the mentally ill from fractious debate to factual data.

—Mental health professionals should be available to consult with and train police to facilitate entry of the mentally ill into psychiatric services.

—As our country moves increasingly from institutional to community-based care, advocacy efforts should shift from exposing abuses and deficiencies in institutions to protecting the basic civil rights and privileges of mentally handicapped persons in the community. Moreover, advocates should promote legislation that would allocate fiscal resources to aid the homeless mentally ill.

—Lastly, the mental health professions must become involved in the legislative process and in advising the courts. Persons with severe chronic mental illnesses are among this nation's most vulnerable citizens, and are unable to advocate for their own needs. No task for mental health professionals is more important than publicly championing the needs of these patients.

References

Bachrach LL: Is the least restrictive environment always the best? sociological and semantic implications. Hosp Community Psychiatry 31:97-103, 1980

Birnbaum M: The right to treatment. American Bar Association Journal 46:499, 1960

Brooks AD: Mental health law, in The Administration of Mental Health Services, 2nd ed. Edited by Feldman S. Springfield, Ill, Thomas, 1980

Callahan LA, Longmire DR: Psychiatric patients' right to refuse psychotropic medication: a national survey. Mental Disability Law Reporter 7:494-499,1983

Chodoff P: The case for involuntary hospitalization of the mentally ill. Am J Psychiatry 133:496-501, 1976

Dixon v Weinberger, 405 F 2d 974 (DC Cir 1975)

Driver v Hinnant, 356 F 2d 761 (4th Cir 1966)

Dusky v United States, 362 US 405 (1960) (per curiam)

Easter v District of Columbia, 361 F 2d 50 (DC Cir 1966)

Guidelines for legislation on psychiatric hospitalization of adults. Am J Psychiatry 140:672-674, 1982

Hedlund et al v Superior Court of Orange County: Wilson et al (real parties in interest) LA 31676, 1983

Hiday VA, Goodman RR: The least restrictive alternative to involuntary hospitalization, outpatient commitment: its use and effectiveness. Journal of Psychiatry and Law: 81-98, Spring 1982

Jackson v Indiana, 406 US 715, 738 (1972)

Lake v Cameron, 364 F 2d 657 (1966)

Lamb HR: Structure: the neglected ingredient of community treatment. Arch Gen Psychiatry 37:1224-1228, 1980

Lamb HR, Grant RW: The mentally ill in an urban county jail. Arch Gen Psychiatry 39:170-172,1982

Lamb HR, Sorkin AP, Zusman J: Legislating social control of the mentally ill in California. Am J Psychiatry 138:334-339, 1981

Miller RD, Fiddleman PB: Outpatient commitment: treatment in the least restrictive environment? Hosp Community Psychiatry 35:147-151, 1984

New York State Association for Retarded Children v Rockefeller, 357 F Supp 752 (1973)

O'Connor v Donaldson, 422 US 563, 95 S Ct 2486 (1975)

Peele R, Keisling R: Commitment to freedom. Presented at the annual meeting of the American Academy of Psychiatry and the Law, Chicago, 1980. Published in St Elizabeths Hospital CME Newsletter 1:1-5, 1983

Perr IN: The most beneficial alternative: a counterpoint to the least restrictive alternative. Bull Am Acad Psychiatry Law 6:iv-vii, 1978

Powell v Texas, 392 US 514 (1968)

Rouse v Cameron, 363 F 2d 451 (DC Cir 1966)

Shelton v Tucker, 364 US 479, 81 S Ct 257, 5L Ed 2d 231 (1960)

Stone AA: Mental Health and Law: A System in Transition. Rockville, Md, National Institute of Mental Health, 1975

Tarasoff v Regents of the University of California, 131 Cal Rptr 14, 551 P2d 334 (1976), vacating 118 Cal Rptr 129, 529 P2d 553 (1974)

Victoroff VM: Collaboration between Ohio psychiatrists and the legislature to update commitment laws. Am J Psychiatry 134:752-755, 1977

Weitzel WD: Legislative liaison as critical intervention. Bull Am Acad
   Psychiatry Law 4:216-220, 1976
Wyatt v Stickney, 325 F Supp 781 (MD Ala 1971); enforced by 344 F
   Supp 373, 376, 379-385 (MD Ala 1972)

Chapter 13

The Family's Perspective
on the Homeless

Agnes B. Hatfield, Ph.D.
Elizabeth Farrell, M.S., M.S.W.
Shirley Starr, M.A.

For families, the issue of homelessness is not only confusing and complex, but personal, and painful as well. To come to the point where one's vulnerable mentally ill relative is forced to survive as best he can in the hostile climate of an urban street is the culmination of a family's worst fear. Families may hear from their homeless relative infrequently or not at all, but by virtue of their imagination and stories in the local press they envision a picture of unremitting cold, hunger, fatigue, and loneliness as the daily lot of their unfortunate relative.

Although the percent of mentally ill who are homeless at a given time may be relatively small, over time many of the mentally ill experience at least temporary periods of homelessness. Thus many families know the sheer agony of it. Those who have not yet experienced homelessness do not discount the fact that it may be a grim possibility for the future, for until we create a caregiving society in which someone besides the family is responsible and accountable, then disablement or death of the caregiver might mean that no one takes over.

Dr. Hatfield is associate professor of education in the Department of Human Development of the University of Maryland College of Education in College Park. Ms. Farrell is director of Work and Leisure Activities, a rehabilitation agency in Takoma Park, Maryland. Ms. Starr is chairman of the mental disability committee of the President's Committee on Employment of the Handicapped. Dr. Hatfield and Ms. Starr are past-presidents of the National Alliance for the Mentally Ill.

In this chapter, devoted to the family's perspective on homelessness, we begin with a description of this phenomenon and some
of the terrors that it holds for both the homeless mentally ill and
their families. We consider how homelessness can occur, even when
patients have caring families anxiously searching for them, and we
conclude with efforts the helping communities can make to develop
meaningful services for the homeless mentally ill and, especially,
to prevent homelessness. We focus on families as a source of important and otherwise unavailable information and as major caregivers
in the system of community care.

The Meaning of Homelessness

The problem of homelessness has attracted much media attention,
but the word "homeless" is rarely defined. Whom do we include
in that term? For the purposes of this discussion, a homeless person
is any person, male or female, over age 18, who has no place to go
for the night and no money to pay for shelter. People move in and
out of conditions of homelessness depending on economic circumstances or the availability of help from families, friends, or the
helping structures. Some people are homeless for a few days or
weeks; for others it may be a matter of years.

Bahr (1970) notes that most people's conceptions of homelessness
have been that of skid row, but Bahr believes the homeless live
everywhere and that skid row is only the tip of the iceberg. What
is significant, he believes, is the lack of affiliative bonds that char-
acterizes the homeless. Bahr uses the terms "withdrawal" or
"retreatism" to characterize this group. Bassuk and others (unpub-
lished paper 1983) see homelessness as a metaphor for profound
isolation and disconnection. It is a collapse, for whatever reason,
of a person's support network.

Essentially all the major cities of this country have a visible quota
of these destitute persons usually congregated in a section of the
inner city where free food, clothing, and day labor offer sustenance.
The media has been diligent in bringing their plight to the attention
of the public. A certain amount of outrage has been expressed, but
no comprehensive solutions to the problem have been forthcoming.
Studies of the homeless indicate that they come from all races,
socioeconomic groups, and age groups, but that they tend to be
disproportionately male, black, of lower socioeconomic origin, and

young. About half are thought to be under 40; (Arce et al. 1983; Farrell 1977).

Some of the most recent studies have made it abundantly clear that a sizable proportion of the homeless are mentally ill. Arce and his associates (1983) estimated the figure to be 84 percent; Lipton and associates (1983) report that about 50 percent are seriously mentally ill; Jones (1983) reports many persons are discharged directly from hospital wards to shelters for the homeless. The plight of the homeless is compounded if they are also afflicted with mental illness. Baxter and Hopper (1982) say:

> Among those who are utterly disaffiliated, madness may compound the hardships of street life to produce a new class of misfits—the so-called "space cases." Their transcience, the chronicity of their affliction, the fact that services are ill suited to their needs, community fear of and distaste for their numbers, and their alleged propensity for violence all conspire to keep them beyond the pale of traditional outreach measures (pp. 393-394).

Bassuk (1983) has also found that a significant percent of the homeless have major psychotic disorders. Many in her study, she notes, were so disorganized that they were unable to put together even a few sentences coherently; their stories were disjointed, rambling, unreal and at times grandiose, and often extremely difficult to follow. It was easy to understand why these people could not handle even the routine aspects of life, let alone hold a steady job. Most lacked family, friends, money. Of the group she studied, nearly three-fourths reported no contact with families. Only 29 percent were involved with any social agency.

The sheer misery of being homeless is hard for those of us with family, friends, and security to grasp. A 1983 *Newsweek* article describes a scene in Chicago in which 79 men and women formed a shivering line, with the temperature in the teens, as they waited to go inside to an emergency shelter for the night. For each there would be a mattress on the floor, a cup of coffee, and a paper towel. There would be toilets but no showers. Many, it was reported, were former mental patients, victims of deinstitutionalization and poor discharge planning. "Life on the street," as this article described it, "is a chaotic, furtive struggle to survive—whole days spent looking for food and a safe place to sleep, intermittent trouble with the police, random violence over pitifully small amounts of money" (Down and Out, p. 29).

Shulman (1981) described homeless women in New York City as "aging women with swollen ankles and ulcerated feet, toting bags, shuffling slowly across the street, poking in garbage cans, slumped on a park bench, dozing in doorways, sprawling across library steps, huddled among their possessions in the dreary waiting rooms of the train and bus stations. Poor, sick, lonely, old, afraid."

In her book entitled *Shopping Bag Ladies*, Rousseau (1981) interviewed a number of homeless women and found they were in a crisis situation in their lives. Alcoholism, mental illness, evictions, family quarrels, mismanagement on welfare, and lost or stolen funds had left them homeless. Many women had no families, but some did have families and a certain amount of contact with them. Some families knew of the plight of their homeless relative, but they were already so overburdened that there was no strength or money to provide for another member who could not carry her full share. Some of the women came from middle-class origins; however, alcoholism and mental illness placed great strains on the families, and often, after years of struggling to sustain and support an ill relative, families gave up for the sake of their own survival. Some of the women chose to leave so as not to be a burden on their families.

Farrell (1981) developed social services in shelters for homeless men and learned from interviews with her clients that many did not get a good night's rest in the shelters, and that two-thirds had transportation difficulties and had to walk everywhere. Access to drinking water and toilets was a problem for two-thirds of the population, and most were bored because they had no daytime activities. The single most pressing personal problem was clothing. More than half carried or hid their clothes and belongings. Laundry services were hard to come by, and people sought new clothes from distribution centers and discarded old ones in alleys. Basic services were inadequate, and life was bitterly harsh for these people.

In his appearance before a Senate hearing on street people, Mitch Snyder (1983) of the Committee for Creative Non-Violence in Washington, D.C., testified about the brutality of the lives of those condemned to be homeless. Drawing on his many years of working directly with street people, Snyder asserted that "there is nothing to equal the indignity and sheer animal terror of homelessness." He stated that "driven by they know not what, the homeless are always on the move; looking for food, clothing, shelter, work." He noted that they search endlessly for the basic necessities of life, constantly evading the voices that urge them to move on. Snyder estimated there were no fewer than 5,000 to 10,000 homeless in the nation's capital. The deinstitutionalized mental patient, he noted, has swelled the ranks of the traditional poor.

That homelessness is a mean and terrifying experience for one condemned to its existence is becoming better known, but it is less well known that for many homeless persons there is a painfully anxious family searching for them. The experiences of one family member illustrate the problem:

> Mrs. A has not seen her son, John, for six months and wonders if he is alive or dead. John split from the hospital he was in, and no one has heard from him since. The last time Mrs. A caught sight of him was when she was on her way to work downtown and noticed a person who resembled John out of the corner of her eye. She stopped the car and shouted, "John, it's me . . . Mom." John looked up, called her a "God-damned bitch," and bolted into the alley. She said he looked like a beggar, unclean and ragged.
>
> Mrs. A still searches for John. Sometimes from her car window she sees someone about the right build, and she calls, "John, is that you?" It never is. She makes the rounds at the medical examiner's offices in Baltimore, and she checks out accident or homicide victims who have ended up at the morgue. One might be John. If she hears about unclaimed bodies of young men who have washed up on the beaches, she checks that out too. She has not found him. She said, "I don't know if it would be easier to know that he was dead or not. At least it would be over, and I wouldn't be watching for him."

How Homelessness Happens

How do we explain this phenomenon of homelessness among our most vulnerable? Clearly something has gone awry in our society. The easy answer is that homelessness is due to deinstitutionalization, which, on one level, is true enough. If people were still in asylums they wouldn't be on the streets, but what society must determine is whether a street existence is a necessary outcome of deinstitutionalization.

Without a doubt, the reasons that people are homeless are many, and we must guard against pointing the finger or looking for a single, simple solution. A great deal of carefully calculated inquiry will have to be undertaken before we know the myriad ways in

284 THE HOMELESS MENTALLY ILL

which people are lost to the streets. In this paper we look to one source for some answers, families of the mentally ill. (The families whose experience we draw on are members of the National Alliance for the Mentally Ill, an organization for families of persons with mental illness.) We learned from these families that temporary homelessness is not an uncommon event, and that some families have had relatives on the streets for long periods of time.

The Need to Escape

Some mentally ill persons take up a life of wandering and living on the streets even when they have families who are trying to care for them and who urge them to stay home. Several families told how they woke up one morning or returned home one day to find their relative gone. They could not account for the disappearance in terms of any special stress or altercation, nor was there any evidence the departure was planned in advance. Rather, it seemed like an act of momentary impulse. Sometimes the missing relative called home after a couple of weeks of misery requesting money or asking the families to come and get him. Sometimes families got calls from hospitals in distant states where the ill person had been picked up on the streets by police. A unique pattern of wandering is revealed in the following story:

> George is in his late thirties. He has an advanced degree in physics and until a few years ago held a responsible job in New York City. For the past five years he has been seriously mentally ill. He was hospitalized once and improved. After coming home, he consistently refused medication and did little but sit in isolation. His one predictable activity was taking off for New York City every few weeks without a discernible purpose; he would return after two or three weeks looking tired and disheveled, and with the soles of his shoes decidedly worn. His parents suspected that he must have walked continuously when he was gone.
>
> Why does he go? His mother says tension seems to build up in him for unexplainable reasons, and he merely announces, "I'm leaving." Sometimes he says that he is "trying to solve his problems," and other times that he wants to stop people from "spying on him." His parents try, to no avail, to persuade him not to leave. Sadly they then tell him, "Well, come back when you are ready." Once he came home with his face bruised and swollen— he said he had fallen off a bench. Later it was learned that he had been mugged.
>
> A few months ago George returned after a six-month absence.

He was in an alarming state. He was thin, haggard, filthy, and wearing the same clothes that he wore when he left. He was disorganized and incoherent. His parents saw this as an opportunity to help him and had him involuntarily hospitalized.

George had a home and a family that welcomed him, yet he was compelled by some inner chaos to escape periodically even though it meant enduring the hardships of street life. Perhaps he could not endure the closeness of family life, or maybe he hoped to leave behind his painful inner torment.

The Failure of the System

Another reason for homelessness is the failure of communities to provide the diversity of living arrangements that are so badly needed for the highly diverse population of the chronically ill. Where housing exists at all, it has been designed by a provider to suit a particular type of client. All others are expected to take it or leave it. There is a failure to acknowledge that when we are dealing with the chronically ill, we are dealing with a population that does not adapt easily—yet we demand of them greater adaptability than we do of ourselves. Hospital staffs, too, rarely listen to the families of patients who have had long experience coping with a disordered son or daughter. A case in point is an elderly widow and her seriously disturbed son:

> Mrs. H is well into her seventies and has frail health, with heart complications that disable her at times. Her son Barry is approaching his forties and has spent years in hospitals, both because of a very traumatic accident and because of a severe psychiatric disorder. The state hospital staff felt that Barry was doing better, and that Mrs. H should take him home to her two-bedroom apartment to live. Mrs. H insisted that Barry was not well enough to come home and that she was not strong enough to manage him. She said staff talked to her unrelentingly for over an hour trying to persuade her to take him; she insisted she couldn't.
> A couple of weeks later Barry appeared at her door—he had been sent home on a weekend pass. He immediately began protesting that he was too heavily drugged and proceeded to flush all his medications down the toilet. Mrs. H awakened next morning to find that her son was gone, leaving no clue about his destination. Although it was late November, and cold, he had not taken a warm coat; neither had he withdrawn any money.
> Weeks went by, and she received no word. Police were alerted.

As the weather brought freezing night-time temperatures, Mrs. H kept remembering the light-weight jacket Barry had taken. Several unnatural deaths were reported, and Mrs. H agonized until the bodies were identified. They were never her son. Four months later word came from a hospital in a distant state. Barry had been apprehended by police and identified as mentally ill. He had been there for many months, but he had not given staff permission to call his mother.

What could have prevented several months of agony for Barry and his mother? Possibly a hospital staff who were willing to listen to the family or were better able to judge a patient's capacity to live on the outside might have spared this family the extended anxiety and the costs of out-of-state hospitalization and return transportation. More to the point, Barry needed housing with considerable supervision by staff who are trained to manage difficult persons like Barry.

Another case illustrates the incredible challenge that a very difficult case can provide to the system:

Joe is a 26-year-old Chippewa male who has been homeless for two years. Before this time he spent seven years in two hospitals. He was first involuntarily hospitalized at age 16 when he was convicted of statutory rape. Joe has slept in a boarded-up house for two winters. He is well known to various social service agencies in the area and receives a monthly Supplemental Security Income (SSI) check, which is mailed to his parents' home.

Recently Joe, who had received leg injuries in a car accident, expressed fear of spending another year in the cold winter on his own and tried to admit himself to the state hospital through a local emergency room. Neither facility would admit him for care. Through advocacy efforts he has been sheltered from night to night at a crisis center. But this is a temporary arrangement. Must Joe survive another bitter winter in the cold? What about his family?

Mrs. B, Joe's mother, says that Joe was an adopted child who had serious developmental and behavioral problems from the beginning. His family pursued all avenues to get a diagnosis of his problem and to find appropriate treatment. He has been variously diagnosed as having an organic personality disorder, mental retardation, and schizophrenia, and he has spent his childhood and young adulthood in special schools and programs. He is frustratingly unable to see the relationship between his behaviors and homelessness, and learns little from his experiences.

Mrs. B feels she has done everything she possibly can. At age 62 she is exhausted and feels she is entitled to a life of her own.

She blames the system. "No one has found out what is wrong with Joe," she said, "and no one ever taught us any ways to manage him."

What could help persons like Joe survive? Is it too late to provide management skills to the family? Mrs. B says they have had ten to 15 years of family therapy. What kind of housing would work for Joe and those like him? Should it be highly structured, or would that only serve to push Joe out? Joe already has been in such a program but couldn't meet the standards, so he was extruded. His mother feels he needs a situation with few restrictions. She has not found an appropriate place for Joe.

The Violent Patient

Some patients have episodic violent outbursts that create danger for the rest of the family. Peter is such a case:

Peter, age 19, has been living for six months in a downtown men's shelter. His family will not let him come home; his mother is afraid of him, as he has struck her. Peter is the only child of his mother, who is a practical nurse, and a stepfather who works as a porter. Peter began having trouble in tenth grade with drugs and alcohol. In 11th grade he had his first manic episode and was arrested.

After a year of institutional treatment and family therapy, Peter came home, stopped taking his medication, became depressed, and suddenly exploded. He began ripping out the walls, tearing out the appliances, and generally wreaking havoc throughout the house. His mother called the police, and he spent the next six months in the hospital. From there he was discharged to a group home. The rules there required that he get a job or find a day activity for himself. He didn't, so he was put out of the program and given names of a couple of shelters in the city, where he continues to live. His mother cries at night and prays a great deal about him, but is terrified to have him home again.

Some mentally ill individuals are too unpredictable, and too volatile, for any family to maintain them in the home. For them the community has little to offer.

Family Therapy and Extrusion From the Home

Several families told us that in seeking advice on the management of their difficult relative, they were told to throw the patient out of the home as a way to teach him that he must conform to the authority of the parents. The following two stories illustrate the risk to the patient of being on the street and the agony suffered by the family:

> Scott was a 25-year-old male who had been involuntarily hospitalized twice when he became so psychotic that he was endangering his own safety and health. Each time he left the hospital, he ceased taking medication and became just as symptomatic again. Neither Scott nor his mother was ever fully alerted to the crucial importance of his staying on medication. For the third time Scott became highly chaotic, lost his rented room, and could not be tolerated in his mother's small apartment.
>
> Mrs. J, Scott's mother, sought guidance from a psychiatrist. He advocated putting Scott out of her apartment. It was cold, rainy, and wintertime. Mrs. J resisted but felt the psychiatrist must know what was best, and was finally persuaded. Scott sometimes stayed in the woods not far from his mother. She often saw him moving furtively through the streets, soaking wet. Several times he appeared at his mother's door, often in the middle of the night. She said she turned him away and then wept bitterly. Once he appeared with a severe cut on his cheek (later she learned he had been attacked).
>
> Finally, after about two weeks on the streets, Scott appeared at 2 a.m. at her door. He was filthy, his cheek was badly infected, and his feet were swollen. She took him in and decided that keeping him away was a crazy solution to a difficult problem. Today, ten years later, Mrs. J is haunted by the terrible experience of keeping her son on the street. She sees his facial scar, feels terribly guilty, and has lost trust in a mental health profession that could offer no better solution to her son's problems.

Are there times when homelessness is palliative? Can it be a treatment of choice? Or is it only evidence of how bankrupt the profession is in its helping skills for certain types of disorders? Perhaps rather than resort to homelessness to bring people to treatment, mental health professionals need to work for less stringent criteria for involuntary treatment, and for better patient and family education. Scott was a person whose condition responded readily to medical treatment—but he had not been persuaded of the importance of staying with his medication. Should he have been compelled to take it?

Another experience of homelessness through professional advice was the case of Tom:

> Tom was a difficult man who drank excessively and then became very hostile. He had been hospitalized several times, and each time returned home and resumed his old behaviors. Finally a doctor sought out by the parents, Mr. and Mrs. S, advised them to tell Tom he could not return home again until he went to see the doctor. After considerable persuasion the family agreed. Tom was not the kind to give in easily. For four bleak months the streets were Tom's home. The family got calls that Tom was sleeping in their neighbors' cars or trucks, and that he entered unlocked houses and slept. Occasionally he went down to missions, but often he was seen rummaging in garbage cans to survive. He was brutalized by policemen and wound up in jail, where he was raped. By the time he surrendered himself to the treatment his family demanded, the doctor pronounced him a severely ill young man—both physically and mentally.
>
> Now, several years later, he has not fully recovered his health. His mother blamed the brutal conditions that were part of bringing him to treatment. Mrs. S said, "It was terrible for us. We decided never again. [Throwing him out] has since been recommended to us by social workers when Tom was difficult. But it is not an option for us. We think families know their relative best and must rely on their own judgments." Tom is home now and they are managing, at least for the present.

Scott and Tom were somewhat similar young men: highly resistant, very negative toward the mental health system, and willing to endure a torturous life on the street rather than give in to the demands made of them. Is homelessness the only treatment we have to offer for persons like them?

These vignettes demonstrate some of the ways in which people can become homeless. We need to know more about the causes of homelessness if we are ever to make real progress with the problems. Families are an untapped source of information because the homeless lived at home at one time, and families have experienced the chain of events that culminated in homelessness.

Developing a Program for the Homeless

It is disturbing to think that we have managed the care of the mentally ill in this country so badly that approximately 5 to 10 percent live on the street at any given time and that several times that figure are homeless at one time or another. The real effort must go into preventing this from happening. Meanwhile more people are on the street, and they must have good emergency care to prevent further suffering and possible death. The helping communities must mobilize themselves.

Making Availability of Shelter a Right

The prevailing notion is that most homeless reject assistance; the assumption is that appropriate help is there to be had. In psychiatric terms homeless behavior has been seen as symptomatic of the illness, a manifestation of paranoia or "flight syndrome." Baxter and Hopper (1982) object to this rationalization for the homeless. "Put simply," they say, "they are charged with not having the good sense to come in out of the rain" (p. 397). In their study, Baxter and Hopper found that no matter what was offered—a chair to rest on, a mattress, or a breadline—always more people came than could be accommodated. Generally people do accept shelter provided under circumstances of care and tolerance. The authors found that women slept in subways when the shelters were full, but they would always come back whenever there was room.

The Coalition for the Homeless in New York City, whose director is lawyer Robert Hayes, believes there should be recognition, with the force of law, of a *right* to shelter. Then the homeless would have remedy through the courts. Hayes believes that the New York State Constitution implies a right to shelter when it states, "the aid, care, and support of the needy are a public concern and shall be provided by the state . . . as the legislature may from time to time determine." Hayes has enlisted some homeless persons to serve as co-litigants; in 1979 the case of *Callahan v. Carey* went to court, resulting in a temporary injunction that required the state to furnish shelter to any person who needed it. This ruling amounted to a recognition of a constitutional right to shelter (Main 1983). Other advocates may want to follow suit and consider litigation on behalf of the homeless in their states.

Making Shelters Livable

Some of the present shelters are so bad that the homeless prefer being on the streets (Baxter and Hopper 1982; Main 1983). There is gross overcrowding, and toilets and showers are filthy or out of order. Guests at the shelter must sleep in their clothes, and they guard their shoes lest they be missing in the morning. Staff may be abrasive and combative, complacent, or cruel. Although there are staff who care, there are others who need training in understanding the mentally ill and the symptoms manifested. There is fear of catching diseases, as some people who use shelters are sick. Sometimes staff verbally abuse the residents, herd them around with night sticks, and eject them onto the streets in the middle of the night for minor infractions of the rules.

Training Shelter Staff

No one can question the difficulties faced by shelter staff, and their need for adequate protection from physical violence, possible contagion, and burnout. But direct service workers, like the public at large, tend to excuse their failures on the grounds that the homeless are so disordered in mind that they cannot be reached, so impaired in judgment that they refuse offers of assistance, and so disruptive in service settings that other more worthy clients are driven away (Baxter and Hopper 1982). It is difficult for the workers to see a human being beneath the disreputable appearance. Service workers need to know how mental illness affects people, what their particular deficiencies are, and what appropriate expectations are so that their services can be helpful and humane.

Workers must learn to accept their clients unconditionally. They may come only for food and shelter and choose not to participate in therapy and counseling. Mental health treatment should not be a condition of shelter (Larew 1980). Workers should not see rejection of treatment as a failure, but rather should see providing food and shelter as a humanitarian accomplishment.

Developing a Continuum of Care

That all homeless are entitled to shelter without conditions attached must be a basic commitment. Humanitarian considerations will permit no less. This premise implies providing outreach teams to go where street people gather and begin initial interviews with them wherever they are—in parks, in subway entrances, on grates, or in cheap restaurants. The most important initial step is to get the homeless into shelters, for little else can happen until this is done.

To the extent that getting them to shelter fails, workers must roam the streets and distribute blankets, sleeping bags, and food to alleviate suffering until trust can be established and the homeless can be persuaded to use shelters (Blumberg et al. 1978).

Beyond simply bringing people to shelter, different levels of shelter and care, varying in the degrees to which they demand regular habits and conformity, must be available. At the minimum level essentially no demands would be made, though staff would try to make conversation and get to know clients individually, gradually developing trust and learning about their needs (Baxter and Hopper 1982; Leach 1979). A second level of care would provide more structure, some screening, and medication for clients who are receptive. Third-stage housing might be provided up to six months or longer while the client is being fully stabilized on medication, entitlements to SSI or public welfare are established, and jobs are found for those who are able. Families can be contacted, and long-term housing at affordable rates located.

Providing Health and Mental Health Care

The homeless suffer from a range of health problems, many of them severely aggravated by exposure and poor nutrition. Medical backup must be available, including emergency room and hospital care when needed. Psychiatric service and the availability of medication has been shown to markedly reduce symptoms of mental illness. Arce and his colleagues (1983) found that 86 percent of the homeless mentally ill accepted medication when it was offered to them.

Facilitating Employment

Many chronically mentally ill persons can work if they are given the opportunity. They need money desperately for a pack of cigarettes, a meal, bus fare, or a phone call and would welcome an odd job, day labor, or even long-term employment. They are, however, at a distinct disadvantage in the competition for scarce jobs. The way they present themselves, their lack of appropriate clothing, and their poor work histories militate against them. Their lack of a telephone, an address, and transportation are further obstacles.

One possibility is the development of a type of sheltered workshop, located near shelters, that could offer day work or work paid at a piece rate to walk-in clients. A warehouse or other empty building could be used. Work could be provided through contracts with employers, similar to the way in which workshops for the retarded are operated. Employment also needs to be recognized as a basic human right.

Connecting With Families

All homeless people at one time in their lives had families. Research data are unclear and contradictory about how many still do. Some researchers see the homeless as nearly universally without family and friends. Others report that some homeless have infrequent contact with relatives and occasionally get support or money from them. In this chapter we have reported cases in which families were searching for their relative, and were concerned about their care. A recent New York study showed that many new arrivals to a shelter had spent the previous night with friends or family or in single-room-occupancy hotels (Main 1983). The authors hasten to add this finding does not imply that the subjects could return to the same resource easily, for they probably are no longer welcome, and it may be a long time before that option is open to them again.

Certainly it is very important for the homeless person and, indeed, for his family to be reconnected again. By their at least finding each other, some pain may be reduced. The risk is that, as with deinstitutionalization, the mental health community would again see sending patients back to their families as a panacea. Some families may remain distant by design, because they know from past experience that if they show any interest in their relative at all, the whole unbearable burden is theirs without help or support. Thus not only is there the problem of winning the trust of the patient if a reconnection is to be made, but it may be equally difficult to win the trust of families.

It should be recognized from the outset that out-of-home placement must be assured wherever it is needed so families can continue to give the emotional support and maintain the kinds of relationships with the homeless person that they have with their other adult children. Nothing can truly substitute for emotional ties with families. But mental health professionals must not jeopardize those ties by overloading a family so they are unable to respond with affection and support. Housing for the handicapped need not be the family home; other places must be found. Where family difficulties have led to homelessness, we cannot push burned-out families to take over again.

Organizing a System of Care

In most places services for the homeless are scattered and piece-meal. A number of charitable agencies and public services may be offering something, but it is difficult to get the various pieces to fit together. An interesting approach that may serve as a model for other communities is a consortium called Concerned Agencies of Metropolitan Los Angeles (CAMLA), which unites 25 public and private agencies that in some way serve skid row residents. CAMLA helps clients get entitlements, does extensive outreach to the severely mentally ill, and helps obtain passes for low-cost transportation so people can seek out medical care or look for jobs and housing. It has linkages with the police and tries to prevent jailing of the mentally ill. CAMLA has developed a *Skid Row Directory* listing more than 100 agencies, with a small pocket size for use by homeless people (Farr 1982).

The Prevention of Homelessness

While the CAMLA approach is an impressive effort to deal with a problem that is overwhelming to most cities, it is disturbing that so much effort must go into treating a problem that should not have been allowed to occur. If it is possible to create a consortium to deal with the failures of community care, why is it not possible to develop an effective system of care that would prevent people from going over the edge?

Without question, we must organize now for the emergency on our hands, and we may always need an additional system of care for mentally ill people who become homeless. But most of our commitment should be adequate community care in the first place. It seems anachronistic that we are now seeking millions of dollars to create an emergency system of care to treat the failures in our mental health and social service systems. Main (1983) estimates that New York City's new program of providing emergency shelters will cost $38 million. In Maryland, advocates are working hard to restore to the budget $3 million for psychosocial centers and housing that could keep the population of street people from growing.

While it is undeniable that more money is needed to provide effective community care, money will not substitute for more imaginative thinking. We will discuss three broad areas that should be a focus of attention: 1) reassessing our policy of deinstitutionalization, 2) developing a system of care that is responsive to the unique characteristics of the mentally ill, and 3) defining the appropriate role for families to play.

Reassessment of Deinstitutionalization

There is a growing backlash from some concerned segments of the community about the lack of evidence that deinstitutionalization really works. If some corrections were made now, we might avoid a groundswell of opinion that could again make state hospitals the primary locus of care. Perhaps it is time that patients' rights groups and civil-liberties lawyers focus more on the rights of patients to housing and care in the community, as New York lawyer Hayes has attempted to demonstrate, and less on forcing discharges from hospitals, which may ultimately put people on the street.

We know now that beyond patients in the "dangerousness to self and others" categories, there are persons so grossly lacking in the ability to care for themselves and in the capacity to make rational decisions that they must be involuntarily cared for by others. The concept of "asylum" for those who really need it is becoming more acceptable when one sees some of the alternatives we have to offer. John Talbott, 1984-85 president of the American Psychiatric Association, is quoted as saying, "Psychiatrists are much more sympathetic to institutional care today" (Nelson 1983). Most families, too, welcome institutional care when their relative is too disturbed to manage at least a minimum degree of rational choices when he is in the community.

Developing an Adequate System of Care

"We need a system of care in this country. No one is in charge" (Nelson 1983). The latter statement seems to identify the fundamental problem. It would appear to be possible to establish through legislation, or through litigation if necessary, some persons or agencies that are ultimately responsible and that can be held accountable for care of the severely mentally ill. With that responsibility must come power to act, and dollars. Someone must be in charge.

The services that are now available are too few, too uncoordinated, and not diverse enough to meet the needs of that heterogeneous population called the severely mentally ill. Bureaucratic agencies are governed by complex and illogical rules difficult for ordinary persons to understand; much less are they intelligible to someone with impaired mental processes. For example, when a patient is hospitalized in a public facility, he automatically loses his Supplemental Security Income, and thus probably his housing and his address. It takes three months to get an SSI check—and if he doesn't have a mailing address, he will not get it at all. Clients do not know how to use social services and do not know how agencies interface. The first step many service agencies take is to try to screen out a potential client. If a client is accepted for a service, responsibility rests with the client to use it. Many fail to do so.

Money management presents great difficulty for some clients. Even if an income is assured, as through SSI, it is the inability to handle their meager checks that lands many persons on the streets. Many need an agency's help in dealing with funds.

Families report that many professionals on the front line of service delivery manifest a serious lack of understanding of the severe mental illnesses, especially schizophrenia. They appear to have little training in the real-life symptomatology and behaviors of severe illness and how to relate to them. These deficiencies become glaringly apparent at points of service delivery, where often little sensitivity is shown to characteristic symptomatology and how it affects the patient's performance. The chances that shelter personnel understand such symptomatology is even more remote. This is clearly a training issue; service workers learn little about severe psychiatric disorders in their preservice programs, and they are forced to catch on as best they can in the process of adjusting to a difficult work situation.

An Appropriate Role for the Family

In the past decade or so the mental health establishment has turned to families to serve as the primary resource—and often the only resource—for persons with mental illness. The consequences of deinstitutionalization were never fully assessed until the late 1970s, when it became known that nearly two-thirds of discharged patients were returning home to live. Although family caretaking was once thought to be a transitional state of affairs, there is now a general feeling that families will always be caregivers. In a strange reversal of theory over a brief span of years, families once considered "noxious," "dysfunctional," "enmeshed," or "pathological" are now lauded as "social networks" and irreplaceable resources—perhaps the only institution that can save a disastrous system of community care.

Recognizing that this is a new direction, it becomes important not to "use" the family to save the concept of deinstitutionalization. Once more it appears we have a new/old panacea for treating the mentally ill: return to the pre-asylum days and let families do it. Families report that they suffer outrageous pressures from hospital staff to resume care of very ill persons in their homes again. Sometimes no discussion has gone on—the patient simply appears at the front door. Little attention has been paid to the studies of burden and risk to families (Arnoff 1975; Doll 1976; Hatfield 1978; Kreisman and Joy 1974).

Some families may be able and willing to care for their relative at home for a few years *if* they have the right kind of support and *if* the family are assured that there will be dependable social care when the family caregiver becomes too frail or dies. We need much contact with these families to find out just what kinds of support will be useful to them. The limited research we do have indicates that families most want education in practical management skills, and they want highly responsive crisis care (Hatfield 1979, 1983; Holden and Lewine 1979). Few mental health professionals are themselves trained in the day-to-day coping techniques that families need. If they are to win the trust of families, they must be able to demonstrate that they themselves are masters of the techniques they are trying to teach.

Some family educational programs are described in the literature (Anderson et al. 1980; Falloon et al. 1981; Kantor 1982; Hatfield in press), but few outcome data have been reported; therefore, we cannot predict the long-term usefulness of these treatments. Whatever help is offered to families must be given in the most cost-effective way. Expensive programs that intrigue providers but provide service for only a select few cannot be condoned when so many families need service and so many patients need food and shelter.

Families need knowledge and skills, but they also need other supportive services in their roles as caregivers. They need a lifeline that is always available in times of crisis. Whether that service should be in the form of a mobile crisis team, a visiting nurse, or something else is not so important as the immediacy of the response, the ability to make home visits, and the skill to deal with a deteriorating situation. Such a service may reduce the likelihood of the disturbed individual's being precipitously expelled from the home.

We have given little consideration in this country to a monetary incentive for families to provide direct care at home. Whether it is a direct subsidy or a tax credit (similar to the extra income tax deduction available for those who are legally blind), such an approach could partly compensate for the costs to families of having to maintain larger living quarters or of having a potential wage earner stay home to care for the ill person. Families of persons with mental illness incur financial losses from damage to property and from wasteful use of heat and electricity and other household resources. Home care, even with compensation, would be cheaper than other shelter to the taxpayer, and financial incentives for the caregivers might reduce substantially the sense of burden that families experience.

Finally, society must find a way to provide respite care to these families. Even as we recognize the risk of burnout for mental health workers, we cannot ignore the toll that caregiving takes when a family is in charge of the ill person for 24 hours of the day without respite.

In our discussion of families we have not really begun to think about the plight of minority families. As we have already noted, a disproportionate number of homeless people are members of minorities. Mental health care for these patients and families must be given on a basis that is affordable, understandable, and acceptable within their cultural systems. We need to know much more about them if we are to meet their needs in an acceptable manner.

With the development of the National Alliance for the Mentally Ill and its various affiliates around the country, families now have a source of support and knowledge not previously available. Members can learn coping strategies from each other, profit from the role models afforded, and learn how to assess available social services. As this rapidly developing consumer movement spreads, more families will learn how to accommodate their difficult relative or advocate for housing that will work for him. The families in the National Alliance are an excellent source of inside information about the family and patient experience and can give specific data about events that lead a disturbed person inexorably down the path to homelessness.

Conclusions

In this chapter we have attempted to give a family perspective on homelessness. Therefore it leans toward the subjective since the sheer horror of it all is forever haunting families. Families are especially aware of the uniqueness of personality of those who have mental illnesses and the unique ways that arrangements fall apart for them. Failure to recognize this diversity explains, in part, why mentally ill persons end up on the streets.

Families are a key part in helping to determine the solutions to homelessness: they are excellent sources of otherwise unavailable information, they serve as temporary caregivers while society is catching up on its obligations to the mentally ill, and they are highly committed advocates for more compassionate and skillful care of the mentally ill.

References

Anderson CM, Hogarty GE, Reiss DJ: Family treatment of adult schizophrenic patients: a psycho-educational approach. Schizophr Bull 6:490-505, 1980

Arce AA, Tadlock M, Vergare MJ, et al: A psychiatric profile of street people admitted to an emergency shelter. Hosp Community Psychiatry 34:812-817, 1983

Arnoff FN: Social consequences of policy toward mental illness. Science 188:1277-1281, 1975

Bahr HM: Homelessness, disaffiliation, and retreatism, in Disaffiliated Man. Edited by Bahr HM. Toronto, University of Toronto Press, 1970

Bassuk EL: Addressing the needs of the homeless. Boston Globe Magazine, Nov 6, 1983

Baxter E, Hopper K: The new mendicancy: homelessness in New York City. Am J Orthopsychiatry 52:393-408, 1982

Blumberg LU, Shipley TF, Barsky SF: Liquor and poverty: skid row as a human condition. New Brunswick, NJ, Rutgers Center of Alcohol Studies, 1978

Doll W: Family coping with the mentally ill: an unanticipated problem of deinstitutionalization. Hosp Community Psychiatry 27:183-185, 1976

Down and out in America. Newsweek, Mar 15, 1983, pp 28-29

Falloon IR, Boyd JL, McGill CW, et al: Family management training in community care of schizophrenia. New Directions for Mental Health Services, no 12: 61-77, 1981

Farr RK: Skid Row Project. Los Angeles County, Department of Mental Health, Jan 18, 1982

Farrell E: A descriptive study of some homeless women. Master's thesis, College Park, Md, University of Maryland, 1977

Farrell E: Service needs as perceived by shelter men. Master's thesis, Washington, DC, Howard University, 1981

Hatfield AB: Psychological costs of schizophrenia to the family. Social Work 23:355-359, 1978

Hatfield AB: Help-seeking behavior in families of schizophrenics. Am J Community Psychol 7:563-569, 1979

Hatfield AB: What families want of family therapists, in Family Therapy in Schizophrenia. Edited by MacFarlane W. New York, Guilford, 1983

Hatfield AB: Family education: a competence approach, in Competence Development in Special Populations: Theory and Practice. Edited by Marlowe HA, Weinberg RB. Springfield, Ill, Thomas (in press)

Holden D, Lewine R: Families of schizophrenic individuals: an evaluation of mental health professionals, resources, and the effects of schizophrenia. Chicago, Illinois State Psychiatric Institute, 1979

Jones RE: Street people and psychiatry: an introduction. Hosp Community Psychiatry 34:807-811, 1983

Kantor J: Coping Strategies for Relatives of the Mentally Ill. Washington, National Alliance for the Mentally Ill, 1982

Kreisman DE, Joy VD: Family response to the mental illness of a relative: a review of the literature. Schizophr Bull, no 10:34-57, 1974

Larew B: Strange strangers: serving transients. Social Casework 63:107-113, 1980

Leach J: Providing for the destitute, in Community Care for the Mentally Disabled. Edited by Wing JK, Olsen R. New York, Oxford University Press, 1979

Lipton FR, Sabatini A, Katz SE: Down and out in the city: the homeless mentally ill. Hosp Community Psychiatry 34:817-821, 1983

Main TJ: The homeless of New York. Public Interest 72:3-28, 1983

Nelson B: Nation's psychiatrists give "high priority" to the homeless. New York Times, May 10, 1983

Rousseau AM: Shopping Bag Ladies. New York, Pilgrim Press, 1981

Shulman AK: Preface, in Shopping Bag Ladies. Edited by Rousseau AM. New York, Pilgrim Press, 1981

Snyder M: Statement Before the Committee on Appropriations, in US Senate Special Hearing on Street People. Washington, US Government Printing Office, 1983

Chapter 14

The Politics of Homelessness

Ellen L. Bassuk, M.D.
Alison S. Lauriat, M.A.

Homeless people serve as a painful reminder of what can become of us. Their plight arouses fears of abandonment and concerns about our connectedness to other people and institutions. Proposals for ameliorating the problem of homelessness reflect these anxieties as well as deeply held philosophical views about how society should care for those who cannot care for themselves.

While most agree about the immediate solution—providing food, clothes, and shelter—there is little consensus about longer-term plans. Many of those now speaking out seem to be guarding partisan beliefs rather than encouraging creative program development. This chapter explores the attitudes, biases, and opinions that shape the debates and that converge to maintain a burgeoning shelter industry, perhaps at the expense of a more broad-based solution.

Nature of the Debate

Whenever the origins of homelessness are described, four factors are often cited: unemployment and governmental economic poli-

Dr. Bassuk is associate professor of psychiatry at Harvard Medical School in Boston. Ms. Lauriat is an independent consultant on issues of public policy and homelessness. The authors thank Paul McGerigle, Stuart Guernsey, Ellen Gallagher, and Ann Louise McLaughlin for their comments about this chapter.

cies; lack of low-cost housing; mental health policies such as deinstitutionalization; and reduced disability benefits (Hopper 1983).
Although most experts agree about the importance of these factors,
there are few data describing the relative contribution of each to
the alarming increase in the numbers of homeless people. Researchers only recently have begun any form of systematic data collection
about the needs of homeless people—which, in itself, may be symptomatic of the problem. The relative lack of rigorous research has
allowed conflicting assumptions and ideologies to pervade analyses
of the problem.

Ostensibly the debate revolves around the origins of homelessness. Although homelessness is almost certainly a final common
pathway reflecting the failure of various federal and state policies,
the controversy about the balance of specific factors has become a
political football. Because definition of the problem delineates
responsibility and jurisdiction for care, the basic question seems to
be whether or not homeless people are disabled and, if so, how
severely.

A related question that is intensely argued is whether homelessness leads to mental illness or vice versa. Because people with special
needs require comprehensive support and rehabilitation, often for
life, these programs are expensive. And even with these costly
programs, many disabled persons cannot ever live independently.
In contrast, if the problem resulted solely from the economic recession or lack of housing, it could be ameliorated by the reallocation
of resources to the poor.

What is known about the characteristics and needs of homeless
people? Researchers have shown that many homeless persons suffer
from severe psychological difficulties. However, the extent of mental
illness among the population remains controversial, with estimates
ranging from 20 to 91 percent (Bassuk 1983b). Reports from Boston
(Lauriat and McGerigle 1983), Los Angeles (Farr 1982), Philadelphia (Arce et al. 1983), and New York City (Men's Shelter Study
Group 1976; Reich and Siegel 1978) indicate that a majority of the
sheltered homeless have diagnosable mental illnesses, particularly
psychoses, chronic alcoholism, and personality disorders, and that
approximately one-third have been psychiatrically hospitalized.

The relationship of mental health policy to the increasing numbers
of homeless mentally ill cannot be demonstrated convincingly, for
several reasons (Bassuk 1983a). First, data about the homeless

chronically mentally ill that span the period of deinstitutionalization are unavailable. Second, the median age of the homeless is approximately 34. Many became psychotic after mental health policy had changed. To avoid "institutionalization," they are now hospitalized for brief periods only. Third, laws authorizing involuntary commitment to mental hospitals are being interpreted more narrowly and refer predominantly to the dangerous mentally ill. Although the law was intended to protect civil liberties, recent interpretations make it difficult for extremely disturbed but not overtly dangerous persons to receive care. Some of them may resist help because of their illness and past experiences.

The rate of hospitalization is confounded by such factors, yet policy-makers and some personnel in departments of mental health have used these figures to argue against the importance of mental health policy as a major factor in the etiology of homelessness. There is no doubt that a significant percentage of the homeless population suffer from chronic mental illness; nevertheless, existing data continue to be used as a basis for arguments on every side of the issue. To understand how this controversy has contributed to the absence of even rudimentary psychiatric services and to the lack of comprehensive and rational long-term planning, we must explore underlying attitudes of politicians, shelter providers, and mental health professionals.

Attitudes of Politicians

Before the early 1980s, policy-makers largely ignored homelessness. Newspaper and periodical articles suggest that although homelessness is not a new phenomenon, the involvement of politicians is relatively recent. During the past three to four years, increasing visibility of homeless people, highlighted by widespread media coverage, has given the issue substantial political value. Most federal, state, and municipal elected politicians have something to say about homelessness. Rhetoric abounds, spanning the ideological spectrum. Conservatives often downplay the problem; for instance, Edwin Meese, when chief counsel to the President, said that, lacking "authoritative figures," hunger may not be a problem in the United States (Guyon 1984). Liberals are likely to bemoan the situation; Governor Michael Dukakis of Massachusetts asked those gathered

to hear his 1982 inaugural address: "Who would have believed it?
. . . Hunger and homelessness in the most affluent nation on the
face of the earth" (Boston Globe, 1983).

The sweeping tide of conservatism and the election of Ronald
Reagan at the beginning of this decade reflected a clear message
from the voters: it's time for the government to support the productive, income-producing segments of society and, at the same time,
to decrease the allocation of resources to those dependent on the
public sector. A columnist captured this view when he wrote: "Too
seldom in the present furor over hunger and homelessness is it
recognized that these conditions are neither the fault of government
nor its responsibility" (Wilson 1984).

Conservative politicians generally believe that they must limit the
size of government and contain costs. They have significantly reduced
traditional welfare programs that aid the poor. Under the current
conservative administration, eligibility requirements for financial
benefits have been narrowed. Many once deemed unemployable are
now considered well enough to work. In just three years Social
Security Disability Insurance (SSDI) and Supplemental Security
Income (SSI) have dropped approximately 350,000 persons from
their rolls (Hopper 1983). These programs most affect the disabled
and mentally ill, but similar cutbacks have occurred in Aid to Families With Dependent Children (AFDC). In addition, the Reagan
administration has substantially reduced housing assistance programs
for the poor.

Although not representative of all conservative politicians, the
notion that government has little obligation to or responsibility for
the homeless has engendered some harsh and punitive reactions.
In Fort Lauderdale, Florida, a municipal commissioner suggested
that the city should institute a program of spraying the garbage
with poisonous substances in order to discourage destitute people
from foraging in dumpsters and barrels (Homelessness in America
1983, 15). A bill was introduced before the Baltimore City Council
prohibiting the homeless from sleeping in or on public buildings,
parks, streets, stations, or parking areas. Conviction would have
carried penalties of fines, imprisonment, or both. Advocates for
the homeless demonstrated against the bill and saw it ultimately
defeated, but its introduction reflected intensely negative feelings
(Homelessness in America 1983, 513). In Phoenix a similar ordi-
nance was passed. Although there are between 3,000 and 7,000

homeless men and women in that city, officials dispersed or closed all programs providing overnight shelters for the homeless. In so doing, they expressed a hope that the needy would go to Los Angeles, or Salt Lake City, or anywhere but Phoenix (Homelessness in America 1983, 670).

Meanwhile, in spite of such measures reflecting the country's new conservatism, liberal officials are calling for government action. Homelessness has become an expedient issue for some politicians. By providing immediate aid in the form of emergency shelter and food, they are doing something almost biblical in its simplicity, and not particularly costly. At the same time, they can use homelessness as a rallying point against the conservative tide and Reagan's economic philosophy. A leading Democrat on the congressional subcommittee considering program proposals for homeless people described the situation as follows: "Since the onslaught of the recession there has been a tremendous growth in the number of people without a place to live, and there has been an expansion of the people who are homeless. Today, people who could not previously conceive of a situation where they would not have a place to live have been forced into streets onto heating grates, in cars, doorways, and caves along rivers. They are indeed victims of our economy" (Homelessness in America 1983, 8). Like the conservative response, such an analysis avoids the troublesome question of how to provide long-term care to disabled persons.

Symptomatic of the avoidance of this fundamental question is that, to varying degrees, each level of government has refused to assume bottom-line responsibility for the homeless, or even to accept a meaningful share. The United States Conference of Mayors devoted considerable time in 1982 to discussing how cities could ameliorate the distress of homeless people. But all the solutions required other levels of government to provide the resources necessary to help the cities (Homelessness in America 1983, 170). The mayors first asked the U.S. Department of Agriculture to send the cities surplus commodities to help feed the hungry; second, they requested $500 million in emergency funds from Congress for food, shelter, heat, medical care, and clothing; third, they sought congressional consideration of ways to provide health insurance to recently unemployed people; fourth, they requested federal housing funds to rehabilitate existing structures for use as emergency shelters; and fifth, they advocated for a federal job creation bill that would allow localities to hire the unemployed to repair aging streets, bridges, sewers, and water systems.

The message of local officials was clear: they were willing to administer the programs to help the homeless, but financial support and other resources had to come from other levels of government. Indeed the mayor of Seattle described the situation just that way when he said, "We are asking Congress to provide a desperately needed CARE package. . . . We are asking for the resources to respond to the crisis of homelessness immediately" (Homelessness in America 1983, 384).

Local public officials obviously are the ones most directly concerned with homelessness. Many of them see the problem clearly and have responded compassionately. Last winter New York's mayor rode around the city trying to coax street people out of the cold and into city shelters—sometimes unsuccessfully (Sullivan 1983). In Boston newly elected Mayor Raymond Flynn ate his Thanksgiving meal at the Pine Street Inn, the city's largest and oldest shelter. The cities provide care at the grassroots level; thus their programs are the final safety nets. But local officials have expressed concern that providing even rudimentary services constitutes an implicit agreement to take full responsibility. They feel that they are assuming responsibilities that rightfully belong to other levels of government. The mayor of Salt Lake City pondered this problem when he said, "We become a blinking neon light of a sort to those who see us caring" (Homelessness in America 1983, 161).

As the distance from city streets increases, understanding of the problem of homelessness decreases. This is particularly true at higher levels of government and corresponds with a greater unwillingness to provide services. Consistent with this feeling is the belief among politicians from different parties and at various levels of government that much of the responsibility for the hands-on, one-to-one caring should be borne by charitable or religious groups. In New York City Mayor Koch has appealed repeatedly to churches and synagogues to open their doors and make room for the homeless. In Massachusetts, in the winter of 1983-84, Governor Dukakis provided encouragement, technical assistance, and some resources to religious groups to make more beds available on an emergency basis. Like the transfer of responsibility among levels of government, such actions reflect a transfer from public to private sectors.

The private sector shares some of the concerns expressed by municipal politicians. Officials in churches and foundations worry about assuming responsibilities that belong in the public sector. Foundations feel they should strike a delicate balance between encouraging private efforts while not providing an excuse for government cutbacks. And although some church officials may have similar misgivings about allowing government to transfer its most difficult and needy clients to the private sector, thus avoiding its obligations, the religious community continues to fill in where others have failed.

Attitudes of Shelter Providers and the Religious Community

In accordance with scriptural injunctions and implicit notions of human kindness and decency, the religious community has traditionally assumed responsibility for homeless and hungry people. The monastic tradition of responsibility, exhibited today by the Catholic Worker movement among others, is rooted in a rich literature of concern for the disempowered. Traditionally churches have founded, supported, and staffed many breadlines and sheltering facilities.

Although not all shelter providers are part of the religious community, religious philosophy permeates their activities. This passage captures the spirit of its commitment to the homeless: "Then the righteous will answer him, 'Lord, when did we see thee hungry and feed thee, or naked and clothe thee? And when did we see thee sick or in prison and visit thee?' And the King will answer them, 'Truly, I say to you, as you did it to one of the least of these my brethren you did it to me'" (Matthew 25:37-40).

The shelters, which began as counter-institutions operated primarily by churches and other nonprofit groups, have evolved into stable components of the human services system. Just five years ago, when homelessness was less politically valuable, it was almost solely the province of the religious community. Because many shelter directors believed that one of the causes of homelessness was the oppression of people by traditional systems and institutions, the experiences they provided in the shelters were humane and decent and hence antidotal; they treated their guests with respect and dignity. Many shelter directors instituted policies of "no questions asked," "no strings attached," and "live and let live." Rules were invoked only to protect the guests and ensure the survival of the community. Paradoxically, although many shelters are frightening and volatile places precisely because of the lack of controls, they are also comforting places because they allow anonymity and invisibility and embrace everyone as equals, without class distinction.

Consistent with these attitudes, some providers believe that research represents further abuse by the system because data collection has not improved the situation of the poor and homeless in the past. They oppose anything that infringes on rights of privacy and autonomy. Accordingly, some shelters will not cooperate with the public sector, even if it means turning down substantial funding.

Although its program is not typical, the Salvation Army may be the best known religious group that follows the Judeo-Christian tradition of providing care for the homeless. The avowed purpose of this sect, founded in the late 19th century, is to bring individuals into a relationship with God through Jesus Christ. The social service program represents the practical application of this philosophy. The Salvation Army offers its services where people most need them—in prisons, in hospitals, and on the streets. According to its tenets, when people have been assisted nonjudgmentally and with compassion and kindness, they will be more receptive to the organization's desire to lead them into a life-enriching spiritual experience.

Two million people worldwide consider the Salvation Army their church. Four thousand officers and 80,000 soldiers, organized in a semimilitary structure, constitute the Army in the United States. The officers, ordained ministers of the Gospel, "spread the word of God, and carry comfort wherever they can" (Fellows 1979, 3).

Although many shelter providers are not organized into formal religious groups or even identified as belonging to a religious community, they adhere to various aspects of religious philosophy. Like politicians, their spectrum of beliefs is extremely broad. However, in contrast to politicians, generally shelter providers are sincerely dedicated to the care of all the disenfranchised.

Attitudes of Mental Health Professionals

The long history of neglect of the long-term mentally ill can be traced from the overcrowded state hospitals to the community, where former patients lead bleak existences in nursing homes, single-room occupancies, and other community residences (Lamb 1979).

Now, in the 1980s, the problem has moved into the shelters—or, even worse, into the streets.

In 1979 Richard Lamb posed the following question when discussing "the roots of neglect" of the severely mentally ill: "How could professionals highly trained and skilled in the understanding of human behavior, and with a major responsibility for the fate of the mentally ill, be so insensitive to the needs of their charges, not once but repeatedly?" (Lamb 1979, 201). He concluded that the needs of these patients clashed with those of the professional staff. Today, with homelessness added to the already long list of unappealing problems, the gap between the professional and the severely mentally ill patient has widened even further.

Physicians often unknowingly share general, sometimes negative, attitudes toward illness—particularly chronic illness. Sociologists and anthropologists have described the way persons with ill health are assigned "a socially deviant status in relation to institutionalized social expectations, sentiments, and sanctions" (Ablon 1981, 6). Patients should not be blamed for their illness and are exempt from various responsibilities when ill, but the sick role is acceptable only if patients do everything possible to overcome it—such as seeking appropriate medical care.

This is not their only burden. In addition to dealing with the obligations of the sick role, patients must cope with the meaning of the illness and the reactions of others. Specific diseases have become metaphors for complex historical and cultural attitudes, values, and beliefs. Mental disorders, like leprosy, tuberculosis, and cancer, are perceived as particularly horrifying. The impact of these illnesses is magnified by their metaphorical meanings (Sontag 1977).

Chronic disorders may be viewed by physicians as unappealing, even repugnant. Because doctors often perceive their primary function as "curing" illness, chronic patients may evoke feelings of frustration, discouragement, helplessness, and vulnerability. These feelings may be intensified when dealing with patients who suffer from chronic mental illness. Lamb has described how "there tends to be a basic moral disapproval in our society of dependency, of a passive, inactive life style and of accepting public support instead of working" (Lamb 1979, 204). Because physicians sometimes feel anxious and disapproving, they may devalue or avoid patients who suffer from progressively deteriorating or chronic conditions. The fact that service demands often outweigh the perceived training or academic value of caring for these patients makes the task even more undesirable.

These concerns are even more exaggerated in relation to chronically mentally ill homeless persons. Such people suffer from a stigmatized illness that implies a moral deficiency or weakness of character. Their poverty and often nonwhite ethnic identity are generally associated with poorer health than that of patients from higher social classes (Hollingshead and Redlich 1958). Because the mentally ill homeless are unlike their caretakers, they are viewed less favorably than those whose backgrounds are similar to those of the caretakers; they enter the health care system as stigmatized patients. Without the accouterments that most people take for granted—an address, cash in one's pocket, a friend—homeless persons lack dignity, respect, and, most important, an identity. As individuals without status in society, they are less recognizable. Within the health care system, they are almost invisible.

Regardless of the reasons, homeless persons have fallen out of society's systems; they have become unwilling or unable to seek and obtain help. Because of their illness and their experiences with an inflexible, illogical, and uncompromising bureaucracy, many of these homeless persons have become passive, numbed, withdrawn, negativistic, and similarly uncompromising. Some of them manifest symptoms, such as paranoia and antisocial behaviors, that make it more difficult to coexist in a society with other people. Therefore, care of homeless mentally ill patients requires activity, outreach, persistence, patience, and advocacy. Many mental health professionals are uncomfortable in assuming the necessary roles, particularly when they involve confronting the irrationality of traditional systems and functioning at times as political activists. Finally, some of these activities are not financially compensated, even for the care of the rare homeless person who has adequate medical insurance.

The end result is that very few mental health professionals have made an effort to become involved with the large numbers of mentally ill people living in the shelters and on the streets. They seem reluctant to acknowledge that homelessness may belong in their bailiwick and that they could assume important roles as advocates for the homeless and as consultants and trainers to front-line service providers.

Discussion

As homelessness became increasingly newsworthy, politicians embraced the issue. But in spite of their promises to develop a comprehensive system of care for homeless people, emergency accommodations remain the essence of the service delivery system. Although these facilities provide food and shelter and are open only at night, they now constitute a separate and stable component of the human services systems in most states. Their importance as life-saving facilities cannot be disputed, nor can the dedication of their staffs. But many who had hoped that the emergency shelters would be replaced by more stable housing accommodations and a full range of support services have resigned themselves to the permanency of this "emergency" arrangement.

How have the attitudes, opinions, and biases of policy-makers and service providers converged to condone the existence of a shelter industry? Paradoxically, although the problem of homelessness reflects broad and deep-rooted social policy problems, the need to deliver shelter services is pressing and immediate. Policy-makers and shelter directors have agreed to this immediate "solution," but the process of effective long-range planning is blocked by factionalism. Because of their intense commitment to the hungry and homeless, some shelter providers have developed a vested interest in maintaining their own facilities. They have identified with the misfortune of their guests, and after years of unique experience as caretakers, some directors have become suspicious of outsiders. This protective instinct can interfere with needed change.

Some shelters have evolved into insular communities with a "we" and "they" philosophy. "They" refers to traditional systems and institutions that are viewed as the symbolic and real oppressors of homeless people. Many mental health professionals and social service agency providers fall into this category. Yet rather than adopting a more moderate position that accepts and incorporates the useful qualities of these systems, some shelter providers have become increasingly radicalized and opposed to any partnership efforts with outside groups. Other shelter directors, who may be less vocal, are cautious.

As a result, shelter providers have unwittingly joined with politicians to maintain the status quo. Although shelters can provide only a minimal standard of care, policy-makers prefer them because

they are less costly than hospitals, community residences, or permanent housing with comprehensive support services. Policy-makers
can also point to the shelter system as evidence that they are absolv-
ing their responsibility for disabled persons.

Caring for the homeless has become a public issue, with various
groups advocating different solutions. In all discussions, however,
the immediate and often desperate need for shelter and food over-
shadows longer-range planning. This outcome, though it may be
expedient politically, guarantees the status quo and the growth of
the shelter industry. What is lacking are nonpartisan advocates to
speak on behalf of those who need lifelong support and care. Such
an advocacy role could be adopted by the mental health professional
who at least understands the role of chronic mental illness and
severe disability in the etiology of homelessness. Without advocates,
the plight of the homeless will continue to be desperate, and public
dialogue about long-range care will continue to be curtailed.

References

Ablon J: Stigmatized health conditions. Soc Sci Med 15B:5-9, 1981
Arce AA, Tadlock M, Vergare MJ, et al: A psychiatric profile of street
    people admitted to an emergency shelter. Hosp Community Psychiatry
    34:812-817, 1983
Bassuk EL: Addressing the needs of the homeless. Boston Globe Maga-
    zine, Nov 6, 1983, pp 12, 80 (1983a)
Bassuk EL: Homelessness/review of the literature. Harvard Medical School,
    Boston (unpublished), 1983b
Boston Globe, Jan 7, 1983, p 1
Farr RK: Skid Row Project. Los Angeles County, Department of Mental
    Health, Jan 18, 1982
Fellows L: The Gentle War: The Story of the Salvation Army. New York,
    Macmillan, 1979
Guyon J: Bread battle. Wall Street Journal, Mar 9, 1984, p 1
Hollingshead AB, Redlich FC: Social Class and Mental Illness: A Commu-
    nity Study. New York, Wiley, 1958
Homelessness in America. Hearing Before the Subcommittee on Housing
    and Community Development of the Committee on Banking, Finance,
    and Urban Affairs, US House of Representatives, Dec 15, 1982. Wash-
    ington, US Government Printing Office, 1983
Hopper K: Homelessness: reducing the distance. New England Journal
    of Human Services, Fall, 30-47, 1983

Lamb HR: Roots of neglect of the long-term mentally ill. Psychiatry 42:201-207, 1979

Lauriat A, McGerigle P: More Than Shelter: A Community Response to Homelessness. Boston, United Community Planning Corporation and Massachusetts Association of Mental Health, 1983

Men's Shelter Study Group: Report on Men Housed for One Night. New York, Human Resources Administration, 1976

Reich R, Siegel L: The emergence of the Bowery as a psychiatric dumping ground. Psychiatr Q 50:191-201, 1978

Sontag S: Illness as Metaphor. New York, Farrar, Straus & Giroux, 1977

Sullivan R: Mayor offers aid and hand to homeless. New York Times, Mar 25, 1983, p B1

Wilson DB: Turning charity to welfare. Boston Globe, Jan 1, 1984, p 64

Index